THE FATHERS
OF THE CHURCH

A NEW TRANSLATION

VOLUME 65

THE FATHERS
OF THE CHURCH

A NEW TRANSLATION

SAINT AMBROSE

SEVEN EXEGETICAL WORKS

Isaac, or the Soul
Death as a Good
Jacob and the Happy Life
Joseph
The Patriarchs
Flight from the World
The Prayer of Job and David

Translated by
MICHAEL P. McHUGH
University of Connecticut

THE CATHOLIC UNIVERSITY OF AMERICA PRESS
in association with
CONSORTIUM PRESS
Washington, D. C.

NIHL OBSTAT:

JOSEPH B. COLLINS, S.S., S.T.D.
Censor Librorum

IMPRIMATUR:

✠PATRICK CARDINAL A. O'BOYLE, D.D.
Archbishop of Washington

May 10, 1971

The *nihil obstat* and *imprimatur* are official declarations that a book or pamphlet is free of doctrinal or moral error. No implication is contained therein that those who have granted the *nihil obstat* and the *imprimatur* agree with content, opinions, or statements expressed.

Library of Congress Cataloging in Publication Data

Ambrosius, Saint, Bp. of Milan
    Seven exegetical works.

    (The Fathers of the church, a new translation, v. 65)
    CONTENTS: Isaac, or the soul.—Death as a good.—Jacob and the happy life. [etc.]
    1. Theology—Collected works—Early church.
I. Title. II. Series.
BR65.A313E55   1972   201'.1   71-157660
ISBN 0-8132-0065-2

CONTENTS

Page

Select Bibliography vi

Acknowledgment viii

General Introduction 1

Isaac, or the Soul *(De Isaac vel anima)*.............. 9

Death as a Good *(De bono mortis)*.................. 69

Jacob and the Happy Life *(De Iacob et vita beata)*.... 117

Joseph *(De Ioseph)* 187

The Patriarchs *(De patriarchis)* 241

Flight from the World *(De fuga saeculi)*............. 279

The Prayer of Job and David
   (De interpellatione Iob et David)................. 327

Indices

   General Index 423

   Index of Holy Scripture........................ 451

v

SELECT BIBLIOGRAPHY*

Texts

Du Frische, J., and Nourry, N. le [Benedictine edition] (Paris 1686, 1690; reprinted PL 14, 15).

Schenkl, Karl. In CSEL 32.1 (Vienna 1896/7) [*Isaac, or the Soul* and *Death as a Good*], 32.2 *(ibid.* 1897) [the other sermons].

Wiesner, W. T., C. M. S. *Ambrosii De bono mortis: A Revised Text with an Introduction, Translation, and Commentary* (Catholic University of America Patristic Studies 100; Washington, D. C., 1970).

Translations

Beyenka, Sr. M. Melchior, O. P. *Saint Ambrose: Letters* (FOTC 26; Washington 1954, repr. 1967).

De Mornay, P. *Six Excellent Treatises on Life and Death* . . . (London 1607) [copies in the Folger Shakespeare Library, Washington, D. C.; Newberry Library, Chicago].

Deferrari, R. J. *Saint Ambrose: Theological and Dogmatic Works* (FOTC 44; Washington 1963).

McCauley, L. P., S. J., et al. *Funeral Orations by Saint Gregory Nazianzen and Saint Ambrose* (FOTC 22; Washington 1953).

Savage, J. J. *Saint Ambrose: Hexameron, Paradise, and Cain and Abel* (FOTC 42; New York 1961).

Thompson, T. *St. Ambrose, On the Sacraments and On the Mysteries* (London 1950).

Wiesner, W. T. (see *Texts*).

Other Works

Campenhausen, H. von. "Ambrose," in his *Fathers of the Latin Church,* translated by M. Hoffman (London 1964) [= *Men Who Shaped the Western Church* (New York 1964)] 87-128.

Courcelle, P. "Anti-Christian Arguments and Christian Platonism: from Arnobius to St. Ambrose," in Momigliano, A., et al. *The Conflict Between Paganism and Christianity in the Fourth Century* (Oxford 1963) 151–92.

―――. "De Platon à saint Ambroise par Apulée," *Revue de philologie* 35 (1961) 15–28.

―――. "Nouveaux aspects du Platonisme chez S. Ambroise," *Revue des études latines* 34 (1956) 220–39.

―――. "Les Pères devant les enfers Virgiliens," *Archives d'histoire doctrinale et littéraire du moyen âge* 30 (1955) 5–74.

vi

————. "Plotin et saint Ambroise," *Revue de philologie* 24 (1950) 29–56.

————. *Recherches sur les* Confessions *de saint Augustin* (Paris 1950, new ed. 1968).

————. "Traditions platonicienne et chrétienne du corps–prison," *Revue des études latines* 43 (1965) 406–43.

De Labriolle, P. *The Life and Times of St. Ambrose* (St. Louis 1928).

Diederich, Sr. Mary Dorothea, S.S.N.D. *Vergil in the Works of St. Ambrose* (Catholic University of America Patristic Studies 29; Washington 1931).

Dudden, F. Homes. *The Life and Times of St. Ambrose,* 2 vols. (Oxford 1935).

Figueroa, G. *The Church and the Synagogue in Saint Ambrose* (Catholic University of America Studies in Sacred Theology, Second series 25; Washington 1949).

Gorce, D. *Saint Ambroise: Traités sur l'Ancien Testament* (Namur 1967).

Gryson, R. *Le Prêtre selon saint Ambroise* (Louvain 1968).

Hadot, P. "Platon et Plotin dans trois sermons de saint Ambroise," *Revue des études latines* 34 (1956) 202–20.

Maes, B. *La Loi naturelle selon Ambroise de Milan* (Analecta Gregoriana 162; Rome 1967).

McGuire, M. R. P. "Ambrose, St.," *New Catholic Encyclopedia* 1 (New York 1967) 372–75.

Moricca, U. *Storia della letteratura latina cristiana* 2.1 (Turin 1928).

Morino, C. *Church and State in the Teaching of Saint Ambrose,* translated by M. Joseph Costelloe, S.J. (Washington 1969).

Otten, R. T. "Caritas and the Ascent Motif in the Exegetical Works of St. Ambrose," *Studia Patristica* 8 (Texte und Untersuchungen 93; Berlin 1966) 442–48.

Palanque, J.-R. *Saint Ambroise et l'empire romain* (Paris 1933).

Paredi, A. *Saint Ambrose: His Life and Times,* translated by M. Joseph Costelloe, S.J. (Notre Dame, Indiana, 1964).

---

* The following abbreviations have been used:

CHP	*The Cambridge History of Later Greek and Early Medieval Philosophy,* edited by A. H. Armstrong (Cambridge 1967).
CSEL	*Corpus scriptorum ecclesiasticorum latinorum* (Vienna 1866—).
Dudden	F. Homes Dudden, *The Life and Times of St. Ambrose.*
FOTC	*The Fathers of the Church: A New Translation* (New York [later Washington, D. C.] 1947—).
Gryson	R. Gryson, *Le Prêtre selon saint Ambroise.*
Palanque	J.-R. Palanque, *Saint Ambroise et l'empire romain.*
Paredi	A. Paredi, *Saint Ambrose: His Life and Times.*
PL	J.-P. Migne, *Patrologiae cursus completus: Series latina* (Paris 1844-1864).

ACKNOWLEDGMENTS

The translator wishes to express his great indebtedness to two professors of The Catholic University of America, both editors of this series and both deceased in the year 1969, for their assistance and inspiration—Dr. Roy J. Deferrari and Dr. Martin R. P. McGuire. Also, he would thank Miss Carolyn Lee, Theology Librarian of The Catholic University of America, for a generous loan of books, and The University of Connecticut Research Foundation for a welcome grant-in-aid to meet the translator's research expenses.

In passing from typescript to the printed page the work has much profited from the interest, diligence, and keenness of Miss Eleanor W. Clough, Executive Assistant to the Editorial Director, to whom special gratitude is due. She has expunged error and clarified obscurity, brought into play dozens of biblical quotations and allusions passed over by editors of Ambrose, and assisted skilfully in the preparation of the Scripture index.

MICHAEL P. MCHUGH

Storrs, Connecticut

November 29, 1971

GENERAL INTRODUCTION

HE CIRCUMSTANCES AND EVENTS of the life of Ambrose (339–397), Bishop of Milan, are so well known as not to need extensive repetition here.[1] It was mostly in the last decade of the saint's life that the sermons contained in this volume were composed and, for the most part, preached, from 386, or perhaps 383, to as late as 394. This was a period in which Ambrose was much involved in the affairs of the imperial court at Milan, first in 383 as legate of the boy-emperor Valentinian (383–392) to the usurper Maximus,[2] and later in the famous conflict with Valentinian's mother, the Arian Empress Justina, who in Holy Week of 385 attempted to gain possession of the cathedral church of Milan for the Arian bishop Auxentius.[3] Justina made a further attempt to force Ambrose to capitulate early in 386; it was at this time, when his church was surrounded by imperial troops, that Ambrose introduced the antiphonal singing of psalms and hymns.[4]

After the deaths of Maximus and Justina (388), but before the murder of Valentinian (392),[5] Ambrose came into conflict

---

1 Standard works are those of Dudden, Palanque, and Paredi (cited in full above, in the Select Bibliography). For a good short survey, see M. R. P. McGuire, "Ambrose, St.," *New Catholic Encyclopedia* 1 (New York 1967) 372–75; and, for an appreciation with further bibliography, Hans von Campenhausen, "Ambrose," *The Fathers of the Latin Church* (London 1964) 87–128 (bibliography 317–19). A handy chronological table appears in *Saint Ambrose: Theological and Dogmatic Works*, translated by R. J. Deferrari (FOTC 44) xv-xxi.
2 See J.-R. Palanque, "Roman Emperors from Spain: The Emperor Maximus," *Classical Folia* 22 (1968) 85–104.
3 See Ambrose, *Letter* 20, translated as Letter 60 by Sister M. Melchior Beyenka, O.P., *St. Ambrose: Letters* (FOTC 26).
4 Cf. Augustine, *Confessions* 9.7.15.
5 The funeral sermon preached by Ambrose on the Emperor Valentinian

1

on two occasions with the Eastern Emperor, Theodosius. The first of these was the unfortunate incident at Callinicum (388), where the Christians had connived with their bishop to burn a synagogue. Theodosius had ordered the synagogue rebuilt at the local bishop's expense, but Ambrose intervened, out of a misdirected zeal, to have this just order revoked. The second intervention of the Bishop of Milan had considerably more justification, however. In 390 a number of imperial officers had been killed in a riot in Thessalonica. Theodosius ordered a brutal reprisal which resulted in the massacre of seven thousand persons; for this offense he was excommunicated by Ambrose and compelled to do public penance. Throughout, Ambrose kept to one course, through maintaining a single principle, that the Church was supreme in its own sphere, that "the emperor is within the Church, and not above the Church."[6]

These momentous events receive only the scantiest notice, and then only by way of vague allusion, in the seven exegetical works before us in the present volume. Ambrose considered preaching an important duty; he addressed his people on all Sundays and feast days, and daily in Lent. The principal source for his sermons is Scripture—Genesis and the Psalms especially for the Old Testament, the Gospels and the Pauline Epistles for the New, although virtually every book of both Testaments receives at least a citation or two. Above all, Ambrose relies upon allegorical exegesis for the entire Old Testament.[7] This

---

is translated by R. J. Deferrari in *Funeral Orations . . .* (FOTC 22) 263–99. Along with the funeral oration for Theodosius, delivered in 395 and translated in the same volume, it is an important source for the political affairs of the period.

6 Ambrose, *Sermon against Auxentius,* paragraph 3.

7 For a brief history of the allegorical method to the time of Ambrose, see Paredi 260–64. For a very comprehensive survey in a remarkably short span, see V. Harris, "Allegory to Analogy in the Interpretation of Scriptures," *Philological Quarterly* 45 (1966) 1–23. The allegorical meanings of virtually all persons and places referred to in the works of Ambrose are listed in W. Wilbrand, "Die Deutungen der biblischen Eigennamen beim hl. Ambrosius," *Biblische Zeitschrift* 10 (1912) 337–50.

system appears as early as the fifth century B. C. in the explanation of the text of Homer and was adopted by educated Jews of the Hellenistic Age, the foremost among them being Philo.[8] Christ Himself used allegorical exegesis in His comparison of the three days spent by Jona in the belly of the fish with His own three days in the tomb.[9] Paul frequently has recourse to it, as in his comparison of Christ to Adam, the new Adam versus the old.[10] Ambrose, relying essentially on Philo and Origen,[11] distinguishes in the Scriptures three senses, the literal, the moral—intended for man's instruction— and the mystical, or spiritual—which pertains to the kingdom of Christ. His primary interest is in the moral sense, although he does not, of course, deny the literal or the spiritual.

Ambrose does indeed make use of the pagan philosophers— in certain sermons more than in others—especially of Plato[12] and, among the Neoplatonists,[13] of Plotinus[14] and his disciple Porphyry.[15] But since he supposed, as perhaps a rather curious corollary of allegorical exegesis, that the sum and substance of natural wisdom appears in one form or another in the biblical text, our saint holds the notion that whatever wisdom is in the works of Plato and his successors is derived from Scripture! Ambrose copies paragraphs from Plotinus but takes care in every case to remove references to the figures of pagan mythology or to philosophical tenets incompatible with Christian teachings. Further study remains to be done in this area, but much has already been achieved in the way of identi-

---

8 See H. Chadwick, "Philo and the Beginnings of Christian Thought," CHP 137–92, especially chapter 8, "Philo," 137–57. See also R. Arnaldez, "Philo Judaeus," *New Catholic Encyclopedia* 11.287–91.

9 Cf. Matt. 12.38–42.

10 Cf. Rom. 5.14; 1 Cor. 15.45–49.

11 See H. Chadwick's chapter "Origen," CHP 182–92.

12 See P. Merlan, "Greek Philosophy from Plato to Plotinus," *ibid.* 14–132.

13 See the article "Neoplatonism," by P. Hadot, *New Catholic Encyclopedia* 10.334–36.

14 See A. H. Armstrong, "Plotinus," CHP 195–268, and the article "Plotinus," by W. H. O'Neill, *New Catholic Encyclopedia* 11.443–44.

15 See A. C. Lloyd, chapters 17 and 18 of Part IV, "The Later Neoplatonists," CHP 272–301, and the article "Porphyry," by P. Hadot, *New Catholic Encyclopedia* 11.593–94.

fication of source material, thanks above all to the work of P. Courcelle.[16]

Among the classical poets, Vergil alone seems to have had any notable influence upon the sermons in question here, and that mostly in similarity of language, only occasionally in likeness of thought.[17] A number of the metaphors—those of the sea and of athletic contests especially—that were popular among the rhetors of the Second Sophistic movement[18] in the late Empire appear also in these sermons, but it is an open question to what extent Ambrose derived them directly from the rhetorical schools, since they were of such frequent occurrence in Christian authors in any case.

We are puzzled somewhat to explain the highly favorable, enthusiastic evaluation of Ambrose's eloquence that appears in Augustine.[19] Our judgment, however, suffers considerably from the fact that, while Augustine was speaking of the sermons as heard from Ambrose's own eloquent mouth, what we have is in every case the author's reworking of the spoken sermon. Much, naturally, was lost in the process; as one biographer of Ambrose puts it, "It is like having a glass of champagne which has been standing too long, and which has lost its seething, sparkling bubbles."[20] In any event, the sermons presented here do not appear to have had any extensive influence in the subsequent history of literature,

---

16 The writings of Courcelle that are especially relevant are listed together under his name in the Select Bibliography. The second and enlarged edition of Courcelle's *Recherches* seems to show the body of the work unchanged from the first; it appeared too late for the added material, the Appendices, to be considered here.

17 Vergilian influence in Ambrose has been studied by Sister Mary Dorothea Diederich, S.S.N.D., *Vergil in the Works of St. Ambrose* (Catholic University of America Patristic Studies 29; Washington 1931), and, with special reference to a number of aspects of content, by P. Courcelle, "Les Pères devant les enfers Virgiliens," *Archives d'histoire doctrinale et littéraire du moyen âge* 30 (1955) 5–74.

18 See, for a good survey of the subject, J. M. Campbell, *The Influence of the Second Sophistic on the Style of the Sermons of St. Basil the Great* (The Catholic University of America Patristic Studies 2; Washington 1922).

19 Cf. *Confessions* 5.13.23–14.24.   20 Paredi 259.

although large portions of *Isaac, or the Soul* and occasional portions of others of them are found in a *Commentary on the Canticle of Canticles* compiled by the twelfth-century Cistercian William of St.-Thierry.[21] Since each of the seven sermons has its own history, and there is no thematic unity among them, it has seemed best to supply for each its own brief introduction.

The text followed in the making of the translation has been that of Karl Schenkl, CSEL 32.1 (Vienna 1896/7) for *Isaac, or the Soul* and *Death as a Good*, and 32.2 (Vienna 1897) for the other sermons. Occasionally, for the sake of clarity, the translation has been based on the Benedictine edition of 1686, 1690 as reprinted in Migne, PL 14 (Paris 1845); each such departure from the Schenkl text has been noted where it occurs.

No single work could be used as source for the English translation of Ambrose's citations from Scripture. Translations from the New Testament could, most of the time, be based on the Confraternity of Christian Doctrine text.[22] The Psalms most often lent themselves to a translation based on the Douay version. After some deliberation, the present translator decided to make his own translations for citations from the other books of the Old Testament, since the text set out by Ambrose followed, as often as not, the Greek of the Septuagint or an Old Latin version of the Septuagint, and the sense would have been distorted or lost entirely, particularly in places where a play on words was involved, had any existing version been followed exactly. Even in these cases, however,

---

21 PL 15.1851–962 (1947–2060). Passages drawn from Ambrose are noted as they occur. For the *Commentary* as a work of William's, see Fr. Stegmüller, *Repertorium biblicum medii aevi* 2 (Madrid 1950) 435 No. 3028. This work is distinct from William's *Exposition on the Canticle of Canticles* brought out in *Sources chrétiennes* 82 (Paris 1962); cf. p. 8 n. 3.

22 The fully developed Confraternity translation found in *The New American Bible* (1970) appeared too late to be available to me. Regrettably, the same is true of *A New Catholic Commentary on Holy Scripture* (London 1969).

the Confraternity version or an early-American translation of the Septuagint[23] has been followed as far as the sense permitted. The abbreviations employed to refer to the books of Scripture are in every case those of the Confraternity version.

Of the modern works that the reader of this translation could, at various points, consult with profit, some are listed in the intentionally brief Select Bibliography, while some are referred to only in the footnotes. The twofold division of the Latin text into "chapters" and "sections" follows Schenkl's edition, save that what Schenkl notes in the margins is here given within the column of text, either at the beginning of a paragraph or in the midst of one. The first of the two numbers that appear within the parentheses in each case indicates the "chapter," the second the "section."

---

23 *The Septuagint Bible,* the translation of Charles Thomson, Secretary of the Continental Congress of the United States of America, 1774-1789, as revised by C. A. Muses (Indian Hills, Colorado, 1954). Where Ambrose clearly based his Latin version on the Septuagint text or on an existing Latin version based on the Septuagint, that fact has been noted by the word "Septuagint" in parentheses after the relevant biblical citation.

ISAAC, OR THE SOUL

(De Isaac vel anima)

INTRODUCTION

WHETHER AMBROSE EVER DELIVERED *Isaac, or the Soul* as a sermon is uncertain, although the weight of scholarship is in favor of considering it solely a written work.[1] Likewise uncertain is its date, which can only be set between 386 and 391.[2] The influence of Plotinus on the work is very extensive,[3] although Origen, Hippolytus, and Porphyry must also be considered as principal sources. Apparently *Isaac,* as well as its companion work *Death as a Good,* was read by Augustine's mother, Monica,[4] and their influence on Augustine himself is now established.[5]

Isaac, while presenting such doctrines of Plotinus as the sovereign good and the ascent of the soul, and apparent references back to Plato, is primarily an allegory, in which the marriage of Isaac and Rebecca is viewed as a figure of the marriage between Christ and the human soul. Much of the work, deriving from Origen and Hippolytus, constitutes a commentary on the *Canticle of Canticles,* interpreted always in one or another allegorical sense.

There is no other translation in English and only one in any other modern language.[6]

---

1 On the work as a whole see Dudden 682; Palanque 441, 444, 540-541; Paredi 349.
2 In addition to the authorities cited above, see W. Wilbrand, "Zur Chronologie einiger Schriften des hl. Ambrosius," *Historisches Jahrbuch* 41 (1921) 12-13.
3 See especially P. Courcelle, *Recherches sur les* Confessions *de saint Augustin* (Paris 1950) 106-38, 154-55; also Courcelle's "Plotin et saint Ambroise," *Revue de philologie* 24 (1950) 29-56, and P. Hadot, "Platon et Plotin dans trois sermons de saint Ambroise," *Revue des études latines* 34 (1956) 202-20.
4 Cf. Courcelle, *Recherches* 132 and n. 3.
5 Cf. Courcelle, *Recherches* 106-38.
6 D. Gorce, *Saint Ambroise: Traités sur l'Ancien Testament* (Namur 1967), which, however, contains only sections 1-2, 5-7, 9, 11-16, 20-27, 35, 38-39, 41-42, 49-53, 55-56, 60-62, 64, 69, 75, 77-79. But Courcelle also translates substantial portions into French in the course of his discussion in *Recherches* 106-38.

9

ISAAC, OR THE SOUL

I HAVE DESCRIBED sufficiently both the origin of holy Isaac and the grace he received in my discussion of his father.[1] He abounds in glory, in that he was born as a reward to Abraham, his incomparably great father. And no wonder, since there were prefigured in him the birth and the passion of the Lord. An aged woman who was sterile brought him to birth according to God's promise,[2] so that we might believe that God has power to bring it about that even a virgin may give birth; he was offered for sacrifice in a singular fashion, that he might not be lost to his father and yet might fulfill the sacrifice.[3] Likewise by his very name he prefigures grace. For Isaac means laughter,[4] and laughter is the sign of joy. Now everyone knows that He is the joy of all who checked the dread of fearsome death, took away its terror, and became for all men the forgiveness of their sins. The one is named and the other denoted, the one portrayed and the other foretold. He is the one that the slave-girl despised even then;[5] for his sake it was said even then, "Cast out the slave-girl; for the son of the slave-girl shall not be heir with my son Isaac."[6] He is the one for whom his father obtained an alien wife.[7]

---

1 This is Ambrose's work *On Abraham*. There is apparently no English translation of it, but selections from it appear in French in D. Gorce, *Saint Ambroise: Traités sur l'Ancien Testament* (Namur 1967).
2 Cf. Gen. 18.11-15; 21.1-2.
3 Cf. Gen. 22.1-19.
4 Cf. Gen. 21.6.—Literally, Ambrose says: "In Latin *Isaac* is interpreted *risus.*" In this case (another like it occurs below at n. 10) it seemed best simply to omit the word *latine* and to translate the Latin by the English equivalent. More frequently, however, the phrase "in our tongue" has been used in these translations to render *latine, Latina interpretatio,* or similar expressions.
5 Cf. Gen. 16.4.
6 Gen. 21.10.   7 Gen. 24.

He is the one, mild, humble, and gentle,[8] who went out into the field to meditate, when there came Rebecca (or patience).[9] For a wise man should remove himself from fleshly pleasures, elevate his soul, and draw away from the body; this is to know oneself a man—*homo* in Latin, but *Enos*[10] in the language of the Chaldaeans. Enos' successor called upon God in hope and so is thought to have been transported.[11] And so only that man seems to be "man" who puts his hope in God. Moreover, the clear and truthful sense of the passage is that one who puts his hope in God does not dwell on earth but is transported, so to speak, and cleaves to God. (1.2) And so Isaac is good and true, for he is full of grace and a fountain of joy.

To that fountain came Rebecca, to fill her water jar. For Scripture says that "going down to the fountain she filled her water jar and came up."[12] And so the Church or the soul went down to the fountain of wisdom to fill its own vessel and draw up the teachings of pure wisdom, which the Jews did not wish to draw from the flowing fountain. Listen to Him as He says who that fountain is, "They have abandoned me, the fountain of living water."[13] The soul of the prophets ran thirsting to this fountain, even as David says, "My soul has thirsted after the living God,"[14] that he might fill his thirst with the richness of the knowledge of God and might wash away the blood of foolishness with watering of spiritual streams. For this is the flow of blood, as the law indicates,[15] that is detected when a man joins with a woman in intercourse during her menstrual period. A woman is a delight, an allurement of the

---

8 Cf. Matt. 11.29, where Christ is similarly described.
9 Rebecca appears also as a figure of patience at *Jacob and the Happy Life* 2.4.14 and *Letters* 63.100. The former is translated in this book; the latter appears as Letter 59 in *Saint Ambrose: Letters* (FOTC 26; Washington 1954, reprinted 1967). For the incident itself, cf. Gen. 24.63.
10 Cf. Gen. 5.6-11.
11 Cf. Gen. 5.18-24.
12 Gen. 24.16.
13 Jer. 2.13.
14 Ps. 41 (42).2-3.
15 Cf. Lev. 20.18.

body. And[16] so watch out that the firmness of your mind not be bent and softened by the bodily pleasure of intercourse and thus dissolve into all her embraces and open up her fountain, that ought to have been shut and closed in by zealous intent and reasoned consideration. "You are an enclosed garden, a fountain sealed."[17] For once the firmness of the mind is dissolved, thoughts of bodily pleasure pour forth; they are very harmful and flare up into an unrestrained longing for grave danger. But if careful attention had been devoted to guarding the lively mind, it would have checked them.

(2.3) Consider then, O man, who you are and to what end you maintain your life and well-being. What, then, is man? Soul, or body, or a union of both? We are one thing, our possessions are something else; he who is clothed is one person, his clothing something else. We read in the Old Testament, "all the souls that went into Egypt,"[1] in reference to men. And elsewhere it was said, "My spirit shall not remain in those men, since they are flesh."[2] And so we read that "man" is used to refer to either of the two, the soul and the flesh. But the difference is this, that when the term "soul" is used to refer to man, the Hebrew who cleaves to God, and not to the body, is meant, as in this passage: "A soul is blessed which is altogether sincere."[3] But when "flesh" is employed in reference to man, a sinner is meant, as in this passage: ". . . but I am carnal, sold into the power of sin. For I do not understand what I do, for it is not what I wish that I do, but what I hate, that I do."[4] This sentiment appears later with reference to both terms, for he who wishes is one; he who hates is another; and he who does, another. There follows: "But if

16 The material translated from this point to the end of this paragraph appears also in the twelfth-century compendium, *Commentary on the Canticle of Canticles* 4.40. See Gen. Intr. p. 5.
17 Cant. 4.12.

1 Gen. 26.46.
2 Gen. 6.3.
3 Prov. 11.25 (Septuagint).
4 Rom. 7.14-15.

I do what I hate, I consent to the law, that it is good. Now therefore it is no longer I who do it, but the sin that dwells in me."[5] This also appears more clearly: "I see a law of my flesh warring against the law of my mind and making me prisoner to the law of sin."[6] Although Paul said that both men were at war in him, the internal and the external, yet he preferred to establish himself in the part that comprises the soul rather than in the body. For when his soul, in which he preferred to exist, was being drawn captive to sin, he confirms his preference, saying: "Unhappy man that I am! Who will deliver me from the body of this death?"[7] Thus he desired to be delivered from an external enemy, so to speak.

(2.4) Therefore the soul is not blood, because blood is of the flesh;[8] nor is the soul a harmony, because harmony of this sort is also of the flesh; neither is the soul air, because blown breath is one thing, and the soul something else. The soul is not fire, nor is the soul actuality, but the soul is living, for Adam "became a living soul,"[9] since the soul rules and gives life to the body, which is without life or feeling. There is also the more excellent man, of whom it is said, "But the spiritual man judges all things, and he himself is judged by no man."[10] Such a one is more excellent than others. On this account David also says, "What is man, that you are mindful of him or the son of man that you visit him? Man is become like to vanity."[11] Man according to the image of God is not

---

5 Rom. 7.16-17.   6 Rom. 7.23.   7 Rom. 7.24.
8 Cf. Cicero, *Tusculan Disputations* 1.9.19. Cicero there identifies the concept of soul as blood with Empedocles; in reality, Empedocles apparently taught that the soul had its seat in the blood, not that it was blood. For "actuality" Ambrose, a few lines further on, uses the Greek word *entelecheia*, as Cicero does, *op. cit.* 1.10.22.
  The entire discussion here on the nature of the soul probably derives from Porphyry, *De regressu animae*. See also Ambrose, *On Noe* 25.92 (not yet translated into any modern language), and Macrobius, *Commentary on the Dream of Scipio* 1.14.19-20, translated into English by W. H. Stahl (Columbia Records of Civilization 48; New York 1952) and the references given there.
9 Gen. 2.7.
10 1 Cor. 2.15.
11 Ps. 8.5; cf. Ps. 143 (144).3-4.

like to vanity, but he who has lost it and has fallen into sin and has tumbled into material things—such a man is like to vanity.

(2.5) The soul therefore is excellent according to its nature, but it generally becomes subject to corruption through its irrationality, so that it inclines to bodily pleasures and to willfulness, while it does not keep to moderation; or else it is deceived by the imagination, turns to matter, and is glued to the body. Thus its visibility is hindered, and it is filled with evil, for while it is intent on evil, it fills itself with vices and grows more unrestrained from the want of goodness. (3.6) Moreover the perfect soul turns away from matter, shuns and rejects everything that is excessive or inconstant or wicked, and neither sees nor approaches this earthly defilement and corruption. It is attentive to things divine but shuns earthly matter. But its flight is not to depart from the earth but to remain on earth, to hold to justice and temperance, to renounce the vices in material goods, not their use. Holy David fled from the face of Saul,[1] not indeed to depart from the earth, but to turn away from the contagion of a cruel, disobedient, and treacherous man. He fled, cleaving to God, just as he himself said, "My soul has stuck fast to you."[2] He withdrew and lifted himself away from the vices of this world, he lifted up his soul, even as Isaac meditated—or, as others have it, walked about—in the field.[3] For this also is evidence of familiar association with the virtues, that each man walks about in the innocence of his own heart, in no wise involves himself in earthly vices, and with his mind's unhindered step takes the path[4] that is without reproach, and does not open up any place in himself to corruption.

(3.7) Such was Isaac as he awaited Rebecca's coming and

---

1 Cf. 1 Kings 19.18.
2 Ps. 62 (63).9.
3 Cf. Gen. 24.63.
4 The phrase, "takes the path," appears in Vergil, *Aeneid* 6.629, in the address of the Sibyl to Aeneas; the Neoplatonists also refer to the path of the intelligence on its journey to happiness.

made ready for a spiritual union.[5] For she came already
endowed with heavenly mysteries, she came bearing mighty
adornments in her ears and on her arms,[6] because in her
hearing and in the works of her hands there is clearly revealed
the beauty of the Church, and we note that it was rightly said
to her, "May you become thousands of myriads and may your
seed possess the cities of their enemies."[7] Therefore the Church
is beautiful, for she has acquired sons from hostile nations.
But this passage can be interpreted in reference to the soul,
which subdues the bodily passions, turns them to the service
of the virtues, and makes resistant feelings subject to itself.
And so the soul of the patriarch Isaac, seeing the mystery of
Christ, seeing Rebecca coming with vessels of gold and silver,[8]
as if she were the Church with the people of the nations, and
marveling at the beauty of the Word and of His sacraments,
says, "Let him kiss me with the kisses of his mouth."[9] And
Rebecca, seeing the true Isaac, that true joy, and true source
of mirth, desires to kiss him.

(3.8) What does it mean, then: "Let him kiss me with the
kisses of his mouth"? Think upon the Church,[10] in suspense
over many ages at the coming of the Lord, long promised her
through the prophets. And think upon the soul, lifting herself up from the body and rejecting indulgence and fleshly
delights and pleasures, and laying aside as well her concern
for worldly vanities. For a long time now she has desired to
be infused with God's presence and has desired, too, the grace
of the Word of salvation, and has wasted away, because he is
coming late, and has been struck down, wounded with love
as it were,[11] since she cannot endure his delays. Turning to

---

5 Cf. Gen. 24.62.   6 Cf. Gen. 24.22.
7 Gen. 24.60 (Septuagint).
8 Cf. Gen. 24.53, 63.
9 Cant. 1.2. The phrase also appears in Ambrose, *On the Sacraments*
2.5-7, where it refers to both Christ and the Church. See *On the Sacraments*, translated by T. Thompson (London 1950) p. 96 n. 2.
10 The text from this point up to 3.9 is found also in the twelfth-century
Commentary (cf. ch. 1 n. 16) 1.4-5.
11 Cf. Cant. 5.8.

the Father, she asks that He send to her God the Word, and giving the reason why she is so impatient, she says, "Let him kiss me with the kisses of his mouth." She asks, not for one kiss, but for many kisses, so that she may fulfill her desire. For as a lover, she is not satisfied with the meager offering of a single kiss, but demands many, claims many as her right, and thus has grown accustomed to recommend herself the more to her beloved. Indeed she has gained approval in the Gospel, for "she has not ceased to kiss my feet."[12] And so "her sins, many as they are, are forgiven her, because she has loved much."[13]

Therefore such a soul also desires many kisses of the Word, so that she may be enlightened with the light of the knowledge of God. For this is the kiss of the Word, I mean the light of holy knowledge. God the Word kisses us, when He enlightens our heart and man's very governing faculty with the spirit of the knowledge of God. The soul that has received this gift exults and rejoices in the pledge of wedded love and says, "I opened my mouth and panted."[14] For it is with the kiss that lovers cleave to each other and gain possession of the sweetness of grace that is within, so to speak. Through such a kiss the soul cleaves to God the Word, and through the kiss the spirit of him who kisses is poured into the soul, just as those who kiss are not satisfied to touch lightly with their lips but appear to be pouring their spirit into each other. (3.9) Showing[15] that she loves not only the appearance of the Word, and his face, as it were, but all his inner parts, she adds to the favor of the kisses: "Your breasts are better than wine and the fragrance of your ointments is above all perfumes."[16] She sought the kiss, God the Word poured himself into her wholly and laid bare his breasts to her, that is, his teachings and the

---

12 Luke 7.45.
13 Luke 7.47.
14 Ps. 118 (119).131.
15 The text from this point to "For there breathes in the Word. . ." appears in the already cited *Commentary* 1.7.
16 Cant. 1.2-3 (Septuagint).

laws of the wisdom that is within, and was fragrant with the sweet fragrance of his ointments. Captive to these, the soul is saying that the enjoyment of the knowledge of God is richer than the joy of any bodily pleasure. For[17] there breathes in the Word the fragrance of grace and the forgiveness of sins. Poured out into all the world, this forgiveness has filled all things and the ointment has been emptied out, as it were, in wiping away the heavy dregs of vice among all men.

(3.10) "Therefore young maidens have loved you. Draw us, let us run after the fragrance of your ointments."[18] Good indeed is prudence[19] but mercy is sweet. Few attain the former, whereas the latter comes to all men. "By reason of your loving-kindness, the souls renewed in the spirit love you." On this account also it is said to the soul, "Your youth shall be renewed like the eagle's."[20] For the psalmist spoke to the soul and said, "Bless the Lord, O my soul."[21] And[22] therefore the soul hastens to the Word and asks that she be drawn to Him, so that she may not, perhaps, be left behind, for "the Word of God runs and is not bound."[23] Indeed "he rejoices as a giant to run the way" and because "his going out is from the end of heaven and his circuit even to the end thereof,"[24] the soul, seeing that she is no match for such great swiftness, says, "Draw us." And good is the soul that asks, not alone for herself, but for all souls. "Draw us." For we have the desire to follow, which we have inhaled from the gracious gift of your ointments. But since we cannot match your course, draw us, so that we can follow in your footsteps through your assistance and support. If you draw us, we will run and will take hold of swift spiritual breezes. For they put aside their

---

17 The text from this point to 3.10 appears in the *Commentary* 1.9.
18 Cant. 1.3-4. On the relationships of the Latin text and its sources see T. Thompson, in his translation of *On the Sacraments,* p. 97 n. 4.
19 The text from this point to "On this account also it is said to the soul. . ." appears in the *Commentary* 1.9.
20 Cf. Eph. 4.23; Ps. 102 (103).5.
21 Ps. 102 (103).1.
22 The text from this point to 4.11 appears in the *Commentary* 1.13-15.
23 2 Thess. 3.1; 2 Tim. 2.9.   24 Ps. 18 (19).6-7.

burden who have your hand as their support, and into them is poured your oil, with which the man who was wounded by robbers was healed.[25] And do not consider shameless her statement, "Draw us," but hear Him as He says, "Come to me, all you who labor and are burdened, and I will give you rest."[26] You see how gladly He draws us, so that we may not be left behind as we follow.

But let him who desires to be drawn so run as to obtain, and let him run forgetting the things that are past and seeking those that are better, for thus he will be able to obtain Christ. On this account the Apostle also says, "So run that you all obtain."[27] The soul too wishes to arrive at the prize that she longs to obtain. And so she wisely asks that she be drawn, because not all are able to follow. Indeed when Peter said, "Where are you going?" the Word of God replied, "You cannot follow me now but you will follow me later."[28] The Lord had entrusted to him the keys of the kingdom of heaven,[29] and yet Peter judged himself unequal to following. The Lord did not put off this soul, however, for Peter was not presuming but asking.

(4.11) Indeed "the king[1] brought me to his inner apartment."[2] Blessed the soul that enters the inner chambers. For, rising up from the body, she becomes more distant from all, and she searches and seeks within herself, if in any way she can pursue the divine. And when she can obtain it, having passed beyond intelligible things, she is strengthened in it and fed by it. Such was Paul, who knew that he had been caught up into paradise but did not know whether he had been caught up in the body or out of the body.[3] For his soul

---

25 Cf. Luke 10.34.
26 Matt. 11.28.
27 1 Cor. 9.24.
28 John 13.36.
29 Cf. Matt. 16.19.

1 The text from this point to "And so a man of this kind. . ." appears in the *Commentary* 1.16.
2 Cant. 1.4 (Septuagint).
3 Cf. 2 Cor. 12.3-4.

had risen up from the body, had withdrawn from the vitals and the bonds of the flesh, and had lifted herself up. And he was made alien to himself by himself and held within his very self the secret words which he heard and could not reveal, because, as he remarked, it was not permitted a man to speak such thoughts.[4] And so the good soul scorns visible and material things and does not linger over them or delay or tarry in despising them. Rather, she rises to things eternal and immaterial and filled with wonders, for she rises with pure thought from pious mind. Intent on perfection, she strives only for the good that is God's and considers none other necessary, because she possesses that which is supreme. And so a man of this kind, in whom there is beauty of soul, has more than enough for himself, though he is alone, for he is himself sufficient for himself. And yet the man is never alone who has the Lord with him as his protector. (4.12) Indeed, when she was brought into the secret place of divinity, the soul said, "Let[5] us rejoice and be gladdened in you. Let us love your breasts more than wine."[6] For the just man rejoices, not in riches and in treasures of gold and silver, not in the proceeds of his property, not in power or in feasts, but in God alone.[7]

(4.13) And[8] yet the selfsame soul, knowing that she has been darkened by her union with the body, says to other souls or to those powers of heaven that have charge of the holy ministry, "Look not on me, because I am of a dark complexion, because the sun has not looked upon me. The sons of my mother have fought against me";[9] that is, the passions of the body have attacked me and the allurements of the flesh have given me my color; therefore the sun of justice has

4 Cf. 2 Cor. 12.4.
5 The text from this point to 4.13 appears in the *Commentary* 1.21.
6 Cf. Cant. 1.4 (Septuagint).
7 Cf. Hab. 3.18.
8 The text from this point to "The sons of my mother. . ." appears in the *Commentary* 1.21.
9 Cant. 1.6 (Septuagint).

not shone on me.[10] Bereft of this protection, I have not been able to maintain my devotion and full obedience. This is the meaning of "My own vineyard I have not kept."[11] For I have produced thorns and not grapes, that is, sins in place of spiritual fruits.[12] (4.14) And when she speaks of the Word, and the brilliance of the Word shines on her, she turns to Him and says, "Where[13] do you pasture your flock? Where do you rest at noon?"[14] She rightly says "Where do you pasture your flock?" because the word of God is natural; "where do you rest?" because it is moral; "at noon" because it is mystical, since it was at noon that Joseph took his place with his brothers at the banquet and revealed the mysteries of the times that were to come.[15] But David also says, "Commit your way to the Lord and trust in him and he will do it. And he will bring forth your justice as the light and your judgment as the noonday."[16] And Paul himself stated that the light had shone round him at noon, when he was converted from persecution to grace.[17]

Therefore the soul is complaining because she has been forsaken, because she has been abandoned and is poor who was rich. For she overflowed with gifts of grace, but she began to be in want when the fullness of the divine presence was denied to her, and so she demands to be treated as if she were a hireling who had previously claimed for herself the favor of a richer union. (4.15) And the Word of God replies to her, "If[18] you do not know yourself, O fair among women"[19] —for you are complaining that you have been abandoned— "if you do not know yourself," that is, unless you repent of

---

10 Cf. Mal. 3.20 (4.2).
11 Cant. 1.6.
12 Cf. Matt. 7.16-20.
13 The text from this point to 4.15 appears in the *Commentary* 1.28-29.
14 Cant. 1.7.
15 Cf. Gen. 43.15.
16 Ps. 36 (37).5-6.
17 Cf. Acts 9.3.
18 The text from this point to 4.16 appears in the *Commentary* 1.33.
19 Cant. 1.8.

your sins, unless you manifest attentive devotion, unless your faith and purity increase, your complaining will be of no help. Or, alternatively, "if you do not know yourself," that you are fair, unless you maintain the beauty of your nature, and the allurements of the body do not overwhelm you and its impediments do not keep you back, the nobility of a better creation will give you no support at all.

(4.16) Therefore[20] know yourself and the beauty of your nature, and go forth as if your foot had been freed of bonds[21] and were visible in its bare step, so that you may not feel the fleshly coverings, that the bonds of the body may not entangle the footstep of your mind, that your foot may appear beautiful. For such are they who are chosen by the Lord to announce the kingdom of heaven, and of them it was said, "How beautiful are the feet of those who preach the gospel of peace!"[22] Such was Moses, to whom it is said, "Remove the sandals from your feet,"[23] so that when he was about to call the people to the kingdom of God he might first put aside the garments of the flesh and might walk with his spirit and the footstep of his mind naked. Therefore this is what the Lord says, "Go forth in the tracks of the flocks and pasture your kids beside the tents of the shepherds."[24] For by the flocks we understand the kingdom, for to exercise the care of flocks implies power. Further, each man exercises the care of himself by a kind of royal power if he checks the excesses of the body in himself and reduces his flesh to servitude. And so it was said, "The kingdom of God is within you."[25] On this account the Lord aptly said to the soul, "Go forth," that is, go forth from slavery,[26] go forth from the rule and domination of the flesh,

---

20 The text from this point to "and seeks victory by the toil of virtue. . ." (prior to 4.17) appears in the *Commentary* 1.34-35.
21 Cf. Vergil, *Aeneid* 4.518.
22 Rom. 10.15; cf. Isa. 52.7.
23 Exod. 3.5.
24 Cant. 1.8.
25 Luke 17.21.
26 Cf. Vergil, *Eclogues* 1.40.

and go forth, not in the flesh, but in the spirit, go forth to the control of power. Likewise He added, "Pasture your kids"; control the things that are on your left hand, for if they are not controlled they easily fall.[27] Check your wantonness, the lust of your body and unreasonable self-indulgence, master your fickle passions, pasture them not in the tents of the body, but by the tents of the shepherds, who have learned how to control the flock.

For "the tents of Israel are lovable, like shady woods beside a river."[28] The soul, lying in them as if in readiness for war, renders good service, searches out the incursions of the foe, and seeks victory by[29] the toil of virtue, so that she may be compared to that steed of Solomon's, swift in running and fit to give birth, because fertility of soul is desirable and sought after. (4.17) Therefore she is a precious steed, and she is Pharao's swift chariots,[30] but some take this passage in reference to the Church and the people. But I have spoken of this mystery quite often elsewhere, especially in discussing Psalm 118,[31] while I have undertaken here to speak of the soul. The soul is judged like this steed—I mean a soul of prophetic or apostolic virtue—because she is counted in the company of those who have filled up all the spaces of the entire earth with the fertility of their preaching; although established in the body, they felt no loss of their spiritual course. And so she gains praise because, under the illumination of heavenly precept, she is now fair and beautiful. On her face she displays the comeliness of chastity, and, as she raises up her necklace,

---

27 Cf. Matt. 25.33.

28 Num. 24.5-6.

29 The text from this point to "The true Isaac loved. . ." (prior to 4.18) appears in the *Commentary* 1.42.

30 Cf. Cant. 1.9.

31 Cf. *Explanation of Psalm 118*, 2.33. There is no complete translation of this work in any modern language; selections appear in D. Gorce, *Exposé sur le psaume* CXVIII (Namur 1963). The reference proves a contemporaneity between *Isaac, or the Soul* and *Explanation of Psalm 118* but does not definitively prove a derivation of the former from the latter, as might appear. Cf. P. Courcelle, *Recherches* 123 and n. 6.

upon her neck there are the marks of patience and humility. The true Isaac loved the comeliness and humility and patience of such a soul and eagerly awaited her offspring.

(4.18) Now Rebecca conceived[32] and by her patience undid the knot of sterility. Let us consider what her prophetic and apostolic soul brought to birth, and how. "She went to consult the Lord,"[33] because the children leapt up in her womb, and received the reply, "Two nations are in your womb."[34] For of herself she presumes nothing but invokes God as supreme protector of her counsels; filled with peace and piety, she joins two nations together by her faith and by prophecy and encloses them in her womb, so to speak. (4.19) Not without reason is she called sister rather than wife, because her gentle and peaceable soul enjoys a reputation for affection common to all rather than for union with one individual, and because she thought that she was bound to all rather than to one.

(4.20) Now Isaac reopened many wells which his father had dug,[35] but strangers had filled them after the death of his father Abraham. Beyond the others he dug the following wells: one in the valley of Gerara, and he found there a well of living water, and the shepherds of Gerara disputed with Isaac's shepherds, because they claimed the water of this well as their own, and he called its name Injustice.[36] And he dug another well over which a quarrel arose, and he called it Enmity.[37] And he dug a third well, over which no dispute began among the shepherds, and he called it Room-enough.[38] He also dug a well and did not find water in it and called that well Well of the Oath.[39] (4.21) Would anyone reading of these things consider that those works were earthly rather than

---

32 Cf. Gen. 25.21.
33 Gen. 25.22.
34 Gen. 25.23.
35 Cf. Gen. 26.18.
36 Cf. Gen. 26.19-20.
37 Cf. Gen. 26.21.
38 Cf. Gen. 26.22.
39 Cf. Gen. 26.25, 32-33.

spiritual?[40] For Abraham dug wells and Isaac too—that is, the mighty patriarchs—and Jacob also, as we find in the Gospel,[41] as if they were fountains of the human race, and specifically fountains of faith and devotion. For what is a well of living water but a depth of profound instruction? On this account Agar saw the angel by a well[42] and Jacob found his wife Rachel by a well;[43] Moses too earned the first rewards of his future marriage beside a well.[44] (4.22) Therefore Isaac undertook to open wells out of a depth of vision and in good order, so that the water of his well might first wash and strengthen the reasoning faculty of the soul and her eye, to make her sight clearer.

He also dug several other wells. On this account it was written, "Drink water from your own vessels and from the fountains of your own wells."[45] The more there are, the richer is the overflow of graces. But he dug a well which his father Abraham had dug, over which the shepherds of Gerara disputed, this in reference to walls of separation, for where there is a wall of separation, there there is division among combatants, and injustice. And so he called it Injustice. He dug another well, and when discord arose, he called it Enmity. In them there seems to appear a moral teaching, for once the wall of separation is removed, the enmities in man's flesh are dissolved and both elements become one—in figure through Isaac, in truth through Christ.[46] Consequently, later there was found in that well pure water, usable for drinking, like moral teaching. And what is the meaning of the Well of Room-enough but an instruction with a natural interpretation? For this reason also it is called Room-enough. For the man who

---

40 Ambrose does in fact offer an allegorical explanation of the wells in his *Explanation of the Gospel According to Luke*, prologue 2 (no English translation available).
41 Cf. John 4.6, 12.
42 Cf. Gen. 21.14.
43 Cf. Gen. 29.2, 9-10.
44 Cf. Exod. 2.15-22.
45 Prov. 5.15.
46 Cf. Eph. 2.14.

has passed beyond worldly and material things is already tranquil and composed, without contention, without strife. On this account, once he has overcome hostile and alien thoughts —and what is more alien than all the things of this world, which cannot endure forever?—the wise man can say, "The Lord has made room for us and has increased us upon the earth,"[47] because he has passed beyond earthly things. The last is the Well of the Oath, where God appeared to him and said to him, "Fear not, for I am with you,"[48] and blessed him. Now this teaching is mystical.

(4.23) You[49] have the like in Solomon, for his Proverbs are moral, Ecclesiastes—in which he despises the vanities of this world—is natural, his Canticle of Canticles is mystical.[50] You have it also in the prophet: "Sow for yourselves for justice, gather in the fruit of life, light up for yourselves the light of knowledge."[51] This is the light of knowledge, to have the perfection of love. And so it was said, "Fear not, for love casts out fear."[52] So that we may know that Solomon interpreted these wells so as to ascribe to them moral, natural, and mystical meanings, he put them in each of the books that he wrote from the viewpoint of the moral and natural and mystical senses, respectively. (4.24) For in Proverbs, when he was saying that the beauty of worldly allurement should be rejected, he said, "Drink water from your own vessels and from the fountains of your own wells, and let the waters from your fountain overflow for you."[53] And below, "Let your fountain of water be for yourself alone, and rejoice with your wife,"[54] because true wisdom is our remedy against the temptations of the world, and moral teaching too, for with the

---

47 Gen. 26.22.
48 Gen. 26.24.
49 The text from this point to 4.27 appears in the *Commentary* 5.43-47.
50 The same thought appears in the *Explanation of the Gospel According to Luke,* prologue 2, and in the *Explanation of Psalm 118,* 1.3.
51 Osee 10.12 (Septuagint).
52 1 John 4.18.
53 Prov. 5.15-16 (Septuagint).
54 Prov. 5.18 (Septuagint).

well-watered stream from its fountain it washes and cleanses man's image, that had been smeared by the harlot's rouge of worldly pleasure, so to speak.

(4.25) With reference to the natural sense, you find it said in Ecclesiastes, "I made for myself pools of water to water from them a flourishing woodland."[55] And do not be concerned that he said "pools" instead of "a well," because Moses said "the Well of Room-enough." For the man who has transcended this world with a pious mind is freed of all care and anxieties. There Ecclesiastes says "pools" with reason, for he sees that there is no abundance under the sun,[56] but if anyone wishes to abound, let him abound in Christ.[57] (4.26) There remains for us the well in the mystical sense, and we find it in the Canticle of Canticles, where the Scripture says, "the fountain of gardens, the well of living water which runs with a strong stream from Lebanon."[58] Indeed if you pursue the depth of the mysteries, the well appears to you to be mystical wisdom set in the deep, as it were. But if you wish to drink in the abundance of love, which is greater and richer than faith and hope, then you have your fountain. For love abounds, so that you can drink it in close at hand and water your garden with its abundance, so that the latter overflows with spiritual fruits. And because the lover is over beyond that very Well of Room-enough, Scripture therefore said that where love is, there a strong stream runs down from Lebanon. And that there may be no concern that the Scripture was speaking of the same well and fountains, let the Gospel also teach you, for there it is written that "Jesus came to a town of Samaria, which is called Sichar, near the field that Jacob gave to his son Joseph. Now Jacob's well was there. Therefore being wearied, he sat thus on the well."[59] On this account also we know that this well can be taken in the mystical sense, be-

---

55 Eccles. 2.6.
56 Cf. Eccles. 9.6.
57 Cf. Phil. 1.26.
58 Cant. 4.15.
59 John 4.5-6.

cause there the Samaritan woman—who is a guardian, I mean a guardian of the heavenly precepts—drew from that well.[60] For she learned the divine mysteries, that God is spirit and is adored, not in a place but in spirit, and that Christ is the Messias and therefore that he who was still awaited by the Jews had already come.[61] Hearing these things, that woman, who manifests the beauty of the Church, learned and believed the mysteries of the law.

(4.27) In the book of Canticles also Solomon clearly portrayed this threefold wisdom, although it was in Proverbs that he commanded that the man who wished to hear his wisdom should write it for himself three times over.[62] And so in the Canticles the bride says, concerning the bridegroom, "Behold, you are comely, my beloved—beautiful indeed! Our bed is shaded, the beams of our houses are cedar, our rafters, cypresses."[63] We can interpret this in a moral sense. For where do Christ and his Church dwell except in the works of His people? Therefore, where there was impurity, or pride, or iniquity, there, says the Lord Jesus, "the Son of Man has nowhere to lay his head."[64] (4.28) And what of the natural sense? "In his shade I took great delight and sat, and his fruit was sweet to my taste."[65] For the man who passes beyond earthly things and dies to worldly things—since the world is crucified to him and he to the world[66]—scorns and shuns all things under the sun. (4.29) Concerning the mystical sense, the passage also says, "O conduct me into the house of wine, and order for me what I love."[67] For just as the vine embraces the trellis, so the Lord Jesus, like an eternal vine,[68] embraces His people with arms of love, as it were.

---

60 For an explicit statement that "Samaritan" means "guardian," cf. Gregory, *Hom. in Evang.* 18.2. Cf. John 4.7.
61 Cf. John 4.21-26.
62 Cf. Prov. 22.20 (Septuagint).
63 Cant. 1.16-17.
64 Matt. 8.20.
65 Cant. 2.3 (Septuagint).
66 Cf. Gal. 6.14.
67 Cant. 2.4.   68 Cf. John 15.1.

(4.30) Reflect on each point. In the moral sense he is a flower, a lily among thorns, just as he himself says, "I am a flower of the field and a lily of the valleys."[69] In the moral sense he is a flower, in the natural sense, the sun of justice,[70] who gives light at his rising and arising again, but casts a shadow at his setting. See that it does not set upon you, because it is written, "Do not let the sun go down upon your anger."[71] In the mystical sense he is love, because Christ is the fulfillment of the law.[72] And so the Church, which loves Christ, is wounded with love.[73] (4.31) And so he rouses her and rouses her again, until she hears his voice and invites his presence, because, when he is sought, he not only comes, but he comes leaping, "leaping over the mountains and bounding across the hills."[74] He leaps over souls which have more grace, bounds over those which have less. Or it may be taken this way: How did he come leaping? He came into this world in a kind of leap. He was with the Father, he came into a virgin, and from a virgin he bounded into a manger. He was in a manger and he shone in heaven, he went down into the Jordan and up onto the cross, he went down to the tomb, rose up from the tomb, and sits at the right hand of the Father.[75] Like the hart who longs for the fountains of water,[76] he went down to Paul and shone around him[77] and leapt up

---

69 Cant. 2.1.
70 Cf. Mal. 3.20 (4.2).
71 Eph. 4.26.
72 Cf. Rom. 13.10.
73 Cf. Cant. 2.5 (Septuagint).
74 Cant. 2.8. The text is derived from that used by Hippolytus and corresponds more to the Septuagint than to the Vulgate. See A. Olivar, " 'Los Saltos del Verbo,' Una Interpretación Patrística de Cant. 2,8," *Analecta Sacra Tarraconensia* 29 (1956) 5-6. The interpretation of the leaping and bounding which follows also depends on Hippolytus.
75 Very similar language, and the same interpretation, appear in *Explanation of Psalm 118*, 6.6. See also G. Nathanael Bonwetsch, "Hippolyt's Kommentar zum Hohenlied," *Texte und Untersuchungen* 8.2 (Leipzig 1902) 55 and note to line 13.
76 Cf. Ps. 41 (42).2.
77 Cf. Acts 9.3.

over his Church, which is Bethel, that is, the house of God.[78]
For the calling of Paul is the strength of the Church.

(4.32) He came then, and at first he is behind the wall, so
that he may destroy the enmity between soul and body by
removing the wall, which seemed to offer an obstacle to harmony.[79] Then he looks through the windows.[80] Hear the
prophet as he tells what the windows are: "The windows are
opened from heaven."[81] Thus he means the prophets, through
whom the Lord had regard for the race of men, before he
should come down on earth himself. (4.33) Today also, if any
soul seeks after him much, she will merit much mercy, because very much is owed to the man who seeks much. Therefore if any soul searches for him with greater zeal, she hears
his voice from afar and, although she inquires of others, she
hears his voice before those from whom she is asking. She
sees that he is coming bounding to her, that is, hastening and
running and leaping over those who cannot receive his strength
from weakness of heart. Then, by reading the prophets and
remembering their words, she sees him looking through their
riddles,[82] looking, but as if through a window, not yet as if
present.

She sees him standing above the nets.[83] What does this
mean, unless perhaps that the nets are ours, not his? Nets,
because the soul is still among material and worldly things,
and these generally capture the mind of a man and wrap it in
a fold of their own, as it were. Therefore he shows himself
through nets to one who is established still among temporal
things but nevertheless is seeking him. (4.34) Then he says to
the soul of this kind, "Arise, come, my dearest one";[84] that is,

---

78 Cf. Mich. 5.1 (2). The interpretation "house of God" appears in *The
   Prayer of Job and David* 4.1.3 (translated in this book), and *On
   Abraham* 1.2.6 and 2.3.11, 2.5.21.
79 Cf. Cant. 2.9; Eph. 2.14.
80 Cf. Cant. 2.9.
81 Isa. 24.18.
82 Cf. Num. 12.8.
83 Cf. Cant. 2.9 (Septuagint).
84 Cant. 2.10.

arise from the pleasures of the world, arise from earthly things
and come to me, you who still labor and are burdened,[85]
because you are anxious about worldly things. Come over the
world, come to me, because I have overcome the world. Come
near, for now you are fair with the beauty of everlasting life,
now you are a dove,[86] that is, you are gentle and mild, now
you are filled entirely with spiritual grace. Now she ought
not to fear the nets, and rightly so, since he who cannot be
captured by the temptations and nets of the world[87] is sum-
moning the soul to himself. For we men walk in the midst
of snares and are subject at once to nets and snares through
our longing for nourishment, whereas He, when He dwelt in
the body, was not afraid of the nets but stood above the nets,
that is, above the temptations of the world and the passions
of the body, and, what is more, He caused others to stand
above the nets.

Accordingly, wishing to make such a soul firm, He said,
(4.35) "Arise, come, my dearest one, do not fear the nets,
for winter is now past";[88] that is, the Pasch has come,[89] pardon
has come, the forgiveness of sins has arrived, temptation has
ceased, the rain is gone,[90] the storm is gone, and the affliction.
Before the coming of Christ it is winter. After His coming
there are flowers. On this account He says, "The flowers appear
on the earth."[91] Where before there were thorns, now flowers
are there. "The time of pruning has come."[92] Where before
there was desert, the harvest is there. "The voice of the dove
is heard in our land."[93] The prophet did well to add "our,"
as if in wonder that where before there was unchasteness,
chastity is there.

---

85 Cf. Matt. 11.28.
86 Cf. Cant. 2.10.
87 Cf. Sir. 9.13 (20).
88 Cf. Cant. 2.11.
89 In this context, the reference is clearly to the advent of Christ and
not directly to an approaching Easter. See Dudden 682.
90 Cf. Cant. 2.11.
91 Cant. 2.12.
92 *Ibid.*   93 *Ibid.*

(4.36) "The fig tree has brought forth its green figs."[94] Before, it was ordered cut down as not bearing fruit,[95] but now it begins to offer its fruits. But why do you hesitate because He said "green figs"? He shook down those that came before, in order to bring forth those better ones that would come after, just as the fruit of the synagogue is rejected, but that of the Church is renewed.[96] (4.37) And although there is perfect tranquillity and the plan of salvation has attained its maturity, still He says again, "Arise safe in the shelter of the rock,"[97] that is, safe under the protection of my passion and behind the bulwark of faith. For "they sucked honey out of the rock, and oil out of the hardest stone."[98] Clothed with this shelter of faith, the souls of the just are not naked now, and this is a wall for them. Accordingly He says to such a soul as this, "Come you also, my dove, in the shelter of the rock near the wall, show me your face and let me hear your voice."[99] He exhorts her to confidence, that she may not be ashamed of the cross of Christ and His seal;[100] He exhorts her to confession, He wishes all the artifices to be thrust aside, that the good odor of faith may be diffused,[101] that the day may shine bright, that the shade of the hostile night may do no harm, because he who is near Christ says, "The night is far advanced, the day is at hand."[102] There is the shade of worldly things, which passes away, and the light of heavenly things, Christ, who shines on His holy ones. Such a soul receives good assurances of love.[103]

---

94 Cant. 2.13.
95 Cf. Luke 13.7.
96 In Ambrose the fig tree is a symbol of the synagogue. See Gregory Figueroa, *The Church and the Synagogue in Saint Ambrose* (Catholic University of America Studies in Sacred Theology, Second series 25; Washington 1949) 31-36.
97 Cant. 2.13-14 (Septuagint).
98 Deut. 32.13 (Septuagint).
99 Cant. 2.14 (Septuagint).
100 Cf. 2 Tim. 1.8; Cant. 8.6.
101 Cf. 2 Cor. 2.15-16.
102 Rom. 13.12.
103 That is, assurances of Christ's love in baptism. See R. T. Otten, "Caritas and the Ascent Motif in the Exegetical Works of St. Am-

(5.38) But because we ought always to be anxious, always attentive, and because the Word of God leaps forth like the gazelle or the hart,[1] let the soul who searches after Him and longs to possess Him always be on watch and maintain her defenses. "In[2] my bed at night I sought him whom my soul loved,"[3] as if He had stolen in upon her. Let one who seeks carefully seek while in his bed, let him seek at night. Let there be neither nights nor holiday, let no time be free from pious service, and if one does not find Him at first, let him persevere in searching after Him. And so the soul says, "I will rise and I will seek him in the city, in the public places, in the streets."[4] And perhaps she still does not find Him, because she sought in the public places, where there are suits at law, and in the streets, where there are markets with goods for sale; for Christ cannot be obtained for any amount of money.

(5.39) We[5] can also interpret the passage this way: That soul searches for Christ in the bed who seeks after Him with tranquillity and peace. She searches at night because He spoke through parables[6]—"for he made darkness his hiding-place[7] and night to night shows knowledge"[8]—and also because "the things we say in our heart we ought also to be sorry for on our beds."[9] But she does not find Him in this way either, and so she says, "I will rise," that is, I will rise and increase my effort, that I may search for Him relentlessly, I will search carefully, I will go into the city. It is the soul, too, that says, "I am a strong city, a city besieged."[10] The city is

brose," *Studia Patristica* 8 (Texte und Untersuchungen 93; Berlin 1966) 422-48, especially 443 and n. 4.

1 Cf. Cant. 2.9.
2 The text from this point to 5.39 appears in the *Commentary* 3.1.
3 Cant. 3.1.
4 Cant. 3.2.
5 The text from this point to "And so take Eve. . ." (prior to 5.44) appears in the *Commentary* 3.10-16.
6 Cf. Matt. 13.13; Ezech. 21.5 (20.49).
7 Ps. 17 (18).12.
8 Ps. 18 (19).3.
9 Cf. Ps. 4.5.
10 Isa. 27.3 (Septuagint).

besieged through Christ, the city is that heavenly Jerusalem,[11] in which there are interpreters of God's law and men skilled in doctrine in great abundance; through them one seeks the Word of God.

"I will seek in the public places of that city"—in the public places, where the lawyers practice law, and where the oil is sold that the virgins in the Gospel buy,[12] so that their lamps may always be lit and the smoke of iniquity may not put them out. "I will seek in the streets," in which the waters overflow, rushing forth from those fountains from which Solomon says man ought to drink.[13] (5.40) Then while she seeks Christ, she finds the watchmen who are in His service.[14] But the soul who seeks God goes beyond the watchmen also, for they are the mysteries which even the angels desire to see. On this account Peter says, "They were revealed to you by those to whom they have preached the gospel, the Holy Spirit being sent down from heaven, on whom the angels desire to look."[15] Therefore the man who has passed beyond the watchmen finds the Word.

John passed beyond, for he found the Word with the Father.[16] (5.41) There are many also who seek Christ in their leisure and do not find Him, but they find Him in persecutions, and they find Him quickly. Accordingly, after the temptations, as it were, because He is present in the perils of His faithful ones, "How little a while," she says, "when I parted from them, and I found him. I took hold of him and did not let him go."[17] For everyone who seeks, finds,[18] and he who finds ought to keep close, so that he cannot lose.

(5.42) And because we see the heavenly mysteries represented allegorically on earth through the Gospel, let us come

---

11 Cf. Heb. 12.22.
12 Matt. 25.8-9.
13 Cf. Prov. 5.15 (Septuagint).
14 Cf. Cant. 3.3.
15 1 Peter 1.12.
16 Cf. John 1.1.
17 Cant. 3.4 (Septuagint).
18 Cf. Matt. 7.8.

to Mary Magdalene and to the other Mary.[19] Let us meditate upon how they sought Christ at night in the bed of His body, in which He lay dead, when the angel said to them, "You seek Jesus, who was crucified. He is not here, for he has risen. Why then do you seek the living one among the dead?"[20] Why do you seek in the tomb Him who is now in heaven? Why do you seek in the bonds of the tomb Him who frees all men of their bonds? The tomb is not His dwelling, but heaven is. And so one of them says, "I sought him and I did not find him."[21] (5.43) Still, as they are going to tell the Apostles, Jesus takes pity on the searchers, meets them, and says to them, " 'Hail!' And they came up and held his feet fast and worshiped him."[22] Jesus is held fast, but He delights to be held fast in such a way, because He is held fast by faith. Moreover, that woman also delighted Him who touched Him and was cured of a hemorrhage. He said of her, "Someone touched me; for I perceive that power has gone forth from me."[23]

Therefore touch Him and hold Him fast by faith and with faith hold tight His feet, so that power may go out from Him and may heal your soul. Although He says, "Do not touch me, for I have not yet ascended to my Father,"[24] hold Him fast. Only once He said, "Do not touch me," at the time of His resurrection, and by chance He said it to one who thought that He had been taken away by stealth and not raised again by His own power. Further, you find in another Gospel that He said to the women who were holding His feet fast and worshiping Him, "Do not be afraid."[25] Therefore do you also hold Him fast, O soul, just as Mary did, and say, "I took hold of him and I will not let him go," just as both women said, "We are holding you fast." Go to the Father, but do not

19 Cf. Matt. 28.1; Luke 24.3, 10.
20 Matt. 28.5-6; Luke 24.5.
21 Cant. 3.1.
22 Matt. 28.9.
23 Luke 8.46.
24 John 20.17.   25 Matt. 28.10.

leave Eve behind; else she may fall again. Bring her with you, for now she is not wandering astray, but holding fast to the tree of life. Seize her as she clings to your feet, so that she may ascend with you. Do not let me go; else the serpent may spread his poisons again and may seek again to bite at the woman's foot so that she may trip up Adam.[26] Therefore let your soul say, "I take hold of you and I will lead you into my mother's house and into the chamber of her that conceived me,"[27] that I may know your mysteries and drink in your teachings. And so take Eve, not now covered with the leaves of the fig tree,[28] but clad in the Holy Spirit and glorious with new grace. Now she does not hide as one who is naked,[29] but she comes to meet you arrayed in a garment of shining splendor, because grace is her clothing. But neither was Adam naked at first, when he was clothed with innocence.[30]

(5.44) The daughters of Jerusalem[31] see her clinging to Christ and still ascending with Him, for He consents to meet and yield to those who seek Him often, so that He may lift them up. And they say, "Who is she who goes up from the desert?"[32] For this earth seems a desert and uncultivated, since it is choked with the brambles and thorns of our sins. They surely wonder how a soul which before was abandoned in hell clings to the Word of God and ascends like the shoot of the vine that rises to the upper regions, or like smoke produced from fire that seeks the heights,[33] and then, moreover, is fragrant with pleasant odors. Now there is emitted the sweet scent of pious prayer, which is directed like incense in the sight of God. And in the Apocalypse we read that "with

---

26 Cf. Gen. 3.5.
27 Cant. 3.4; 8.2.
28 Cf. Gen. 3.7.
29 Cf. Gen. 3.8-13.
30 The entire passage, 5.40-43, is a development of the *Explanation of the Gospel According to Luke* 10.154-58. See Palanque 540 n. 325.
31 Cf. Cant. 3.5.
32 Cant. 3.6.
33 The phrase "that seeks the heights" ("alta petens") is Vergilian, being found at *Aeneid* 5.508 and 7.362, although used here in a different sense. It appears also at *Death as a Good* 5.16 (translated in this book).

the prayers of the saints there went up the smoke of the incense."[34] The incense—that is, the prayers of the saints—is offered through the angel "upon the golden altar which is before the throne"[35] and is, as it were, fragrant with the sweet ointment of pious prayer, because it had been prepared from prayer for things eternal and invisible, and not for bodily things. And above all, the soul is fragrant with frankincense and myrrh,[36] because she is dead to sin and alive to God.[37]

(5.45) They[38] see her ascending and not resisting, and they take delight in the pleasant fragrances of her merits, for they know too that she is the bride of Solomon the peacemaker. Therefore they follow her in loyal escort even to the couch of Solomon,[39] because true rest in Christ is due her. For Christ is the couch of the saints, on whom the hearts of all, weary with the battles of the world, find rest. On this couch Isaac rested, and he blessed his younger son,[40] saying, "The elder shall serve the younger."[41] Reclining on this couch, Jacob blessed the twelve patriarchs;[42] reclining on this couch, the daughter of the ruler of the synagogue rose from death;[43] lying on this couch, the dead son of the widow broke the bonds of death when he was called by the voice of Christ.[44]

(5.46) Then when the bride has been led to the resting place of her bridegroom, they sing the nuptial song and express love from the daughters of Jerusalem: "Come forth and look upon King Solomon in the crown with which his mother has crowned him on the day of his marriage."[45] They sing

---

34 Apoc. 8.4. The preceding sentence reflects Ps. 140 (141).2.
35 Apoc. 8.3.
36 Cf. Cant. 3.6.
37 Cf. Rom. 6.2, 11.
38 The text from this point to 5.47 appears in the *Commentary* 3.33-35.
39 Cf. Cant. 3.7.
40 Cf. Gen. 27.27.
41 Gen. 25.23.
42 Cf. Gen. 48.2; 49.
43 Mark 5.35-43.
44 Luke 7.11-17.
45 Cant. 3.10, 11.

the epithalamium and call upon the other heavenly powers or souls to see the love that Christ has toward the daughters of Jerusalem.[46] On this account He deserved to be crowned by His mother, as a loving Son, as Paul shows, saying that "God has rescued us from the power of darkness and transferred us into the kingdom of his loving Son."[47] Thus He is the Son of love, and He is love; He does not possess love by way of accidents, but possesses it in His substance[48] like the kingdom, of which He says, "In this I was born."[49] Therefore they say "Come forth," that is, go out from the limitations of the body, go out from the vanities of the world, and see how the King of Peace[50] possesses love on the day of His marriage, how filled with glory He is, because He has given resurrection to the body and has united the soul to Himself. This is the crown of the mighty contest, this the magnificent gift of the marriage of Christ, His blood and passion. What more could He give? He was not sparing of Himself but offered His own death on our behalf.[51]

(5.47) The Lord Jesus Himself, delighted with the faith of such a soul, her confession and her grace, praises her merits and calls her nearer, saying, "Come[52] from Lebanon, my bride, come from Lebanon. You will come, yes come safely, from the source, which is faith, from the peak of Sanir and Hermon, from lions' dens, from leopards' mountains";[53] that

---

46 Cf. Cant. 3.11.
47 Col. 1.13.
48 Christ is here identified as one in substance with the Father. See R. T. Otten, "Amor, Caritas and Dilectio: Some Observations on the Vocabulary of Love in the Exegetical Works of St. Ambrose," *Mélanges offerts à Mlle. Christine Mohrmann* (Utrecht 1963) 73-83, especially 81 and n. 28.
49 John 18.37. The sense is, "In this, that is, the state of kingship, I was born." The phrase "in this" rather than the more familiar "for this" appears in the Vulgate, and also in Ambrose, *Joseph* 12.67 (translated in this book) and *On the Sacraments* 5.22, where see the note (p. 103 n. 3) of T. Thompson in his translation.
50 Cf. 1 Par. 22.9; Heb. 7.2.
51 Cf. Rom. 8.32.
52 The text from this point to 5.48 appears in the *Commentary* 4.25.
53 Cant. 4.8 (Septuagint). The passage is also quoted by Ambrose, *On the Mysteries* 7.39. See Thompson's translation p. 140 n. 1.

is, go out from the body and divest yourself of it wholly, for you cannot be with me, unless you are first absent from the body, because those who are in the flesh are absent from the kingdom of God.[54] "Come, come." The repetition is good because, whether present or absent, you ought to be present to the Lord your God and to please Him. Come when you are present, come when you are absent, although you are still in the body—for to me all those are present whose faith is with me. He is present to me who goes out from the world; he is present to me who thinks of me, looks on me, has hope of me, he whose portion I am. He is present to me who has been absent to himself, he is present to me who has denied himself.[55] He is with me who is not within himself, because he who is in the flesh is not in the spirit. He is with me who goes out from his own self, he is near me who has been outside of himself, he is whole to me who has lost his life on account of me.[56]

And so, "Come, come, my bride; you will come, yes come safely, from the source, which is faith. She comes, yes comes safely, from the earth, and comes safely, who comes to Christ. She comes with the merit of faith and the glory of works that shine like Sanir and Hermon; that is, she comes by a path of light, having conquered the temptations of the world and having overcome the spirits of wickedness,[57] seeking the crown of lawful contest, and therefore she has deserved to be praised with Christ as the judge.

(5.48) "You[58] are an enclosed garden, my sister bride, an enclosed garden, a fountain sealed. What you put forth is a paradise of pomegranates with the fruit of the trees; aromatic plants."[59] The bride is praised, because she is a garden having

---

54 Cf. 2 Cor. 5.8.
55 Cf. Mark 8.34.
56 Cf. Matt. 10.39.
57 Cf. Eph. 6.12.
58 The text from this point to "There is also praise for the gifts of the soul. . ." (prior to 5.49) appears in the *Commentary* 4.34.
59 Cant. 4.12-13 (Septuagint).

in herself the fragrance of the plentiful field, of which Isaac says, "The fragrance of my son is like the fragrance of the plentiful field."[60] Therefore the soul that is good pours forth the fragrances of justice. And perhaps the field is the patriarch, the garden is the soul of someone lesser, a portion of the field, as it were, and the garden is enclosed, so that the soul may not be invaded by wild animals, and the fountain is sealed, so that she may wash away her own sins by the integrity of the seal[61] and by perseverance in faith. For the fountain which draws from the Church has what it may attribute to the grace of virginity, because the soul is set in a paradise of delight and gathers spiritual fruits without toil. Thus the souls of the patriarchs bestow their own fruits upon her by working the land, as it were, in order for her to enjoy the constant sweetness of them. She is rightly called a fountain sealed, because the image of the invisible God[62] is represented in her. There[63] is also praise for the gifts of the soul, which were sent by the bridegroom, with which she came endowed. Now the gifts of the pious soul are good fragrances, myrrh and aloe and saffron, which beautiful gardens exhale and with which the stench of sins is destroyed.

(5.49) Accordingly, untroubled by so great a proclamation, she asks the heavy north wind to be at rest, so that it may not destroy the flowers, but the south wind to blow; that is, she wishes the winter to pass and the season of gentler breezes to burst into springtime.[64] She invites the bridegroom into her garden.[65] The bridegroom comes down[66] and takes delight in the diversity of her fruit; he rejoices because he has found a stronger food and one that is sweeter, too.[67] For there is a kind of bread of the word, and a honey, one speech more

---

60 Gen. 27.27.
61 That is, the seal of baptism.
62 Cf. Col. 1.15.
63 The text from this point to 6.51 appears in the *Commentary* 4.41-42.
64 Cf. Cant. 4.16; 2.11.
65 Cf. Cant. 4.16.
66 Cf. Cant. 5.1.
67 Cf. 1 Cor. 3.2; Cant. 5.1.

ardent, another more persuasive. There is also one faith that is more hot like wine, another that is more clear like the taste of milk. Christ dines on such food in us, He drinks such drink in us; with the intoxication of this drink, He challenges us to make a departure from worse things to those that are better and best.

(6.50) Hearing this, the soul drank in the intoxication of the heavenly mysteries; as if put to sleep by the wine and as if lying in a trance or stupor, she says, "I sleep, and my heart keeps watch."[1] Then, struck by the enlightenment afforded by the presence of the Word, once she had rested with open eyes, she is awakened by the Word. Now this is the fourth advance of the soul. First, impatient of love and not bearing the delays of the Word, she asked that she might deserve his kisses[2] and she deserved to see her beloved, and was also led into the king's chamber. Second, as they were speaking with one another, she rested in his shadow,[3] and suddenly the Word departed from her in the middle of their conversation, yet he was not absent for long, for as she sought him, he came leaping over the mountains and bounding over the hills.[4] Soon after, like a gazelle or hart,[5] while he was speaking to his beloved, he leapt up and left her. Third, although she had not found him by searching in bed and at night,[6] in the city and public places and streets,[7] she finally summoned him back with her prayers and grace, so that she was even called closer by the bridegroom. Fourth, she is now awakened from sleep by him, although she was keeping watch with her heart so that she might hear his voice at once when he knocked.[8] But while she was rising, she experienced a delay, because she could not match the swiftness of the Word. While she was

1 Cant. 5.2.
2 Cf. Cant. 1.2.
3 Cf. Cant. 2.3.
4 Cf. Cant. 2.8.
5 Cf. Cant. 2.9.
6 Cf. Cant. 3.1.
7 Cf. Cant. 3.2.
8 Cf. Cant. 5.2.

opening the door, the Word passed by;[9] she went out at his word, sought for him through wounds, but wounds of love, and, finally and with difficulty, found him and embraced him, so that she might not lose him. I have touched upon these matters briefly and summarily; now let us examine them one by one.

(6.51) Even[10] though you are asleep, if only Christ has come to know the devotion of your soul, he comes and knocks at her door and says, "Open to me, my sister."[11] "Sister" is well put, because the marriage of the Word and the soul is spiritual. For souls do not know covenants of wedlock or the ways of bodily union, but they are like the angels in heaven.[12] "Open to me," but close to strangers. Close to the times, close to the world, do not go out of doors to material things, do not abandon your own light and search for another's, because material light pours out a dark mist, so that the light of true glory is not seen. "Open," therefore, "to me"; do not open to the adversary or give place to the devil. "Open yourself to me," do not be confined, but expand, and I will fill you. And because, in my passage through the world, I have found very much trouble and vexation and have not readily had a place to rest, do you then open, that the Son of Man may rest his head on you, for he has no rest[13] save on one who is humble and quiet.

(6.52) The[14] soul, hearing "Open to me" and "My head is wet with dew,"[15] that is, the soul which was suddenly disturbed by the temptations of the world and was bidden to rise, and indeed is on the point of rising, as it were, speaks; fragrant with aloe and myrrh,[16] signs of burial,[17] she says, "I

---

9 Cf. Cant. 5.5-6.
10 The text from this point to 6.52 appears in the *Commentary* 5.14.
11 Cant. 5.2.
12 Cf. Matt. 22.30.
13 Cf. Luke 9.58.
14 The text from this point to 6.53 appears in the *Commentary* 5.27-29.
15 Cant. 5.2.
16 Cf. Cant. 5.5.
17 Cf. John 19.39.

have taken off my robe, how shall I put it on? I have washed my feet, how shall I defile them?"[18] For she is afraid that she may rise again into temptations and may return again into guilt and sin and may begin to defile her own commencement and advance in the virtues with worldly footsteps. Surely in this way she is also giving evidence of her perfection in virtue, which deserved Christ's great love, so that he comes to her and knocks at her door and comes with the Father and dines with that soul and she with him, just as John said in the Apocalypse.[19] Indeed since she had heard in one of the previous passages, "Come from Lebanon, my bride, come from Lebanon,"[20] and since she observed that she could not be present with Christ in the flesh but could be with him then, if she were present in the spirit, she conformed herself to his will, that she also might be conformed to the image of Christ.[21] Now she is not aware of the remnants of the flesh; now, like a spirit, she has divested herself of the connection with the body; now, as if she had forgotten and could not remember their union even if she wished, she says, "I have taken off my robe, how shall I put it on?" For she took off that robe of skins which Adam and Eve had received after their sin,[22] the robe of corruption, the robe of the passions. "How shall I put it on?" She does not seek again to put it on, but by this she means that it has been thrown away, so that it cannot now be her covering. "I have washed my feet, how shall I defile them?"; that is, I have washed my feet, to go forth and lift myself up from association with the body; "how shall I defile them?" to return to the enclosure of the body and the gloomy prison[23] of its passions?

---

18 Cant. 5.3.   19 Cf. Apoc. 3.20; John 14.23.
20 Cant. 4.8.
21 Cf. Rom. 8.29.
22 Cf. Gen. 3.21.
23 The well-known Platonic concept of the body as a prison receives considerable development in the works of Ambrose. See P. Courcelle, "Traditions platonicienne et chrétienne du corps-prison," Revue des études latines 43 (1965) 406-43, especially 423-26, where the relevant passages from Ambrose are cited.

(6.53) While she was saying this, the Word sent his good work through the opening in the door, as it were, still not face to face, but sent it as his hand, so to speak.[24] "And my heart was confounded over him, and I[25] rose to open to my brother. My hands dripped myrrh, my fingers filled with myrrh are upon the handles of the bar."[26] Let us meditate on the meaning of this. First, God the Word is seen in his works, as I said, as if through an opening in the door, and not completely and perfectly. Then[27] her love increases, and once implanted, grows to maturity; from his seeds which the soul received in a spiritual womb, as it were, she longs to see the entire fullness of his divinity dwelling in him in bodily form, as we have read.[28] She rose, that she might see the wonderful Word of God more closely. And in this her advance is being represented, because she rose through the power of virtue. For from the presence of the Word the soul drank in virtue, just as by the presence of Mary, when she was heavy with child, He gave instruction to John, who was in the womb, so that he leapt in the womb and rejoiced to know the presence of the Lord.[29] She rose to open, and her works and deeds were dead to the world. The soul who is about to receive the Word should be such that she dies to the world[30] and is buried together in Christ.[31] So it is that Christ is found, and such is the reception he asks for himself.

Then the very agents of good works, that is, the hands and fingers, with which Christ is grasped, are put to death—and we can consider those fingers as the good works evident in our actions. And so, although now she was already opening wide

---

24 Cf. Cant. 5.4; 1 Cor. 13.12.
25 The text from this point to "For she has come to know that he delays. . ." (in 6.56) appears in the *Commentary* 6.7-9.
26 Cant. 5.4-5.
27 Ambrose's language and imagery in his *Explanation of Psalm 118,* 12.16, are quite similar to those in this sentence.
28 Cf. Col. 2.9.
29 Cf. Luke 1.44.
30 Cf. Gal. 6.14.
31 Cf. Rom. 6.4; Col. 2.12.

her spiritual hands and fingers from their interlocking embrace, in order to grasp the Word, the pious soul says that he was gone, but not that he was still passing through.[32] And this marks an advance, for the Word of God goes and passes through the soul, because it is written, "And your own soul a sword shall pass through, that the thoughts of many hearts may be revealed."[33] In this case there is still the act of going, and not that of passing through, as perhaps Mary's soul is passed through in later times, when the Lord Jesus is set as a seal in her midst.[34]

(6.54) Then there is at once another advance in the going of the Word, because the soul went out at his word. That is, following his word, she went out of the body, lifting herself up from its dwelling and making herself a stranger to it, so that she might be with God and be a citizen with the saints,[35] for we cannot at one time be servants both of the flesh and of God. Therefore in this passage the meaning is, as I said, that the soul goes forth when it withdraws from bodily pleasures. Further, it is written, "Come forth from Babylon, flee from the Chaldaeans."[36] The Hebrew is warned by the words of the prophet, not indeed that he should flee the lands of Babylon, but its moral conduct, since there are Hebrews who are in Babylon and they show by moral conduct that they have departed from Babylon. For those of whom the psalmist says that they sat by the rivers of Babylon,[37] did indeed sit in the land of Babylon, but they were not in its shameful vices. How were they *in* those shameful vices when they wept and did penance because they had fallen from the ark of faith and devotion and from the virtue and merits of their fathers?

Moreover, the soul that goes forth at his word is searching for the Word. (6.55) On this account too, when she was

---

32 Cf. Cant. 5.6.
33 Luke 7.35.
34 Cf. Cant. 8.6.
35 Cf. Eph. 2.19.
36 Isa. 48.20.
37 Cf. Ps. 136 (137).1.

searching, she came upon the watchmen who go about the city. "They struck me, and wounded me, they took my mantle from me, the watchmen of the walls."[38] Well put, her coming as if a bride with a mantle to cover her head, when the bridegroom should meet her. Rebecca, when she knew that Isaac was coming to meet her, dismounted from her camel and covered herself with a mantle.[39] Just so this soul anticipated the mark of the wedding garment, so that she might not be cast out as one not having a wedding garment,[40] or else wore it to cover her head on account of the angels.[41] But the watchmen struck her so that she might be tested the more, for souls are tried by temptations. They took the mantle from her, for they were searching whether she bore the true beauty of naked virtue, or else because everyone ought to enter the celestial kingdom without clothing and not bring any covering of deceit with him. There are also those who demand that no soul carry with herself the remnants of carnal delight and the concupiscence of the body. She is stripped of the robe when her conscience is revealed. But there is also the soul which is stripped with good intent, the soul that is allowed to imitate Christ when he says, "The prince of this world is coming, and in me he will find nothing."[42] True, because he finds nothing only in him who did not sin.[43] Blessed is the soul in whom he does not find grave sins, or many, but on her he finds the cloak of faith and the rule of wisdom.

(6.56) And so she suffered no loss, because no one can make off with true wisdom even if he wishes; although the adversary may raise a commotion, still the true integrity of a blameless way of life shines forth in such a case. Thus, without suffering loss, she passed beyond the watchmen. Joining the daughters of the heavenly city, she seeks after the Word; by her

---

38 Cant. 5.7.
39 Cf. Gen. 24.65.
40 Cf. Matt. 22.12-13.
41 Cf. 1 Cor. 11.5-10.
42 John 14.30.
43 Cf. 1 Peter 2.22.

search she arouses his love for her, and she knows where to search for him. For she has come to know that he delays among the prayers of his saints and remains close to them, and she understands that he feeds his Church and the souls of his just ones among the lilies.[44] The Lord showed this mystery to you in the Gospel, when he led his disciples through the standing grain on the Sabbath.[45] Moses led the people of the Jews through the desert; Christ leads them through the standing grain, Christ leads them through the lilies, because through his passion the desert blooms like a lily. Let us follow, therefore, so that we may gather the fruits on the Sabbath day, the great Sabbath day, on which there is great rest.[46] Do not be afraid that the Pharisees may accuse you of gathering standing grain.[47] Even if they accuse, yet Christ excuses,[48] and he makes the souls that he wishes, that follow him, like to David, who ate the loaves of proposition outside of the law[49]—for even then he foresaw in his mind the prophetic mysteries of a new grace.

(7.57) Accordingly,[1] she is praised by the bridegroom, because she sought after him so well and so steadily, and now not only is she called sister, but also well-pleasing—for she is pleasing to him who was pleasing to the Father[2]—and beautiful as Jerusalem, an object of admiration in her array.[3] For she possesses all the mysteries of the heavenly city and arouses admiration in all who see her. Because she is like the full and perfect justice, having borrowed her splendor from the light of the Word, while she strives always toward him, she becomes

---

44 Cf. Cant. 2.16.
45 Cf. Matt. 12.1; Mark 2.23; Luke 6.1.
46 Cf. Lev. 23, 25; John 19.31.
47 Cf. Luke 6.2.
48 Cf. Luke 6.3-5.
49 Cf. 1 Kings 21.6.

---

1 The text from this point to "And so he says to her. . ." appears in the Commentary 6.6.
2 Cf. Matt. 17.5.
3 Cf. Cant. 6.4.

terrible too as she advances in a certain array[4] to the heights of virtue.

And[5] so he says to her, as if to one who is perfect, " 'Turn your eyes from me,'[6] do not strive against me." Out of an excess of faith and devotion, she has passed beyond the capacity of her own natural state, because it is a weighty matter to look directly upon the inaccessible light.[7] "Turn your eyes from me," because she cannot withstand the fullness of his divinity[8] and the splendor of the true light.

Yet we can also take "Turn your eyes from me" as follows: "Although you have been perfected, I must still redeem other souls and strengthen them. For you exalt me by looking upon me, but I have descended so that I may exalt all men.[9] Although I have risen up and possess the throne of the Father,[10] still I will not leave you orphans,[11] bereft of a father's help, but by my presence I will strengthen you. You find this written in the Gospel: 'I am with you even unto the consummation of the world.'[12] Turn your eyes from me, therefore, because you exalt me." The more anyone strives toward the Lord, the more he exalts the Lord and is himself exalted. On this account also the psalmist says, "I will extol you, O Lord, because you have upheld me."[13] For the holy man extols the Lord; the sinner brings Him low. Therefore He wishes that she turn her eyes away. Otherwise, by contemplating her He may be exalted—for now He can attain to the higher regions —and may leave the other souls behind. Likewise in the Gospel He showed His glory, not to all the disciples, but to those who were more nearly perfect.[14]

---

4 Cf. *ibid.*
5 The text from this point to 7.58 appears in the *Commentary* 6.7-9.
6 Cant. 6.5.
7 Cf. 1 Tim. 6.16.
8 Cf. Col. 2.9.
9 Cf. John 6.38-40.
10 Cf. Heb. 8.1; 12.2.
11 Cf. John 14.18.
12 Matt. 28.20.
13 Ps. 29 (30).2.   14 Cf. Matt. 17.1-8.

Now imagine some teacher who desires to explain an obscure matter to his hearers. Although he is himself an accomplished speaker and well informed, nevertheless, let him lower himself to the ignorance of those who do not understand, and let him use simple, rather plain, everyday speech so that he can be understood. Then whoever is more quick-witted among his hearers, and can follow easily, disparages and questions him. Looking on such a one, the teacher restrains him, so that the latter may permit him to spend time rather on those who are more humble and lowly, in order that the rest may also be able to follow.

(7.58) The phrase of Acylas,[15] "resounding as one revealed,"[16] referred to her as "resounding" to due admiration on the grounds of having mighty, sonorous works; "revealed" referred to the brightness of her works, or the fact that the works of the soul shine in the presence of the Father, who is in heaven.[17] On this account you understand that her mantle was not taken without purpose, but so that she, uncovered and bare, might be resplendent in her merits.

(7.59) She[18] is praised, moreover, because she is faithful and strong in speech, prolific in diverse fruits, like the one dove[19] having unity of spirit, in whom there is peace, who has made both one[20] and who is not composed of unlike elements of a separate and contending nature. For what is so unlike as fire and water, air and earth, of which the creature that is our body consists? Further, "a soul is blessed which is altogether

---

15 The name Acylas is adopted here by the editor of the Vienna edition from 7.63, where the form of the name is also in some doubt. The reference may well be to Aquila, author of a Greek translation of the Old Testament familiar to Ambrose. See Dudden 456 and notes 8, 10. The text of Aquila was included by Origen in his *Hexapla* (= sixfold Bible); while familiar to Ambrose, the work has survived only in fragments.
16 Cf. Cant. 6.9.
17 Cf. Matt. 5.16.
18 The text from this point to "To use the testimony of Scripture. . ." (7.60) appears in the *Commentary* 6.10-11.
19 Cf. Cant. 6.8 (9).
20 Cf. Eph. 2.14.

sincere,"[21] which imitates Him who says, "That all may be
one, even as you, Father, in me and I in you, that they also
may be one in us,"[22] for this is the completion and perfection.
On this account He also added, "That they may be one, even
as we are one, I in them and you in me, that they may be
perfected in unity."[23] Therefore such a soul is a dove and is
perfected, that is, sincere and spiritual and not disturbed by
the passions of the body, in which there are "conflicts without
and anxieties within."[24] Scripture teaches us that by the word
"unity" concord and peace are meant, for it says, "Now the
multitude of the believers had one heart and one soul, and
there was not any separation in them."[25]

(7.60) The soul is praised for her fertility, and not without
reason, both because she is prolific in virtues and also because
she has no evil in herself. For that is becoming and beautiful,
in which there is no evil; that is becoming which is good, but
what is unbecoming is evil. Fertility in good works is beautiful.
Sterility then is the opposite of beauty, because there is evil
in one who is deprived of beauty and of that which is becoming. Further, what is evil is sterile and infertile. What evidence of this fact is clearer than that afforded by nature? For
the land which is good is fertile and prolific, but that which
is bad is barren and sterile; that which is fertile is also becoming. What is more beautiful than a full field, when the
grain is waving, when the fruits are ruddy and garlands of
grapes hang down, and the olive tree bends heavy with its
fruits, and the peaks are clothed with verdant mountain
grasses, the lowlands with the grasses of the valley? To use
the testimony of Scripture, Jacob was becoming and his fragrance was like the fragrance of a full field,[26] whereas Esau was

---

21 Prov. 11.25 (Septuagint).
22 John 17.21.
23 John 17.22-23.
24 2 Cor. 7.5.
25 Acts 4.32.
26 Cf. Gen. 27.27.

hairy and unbecoming,[27] and so a man of the open field,[28] who could not have any crops. It was aptly said in reference to the Lord Himself, after He made the Church to increase in fertility, "The Lord has reigned, he has clothed himself in beauty,"[29] and in another passage, "You have clothed yourself in praise and beauty."[30] Therefore it is clear that what is prolific is also becoming, what is not prolific is also unbecoming.

The case of the soul is like that of the soil, because that soul is becoming which is prolific in merits, prolific in counsels, but the one that is sterile is unbecoming. For sterility and matter are weaknesses of the soul. Sterility cheats the soul of her fruit, introduces want, arouses fear, and magnifies greedy desires and idle thoughts; thus the soul falls. And what is wickedness but the lack of good?[31] Cheated of what is hers, she has need of what belongs to another; she is emptied and filled with no measure or limit. Moreover, vices of matter darken the grace of the soul. Ignorance and concupiscence are illnesses of the soul but are ascribed more to form than to matter. The flesh is matter, ignorance and concupiscence form. Then why is the flesh blamed when there are such great blemishes in the form? Because the form can do nothing without the matter. Indeed the form accomplishes nothing in the case of those who are tranquil because they are without the matter. For what would concupiscence be if the flesh did not inflame it? It is cold in old men, in boys too, because their body is weak; it is hot in young men, because their bodily strength is at fever pitch. Evils, then, arise from goods,[32]

---

27 Cf. Gen. 27.11.
28 Cf. Gen. 25.27.
29 Ps. 92 (93).1.
30 Ps. 103 (104).2.
31 The development of the concept of evil as deprivation of good is based on Plotinus, *Enneads* 1.8.1. For detailed comparison, see P. Courcelle, *Recherches* 107 and L. Taormina, "La dottrina del male come privazione di bene," *Convivium Dominicum* (Catania 1959) 425-37, especially 428-29. Cf. Augustine, *Contra Iulianum Pelagianum* 1.9.44.
32 Cf. Augustine, *Contra Iulianum Pelagianum* 1.9.44 and *Contra secundam Iuliani responsionem opus imperfectum* 4.109.

for there are no evils but deprivations of goods. Yet through evils it came about that goods became apparent. Thus the lack of good is the root of wickedness, and, in the definition of good, wickedness is detected, because evil is found through the knowledge of good. But good is in want of nothing, it abounds to itself, it allots to all things their measure and perfection, their end too; in it all things subsist, and on it all things depend. Such is the nature of the good, and it fills the mind.

(7.61) Such is the concern of the soul that is pure, such is what it perceives within; it discerns God and abounds in all good things. On this account, "His mouth is sweetness and he is all delight."[33] For[34] God is the author of all good things and all things which are, are His. Nowhere is there evil there, and, if our mind dwells in Him, it does not know evil. Therefore the soul that does not dwell in God is the author of her own evils, and so she sins, but the soul that sins will herself die.[35] Freed of the golden bonds of virtue, she is carried headlong to the precipice and falls to the lower regions. But the soul is blessed that is not overcome by any hostile strife in the body. Such a soul flies out like a sparrow from the broken snare[36]—for the pleasures of the body are the nourishment of evils. Whoever turns to these, binds his soul in a snare. (7.62) But as for the man who abstains from that nourishment and from that darkness, his soul is resplendent like the dawn, and of her it is said: "Who is she that is looking forth like the dawn, beautiful as the moon?"[37] For she looks forth as if from a house that is free, and she does not say, "Darkness covers me and walls surround me, and who knows if the Most High sees?"[38] Rather, she is herself seeking the light. Set above the world as if she were in the upper parts of her

33 Cant. 5.16.
34 The text from this point to 7.63 appears in the *Commentary* 6.12-13.
35 Cf. Ezech. 18.4, 20.
36 Cf. Ps. 123 (124).7.
37 Cant. 6.9 (Septuagint).
38 Sir. 23.18 (26).

house—that is, her body—she gazes on things divine and raises herself to things eternal, so that she may be with God; now she displays the light of her works, just as the moon displays its surface, over the whole world.

(7.63) As for the phrase of Acylas, "resounding like the sun,"[39] it seems that the turning of heaven's axis, the course of the sun, moon, and stars, and the harmony of the spheres are being represented, and this met with approval on the part of certain Christians. Whereas the harmony does not meet with credence,[40] at least, since it is pleasant and charming, it does not seem inimical.

(8.64) While she is receiving praise from the bridegroom, she modestly refuses to receive it in his presence. But then she is called back out of love of the bridegroom and says, "I went down to the nut garden to look on the birth of the torrent."[1] Now where is the Church, save where the bishop's staff flourishes[2] and his charism?[3] Often she is there, so that she may be put to the proof in bitterness and temptation. We take the nut to mean bitterness, the torrent temptation, but temptation that is endurable, because it is written, "Our soul has passed through a torrent."[4] And so she went down into a place of bitterness, where the vine flourishes, as well as a various and manifold fruit in the likeness of pomegranates,[5] which is sheltered by faith and charity like the one covering of the entire body. In that bitterness the soul did not know

---

39 Cf. note 15 above.
40 The Latin text is unclear, and could mean "Whereas the harmony does not pertain to faith. . ." In any case, Philo and Origen accepted the concept. The matter is discussed further by Ambrose in *Hexameron* 2.2.6-7 (English translation by J. J. Savage, *Saint Ambrose: Hexameron, Paradise and Cain and Abel* [FOTC 42; New York 1961]) and *On Abraham* 2.8.54, where Origen is cited as an authority.

---

1 Cant. 6.11.
2 Cf. Num. 17.23 (8).
3 Cf. C. Morino, *Church and State in the Teaching of Saint Ambrose* (Washington 1969) 73: "It is obvious that Ambrose frequently stresses and emphasizes in every way the dignity and authority of bishops."
4 Ps. 123 (124).5.
5 Cf. Cant. 6.11.

herself, for the corruptible body burdens her and her earthly dwelling swiftly declines. Yet she ought always to know herself. But Peter was tempted, and Peter did not know himself; for if he had known himself, he would not have denied his Creator.[6] But Christ knew him; indeed He knew him, for He also looked upon him[7]—"the Lord knows who are his"[8]—and, like a good master, He drew him back from his fall with the reins of His mercy, so to speak. Therefore Christ is our master.

(8.65) Thereupon the soul says, "It[9] made me like the chariots of Aminadab."[10] Now the soul is the chariot which carries its good master. If the soul is a chariot, she has horses that are either good or bad. The good horses are the virtues of the soul, the bad horses the passions of the body. So the good master restrains the bad horses and draws them back but urges on the good. The good horses are four:[11] prudence, temperance, fortitude, justice; the bad horses: wrath, concupiscence, fear, injustice.[12] Sometimes these horses are in dissension with one another, either wrath or fear strains forward, and they hinder one another and slow their progress.[13] But the good horses fly up, ascend from earth to the higher regions, and raise up the soul, especially if they have the sweet yoke and light burden of Him who says, "Take my yoke upon you, for

---

6 Cf. Luke 22.54-62.

7 Cf. Luke 22.61.

8 2 Tim. 2.19.

9 The text from this point to 8.67 appears in the *Commentary* 6.19-22. Further, the text of 8.65 seems to be a development of *Explanation of Psalm 118*, 2.34-35.

10 Cant. 6.12 (Septuagint). The Hebrew text causes difficulty, being variously taken as the proper name Aminadab, or as "noble people," "prince of my people," "princely cortege." The bridegroom ran out in haste at the sudden appearance of his bride—that much is clear.

11 Ambrose makes several attempts elsewhere in his works to base the cardinal virtues on the Bible. See *Paradise* 3.14 (translated by J. J. Savage, *Saint Ambrose: Hexameron* . . . [cited above, ch. 7 n. 40]), and *On Abraham* 2.5.54. The imagery is derived from Philo. See Baziel Maes, *La Loi naturelle selon Ambroise de Milan* (Analecta Gregoriana 162; Rome 1967) 133 (with n. 45), 134.

12 Cf. Augustine, *Contra Iulianum Pelagianum* 2.5.12; 3.14.28.

13 Cf. Plato, *Phaedrus* 247 B.

my yoke is sweet and my burden light."[14] He is the master
who knows how to rule his own horses, so that all keep the
same pace. If prudence is too swift, and justice too slow, he
admonishes the one that is more sluggish with his own whip.
If temperance is too gentle, and fortitude too severe, he knows
how to unite those that are in discord, so that they may not
perhaps lose their progress. And thus it is allowed to the sight
of the intellect to see that each soul is hastening to heaven
with the keenest rivalry, that the horses are hurrying to be
the first to come to the prize, which is Christ,[15] so that the
palm may be put on their necks first. Those horses are subject
to the yoke of faith, bound with the bond of charity, the reins
of justice, the halter of moderation.

Therefore it is well put, "It made me like the chariots of
Aminadab," which name is, "the father of a people." Now he
that is the father of a people is likewise the father of Nahasson,[16] which is, "of the serpent."[17] Now recall who hung like
a serpent upon the cross for the salvation of all men[18] and
you will understand that the soul is at peace that has God as
her protector and Christ as her driver, for this word "driver"
is also written in our Scriptures: "Father, father, the driver of
Israel."[19] (8.66) And so this driver says, "Turn, turn, O Sulamite,"[20] which name is, "at peace."[21] For the soul that is at
peace swiftly turns and corrects herself, even though she
sinned before, and Christ mounts her, rather, and considers
it appropriate to guide her. To Him it is said, "Mount your
horses, and your riding is salvation,"[22] and in another passage,

14 Matt. 10.29-30.   15 Cf. Phil. 3.14.
16 Cf. Num. 1.7; 2.3.
17 Nahasson's name appears with the same interpretation at *Explanation
of Psalm 118*, 2.34.
18 Cf. John 3.14; Num. 21.9.
19 4 Kings 2.12.
20 Cant. 6.12.
21 "Sulamite" appears with the same interpretation at *Consolation on
the Death of Valentinian* 65 (translated by R. J. Deferrari in *Funeral
Orations by Saint Gregory Nazianzen and Saint Ambrose* [FOTC 22;
New York 1953]).
22 Hab. 3.8 (Septuagint).

"I have sent your horses into the sea."[23] These are the horses of Christ. Therefore Christ mounts His horses, the Word of God mounts pious souls.[24]

(8.67) On[25] this account, know that he also mounted the soul of the bride and led her to the place of the victor's palm, when he says to her, "How beautiful you have become, how pleasing, my love, in your delights! Your stature is like a palm tree."[26] And she says, "I said, 'I will climb the palm tree.' "[27] Now love itself is the palm tree, for it is itself the fullness of victory; "love, therefore is the fullness of the law."[28] Let us run, then, so as to obtain it; [29] let us run, so as to win it. He who has overcome goes up to receive the palm and acquires its fruits. He who has overcome is not now in the race, as it is written, "He who has overcome, I will permit him to sit with me upon my throne, as I also have overcome and sit with my Father on his throne."[30] From this source the philosophers portrayed those chariot-races of souls in their books;[31] nevertheless they could not attain to the victor's palm, because their souls did not know the summit of the Word and His height. But the soul in whom the Word dwelt knew this, (8.68) for she speaks thus: "I am my dear brother's, and toward me is his desire."[32] She repeated this thought three times in various ways in the Canticle of Canticles. In the beginning she says, "My brother is mine and I am his; he is

---

23 Hab. 3.15. (Septuagint). The Latin text reads *Tharsis* at this point; Schenkl, the CSEL editor, suggests that the word may perhaps stand for the phrase "in the sea."
24 On 8.65 and 8.66, see R. T. Otten, "Caritas" (cited above, ch. 4, n. 103) 447: "The figure of the horse and of the chariot are also deeply rooted in both the Scriptures and the philosophic literature of Platonic tradition as symbols of ascent."
25 The text from this point to 8.72 appears in the *Commentary* 7.12-16.
26 Cant. 7.6-7.
27 Cant. 7.8.
28 Rom. 13.10.
29 Cf. 1 Cor. 9.24.
30 Apoc. 3.21.
31 Cf. Plato, *Phaedrus* 246 A-248 B.
32 Cant. 7.10 (Septuagint).

feeding among the lilies, till the day blows fresh and the shades are removed."[33] Then she says, "I am my dear brother's and my dear brother is mine; he is feeding among the lilies."[34] Toward the end, she says, "I am my dear brother's, and toward me is his desire."[35]

The first instance has to do with the formation of the soul, and therefore she said first, "My brother is mine." For once He reveals Himself, the soul of one who cleaves to God has also entered upon the way of love. What follows refers to the soul's advance, what is third refers to her perfection. In the first stage, that of formation, the soul still sees shadows not yet parted by the revelation of the Word's approach,[36] and therefore hitherto the daylight of the Gospel did not shine upon her. In the second, she enjoys sweet fragrances without the confusion of the shadows.[37] In the third, now perfected, she offers to the Word a resting place in herself, so that he may turn toward her, rest his head upon her[38] and find repose. Now she possesses the reward that she had not been able to find when she searched before, and she invites him to her field, saying, (8.69) "Come, my brother, let us go out into the field, let us find rest in the villages."[39] She invited him before to her garden, and in this passage to a field that has not only beautiful flowers, but wheat and barley as well, that is, the foundations of stronger virtues, in order to see her fruits. "Let us find rest in the villages," to which Adam had been exiled when he was cast out of paradise. In them he found rest, but he worked upon the land. Our comprehension of the reason why she wishes him to go forth to the field is clear—so that he may feed his flock like a good shepherd,[40]

---

33 Cant. 2.16-17 (Septuagint).
34 Cant. 6.2 (Septuagint).
35 Cant 7.10 (Septuagint).
36 Cf. Cant. 2.17.
37 Cf. Cant. 1.12-13.
38 Cf. Cant. 8.3; Luke 9.58.
39 Cant. 7.12.
40 Cf. John 10.11; Isa. 40.11; Ezech. 34.23.

lift up those that are weary, and call back those that are going astray. For although that soul saved for him both the new and the old,[41] yet they are still like lambs, who have to be nourished with a drink of milk.[42]

It was as if she had been made perfect, not for herself, but for others. Therefore she interceded so that he would go forth from the bosom of the Father, go out of doors like the bridegroom coming out from his chamber, and run his course;[43] she interceded, too, that he would win those who were weak, would not linger on the distant throne of the Father and in that light, for those without strength cannot follow there, but that he would be taken up and led into the dwelling of the bride and her chamber,[44] that he would be out of doors for her but within for us, would be in our midst, even though unseen by us.[45] (8.70) On this account she says, "Who shall give you to me for my brother, O my brother, sucking the breasts of my mother? Finding you out of doors, I will kiss you."[46] Good is the soul that is out of doors, that the Word may be within. She is outside the body, that the Word may dwell in us.[47]

(8.71) "I will take you up and lead you in."[48] It is right to take up the Word of God and lead Him in, because He knocks at the soul, that the door may be opened to Him, and, unless He finds the door opened to Him, He does not enter. But if anyone opens the door, He enters and dines.[49] The bride takes up the Word in such a way that she is taught in the taking up. On this account it is not without reason that the soul is still rising to the mansions that are above and is always under-

---

41 Or, "the fresh and the mellowed fruits." Cf. Cant. 7.14.
42 Cf. 1 Cor. 3.2.
43 Cf. Ps. 18 (19).6.
44 Cf. Cant. 8.2 (Septuagint).
45 Cf. John 1.26.
46 Cant. 8.1.
47 Cf. Col. 3.16.
48 Cant. 8.2.
49 Cf. Apoc. 3.20.

going an advance. (8.72) This is what the virtues mean when they say to the soul, "Who[50] is this that comes up clothed in white, leaning on her brother?"[51] Earlier they had said, "Who is she that is looking forth like the dawn, beautiful as the moon, choice as the sun?"[52] In this passage we find that more is added, because she ascends leaning on the Word of God. For those who are more perfect recline upon Christ, just as John also was reclining at Jesus' bosom.[53] So then she either rested in Christ or reclined upon Him or even—since I am speaking of a marriage—as if already given into the power of Christ, she was led to the bridal couch by the bridegroom.

(8.73) Because there is now a union of love, the bridegroom caresses her and says, "Under the apple tree I raised you up. There your mother brought you forth, there she brought you forth who bore you."[54] Good is the soul that rests under the tree that is fruitful and especially the tree of a good fragrance. For if good Nathanael, in whom there was not any guile, was seen under a fig tree,[55] surely the soul is good that was raised up by her bridegroom under an apple tree. It is a greater thing to be raised up than to be seen, and greater still to be raised up by the bridegroom.[56] For although Nathanael was seen under a tree, still his soul was not a bride, for he came to Christ secretly because he was afraid of the Jews. She was not beautiful as the moon, choice as the sun,[57] for she was in the shadow, whereas the bride is married in the day and declares it openly. And so the one was under an apple tree, the other under a fig tree, because the one spread the fragrance of her profession of belief over a wider area, the other possessed

50 The text from this point to "This only did he desire to see . . ." (8.78) appears in the *Commentary* 8.6-14.
51 Cant. 8.5 (Septuagint).
52 Cant. 6.9 (Septuagint).
53 Cf. John 13.23.
54 Cant. 8.5 (Septuagint).
55 Cf. John 1.47-50.
56 Cf. Cant. 8.5.
57 Cf. Cant. 6.10.

the sweetness of purity and blamelessness but did not possess fragrance of spirit.[58]

(8.74) "There your mother brought you forth, there she brought you forth who bore you." For we are born there, where we are born again. Moreover, they are brought forth in whom the image of Christ is formed. On this account the Apostle also says, "my dear children, with whom I am in labor until Christ is formed in you."[59] Now she is in labor who receives the spirit of salvation in her womb and pours it out to others. (8.75) On this account, since Christ was already formed in her, the bride says, "Set me as a seal on your heart, as a seal on your arm."[60] Christ is the seal on the forehead, the seal in the heart—on the forehead that we may always confess Him, in the heart that we may always love Him, and a sign on the arm, that we may always do His work. Therefore let His image shine forth in our profession of faith, let it shine forth in our love, let it shine forth in our works and deeds so that, if it is possible, all His beauty may be represented in us. Let Him be our head, because "the head of man is Christ";[61] let Him be our eye, that through Him we may see the Father; let Him be our voice, that through Him we may speak to the Father; let Him be our right hand, that through Him we may bring our sacrifice to God the Father. He is also our seal, which is the mark of perfection and of love, because the Father, loving the Son, set His seal on Him, just as we read, "Upon him the Father, God himself, has set his seal."[62]

And so Christ is our love. Good is love, since it has offered itself to death for transgressions; good is love, which has forgiven sins. (8.76) And so let our soul clothe herself with

---

58 For a different interpretation of the name Nathanael, see *Explanation of the Gospel According to Luke* 8.90, and P. Courcelle, *Recherches* 193 (with n. 1), 194.

59 Gal. 4.19.

60 Cant. 8.6. For discussion of the text of this Scripture quotation, which appears also in *On the Sacraments* 2.6 and *On the Mysteries* 7.41, see Thompson's translation of the latter work, p. 110, n. 4.

61 1 Cor. 11.3.

62 John 6.27.

love,[63] and love of a kind that is "strong as death."[64] For just as death is the end of sins,[65] so also is love, because one who loves the Lord ceases to commit sin. For "charity thinks no evil and does not rejoice over wickedness, but endures all things."[66] For if one does not seek his own goods, how will he seek the goods of another?[67] Strong, too, is that death through the bath[68] through which every sin is buried and every fault forgiven. Such was the love which that woman in the Gospel brought, of whom the Lord says, "Her many sins have been forgiven her, because she has loved much."[69] Strong, too, is the death of the holy martyrs, that destroys earlier fault, and therefore—since it involves a love not less than theirs—death that is equal to the martyrs' suffering is just as strong for taking away the punishment of sins.

(8.77) Also, "zeal is like the nether world,"[70] because one who has zeal for God for Christ's sake is not sparing of what is his own. And so love encompasses death and love encompasses zeal and love possesses wings of fire.[71] Indeed, Christ, loving Moses, appeared to him in fire,[72] and Jeremia, having in himself the gift of divine love, said, "There was a burning fire in my bones and I have become weakened on every side and I cannot bear it."[73] Good then is love, having wings of burning fire, that flies through the breasts and hearts of the

---

63 There is a reference here to baptism, which is a clothing of oneself with, or putting on of, Christ. Cf. Gal. 3.27, and see R. T. Otten, "Caritas" (cited above, ch. 4 n. 103) 443 (with n. 6), 444; for the concept of purgation involved, see *ibid*. 445, n. 1.

64 Cant. 8.6.

65 The concept of death as "end of sin" appears also at *Death as a Good* 4.15 (translated in this book); *Cain and Abel* 2.9.32 (translated by J. J. Savage in FOTC 42 [cited above, ch. 7 n. 40]); *Explanation of Psalm 118*, 18.3; and *On the Sacraments* 2.6.17.

66 1 Cor. 13.5-7.

67 Cf. 1 Cor. 13.5.

68 Cf. Titus 3.5.

69 Luke 7.47.

70 Cf. Cant. 8.6.

71 Cf. *ibid.*

72 Cf. Exod. 3.4.

73 Jer. 20.9 (Septuagint).

saints and consumes whatever is material and earthly but tests whatever is pure and with its fire makes better whatever it has touched. This fire the Lord Jesus sent upon earth,[74] and faith shone bright, devotion was enkindled, love was illuminated, and justice was resplendent. With this fire He inflamed the heart of His Apostles, as Cleophas bears witness, saying, "Was not our heart burning within us, while he was explaining the scriptures?"[75] Therefore the wings of fire are the flames of the divine Scripture.

Indeed, He explained the Scriptures, and the fire went forth and entered into the hearts of His hearers. And truly they were wings of fire, because "the words of the Lord are pure words, as silver tried by the fire."[76] And when Paul was selected by Christ, he saw that a light had shone down around himself and over those who were with him; he fell down out of fear and rose approved; he who had come as a persecutor became an apostle.[77] The Holy Spirit also came down "and filled the whole house, where very many were sitting, and there appeared parted tongues as of fire."[78] Good are the wings of love, the true wings that flew about through the mouths of the Apostles, and the wings of fire that spoke the pure word.[79] On these wings Henoch flew when he was snatched up to heaven;[80] on these wings Elias flew when he was transported by the fiery chariot and the fiery horses to the regions above;[81] on these wings the Lord God led the people of the patriarchs by the pillar of fire.[82] These wings the Seraphim had, when he took the coal of fire from the altar, touched the mouth of the prophet, and took away his iniquities and cleansed his sins;[83] with the fire of these wings

74 Cf. Luke 12.49.
75 Luke 24.32.
76 Ps. 11 (12).7.
77 Cf. Acts 9.3-7; 1 Tim. 1.13.
78 Acts 2.2-3.
79 Cf. Ps. 11 (12).7.
80 Cf. Gen. 5.24.
81 Cf. 4 Kings 2.11.
82 Cf. Exod. 13.21.   83 Cf. Isa. 6.6-7.

the sons of Levi were purified[84] and the tribes of the Gentiles are baptized, as John bears witness when he says of the Lord Jesus, "He will baptize you with the Spirit and with fire."[85] David rightly wished that his loins and heart be burned,[86] for he knew that he need have no fear of the fiery wings of love. The Hebrew young men in the white-hot furnace did not feel the burning fire, and with good reason, because the flame of love cooled them.[87] And that we may know better that perfect charity has wings, hear now Christ saying, "How often I would have gathered your children together, as a hen gathers her young under her wings."[88]

(8.78) Let[89] us then take up these wings, since like flames they aim for the higher regions. Let each man divest his soul of her baser coverings and approve her when she is cleansed of the mire just as he would approve gold cleansed by fire. For the soul is cleansed just like the finest gold. Moreover the beauty of the soul, her pure virtue and attractiveness, is her truer knowledge of the things that are above, so that she sees the good on which all things depend, but which itself depends on none.[90] There she lives and receives her understanding. For that supreme good is the fountain of life; love and longing for it are enkindled in us, and it is our desire to approach and be joined to it, for it is desirable to him who does not see it and is present to him who sees it, and therefore he disregards all other things and takes pleasure and delight in this one only. This it is that supplies to all things their being; itself remaining in itself, it gives to others but receives nothing into itself from others.[91] Of this the psalmist says, "I have said to

---

84 Cf. Mal. 3.3.
85 Matt. 3.11; cf. John 1.33, but the quotation does not appear in John in this form.
86 Cf. Ps. 25 (26).2.
87 Cf. Dan. 3.50.
88 Matt. 23.37.
89 This passage (8.78) is modelled on Plotinus, *Enneads* 1.6.5. The parallels between the two passages are fully set out by P. Courcelle (*Recherches* 107-109).
90 Cf. Plato, *Symposium* 211 A.
91 Cf. Augustine, *Confessions* 7.11.17.

my Lord, you are my God, because you have no need of my goods."[92] This only did he desire to see, just as he says in another passage, "One thing I have asked of the Lord, this will I seek, that I may dwell in the house of the Lord all the days of my life and see the delight of the Lord and contemplate his temple."[93]

If anyone then has deserved to see that pure and incorporeal supreme good, what else would he have to desire?[94] Indeed Peter saw the glory of Christ's resurrection and did not wish to go down, for he said, "Lord, it is good for us to be here."[95] And how much more beyond compare is the glory of divinity and the inaccessible light[96] than anything else one may see and desire?[97] Kingdoms are not comparable, nor riches nor honors nor glory nor powers; for in the use of them there is no blessedness, but the employment of this supreme good is blessed, that a man may look down on such things, turn to this good, and remain in it. And so, seeing this fair image, let him enter within but leave the likeness of the body outside. For a man who looks to bodily things ought not to look inward; else he may be caught up like one who is sinking in a whirlpool and be swallowed and appear nowhere in sight, like a man plunged into the depths.

Let[98] us flee therefore to our real, true fatherland. There is our fatherland and there is our Father, by whom we have been created, where there is the city of Jerusalem, which is the mother of all men.[99] (8.79) But what is this flight? Not at all a flight with the feet, which belong to the body; for wherever they run, they run upon the earth and pass from one soil to another. Let us not flee either on ships or chariots or

---

92 Ps. 15 (16).2. Augustine cites the same psalm at *Confessions* 7.11.17.
93 Ps. 26 (27).4.
94 Cf. Plato, *Symposium* 210 E.
95 Matt. 17.4.
96 Cf. 1 Tim. 6.16.
97 Cf. Plato, *Symposium* 211 D, E.
98 The text from this point to the conclusion of the work appears in the *Commentary* 8.33-35.
99 Cf. Gal. 4.26; Heb. 12.22.

horses, which are impeded and fall, but let us flee with the spirit and the eyes and feet that are within. Let us accustom our eyes to see what is bright and clear, to look upon the face of continence and of moderation, and upon all the virtues, in which there is nothing scabrous, nothing obscure or involved. And let each one look upon himself and his own conscience; let him cleanse that inner eye, so that it may contain no dirt. For what is seen ought not to be at variance with him who sees, because God has wished that we be conformed to the image of His Son.[100] Thus the good is known to us and it is not far from anyone of us, for "in him we live and move and have our being, for we are also his offspring,"[101] as the Apostle asserted that the pagans said.[102]

This is the good that we seek, the only good, for no one is good but the one God.[103] This is the eye that looks upon the true and great beauty. Only the strong and healthy eye can see the sun; only the good soul can see the good. Therefore let him become good who wishes to see the Lord and the nature of the good. Let us be like this good and do good works according to it. This is the good that is above every work, above every mind and understanding. This it is that endures always, and toward it all things are directed, "in which dwells the fullness of divinity,"[104] and through it all things are reconciled to it. To define the nature of the good more fully, life is the good, because it always endures, giving to all their existence and being, because the source of the life of all is Christ, of whom the prophet says, "We shall live in his shadow";[105] for now "our life is hidden in Christ, but when Christ, our life, shall appear, then we too will appear with him in glory."[106] Accordingly, let us not be afraid of

---

100 Cf. Rom. 8.29.
101 Acts 17.28. For Ambrose's fairly extensive use of this passage, see Courcelle, *Recherches* 131 n. 2.
102 The "pagans" include the poets Aratus and Cleanthes; they were referring to Zeus.
103 Cf. Mark 10.18; Luke 18.19.
104 Col. 2.9.　　　　　105 Lam. 4.20.　　　　　106 Cf. Col. 3.3-4.

death,[107] because it is rest for the body, and for the soul a freedom or separation. And let us not be afraid of him who can kill the body but cannot kill the soul,[108] because we do not fear him who can carry off our clothing, we do not fear him who can steal our property but cannot steal us. We therefore are souls, if we wish to be Hebrews of those who are companions of Jacob,[109] that is, imitators of him. We are souls, but our members are our clothing. The clothing is indeed to be protected, that it not be torn or wear out,[110] but he who uses it ought the more to protect and guard himself.

---

107 This is the principal theme of *Death as a Good,* which follows.
108 Cf. Matt. 10.28.
109 Cf. Gen. 46.26-27.
110 Cf. Heb. 1.11; for the passage as a whole, cf. Porphyry, *De antro nympharum* 66.13, and *De abstinentia* 109.15.

DEATH AS A GOOD

(De bono mortis)

INTRODUCTION

THE WORK *Death as a Good* was composed at some point between 387 and 391[1] and was certainly intended as a supplement to *Isaac*.[2] Probably intended as two sermons, perhaps for the catechumens awaiting baptism at Easter,[3] the work has been described as "pervasively Neo-platonic."[4] It is undoubtedly influenced heavily by Plotinus,[5] and reliance on Origen and Porphyry must be admitted as well.[6] The tone throughout is as much philosophical as exegetical, although there is heavy reliance toward the end on the Fourth (Second) Book of Esdras, which Ambrose considered canonical.

There is another translation in English, dating from 1607;[7] there are a few in other languages,[8] and a few brief discussions.[9]

---

1 For the dating, and discussion of the work as a whole, see Dudden 682-683; Paredi 425 n. 16; Palanque 441, 444, 540-541.
2 Cf. *Death as a Good* 1.1.
3 The division, then, is 1-29 and 30-57.
4 R. T. Otten, "Caritas and the Ascent Motif in the Exegetical Works of St. Ambrose," *Studia Patristica* 8 (Texte und Untersuchungen 93; Berlin 1966) 445; whole article 442-448.
5 Cf. P. Courcelle, *Recherches sur les* Confessions *de Saint Augustin* (Paris 1950) 110-138, *especially* 120, 122, and 251.
6 On Origen and Porphyry, see the brief but important review of F. Portalupi's translation by P. Hadot in *Latomus* 21 (1962) 404-405.
7 In *Six Excellent Treatises on Life and Death, collected (and published in French) by P. Mornay . . . and now (first) translated into English.* (H. L. for M. Lownes, London 1607). Philippe de Mornay (1549-1623) was a French Huguenot. I have not had the opportunity to consult this translation. After the present translation was made, there appeared that of W. T. Wiesner, *S. Ambrosii De bono mortis: A Revised Text with an Introduction, Translation, and Commentary* (Catholic University of America Patristic Studies 100; Washington, D.C., 1970).
8 See Gryson 17-18 and below, *Flight from the World* Intr. n. 6.
9 See U. Moricca, *Storia della letteratura latina* 2.1 (Turin 1928) 368-371 and J. E. Niederhuber, "Das 'Bonum Mortis,'" *Forschungen zur christlichen Literatur- und Dogmengeschichte* 6 (1907) 11-20.

DEATH AS A GOOD

BECAUSE I HAVE WRITTEN a kind of homily concerning the soul in the previous book, I think the way is more open to compose something about death as a good. Should death do injury to the soul, it can be considered an evil, but should it do the soul no harm, it cannot. Moreover, what is not an evil is also a good, because what is wicked is evil, but what is without wickedness is good, and so good is opposed to evil and evil to good. Accordingly, where there is not the intention to do harm, there is innocence, and one who is not blameless is blameworthy; one who grants pardon, merciful; one who does not know how to forgive and to bend, merciless.

(1.2) But someone may perhaps say: "What is so opposed to death as life is? If then life is reckoned a good, how is death not an evil?"[1] And therefore let us ponder the nature of life and that of death. Life is the enjoyment of the gift of breath, death the deprivation of it. Further, this gift of breath is considered by most people as a good. And so life is this, the enjoyment of goods, but death is the divestiture of them. And Scripture says: "Behold, I have set before your face life and death, good and evil,"[2] for it calls life good and death evil and attributes to each its proper deserts. Further, to use an example from the Scripture reading, man was placed in paradise "to eat of the tree of life and the other trees of the garden, but not to eat from the tree in which there was the knowledge of good and evil, for on the day he would eat, by death he would die."[3] He did not keep the commandment and was without

---

1 Cf. Plotinus, *Enneads* 1.7.3.
2 Deut. 30.15.   3 Gen. 2.16-17.

fruit; he was cast out of paradise and tasted death. Therefore death is the evil which is introduced as the price of condemnation.

(2.3) But there are three kinds of death.[1] One is the death due to sin, concerning which it was written: "The soul which sins shall itself die."[2] Another death is the mystical, when someone dies to sin and lives to God;[3] concerning this the Apostle likewise says: "For we were buried with him by means of Baptism into death."[4] The third is the death by which we complete our life-span with its functions—I mean the separation of soul and body.[5] Thus we perceive that the one death is an evil, if we die on account of sins, but the other, in which the deceased has been justified of sin, is a good, while the third stands midway, for it seems good to the just and fearful to most men; although it gives release to all, it gives pleasure to few.

But this is not the fault of death but of our own weakness. We are taken with bodily pleasure and delight in this life and are afraid to complete this journey in which there is more bitterness than pleasure. But the saints and wise men, who lamented the longevity of this pilgrimage, since they considered it more glorious "to depart and to be with Christ,"[6] did not curse the day of their generation, as someone says: "Perish the day, on which I was born."[7] (2.4) For what is the pleasure of this life? It is full of troubles and cares, and in it are countless injustices and many vexations and many tears from those who

---

1 The first kind, "the death due to sin," is derived from Philo, the other two types from Porphyry, relying on Plato and Plotinus. See Baziel Maes, *La Loi naturelle selon Ambroise de Milan* (Rome 1967) 43-44 and n. 108.
2 Ezech. 18.4.
3 Cf. Rom. 6.2; Gal. 2.19. The words used to introduce this citation are a probable indication of the homiletic origin of the work.
4 Rom. 6.4.
5 The definition of death as "separation of soul and body" is frequent in Ambrose and ultimately derives from Plato, *Phaedo* 64 C, 67 D. See P. Courcelle, "De Platon à saint Ambroise par Apulée," *Revue de philologie* 35 (1961) 23-24 and especially 23 n. 4. See also 8.31 below.
6 Phil. 1.23.   7 Job 3.3. The speaker is Job.

are afflicted with vexations, and "there is no one to comfort them."[8] And so Ecclesiastes praises the dead rather than the living and says, "And better off than both is the yet unborn, who has not seen this evil."[9] And elsewhere the same Ecclesiastes affirmed that the child born dead was better off than the man of great age, because he did not see the evils that take place in this world, did not come into this darkness, nor walk in the vanity of the world, and so he who did not come into this life will have rest rather than he who came into it.[10] Really, what good is there for a man in this life? He lives in darkness and cannot be satisfied in his desires. And if he is sated with riches, he loses the enjoyment of his rest, because he is forced to guard the possessions he has acquired through his wretched greed. Thus he possesses them in greater wretchedness, seeing that they can do him no good. For what is more wretched than to be tormented with guarding them and derive no advantage from their abundance?

(2.5) And so if life is full of burden, its end comes as a relief. Now the relief is a good, death is the end—death therefore is a good. Just so did Simeon rejoice, for he had received the revelation that "he should not see death before he had seen the Christ of the Lord."[11] And when Christ's parents brought Him into the temple, "he received him into his arms and said: 'Now do you dismiss your servant in peace,' "[12] as if he were kept in this life by a kind of compulsion and not by choice. And so he sought to be dismissed, as if he were hastening to his freedom from some kind of fetters. For there are, so to speak, fetters of the body, and—what is worse—fetters of temptation, that bind us and fasten us to a harmful bondage by a law of sin. And at last, in its departure, we see how the soul of the dying man gradually frees itself from the bonds of

---

8 Eccles. 4.1.
9 Eccles. 4.2-3.
10 Cf. Eccles. 6.3-5.
11 Luke 2.26.
12 Luke 2.28-29.

the flesh and, passing out from the mouth, flies away as if freed from the prison, the poor abode that is the body.[13]

And so holy David hastened to depart from this place of pilgrimage and said: "I am a wayfarer before you on the earth and a pilgrim like all my fathers."[14] And so, like a pilgrim, he hastened to that common homeland of all the saints; in view of the defilement of his stay here, he sought the forgiveness of his sins before his departure from life. For whoever has not received the forgiveness of his sins here, will not be there; and no one will be there who cannot attain to eternal life, because eternal life is the forgiveness of sins.[15] And so he says: "Forgive me that I may find respite ere I depart and be no more."[16]

(2.6) Why then do we desire this life so much? The longer anyone is in it, the greater the burden that weights him down. The Lord Himself says: "Sufficient for the day is its own evil";[17] and Jacob said: "The days of the years of my life which I have now reached are a hundred and thirty years, few and evil,"[18] not because the days were evil but because evils pile up for us in increasing number with the advance of the days. (2.7) For not a day passes without sin on our part. And so the Apostle says quite rightly: "For to me to live is Christ and to die is gain."[19] The one statement refers to the anguish of life, the other to the benefit of death; to us Christ is to live, and we serve Him, and it is right that homage be given to Him by His holy people in the preaching of the Gospel. So too Simeon, who says "Now you dismiss your servant,"[20] was waiting on account of Christ. For Christ is our king; there-

---

13 On the concept of the body as prison of the soul, frequent in Ambrose and many other Christian writers, see P. Courcelle, "Traditions platonicienne et chrétienne du corps-prison," *Revue des études latines* 43 (1965) 406-43, especially 425-26 and 426, n. 1.
14 Ps. 38 (39).13.
15 For a full treatment of the phrase "eternal life" *(vita aeterna)* with reference to this passage, see P. J. Couvée, *Vita Beata en Vita Aeterna* (Baarn 1947), especially p. 173.
16 Ps. 38 (39).14.
17 Matt. 6.34.
18 Gen. 47.9 (Septuagint).
19 Phil. 1.21.   20 Luke 2.29.

fore we cannot abandon and disregard His royal command. How many men the emperor of this earth orders to live abroad in the splendor of office or to perform some function! Do they abandon their posts without the emperor's consent? Yet what a greater thing it is to please the divine than the human! Thus for the saint "to live is Christ and to die is gain."[21] He does not flee the servitude of life like a slave, and yet like a wise man he does embrace the gain of death. For it is a gain to have avoided the increase in sins, a gain to have avoided the worse and passed to the better. And the Apostle adds: "To depart and to be with Christ, a lot by far the better; yet to stay on in the flesh is necessary for your sake."[22] The one course is better, the other is necessary—one necessary by reason of the profit of the work, the other better by reason of the grace and union with Christ.

(3.8) Therefore since the Apostle taught that a man who has passed out of this body will be with Christ, provided he deserves it, let us consider the nature of life and of death. We know from the teaching of Scripture that death is a freeing of the soul from the body, a kind of separation in man. For we are freed from this bond between soul and body, when we depart. For this reason David also says: "You have loosed my bonds. To you will I offer sacrifice of praise."[1] The preceding verse of that psalm, "Precious in the sight of the Lord is the death of his holy ones,"[2] shows that the bonds of this life are meant—the bonds of that union which consists of body and soul. And so he rejoices, foreseeing like a prophet that he will be with the saints and those who have laid down their lives in Christ out of devotion, because he also offered himself in faith for the people of God, when he fought in single combat against Goliath and alone repelled the peril and the reproach that were common to all.[3] He readily offered himself to death

---

21 Phil. 1.21.   22 Phil. 1.23-24.

1 Ps. 115 (116B).7-8.
2 Ps. 115 (116B).6.
3 Cf. 1 Kings 17.40-54.

to atone for his offense against the Lord and presented himself, prepared to suffer God's vengeance for the well-being of his afflicted people.[4] He knew that it was more glorious to die for Christ than to rule in this world, for what is more excellent than to become a victim for Christ?

While we often read that sacrifices were offered by David to the Lord, he adds in this passage: "To you I will offer sacrifice of praise."[5] He does not say "I offer sacrifice," but "I will offer sacrifice," meaning that the sacrifice will have been completed when each one stands before the Lord, freed of the fetters of this body, and offers himself as a victim of praise. For before death no praise is completed nor could anyone in this life be praised with final praise, since his later actions are uncertain. Death then is the freeing of the soul from the body. And so we have taught what was written in the Apostle: "by far the better to be dissolved and to be with Christ."[6] And what is the effect of that dissolution? The body is released and at rest, while the soul turns to its place of repose and is free, and if it is devout, it is going to be with Christ.

(3.9) What do the just accomplish in this life but to divest themselves of the contagions of the body, that bind us like fetters? They strive to free themselves from these vexations, they renounce luxury and pleasures, they flee the fires of lust. Doesn't each person who dwells in this life undergo something like death, if he is able so to act that all his bodily pleasures die and he himself dies to all his desires and the allurements of the world, as Paul had died,[7] saying "The world has been crucified to me and I to the world"?[8]

That we may know that there is death in this life, and a good death, he urges us to bear the death of Jesus in our body.

---

4 Cf. 2 Kings 24.17. 5 Ps. 115 (116B).8. 6 Phil. 1.23.
7 See Ambrose, *On his Brother, Satyrus*, 2.35: ". . . Paul practiced the actual experience of dying." The work is translated into English by J. J. Sullivan and M. R. P. McGuire in *Funeral Orations by Saint Gregory Nazianzen and Saint Ambrose* (FOTC 22; New York 1953) 197-259.
8 Gal. 6.14.

"Whoever has in himself the death of Jesus, he will also have
in his body the life of the Lord Jesus. Let death then work in
us, that life also may work, the good life after death,"[9] that
is, the good life after the victory, the good life once the contest has been completed.[10] Then the law of the flesh will not
know how to war against the law of the mind,[11] then we will
have no strife between death and the body, but the victory
over death in the body. And I wonder if such a death is not
more excellent than life. At any rate, I am moved by the authority of the Apostle, who says: "Thus death is at work in
us, but life in you."[12] The death of one has built up the life
of so many peoples! And so he teaches that such a death should
be sought by those who dwell in this life, so that the death of
Christ may be manifest in our body, and that that death is
happy in which "our outer man is decaying that our inner
man may be renewed,"[13] and our earthly dwelling is being dissolved that a dwelling-place in heaven may be opened to us.
And so a man prefigures death when he withdraws from the
sharing of this body and frees himself from the fetters about
which the Lord spoke to you through Isaia: "But loose every
bond of iniquity; dissolve the obligations of onerous contracts,
set at liberty those who are oppressed, and tear in pieces every
unjust stipulation in writing."[14]

(3.10) He does the same who divests himself of pleasures,
lifts himself up from earthly delights, arises and sets himself in
that heavenly dwelling-place where Paul dwelt while he was
still living. Else the Apostle would not have said "Our way of
life is in heaven,"[15] for this could be set down to a presump-
tion of merit as well as to meditation. Indeed his meditation
was in heaven, and the dwelling of his soul was there. His

---

9 Paul's exhortation is adapted from 2 Cor. 4.10-12.
10 A portion of this passage is cited (*ca.* 420) in Augustine, *Contra duas
   epistulas Pelagianorum* 4.11.31.
11 Cf. Rom. 7.23.
12 2 Cor. 4.12.
13 2 Cor. 4.16.
14 Isa. 58.6 (Septuagint).   15 Phil. 3.20.

wisdom was there, for it generally did not remain within the
confines of this flesh. For the wise man, when he seeks after
the divine, frees his soul from the body and foregoes its company. He is dealing with knowledge of the truth, of such a
kind that he longs for it to be revealed to him naked and
clear, and so he seeks to divest himself of certain snares and
obscurities of the body. And we cannot comprehend such
heavenly truth with hands or eyes or ears, because what is
seen is temporal, but what is not seen is eternal.[16]

Indeed we are often deceived by sight and we see things for
the most part other than they really are; we are deceived by
hearing too, and so, if we do not wish to be deceived, let us
contemplate, not what is seen, but what is unseen. But when
is our soul not deceived, when does it attain the throne of
truth, save when it separates itself from the body and is not
deceived and led astray by it? For it is led astray by the sight
of the eyes, it is led astray by the hearing of the ears, and so
let it leave and abandon them. On this account the Apostle
also cries out: "Do not touch, nor taste, nor handle, things
which must all perish";[17] for things which are for the body's
indulgence are also for its corruption. Thus he shows us that
he has found the truth—not through bodily indulgence, but
through elevation of soul and humility of heart—and he continues: "But our way of life is in heaven."[18] And so he would
seek there what is true, what exists and endures, would gather
himself into himself and would assemble all the insight at
his command. He would not entrust himself to others or
believe them but would know and understand himself and
know that he must follow what he thought to be true. He
would know that what he had thought desirable out of carnal
pleasure is false and would retreat and fly from it, because it
is full of deceit. (3.11) Therefore he rightly devalued and dishonored this body, and called it "the body of death."[19]

16 2 Cor. 4.18.
17 Col. 2.21-22.
18 Phil. 3.20.   19 Rom. 7.24.

Who then could see the splendor of the virtues with his eyes, could lay hold of justice with his hands, could gaze upon wisdom with the sight of his eyes? Indeed, when we are thinking of something, we do not want anyone to appear before us or to raise a din against our ears, and we concentrate in such a way that we generally do not see what is present. Moreover, we think more clearly at night and at that time we meditate better in our hearts upon what is dear to us. On this account too the psalmist says: "What you say in your hearts and on your beds, be sorry for."[20] Some often close their eyes if they wish to dig out anything by profound mental effort, for they shun sight as a hindrance. Often too we search after solitude, so that no one's conversation may be whispered into our ears and, like a kind of bypath, lead the soul away from the truth while it is deeply engaged in thought or turn it aside from its concentration.

(3.12) And so the needs of the body beget many concerns and introduce pursuits that impede the strength of the soul and hinder its concentration. Holy Job puts this well: "Remember that you fashioned me from clay!"[21] So if the body is clay, it surely soils us and does not wash us, for it contaminates the soul with the contamination of intemperance. "With skin and flesh you clothed me, with bones and sinews knit me together."[22] So our soul is bound and tormented by the sinews of the body and sometimes hardens, while it often bends. And further, "From my guilt you did not absolve me. If I should be wicked, alas for me! If righteous, I dare not hold up my head, for I am full of ignominy. You have brought against me tortures."[23]

What is this life but full of snares? We walk among snares,[24] we live among many trials. "Is not man's life on earth a state of trial?"[25] He does well to add "on earth," because there is a

20 Ps. 4.5.
21 Job 10.9.
22 Job 10.11.
23 Job 10.14-15, 17 (Septuagint).
24 Cf. Sir. 9.13.   25 Job 7.1 (Septuagint).

life of man also in heaven. "His life is the wages of a hireling, in toil and in warmth, lighter than idle tales,"[26] and floating in words and overflowing with words. Its dwelling is in the abodes of slime, and life itself is in the slime. There is no stability of thought, no constancy. By day man longs for the night, at night he searches for the day.[27] Before he takes food he groans; amid his nourishment there are weeping and tears and sorrows and fears and anxieties, with no respite from troubles, no repose from toils. The passion of anger and indignation is more terrible. Many desire death and do not obtain it; if they do obtain it, they rejoice, because death alone brings rest to man.

(4.13) But someone will say that it has been written that "God did not make death."[1] There was life in paradise, where there was the tree of life,[2] and "the life was the light of men."[3] Death then is an evil which befell and entered in secretly. But how is death an evil if, as the pagans say,[4] it is the lack of feeling, or, according to the Apostle, the gain is Christ,[5] "to be with whom is by far the better"?[6] How, then, is death an evil for us, if there is no feeling after death? For where there is no feeling, there is no grief at injustice, since grief is a feeling. Or, because there is feeling after death, it follows that

---

26 Job 7.1-2, 6 (Septuagint).
27 Cf. Job 7.4.

---

1 Wisd. 1.13.
2 Cf. Gen. 2.9.
3 John 1.4.
4 On the pagan views of death, see P. Courcelle, "Anti-Christian Arguments and Christian Platonism: from Arnobius to St. Ambrose," in A. Momigliano *et al., The Conflict between Paganism and Christianity in the Fourth Century* (Oxford 1963) 151-192, especially p. 161: "Though the pagans were united in denying the resurrection, which to them belonged in the realm of poetic myth, they were divided on the question of the eventual fate of the human soul. Some believed it to be mortal." The relevant passages from Ambrose are assembled at p. 182 n. 121.
5 Cf. Phil. 1.21. A somewhat different reading of the text, advocated by O. Bardenhewer in *Literarische Rundschau* 24 (1898) col. 200, gives the sense "it (death) is . . . the gaining of Christ."
6 Cf. Phil. 1.21, 23.

there is a life after death and the soul survives death, for it possesses feeling and enjoys life. But since the life of the soul remains after death, there remains a good which is not lost by death but is increased. The soul is not held back by any obstacle placed by death but is more active, because it is active in its own sphere without any association with the body, which is more of a burden than a benefit to it. And so what evil does the soul suffer, if it has guarded its integrity and maintained the rule of the virtues? But if it has not done so, death is not the evil, but life is, because the soul did not have life. For what is a life choked with vices and sins? Why do we blame death, which merely pays the wages of life or else destroys life's pain and torment? Therefore death either enjoys a good, which is its own repose, or suffers under an evil not its own.

(4.14) Now consider this: If life is a burden, death is a release; if life is a punishment, death is a remedy; and if there is a judgment after death,[7] there is also life after death. And so is not such a life a good? Or if life here is a good, how is death there not a good, when no fear of dread judgment remains? But if life here is a good, in what does its goodness consist? In virtue and in good moral conduct. And so life is a good, not by reason of the union of soul and body, but because through virtue it rejects what is evil to itself but obtains the good that is in death. Thus it achieves what pertains to the soul rather than to the dwelling together and union of soul and body.

But if life is a good—and it is the image of the soul separating itself from the body—and if the soul is a good—and it raises itself and draws away from dwelling with the body—indeed death also is a good, for it releases and frees the soul from this union with the flesh.[8] (4.15) Therefore death is in every way a good, both because it separates elements in conflict, so that they may not fight with one another, and because it is

---

7 Cf. Heb. 9.27.
8 On the entire passage 4.13-14, cf. Plotinus, *Enneads* 1.7.3.

a kind of harbor for those who seek an anchorage of trusty rest after they have been tossed about on the sea of this life,[9] and because it does not make man's condition worse. Just as it finds each one, so it keeps him for the judgment that is to come and comforts him with its repose; it draws him away from envy of things present and calms him with the expectation of those that are to come. Further, men vainly fear death as if it were an end set by nature. But let us recall that "God did not make death"[10] but after man fell into the disgrace of prevarication and fraud, He took hold of him with the sentence that "earth should return into its kindred earth."[11] Thus we will find that death is the end of sin;[12] else, the longer life was, the more numerous its faults might have become.

Therefore the Lord permitted death to steal in, that guilt might cease. But so that the end set by nature might not also be in death, there was granted a resurrection of the dead, that the guilt might fail through death, but the nature be continued through resurrection. And so death is a passage for all men, but you must pass with constancy—a passage from corruption to incorruption, from mortality to immortality, from disquiet to tranquillity.[13] And so let not the word "death" give you offense, but let the benefits of a good passage give you pleasure. What indeed is death but the burial of vices and the awakening of virtues? For this reason "may my soul depart

---

9 On the metaphor of the sea, cf. P. Courcelle, "De Platon à saint Ambroise par Apulée," *Revue de philologie* 35 (1961) 22 n. 1, where relevant passages are set out. The metaphor reappears frequently, for example in pseudo-Prosper, *Carmen de Providentia Dei* 772-776. For the possible influence of Sophistic rhetorical training see J. M. Campbell, *The Influence of the Second Sophistic on the Style of the Sermons of St. Basil the Great* (The Catholic University of America Patristic Studies 2; Washington 1922).
10 Wisd. 1.13.
11 Cf. Gen. 3.19.
12 The concept of death as "end of sin" appears also in several other passages in Ambrose. See *On the Sacraments* 6.17; *On Cain* 2.9.32; *Explanation of Psalm 118.*18.3, and *Isaac* 8.76, all cited in the handy translation of *On the Sacraments* by T. Thompson (London 1950) at p. 65 n. 4.
13 Cf. 1 Cor. 15.42.

among the souls of the righteous," that is, "may it be buried together with them,"[14] that it may lay down its sins and take up the grace of the just, who "bear about the dying of Christ in their body"[15] and soul. Moreover, the dying of Christ is the forgiveness of sins, the abolition of faults, the forgetting of error, the taking on of grace. What more can I say about the good which is death, except that it is death which has redeemed the world?

(5.16) But let us speak of death as common to all men. Why should we be afraid of it, when it generally does not harm the soul? For it is written: "Do not be afraid of those who kill the body but cannot kill the soul."[1] Now through death the soul is freed, while it separates itself from the dwelling-place of the body and divests itself of the wrappings of disquiet. And so let us too, while we are in the body, following the way of death, raise up our bodies from this fleshly couch and arise from the tomb, as it were. Let us withdraw from the bond of the body, and leave all things whatsoever which are of earth, so that when the adversary comes he may find nothing of his in us.[2] Let us strive for the eternal, and fly up to the divine on the wings of love and the oars of charity. Let us rise up from here, that is, from the things of the age and those of the world. For the Lord has said: "Arise, let us go from here,"[3] teaching that each one should arise from the earth, raise up his soul that lies upon the ground, lift it to the things that are above, and call forth his eagle, the eagle of whom it is said: "Your youth will be renewed like the eagle's."[4]

The foregoing is addressed to the soul. And so let our soul seek the heights like the eagle, let it fly above the clouds, let it glisten in its new skin, let it carry its flight to heaven,

---

14 Num. 23.10 (Septuagint); cf. Col. 2.12.
15 2 Cor. 4.10.

---

1 Matt. 10.28.
2 Cf. John 14.30.
3 John 14.31.
4 Ps. 102 (103).5.

where it cannot fall into snares. For a bird that goes down from the heights or cannot lift itself to them is often taken in the nets or tricked with the lime or snared by some sort of ambush.[5] So also let our soul beware of going down to the things of this world. The snare lies in gold, the lime in silver, the bond in an estate, the nail in love. When we seek the gold, we choke; when we search after the silver, we are stuck in the lime; when we enter upon the estate, we are bound to it.

Why do we search after idle gain to the loss of our precious souls? The whole world costs you dear at the price of a single soul. "For what does it profit a man, if he gain the whole world, but suffer the loss of his soul? Or what exchange will you give for your soul?"[6] It is not redeemed for gold or for silver; on the contrary, it is lost for gold. Feminine beauty, too, binds man fast while he is putting it to the test. The nail is lust and moroseness and wrath, the nails are all the passions that penetrate our soul like a kind of stake, fasten on to the body, and bind themselves to its vital organs.

(5.17) Therefore let us flee these evils and elevate our soul to the image and likeness of God. The flight from evils is the likeness of God, and the image of God is gained through the virtues.[7] And so, like a painter, He has painted us with the colors of the virtues. "See, I have painted your walls, Jerusalem."[8] Let us not wipe away with the brush of neglect the props of the painted walls of our soul. And so "I have painted the walls,"[9] with which we can turn away the enemy. (5.18) The soul has its walls; from them it stands forth and concerning them it says: "I am a strong city, a city besieged."[10] By these walls it is guarded, and by them it is protected under siege. And truly the soul is a wall, which stretches forth over the

---

5 This passage is Vergilian in tone. For the concept of the bird in flight, see Vergil, *Aeneid* 5.508; 9.564 and *Georgics* 1.364. For the bird as ensnared, see *Georgics* 1.139.
6 Cf. Matt. 16.26.
7 Cf. Ambrose, *Flight from the World* 17.
8 Cf. Isa. 49.16.
9 Cf. *ibid.*
10 Isa. 27.3 (Septuagint).

camp. And therefore the bride says in Canticles: "I am a wall, and my breasts are like towers."[11] The wall which the Lord painted is good, even as He says: "On my hands I have painted your walls, and you are always in my sight."[12]

The soul which has God as its watchman and is in His hands is good, just as the soul of the psalmist, which is commended into the hands of the Lord[13] as a spirit, and which is in the sight of God. "For the eyes of the Lord are upon the just,"[14] even as the bride says, "I was in his eyes as one finding peace."[15] And she had good towers, for she has both the word, as regards intelligibles, and the rule of conduct, as regards moral questions. And so such a soul, having grace in its breasts, enters into the gardens: there it finds its bridegroom sitting and conversing with His friends,[16] and says: "You who are sitting in the garden, let me hear your voice."[17] It says "me," not "my friends." "Away, my brother"[18]—it urges that the bridegroom flee, because already, although it is of earth, it can follow Him in His flight. It says this so that it may be like the young deer that escapes the nets; for it desires also to flee and to fly away above the world.[19]

(5.19) From this source Plato fashioned the well-known garden for himself. Sometimes he called it Jupiter's garden, other times the garden of the mind, for he said "Jupiter" and "god" and "mind" indifferently. And the soul, which he calls "Venus," had entered into it to be filled with the abundant wealth of the garden, in which there lay Porus filled with drink, who poured forth nectar.[20] And this account he fashioned from the book of Canticles, insofar as the soul that

---

11 Cant. 8.10.   12 Cf. Isa. 49.16.   13 Cf. Ps. 30 (31).6.
14 Ps. 33 (34).16.   15 Cant. 8.10.
16 This portion of the sentence appears also in the *Commentary on the Canticle of Canticles* (8.28), for which see above, p. 5.
17 Cant. 8.13.   18 Cant. 8.14 (Septuagint).
19 The entire passage 5.17-18 is modeled on Ambrose, *Hexameron (Creation)* 6.49, translated by J. J. Savage in *Saint Ambrose: Hexameron, Paradise, and Cain and Abel* (FOTC 42: New York 1961).
20 In Plotinus' allegorical interpretation, Porus (Plenty) was identified as the Logos, the rational principle of all things.

cleaves to God entered into the garden of the mind, in which there were an abundance of various virtues and the choicest discourse.[21] From that paradise which, as we read in Genesis,[22] contained the tree of life and the tree of the knowledge of good and evil and the other trees—does not everyone know that Plato thought that from there he should transplant that abundance of virtues and plant them in the garden of the mind which in his Canticles Solomon called the garden of the soul or the soul itself? For thus is it written: "You are an enclosed garden, my sister spouse, an enclosed garden, a fountain sealed; what you yield is a paradise."[23] And later the soul says: "Awake, O north wind, come also, O south wind, and blow gently through my garden and let my aromatic spices flow. Let my brother go down into his garden."[24] The sentiment is the finer on this account, that the soul, bedecked with virtues as with flowers, is a garden and has a paradise flowering in itself.

Into that garden the soul invites the Word of God to come down, so that it may be watered by the abundant heavenly rain of the Word and thus bear fruit. Now the Word of God is nourished on the virtues of the soul. Whenever He finds the soul fertile and manageable, He gathers its produce and takes pleasure in it. And when the Word of God has gone down into the soul, there flow out from it the ointments of the words of salvation, while the fragrant scents of various graces spread far and wide.

(5.20) On this account the spouse says—and the spouse of the soul is the Word of God, for the soul is united to Him in a bond of lawful matrimony, so to speak—"I have come to my garden, my sister spouse. I have gathered my myrrh with my spices, I have eaten my bread with my honey, I have drunk

---

21 Ambrose is relying here on the account in Plotinus, *Enneads* 3.5, derived from the *Symposium* of Plato. For a thorough discussion of the complex relationship involved, see P. Courcelle, *Recherches sur les Confessions de Saint Augustin* (Paris 1950) 120-122.
22 Cf. Gen. 2.9.　　　23 Cant. 4.12-13 (Septuagint).
24 Cant. 4.16 (Septuagint).

my wine with my milk. Eat, my friends; drink, yes, drink plentifully, my brethren. I sleep, but my heart is awake."[25] Let us learn what food and produce God feasts upon and in which ones He takes pleasure. He takes pleasure in this, if anyone dies to his sin, blots out his guilt, and destroys and buries his iniquities. The myrrh represents the burial of the dead, but sins are dead, for they cannot possess the sweetness of life. Moreover, some wounds of sinners are moistened with the ointments of Scripture and the stronger food of the word as with bread,[26] and are treated with the sweeter word like honey. Elsewhere, too, Solomon teaches that there is food in words, when he says: "Good words are a honeycomb."[27]

And so in that garden there are good words, one to check fault, another to reprove iniquity, another to bring on the death of insolence and to bury it, when someone has been reproved for his errors and renounces them. There is also a stronger word, that strengthens the heart of man with the more powerful nourishment of heavenly Scripture. There is as well a word of persuasion, sweet like honey and still afflicting the conscience of the sinner in its very sweetness. There is also a word of more ardent spirit, that inebriates like wine and gladdens the heart of man,[28] and also a word like milk, that is pure and clear. The bridegroom is saying to His friends that they should feast on these foods, these sweet and useful words.[29] Now His friends are those who follow Him and attend His wedding. The soul was filled with that food and drink— for "each one drinks water from his own vessels and from the fountains of his own wells"[30]—and it was sleeping, drunk to the world, but it was keeping watch for God. And so, as

---

25 Cant. 5.1-2 (Septuagint). Much of this passage appears with slight variation at *On the Sacraments* 3.15. See Thompson's translation (cited in ch. 4, n. 12, above) p. 100 n. 1. for further discussion of the text of the Scripture passage.
26 Cf. Ps. 103 (104).15.
27 Prov. 16.24 (Septuagint).
28 Cf. Ps. 103 (104).15; Sir. 40.20.
29 Cf. Cant. 5.1 (probably in the Septuagint version).
30 Prov. 5.15 (Septuagint).

the later verses show, God asked that the door, His word, be opened to Him, that He might fill it in His coming. (5.21) And from this source are derived the banqueters of Plato, the nectar is derived from the wine and the honey of the psalmist, the sleep too, and the everlasting life that Plato said his gods spent in feasting,[31] because "Christ is the life."[32] Thus the belly of that soul was filled from the seeds of those words[33] and the soul itself went forth in the Word. And the soul that goes forth from that slavery[34] and raises itself from the body follows the Word.

(6.22) But there are powers of the air and powers of the world,[1] who strive to cast us down from the wall of the soul, to keep us from walking in the right way, to put us aside from aiming for the higher realms, and to call us back to earthly things. But let us follow the Word of God and rouse the mind much more to lofty concerns. Those principalities pour forth the goods of the world to warp your mind with them. Then do you, O soul, direct your steps the more to Christ. They introduce the greedy desire for gold and silver and the neighbor's property, so that, in order to gain it, you may excuse yourself from the dinner of him who invited you to the wedding feast of the Word. See that you do not excuse yourself, but put on the wedding garment and enjoy the rich man's banquet. Otherwise, when you have excused yourself and while you are occupied with worldly concerns, the rich man who invited you may invite others and you may be kept out.[2]

Those powers of the world also introduce the competition for position, so that you may exalt yourself like Adam; while you desire to be equal to God by possessing similar

---

31 Cf. Plato, *Symposium* 203 B. See also n. 21 above.
32 John 14.6.
33 Cf. Ps. 16 (17).14.
34 The phrasing is modeled on Vergil, *Eclogues* 1.40.

1 Cf. Eph. 6.12.
2 Cf. Luke 14.18-24; Matt. 22.1-14.

power, you despise God's commandments and begin to lose
what you possessed. For "from him who does not have, even
that which he has shall be taken away."[3] (6.23) So many times
when we are at prayer, where we approach closest to God,
things are offered us that are full of some dishonor or wrong,
so as to turn us away from the desire to pray! So often the
enemy tries to creep into our heart to turn us back from our
holy purpose and pious intentions! So often he sets afire the
passions of the body, so often he makes our eyes wander in
meretricious fashion, to test the pure disposition of the just
man and strike him unprepared with love's sudden dart! How
often he sets in your soul the wicked word and the hidden
thoughts of the heart! Concerning this the law says to you:
"Take heed to yourself that there not be a wicked word hid
in your heart"[4] and Jesus may say to you: "Why do you
harbor evil thoughts in your heart?"[5] Otherwise, when you are
overflowing with gold and silver and the rich produce of the
fields or with honors, you may say: "My own might has
achieved all these things for me,"[6] and may be forgetful of the
Lord your God.

(6.24) And so the soul which desires to fly away is brought
down by these allurements. But you must struggle like a good
soldier of Jesus Christ; despise lesser things, forget the things
of earth, strive for the celestial and eternal. Lift up your soul,
so that the bait in the snares does not entice it. The pleasures
of the world are a kind of bait—and what is worse—the bait
of evils, the bait of temptations. While you seek pleasure, you
are running into the snares. For "the harlot's eye is the lover's
snare." And so the eye of the harlot is a snare; the harlot's
speech is a snare too, for it sweetens your lips for a time and
later roughens them with the bitter knowledge that you had a
share in her sin. The possession of what belongs to another,
full of delight as it is, is a snare. Every path of life is filled

---

3 Matt. 13.12.
4 Deut. 15.9 (Septuagint).
5 Matt. 9.4.   6 Deut. 8.17.

with snares. On this account the just man says: "In the way I was going they had hid snares for me."[7] He says: "In the way, they had hid. . ." And so you must walk the way that says: "I am the way, and the truth, and the life,"[8] so that you may say: "He has converted my soul; he has led me on the paths of justice for his own name's sake."[9]

(6.25) Therefore let us die to this world, let us die to "the wisdom of this flesh, which is hostile to God."[10] Let us make our soul subject to Christ alone, so that each man may say: "Is not my soul subject to God?"[11] (The passage does not say "subject to the age, subject to the world.") The wealthy man cannot say this, the greedy man cannot, but the just and temperate man says it. The greedy man says: "Soul, you have many good things laid up for many years; take your ease, eat, drink and be merry,"[12] because the soul of the greedy man is subject to the luxury of the body, but the just man employs the body as an instrument or tool. Like a highly skilled artisan, the soul leads the body in its service where it will, fashions out of it the form it has chosen, and makes the virtues it has willed resound in it:[13] now it composes the melodies of chastity, again those of temperance, the song of sobriety, the charm of uprightness, the sweetness of virginity, the seriousness of widowhood.

But sometimes the musician has compassion on his instrument. Therefore play what is honorable, that your compassion may be honorable. For one who sees is much affected by what he sees, and one who hears by what he hears. And so Scripture says: "Let your eyes look straight ahead"[14] and later: "Be not devoted to a strange woman."[15] Do not turn to the eyes of a young girl, do not turn to the words of a harlot.

---

7 Ps. 141.4.   8 John 14.6.   9 Ps. 22 (23).3.
10 Rom. 8.7.
11 Ps. 61 (62).2.
12 Luke 12.19.
13 The image of the body as a musical instrument which resounds when struck appears in Porphyry, *De abstinentia* 1.43.
14 Prov. 4.25.
15 Prov. 5.20 (Septuagint).

(7.26) But why speak of snares that are from outside? We must beware of our own internal snares. In this body of ours we are surrounded by snares, and we ought to avoid them. Let us not trust ourselves to this body, let us not join our soul with it. "Join your soul with a friend, not with an enemy."[1] Your enemy is your body, which "wars against your mind,"[2] and its works are enmities, dissensions, strifes and disorders.[3] Do not join your soul with it; else you may bring both into disorder. For if there is a joining, the flesh, which is the lesser element, becomes better than the soul, which is the greater, because the soul gives life to the body, but the flesh pours death into the soul. And so the working of each element is brought into disorder; indeed the very nature of each is in effect brought into disorder. And so the soul receives into itself the insensibility of the dead body, and the body performs all the functions of the soul.

But do not think that disorder occurs merely because the soul is infused into the body. Take for example the gift of light, for the light is poured out upon the earth and yet is not confounded with it. And so let the working of elements whose nature is unlike not be confounded, but let the soul be in the body to give it life, to rule and enlighten it. (7.27) Yet we cannot deny that it should have compassion on its body. For it also is afflicted, since Jesus says: "My soul is sad, even unto death,"[4] thus expressing human emotion in Himself, and elsewhere He says: "My soul is troubled,"[5] since He shows compassion by His attitude and disposition. Just so the singer shows compassion with his melodies and with the sound of his pipe or cithara or organ, when he is sad at the sad sounds, joyful at the joyful ones, more excited at those that are sharper,

---

1 Cf. Sir. 6.13; Prov. 25.9. The exact source of the quotation is unclear, as perhaps it also was to Ambrose.
2 Cf. Rom. 7.23.
3 Cf. Gal. 5.19-20.
4 Matt. 26.28.
5 John 12.27.

more calm and gentle at those that are calmer. Thus in his own person he gains favor for the sounds of his songs and in some way controls their moods. The soul too, playing in moderation on the body as if on a musical stringed instrument, strikes the passions of the flesh as if they were notes on the strings, but with its fingertips,[6] so to speak. Thus it produces music in euphonious accord with a virtuous way of life, and in all its thoughts and works sees to it that its counsels harmonize with its deeds.

The soul, then, is the user, the body that which is being used, and thus the one is in command, the other in service; the one is what we are, the other what belongs to us. If anyone loves the beauty of the soul, he loves us; if anyone loves the grace of the body, he loves not the man himself, but the beauty of the flesh, which quickly wastes away and disappears.

(7.28) Therefore incline to him of whom the psalmist says: "He has not taken his soul in vain."[7] To speak now of the troubles of this life, the man has taken his soul in vain who is constructing the things of the world and building the things of the body. We arise each day to eat and drink; yet no one is filled so that he does not hunger and thirst after a short time. Daily we seek profit, and to greed there is set no limit. "The eye will not be satisfied with seeing, nor the ear with hearing."[8] He that loves silver will not be satisfied with silver. There is no limit to toil, and there is no profit in abundance. We desire each day to know what is new, and what is knowledge itself but our daily sorrow and abasement? All things which are have already been and "nothing is new under the sun," but "all is vanity. Therefore I hated the whole of this life," said Ecclesiastes.[9] He who hated his life certainly commended death. And so he praised the dead rather than the living and

---

6 The phrase is proverbial. Cf. A. Sonny, "Zu den Sprichwörtern und sprichwörtlichen Redensarten der Römer," *Archiv für Lateinische Lexikographie und Grammatik* 9 (1896) 60, under *digitus*.
7 Ps. 23 (24).4.
8 Eccles. 1.18.
9 Eccles. 1.9-10; 2.17 (Septuagint).

judged him happy that did not come into this life nor take up this vain toil.[10] "My heart took a circuit to know the joy of the impious man and to examine carefully and to seek wisdom and a mode of calculating and to know joy through the impious man and trouble and disquietude, and I find that it is bitterer than death"[11]—not because death is bitter, but because it is bitter for the impious one. And yet life is bitterer than death. For it is a greater burden to live for sin than to die in sin, because the impious man increases his sin as long as he lives, but if he dies, he ceases to sin.

(7.29) Many rejoice in absolution from their crimes, and rightly so, if they are going to reform, but foolishly, if they are going to continue in them. For damnation would have been far more to their advantage, so that they would not increase the number of sins. Concerning this we have the exalted thought of the Apostle, who says that not only those who commit the outrages but those who approve of them are deserving of death.[12] And also he says that those who condemn in others what they do themselves are reckoned inexcusable and are condemned by their own sentence, for when they condemn others, they are condemning themselves.[13] And they ought not to flatter themselves because they seem exempt from punishment for the moment and free of charges, since they are paying heavier penalties within themselves and are criminals to themselves, although they do not seem so to others. When they make judgments about the sins of others, they are casting a heavier sentence of conscience upon themselves.

"But do not, O man," the Apostle says, "despise the riches of God's goodness and patience; for the goodness of God calls you to repentance and invites you to correction."[14] But your hardness, by which you persist in the obstinacy of error, in-

---

10 Cf. Eccles. 4.1-2.
11 Cf. Eccles. 7.25-26 (Septuagint).
12 Cf. Rom. 1.32.
13 Cf. Rom. 2.1, 3.
14 Rom. 2.4.

creases the severity of the judgment that is to come, so that you may receive fit retribution for your offenses.[15]

(7.30) And so death is not an evil. For death is not with the living nor with the departed. It is not with some, because they are still living, but the others have departed. And so death is not bitter in the case of those who still do not know it, for the very reason that they do not know it, nor in the case of those who already have no sensation in regard to the body and have been freed as regards the soul.

(8.31) But if death is considered frightening among the living, it is not death itself that is frightening, but conjecture about death,[1] which each person interprets according to his disposition or holds in dread according to his conscience. And so let each one find fault with the wound made by his own conscience, not with the bitterness of death. To the just, death is a harbor of rest; to the guilty, it is reckoned a shipwreck. Surely for those who have a grievous fear of death, it is not death that is grievous, but life under the fear of death. And so death is not grievous, but the fear of death.

Now fear is a matter of the imagination, and the imagination, opposed to the truth, is a matter of our weakness. For through the truth is strength, but through the imagination weakness. Moreover, the imagination belongs, not to death, but to life. And so the burden is found to belong rather to life. Therefore it is clear that the fear of death is to be ascribed, not to death, but to life. For we do not have anything to fear in death if in our life we have done nothing to be afraid of. For indeed the punishment of offenses causes dread to wise men, whereas the offenses are not actions of the dead, but of the living. Life then is ascribed to us, and its living is in our power, but death is in no way attributable to us. Death is the separation of body and soul;[2] the soul is freed, the body dis-

---

15 Cf. Rom. 2.5.

---

1 Cf. Epictetus, *Enchiridion* 5.
2 Cf. n. 5 to chapter 2, above.

sipated. What is freed rejoices, what is dissipated into its clay feels nothing. What feels nothing is nothing to us.

(8.32) But if death is an evil, why are young men not afraid to become old men and not terrified of an age that is near to death? And why does a man depart with greater endurance who departs in a death that is foreseen than one who departs in an unexpected death? For those who consider death an evil, I think it also a suitable reply that through life there is a passage to death, but through death a return to life—only those who have died can rise again. And the foolish are afraid of death as the greatest of evils, but wise men seek it as a rest after their toils and as the end of evils.

(8.33) Moreover, the foolish are terrified of death for two reasons. One, because they call it a destruction. But there cannot be a destruction of man, since the soul survives the body, with the reservation that a resurrection awaits the body itself. The other reason is that they are terrified of the punishments—doubtless because they have been frightened by the fabulous stories of the poets—the baying of Cerberus[3] and the grim whirlpool of Cocytus' stream, Charon yet more grim,[4] the Furies in battle array[5] or the heights of Tartarus,[6] then the vestibules wherein the Hydra, more cruel, has her abode,[7] the vitals of Tityos too, so productive for repaying penalties, on which a monstrous vulture feasts endlessly,[8] and the everlasting turning of Ixion's wheel, cruel punishment! and the destruction that threatens those reclining at the feast from the rock that hangs down over their heads from above.[9]

---

3 Cf. Vergil, *Aeneid* 6.401, 417.
4 Cf. *ibid*. 296-98.
5 Cf. *ibid*. 572.
6 Cf. *ibid*. 577-78.
7 *Cf. ibid.* 576-77. The phrase translated as "the vestibules wherein" is suggested by Schenkl to fill a lacuna in the text at this point.
8 Cf. *ibid*. 595-600.
9 Cf. *ibid*. 601-16. For a full discussion of the passage, see P. Courcelle, "Les Pères devant les enfers virgiliens," *Archives d'histoire doctrinale et littèraire du moyen-age* 30 (1955) 5-74, especially 28-29.

Such stories are full of the fabulous. Yet I would not deny that there are punishments after death. But what has that which comes after death got to do with death? If what comes after death is ascribed to death, likewise what comes after life is ascribed to life. Then there will be no punishments to be ascribed to death. For death, as I said above, is a freeing and separation of soul and body; but it is not an evil separation, because "to depart and to be with Christ is a lot by far the better."[10] And so death is not an evil. Indeed, "the death of sinners is wretched,"[11] not that death in general is wretched, but that that of sinners in particular is wretched. Indeed, "precious is the death of the just."[12] On this account it is clear that the bitterness comes, not from death, but from guilt.

(8.34) Further, the Greeks did well to term death an end. They call death an end, because it is the end of this life.[13] But Scripture also calls death sleep, as in this passage: "Lazarus, our friend, sleeps; but I go that I may wake him."[14] Now sleep is good, because it is rest, just as it is written: "I have slept and have taken my rest and have risen up, because the Lord will receive me."[15] Sweet indeed is the rest that is death.[16] The Lord raises those who are at rest, because the Lord is the resurrection.[17] (8.35) Scripture puts it well: "Praise no man before death."[18] For each man is known in his last end and is judged in his children, if he has trained his children well and has taught them with suitable teachings, since the dissoluteness of the children is ascribed to the negligence of the father. And because everyone, as long as he lives, is subject to a fall, not even old age is immune to guilt. Thus you read

---

10 Phil. 1.23.
11 Ps. 33 (34).22.
12 Ps. 115 (116B).6.
13 Cf. ch. 2 n. 5, above, and Plato, *Gorgias* 516 A.
14 John 11.11.
15 Ps. 3.6.
16 Cf. Vergil, *Aeneid* 6.520-522, and P. Courcelle, "Les Pères devant les enfers virgiliens," p. 16 and n. 10.
17 Cf. John 11.25.
18 Sir. 11.28.

that "Abraham died at a good old age"[19] because he persisted in his good purpose.

Death is therefore a witness to life. For if the pilot cannot receive praise before he has brought the ship into port, how will you praise a man before he has passed into the anchorage of death? He is the pilot of his own self and is himself tossed about on the depth that is this life, amid shipwrecks so long as he is on this sea. Even the general does not take the laurel wreath unless the battle has been finished, nor does the soldier lay down his arms and receive pay for his service unless the enemy has been conquered. And so death is the fullness of service, the total of pay, the thanks of discharge.

(8.36) How highly holy Job valued death, for he said: "Let the blessing of him who is about to die come upon me!"[20] Although Isaac blessed his sons at his death,[21] and Jacob blessed the patriarchs,[22] still the grace of that blessing could be attributed to the singular merits of those who gave it or to paternal piety. But in the present instance there is no prerogative of merit involved, and none of piety, but only the privilege of death. For the blessing of someone on the point of death has such power that the holy prophet desired it for himself.

And on this account let us meditate upon this verse and hold it in our heart. (8.37) If we see any poor person on the point of death, let us help him at our expense. Let each person say: "Let the blessing of the person who is about to die come upon me!"[23] If we see anyone infirm, let us not abandon him; if we see anyone in his final agony, let us not leave him. Let it befall us also to say: "Let the blessing of the person who is about to die come upon me!"[24] Let each person who is about to die give you praise, each person dying of old age, each

---

19 Gen. 25.8.
20 Job 29.13 (Septuagint).
21 Cf. Gen. 27.27-40.
22 Cf. Gen. 49.28.
23 Job 29.13.
24 *Ibid.*

person afflicted with a deadly wound, each person consumed with disease and by now on the point of death. This verse has brought a blessing on so many! How often it has inspired in me a sense of shame, if I have passed by someone who was about to die, if I have not visited one who was gravely ill, if I have scorned one who was needy, if I have not redeemed the captive and have despised the aged man! Let it then remain always in the heart, to spur those who are hard of heart, to admonish those who are better disposed. Let the last words of the one who is about to die reecho your name, and as his soul departs from the body let it bear with itself a blessing on you. And rescue him who is being led to death, who would have perished unless you had helped, so that you may say: "May the blessing of him that was about to perish come upon me!"[25]

(9.38) Who would doubt that death is a good? Whatever is unquiet, or shameworthy, or hostile to us, whatever is boisterous or stormy or entices to vice of every kind, is at rest; it lies still and is shut in the hollow tomb like a wild beast. Its savagery is bereft of life, while the union of the vital parts is dead and dissolved into clay. But that part that is intimate with the virtues, friendly to the rules of right conduct, zealous for glory, in pursuit of the good and subject to God—that part flies away to what is on high; it remains with the pure and everlasting good that is immortal, cleaves to Him and is with Him from whom it takes its likeness, "whose offspring," as someone says, "we also are."[1]

For it is clear that the soul does not die with the body, because it is not of the body. And that it is not of the body Scripture teaches us in many ways. For Adam received the breath of life from the Lord God "and became a living soul,"[2]

---

25 *Ibid.*

---

1 Cf. Acts 17.28 and above, *Isaac* ch. 8 nn. 101, 102. For further treatment of Ambrose's use of this Scripture passage and for the relationship of it to Plotinus, see P. Courcelle, *Recherches sur les* Confessions *de Saint Augustin* (Paris 1950) 131 (with n. 2), 132.

2 Gen. 2.7.

and David says: "Turn, O my soul, into your rest, for the Lord has been good to me."[3] And learn the nature of God's goodness: "For he has freed my feet from falling."[4] You see that David rejoices in the remedy of such a death, because an end has been put to error, because guilt has perished, but not nature. (9.39) And so he says, as if liberated and free: "I shall please the Lord in the land of the living."[5] For that is the land. . . . Further, he says that the land of the living is that resting place of souls,[6] where sins do not enter in and where the glory of the virtues lives. Now that land is filled with the dead, because it is filled with sinners, and it was rightly said: "Leave the dead to bury their own dead."[7] But likewise he also said above: "His soul shall dwell in good things, and his seed shall inherit the land";[8] that is, the soul of one who fears God will dwell in good things, so that it is always in them and in conformity with them. The passage can also be taken to refer to one who is in the body, so that he too, if he fears God, dwells in good things and is in heavenly things, for he possesses his body and enjoys mastery over it as if it had been reduced to slavery, and he possesses the inheritance of glory and of the heavenly promises.

(9.40) On this account, if we desire to be in good things after the death of this body, let us take care that our soul not be glued to the body, nor mingled with it, that it not cleave to it nor be pulled by it, that it not totter and stagger as if drunk under the passions of the body nor trust itself to bodily pleasures, to commit itself to the feelings of the body. For the eye of the body is error and fraud, because sight is deceived, and its ear is deception, because hearing too is mocked, and its

---

3 Ps. 114 (116A).7.
4 Ps. 114 (116A).8.
5 Ps. 114 (116A).9. It is not clear what text should be supplied to fill in the lacuna noted by Schenkl in the following sentence.
6 Cf. Ps. 26 (27).13.
7 Matt. 8.22.
8 Ps. 24 (25).13.

taste is deception. Further, the saying is not an idle one: "Let your eyes look straight ahead"[9] and "Keep your tongue from evil."[10] This would not have been said unless they frequently went astray.

You have seen the harlot; you have been taken by her countenance and have considered her features beautiful. Your eyes have gone astray; they have seen evil but have declared otherwise. For if they had seen truly, they would have seen the harlot's ugly condition, her bristling impudence and unsightly impurity, her withering lusts and foul pollution, the wounds of the spirit, the scars of conscience. "Whosoever shall look at a woman to lust after her. . . ."[11] You see that the man who did not seek after truth but after adultery sought falsehood. For he sought to see in order to lust, not in order to learn the truth. And so his eye goes astray where his passion goes astray. Thus passion is a deception, and sight is a deception, and so it is said to you: "Be not captivated by your eyes";[12] that is, do not let your soul be captivated; for "the woman catches the precious souls of men"[13]—hearing is a deception. Further, "with much fawning discourse"[14] the harlot has often led the heart of the young man astray and deceived and mocked it.

(9.41) And so let us not trust these snares and nets that deceive and mock because our hearts are tempted and our thoughts are impeded. And the impediments to sight are also the impediments to hearing, smell, touch, and taste. Let us not follow after enticements and seductions, but follow after the good, cleave to it, imitate it, let its presence that we share make us better and color our way of life, let us be molded in a kind of union with it. For the man who cleaves to the good takes from it what is good, because it is written: "With the

---

9 Prov. 4.25.
10 Ps. 33 (34).14.
11 Matt. 5.28.
12 Prov. 6.25 (Septuagint).
13 Prov. 6.26 (Septuagint).
14 Prov. 7.21 (Septuagint).

holy you will be holy and with the perverse you will be perverted and with the innocent man you will be innocent,"[15] for with persevering imitation a kind of image and likeness develops. And so further: "You indeed give light to my lamp, O Lord."[16] For one who draws near the light receives the light more quickly, and the splendor of the everlasting light shines more in him from nearby.

Therefore the soul that cleaves to the invisible God, good and immortal, flees from the things of this body, abandons earthly and mortal concerns, and becomes like to the object of its desire, in which it lives and has its sustenance. And because it aims for the immortal, it is not itself mortal. For the soul that sins, dies, not through some dissolution of itself, but it deservedly dies to God, because it lives to sin. And so the soul that does not sin does not die, because it remains in its own nature, it remains in virtue and in glory. (9.42) For how can its nature perish, seeing that it is the soul that infuses life? One who receives a soul, receives life, and when the soul departs, life departs. The soul therefore is life. How then can it admit death, when it is the opposite of death? Snow does not suffer heat—for it melts at once; light does not suffer darkness—it dissipates it at once, for with the introduction of light the dread of darkness is removed, just as the chill of snow ceases when fire is employed. Just so the soul, which creates life, does not suffer death, does not die. Therefore the soul does not suffer death; it does not die.[17]

(10.43) And so we have the proof. But this is of man, and what the Lord says is of God: "I have the power to lay down my soul and I have the power to take it up again."[1] You see then that what is put down and taken up and commended into the hands of God[2] the Father does not die. But perhaps you

---

15 Ps. 17 (18).26-27.
16 Ps. 17 (18).29.
17 Cf. Plato, *Phaedo* 106 A-B.

---

1 John 10.18.
2 Cf. Luke 23.46.

may say: "That is to be understood in a special sense, because
it refers to Christ." Although Christ did assume our human
nature, still, because a different point is in question here,[3]
and not to spend time in proving the former one, listen as He
says: "How do you know whether your soul may be demanded
from you in the night?"[4] He did not say "whether your soul
may die in you" but "whether it may be demanded from you."
What has been given "is demanded," that is, "they claim it
back from you." The soul is demanded, then, but it is not
destroyed. What is demanded endures; what is destroyed does
not endure. For how is it destroyed, when the Wisdom of
God said that no one should be feared "who is able to kill
the body, but cannot kill the soul"[5] and when the psalmist
says, "My soul is always in your hands"?[6] He says "always,"
not "for a time."

(10.44) Do you, then, entrust your soul to the hands of the
Lord. Not only when it departs from the body, but also when
it is in the body, it is in the hands of the Lord, because you
do not see it, its source or its destination. It is both in you
and also with God. Therefore "the heart of the king is in the
hand of the Lord,"[7] who guides and rules it. The heart is
filled with the spirit, because the spirit is the ruling part of the
soul and the strength of the soul. I say that strength lies, not
in the arms, but in counsel, temperance, piety and justice. If
the heart of a man is in the hand of the Lord, much more is
his soul. If the soul is in the hand of God, surely our soul is
not shut up in the tomb with the body nor is it held by the
funeral pyre, but enjoys a holy repose. And so men build
rich tombs in vain, as if they were receptacles for the soul
and not just for the body.

---

3 The Latin text is unclear at this point. The translation assumes a
slightly different reading (alterius est causae) from that found in the
Vienna edition (alterius est causa).
4 Luke 12.20.
5 Matt. 10.28.
6 Ps. 118 (119).109.
7 Prov. 21.1.

(10.45) That there are chambers for souls up above receives abundant proof in the testimony of Scripture, since in the books of Esdras we read that when the day of judgment comes, "the earth will give up the bodies of the departed and the dust will give up those that rest in the graves, the remains of the dead. And the chambers will give up the souls that have been committed to them, and the Most High will be revealed on his judgment seat."[8] These are the chambers concerning which the Lord says that there are many mansions in His Father's house, which He is going to the Father to prepare for His disciples.[9]

Now I have used the writings of Esdras so that the pagans may know that the marvelous contents of their philosophical works have been taken over from ours.[10] And would they had not mixed them with superfluous and useless matter, so as to assert that men had souls in common with those of the beasts, and that it was their greatest reward if the souls of distinguished philosophers should pass into bees or nightingales. Thus those who had previously fed the human race with their discourse, afterwards could charm it with their sweet honey or pleasant singing![11]

It would have been sufficient for them to have said that souls freed from their bodies sought *Haïdēs,* that is, a place that is not seen and that we call in our tongue "hell."[12]   (10.46)

---

8 4 (2) Esd. 7.32-33.   9 Cf. John 14.2.

10 The view that pagan philosophers—Plato and Cicero are mostly in question—derived their valid concepts from the Old Testament probably originated among the Jews in Alexandria. It is frequent in Ambrose; cf. *On Abraham* 2.2-6; 2.7; 37; *On Psalm 118*.2.3; *Letters* 28.1. P. de Labriolle, in *The Life and Times of St. Ambrose* (St. Louis 1928) 188, remarks: "He [Ambrose] is much more aware of the elements separating him from his models than of those which bring him nearer to them. And on every occasion he accentuates the difference between the principles underlying the two systems of morals, his own and that of the pagans."

11 Cf. Plato, *Republic* 10.620 A.

12 In the Greek word here used Ambrose finds two parts—"not" and "see." The etymology is derived from Plato through Plotinus. See P. Courcelle, "Anti-Christian Arguments and Christian Paganism: from Arnobius to St. Ambrose," in A. Momigliano *et al., The Conflict*

Further, the Scripture calls those dwellings "repositories of souls."[13] Meeting the complaint of men that the just who have gone before seem to be cheated of their due reward for a very long time, even to the day of judgment,[14] it admirably says that the day of judgment is like the day when the crown is awarded, when "just as there is no slowness on the part of those who are last, there is no swiftness on the part of those who are first."[15] For all await the day when the crown is given, so that during that day the defeated may manifest their shame and the victors obtain the palm of victory. And the text quoted made no secret of the fact that those who were created earlier seem stronger, while those of later creation seem weaker. For it compared the births of this world to those of a woman's uterus, since those are stronger "who were born in the vigor of youth," but weaker "who were born in the time of old age."[16] For this world, like the womb of one who procreates, has been enervated from the multitude of begettings, and like a creature growing old, it has laid aside the vigor of its youth, for the powers it possessed in its prime have withered away.

(10.47) And so while we await the fullness of time, the souls await their due reward. Some await punishment and others glory. And yet in the meantime the one group is not without harm nor the other without gain. For the former will be dismayed[17] upon seeing that the reward of glory has been stored up for those who keep the law of God,[18] that the chambers of those souls are being preserved by the angels, that shame and ruin will be the punishments of their negli-

---

between *Paganism and Christianity in the Fourth Century* (Oxford (1963) 183 n. 123.

13 4 (2) Esd. 7.32.

14 This objection, frequent in anti-Christian polemic, was advanced to show the incompatibility of the Old and New Testaments. Cf. Courcelle in Momigliano (*op. cit.* n. 12 above) pp. 159-60.

15 4 (2) Esd. 5.42.

16 Cf. 4 (2) Esd. 5.53.

17 The phrase "will be dismayed" *(conturbabuntur)* is inserted here, following Schenkl's suggestion, to fill a lacuna in the text.

18 Cf. 2 Tim. 4.8.

gence and rebellion, so that they may gaze on the glory of the Most High and blush to come into His sight, for they have profaned His commandments. For Adam's sin was also his ruin. He fell through heedlessness of the commands of heaven and hid himself out of shame at his fall and did not dare to approach the splendor of God's presence by reason of the shame of his sinful conscience.[19] Just so, the souls of sinners will not withstand the brilliance of God's dazzling light, but with Him as their witness, they will remember that they have gone astray.

(11.48) The joy of just souls is apportioned over certain orders.[1] First, that they have overcome the flesh and have not bent to its enticements. Then, that as the reward of their perseverance and their innocence they possess a composure and are not involved in any vices and disorders, as the souls of the unholy are, nor are they tormented with the recollection of their vices or tossed about, as it were, on tides of anxiety. Third, that they are supported by God's testimony that they have kept the law so that they have no fear of any uncertain outcome of their deeds at the last judgment. Fourth, that they begin to understand their rest and to foresee their future glory. They find it a soothing consolation, and they rest in much quietness in their chambers, where they are attended by escorts of angels. The fifth stage moreover is one of the most delightful and rich exaltation, because the souls have come from the prison of this corruptible body into light

---

19 Cf. Gen. 3.8.

1 Cf. 4 (2) Esd. 7.91-99 on the seven stages of the just. The correspondences between this passage and that in Esdras increase as the later stages of the just are described. Owing to a lacuna in many MSS, the passage cited here and in nn. 4-8 below may not be available in the ordinary text of 2 (4) Esd. published in the Vulgate as an appendix. It is found in the recent critical edition, the *Biblia Sacra iuxta Vulgatam versionem*, R. Weber ed., 2 (Stuttgart 1969) 1947-48. For information and a translation, see *The Apocrypha and Pseudepigrapha of the Old Testament*, ed. by R. H. Charles, 2 (Oxford 1913) 542-624. It is also translated in the *Oxford Annotated Apocrypha: The Apocrypha of the Old Testament, Revised Standard Version*, ed. by B. M. Metzger (New York 1965).

and liberty and they possess the inheritance promised to them. It is the stage of tranquillity because it is also the stage of resurrection. "For as in Adam all die, so in Christ all will be made to live, but each in his own turn, Christ as firstfruits, then they who are Christ's, who have believed in his coming, then the end."[2] And so the order of splendor and of glory will differ, as will the order of merit. The advance in the stages represents also the advance in splendor. Then in the sixth stage it will be shown to them that their face is beginning to shine like the sun and to be like the light of the stars; only their splendor cannot suffer decay henceforth. The seventh stage will be such that they exult confidently and trust without any hesitation and rejoice fearlessly, as they hasten to see the face of Him to whom they have offered their devoted and faithful service. With the recollection of a clear conscience, they trust to receive from Him a glorious reward for their poor toil. As they begin to receive it, they come to know that the sufferings of this age do not deserve the glorious and eternal reward that is given for them.[3]

"Such is the way of the souls of the just,"[4] the Scripture says, and it did not hesitate to call them immortal in the fifth stage, "because of the spaciousness they are destined to receive and enjoy in immortality."[5] Such is their repose through the seven stages, and such is their first accomplishing of the glory that is to come, before they enjoy to the full the gift of tranquil assembly in their dwellings. On this account the prophet says to the angel: "Then will time be given the souls after they are separated from the bodies to see what you have told me of?"[6] And the angel said: "They will have freedom for seven days, to see in the seven days the words that have been foretold, and afterward they will be gathered in their dwell-

---

2 1 Cor. 15.22-24.
3 Cf. Rom. 8.18.
4 4 (2) Esd. 7.99.
5 4 (2) Esd. 7.96.
6 4 (2) Esd. 7.100.

ings."[7] And these matters are more fully described in relation
to the stages of the just than to the sufferings of the unholy,[8]
because it is better to know how the guiltless are saved than
how sinners are tormented.

(11.49) Therefore because the just have the reward of seeing the face of God and "the light that enlightens every
man,"[9] let us henceforth clothe ourselves in zeal that our soul
may draw near to God, that our prayer may draw near to Him,
that we may cleave to Him in desire and may not be separated
from Him. And taking this stand, let us be united to God by
meditating and reading and searching, and let us come to know
Him according to our ability. For only in part have we come
to know Him here, because here all things are imperfect, but
there all are perfect; here we are slight, but there we are
strong. "We see now through a mirror in an obscure manner,
but then face to face."[10] Then we will be allowed to look
upon the glory of God, and His face will be revealed, but now
we are enveloped in the thick substance of the body and covered over by the stains and pollutions of the flesh, as it were,
and we cannot see with total clarity. "Who shall see my face
and live?" Scripture said,[11] and rightly so. For our eyes cannot
bear the sun's rays and whoever turns too long in its direction
is generally blinded, so they say. Now if one creature cannot
look upon another creature without loss and harm to himself,
how can he see the dazzling face of his eternal Creator while
covered with the clothing that is this body? For who is justified
in the sight of God,[12] when the infant of but one day cannot
be clean from sin[13] and no one can glory in his uprightness
and purity of heart?[14]

---

7 4 (2) Esd. 7.101.
8 These are described in 4 (2) Esd. 7.78-87.
9 John 1.9.
10 1 Cor. 13.12.
11 Exod. 33.20.
12 Cf. Ps. 142 (143).2.
13 Cf. Job 14.5 (Septuagint).
14 This passage (11.49) is cited in Augustine, *Contra duas epistulas Pelagianorum* 4.11.31. For "no one can glory. . ." cf. Prov. 20.9.

(11.50) And so let us not be afraid to be taken from among men, let us not dread the end that is due to all; in it Esdras finds the recompense of his devotion when the Lord says to him: "You will be taken up from among men and henceforth you will live with my Son and those who are like you."[15] Now if it was glorious and pleasing for him to live with those who were like him, how much more glorious and more pleasing it will be for us to go on to our betters and to live with those whose deeds we hold in admiration. (11.51) And who indeed is first, Esdras or Plato? For Paul followed the words of Esdras, not those of Plato.[16] Esdras revealed according to the revelation bestowed on him that the just would be with Christ and with the saints. Hence Socrates too says that he is hastening to those gods of his, those most excellent heroes.[17] Likewise, what is admirable in the writings of the philosopher belongs to us. Socrates indeed set down these matters while he did not have his own proof of them, but we have the weight of God's instruction. Moses and Elias appeared with Christ.[18] Abraham hospitably received God and two others,[19] Jacob looked upon God's camp,[20] and Daniel, at the revelation of the Holy Spirit, said that the just shone in heaven like the sun and the stars.[21]

(12.52) Trusting in them, let us go on without fear to Jesus our redeemer, and without fear let us advance to the council of the patriarchs and to our father Abraham, when the day comes, and let us go on without fear to the assembly of the saints and the congregation of the just. For we will go to our fathers, we will go to our instructors in the faith; even though our works are deficient, our faith will come to our aid and our inheritance will be maintained. We will go too where holy

---

15 Cf. 4 (2) Esd. 14.9.
16 Cf. ch. 10 n. 10 above.
17 Cf. Plato, *Phaedo* 63 C, *Apology* 41 A.
18 Cf. Matt. 17.1-13.
19 Cf. Gen. 18.1-15.
20 Cf. Gen. 32.1-2.
21 Cf. Dan. 12.3.

Abraham opens his bosom to receive the poor, as he also received Lazarus;[1] in his bosom those who have endured bitter hardships in this world find rest. (12.53) But now, father Abraham, reach out your hands again and again to take up the poor man from here, open your lap, open out your bosom to receive more, because very many have believed in the Lord.

But although faith has grown, iniquity abounds and charity grows cold.[2] We will go to those who recline in the kingdom of God with Abraham and Isaac and Jacob[3] because they did not make excuses when they were invited to the banquet.[4] We will go there, where there is a paradise of delight, where Adam, who fell among thieves,[5] cannot now weep for his wounds, where the robber as well rejoices in the fellowship of the heavenly kingdom,[6] where there are no clouds, no thunderstorms, no lightning flashes, no windstorm nor darkness nor evening nor summer nor winter, nor changing course of seasons, no cold, no hail, no rains, no need of sun or moon or mass of stars, but only the brightness of God will shine. For the Lord will be the light of all,[7] and "the true light that enlightens every man"[8] will shine for all.

We will go there, where the Lord Jesus has prepared mansions for His servants, that where He is, we also may be, for such is His will. Listen to Him telling what those mansions are: "In my Father's house there are many mansions,"[9] and telling His will: "I am coming again and am taking you to myself, that where I am, you also may be."[10] (12.54) But you say that because He was speaking only to His disciples, He promised many mansions only to them; therefore He was pre-

---

1 Cf. Luke 16.23.
2 Cf. Matt. 24.12.
3 Cf. Matt. 8.11.
4 Cf. Luke 14.18.
5 Cf. Luke 10.30.
6 Cf. Luke 23.43.
7 Cf. John 1.4.
8 John 1.9.
9 John 14.2.
10 John 14.3.

paring the mansions for the eleven disciples alone.[11] And what of the statement that they shall come from all directions and recline in the kingdom of God?[12] On what account do we doubt the realization of God's will? But for Christ, to will is to have acted. Therefore He showed the way and He showed the place, when He said: "And where I go you know and my way you know."[13] The place is with the Father, the way is Christ, just as He said: "I am the way, and the truth, and the life. No one comes to the Father but through me."[14] Let us enter upon this way, let us hold to the truth, let us follow the life. He is the way that leads, the truth that strengthens, the life that is restored through Himself. And so that we may know His true will, in what follows He added this: "Father, I will that where I am, they also whom you have given me may be with me, that they may behold my glory, Father."[15] The repetition is a confirmation, as is "Abraham, Abraham!"[16] and again: "It is I, I, who wipe out your offenses."[17]

Further, He aptly asked here what He promised before. And because He promised before and asked accordingly—and did not ask before and promise accordingly—He promised like a judge, aware of His power, and asked from the Father like an intermediary of piety. He promised before, so that you may know His power, but asked afterward, so that you may understand His piety. He did not ask before and promise accordingly; else He might have appeared to promise what He had obtained rather than to have fulfilled what He had promised. And do not consider His asking unnecessary, since it expresses to you the sharing of His Father's will, in which there is the sign of unity, not the increase of power.

---

11 This was a known anti-Christian argument. Cf. P. Courcelle in Momigliano (*op. cit.* ch. 10 n. 12 above) p. 160.
12 Cf. Matt. 8.11.
13 John 18.4.
14 John 14.6.
15 John 17.24.
16 Gen. 22.1.
17 Isa. 43.25.

(12.55) We follow You, Lord Jesus, but summon us to follow, because without You no one may ascend. For You are "the way, truth, life,"[18] the power, faith, reward. As the way, receive Your own; as the truth, strengthen them; as the life, give them life. Reveal that goodness of Yours that David desired to see when dwelling in the house of the Lord,[19] so that he said: "Who will show us good things?"[20] and again: "I believe to see the good things of the Lord in the land of the living."[21] For the good things are there, where there is everlasting life, life without sin. Elsewhere he also says: "We shall be filled with the good things of your house."[22] He repeated this so often, so that you could know that the philosophers borrowed from this source their concept of the good, the good they assert is supreme. Reveal then the true good that is Yours, the divine good, in which "we live and move and have our being."[23] We move as if on the way, we have our being as if in the truth, we live as if in the eternal life. Show us that which is the good, the equal of itself, always indestructible and immutable, in which we may be forever in the recognition of every good, as Paul, Your chosen vessel,[24] bore witness when he said: "Perhaps indeed he departed for a short while so that you might receive him forever."[25] And so he said that the servant of God was forever in the letter to Philemon, and asked that the latter's faith be made more evident in the full knowledge of all the good that is in the saints, in Christ Jesus.[26]

In that good there is pure repose, immortal light, everlasting grace, a pious inheritance of the soul, a carefree tranquillity, not subject to death but snatched away from death, where there are no tears, where there is no weeping—for what reason is there for weeping there, where there is no sin? There Your

---

18 John 14.6.
19 Cf. Ps. 22 (23).6.
20 Ps. 4.6.
21 Ps. 26 (27).13.
22 Ps. 64 (65).5.
23 Acts 17.28.
24 Cf. Acts 9.15.   25 Philemon 15.   26 Cf. Philemon 6.

saints are free of faults and anxieties, of foolishness and ignorance, of fear and dread, of greed and all the defilements and
passions of the body, where the land of the living is. To add
weight to this assertion, the psalmist said in regard to this
good: "Turn, O my soul, into your rest, for the Lord has been
bountiful to me, because he has delivered my soul from death,
my eyes from tears, my feet from falling. I will please the Lord
in the land of the living."[27] He said "I will please," not "I
please," that is, he encourages himself in regard to the time that
is to come. Now what is to come is opposed to what is here
present, and things eternal to things temporal. And so, because the land of the living is there, surely the land of the
dead is here.

(12.56) Or is this not the land of the dead, where there is
the shadow of death, the gate of death, the body of death?[28]
Therefore it is granted to Peter that "the gates of hell shall
not prevail against him."[29] The gates of hell are these earthly
gates, on which account the psalmist also says: "You raise me
up from the gates of death."[30] For just as there are gates of
justice, in which the saints confess to the Lord, so there are
gates of sin, in which the unholy have denied the Lord. Hear
that the land of the dead is such: "Whoever touches the dead
shall be unclean,"[31] and every evildoer is unclean in the sight
of the Lord. And so whoever touches iniquity will be unclean,
and whoever gives himself up to pleasures will be dead, for
"she who gives herself up to pleasures is dead while she is still
alive."[32] And those who are without faith go down while alive
into hell; even though they appear to live with us, yet they are
in hell. Whoever commits usury or theft is not alive, as you
find in Ezechiel.[33] Whatever just man keeps the ordinances of

---

27 Ps. 114 (116A).7-9.
28 Cf. Matt. 4.16.
29 Cf. Matt. 16.18.
30 Ps. 9A.14.
31 Num. 19.11.
32 1 Tim. 5.6, a verse referring to widows.
33 Cf. Ezech. 33.18.

the Lord that he may do them "will live, and will live in
them."[34] And so such a one is in the land of the living, in the
land where life is not hid, but free, where there is not shade,
but glory. For here below not even Paul himself was living in
glory. Indeed he groaned in the body of death. Hear him as
he says: "For now our life is hidden with Christ in God; when
Christ, our life, shall appear, then we too will appear with
him in glory."[35]

(12.57) Let us therefore hasten to life. Whoever touches
life, lives. And indeed the woman touched it, who touched
the fringe of His cloak and was released from death. And to
her it is said: "Your faith has saved you. Go in peace."[36] For
if one who touches the dead man is unclean, then surely one
who touches the living man is saved. Therefore let us seek the
living man. But let us watch out that we do not seek Him
among the dead and it be said to us as it was to those women:
"Why do you seek the living one among the dead? He is not
here, but has risen."[37] And the Lord Himself shows where He
wishes to be sought when He says: "Go to my brethren and
say to them: 'I ascend to my Father and your Father, to my
God and your God.' "[38] So let us seek Him there, where John
sought and found Him. He sought Him in the beginning[39]
and found Him living with the living, the Son with the
Father.[40] Let us seek Him at the end of the ages and "embrace
his feet and worship him,"[41] so that He may say to us also:
"Do not be afraid,"[42] that is, "Do not be afraid about the sins
of the age, do not be afraid about the iniquities of the world,
do not be afraid about the surges of the bodily passions; I

---

34 Ezech. 33.19.
35 Col. 3.3-4.
36 Luke 8.48; cf. Matt. 9.22.
37 Luke 24.5-6.
38 John 20.17.
39 Cf. John 1.1.
40 Cf. John 1.18.
41 Matt. 28.9.
42 Matt. 28.10.

am the forgiveness of sins. Do not be afraid of the darkness;
I am the light. Do not be afraid of death; I am life. Whoever
comes to me will not see death forever,"[43] because He is the
fullness of divinity, and to Him is honor and glory and perpetuity in the ages, both now and always and forever and ever.

---

43 John 8.51.

JACOB AND THE HAPPY LIFE

(De Iacob et vita beata)

INTRODUCTION

HILE WE CAN HAVE no absolute assurance of the date of this sermon, the extensive treatment given to Eleazar as an example of endurance under persecution suggests a very possible date of 386,[1] when Ambrose and the Church at Milan were offering resistance to the reestablishment of Arianism there.[2] Internal evidence suggests that the two books were originally given as sermons.[3]

The principal sources of the work, apart from the Bible, are the apocryphal Fourth Book of Machabees, which contains the story of Eleazar and that of the seven brothers,[4] and the *Enneads* of Plotinus;[5] references to classical authors are very rare.

The purpose of *Jacob and the Happy Life* is in part philosophical, since Ambrose wishes to show the importance of right reason for the attainment of perfection, which is identified with true happiness. The examples, developed at greater

---

1 On the work as a whole, see Dudden 2.683, Palanque 514–15, and Paredi 249.
2 See Dudden 1.281–93; Paredi 237–55.
3 Cf. *Jacob* 1.5.17: "And so, to return to the beginning of this discourse . . ." (the Latin word translated "discourse" is *sermo*) and 2.5.23: ". . . as you have heard in today's reading. . ." Such a phrase as "the preceding *book,*" in the first sentence of Book II, is proof enough that the sermons were adapted for publication as a unit.
4 See C. W. Emmet, *The Fourth Book of Maccabees* (London 1918), with a useful introduction. Most reliance is placed on 4 Machabees for *Jacob* 1.1.1–2.7 and 2.10.43–12.58.
5 Discussion of the Plotinian influence has developed fairly recently. It is certain that considerable resemblances exist between *Enneads* 1.4 and *Jacob* 1.7.28–8.39. See especially A. Soulignac, "Nouveaux parallèles entre saint Ambroise et Plotin," *Archives de philosophie* N.S. 19 (1956) 148-56, and P. Courcelle, "Nouveaux aspects du platonisme chez saint Ambroise," *Revue des études latines* 34 (1956) 220–39.

length in the second book, are chiefly such Old Testament figures as Jacob, Rebecca, Isaac, Joseph, and those from Machabees.

There is a good, but relatively inaccessible, translation of the first book into English, which contains useful explanatory and supplemental material;[6] selections only from the second book have been translated into French.[7]

---

6 Rev. Mark Edwards, S.M., *S. Ambrosii De Jacob et vita beata* I (unpublished master's thesis, The Catholic University of America, Washington 1952).
7 D. Gorce, *Saint Ambroise: Traités sur l'Ancien Testament* (Namur 1967). The sections of Book II translated are 1, 3–9, 16–20, 22–23, 26–28, 35–38, 40–42.

JACOB AND THE HAPPY LIFE

Book One

ECESSARY FOR THE TRAINING of all men is good discourse, full of prudence, while the mind given to
reason excels in virtue and restrains its passions, for
virtue is teachable.[1] Further, one seeks it by study and learning and loses it by neglect. Otherwise, unless good discourse
were necessary for correction, the law would never say, "You
shall not commit adultery."[2] But because discourse alone is
helpful by way of admonition but weak by way of persuasion,
therefore right reason must be employed with due reflection.
Thus reason, given fuller consideration, may persuade us to
the command laid down by good discourse. For man is not
bound to obedience out of servile necessity, but by free will
we either incline to virtue or lean to vice.[3] And thus either
our affections, which are free, draw us into error, or our will,
following upon reason, calls us away. Now the most severe
of the guilty passions is concupiscence,[4] but reason mitigates
and restrains it. For it is able to mitigate but cannot uproot
it, because the soul that is capable of reason is not the master
of its passions but can only restrain them. And it is not possible that the irascible man not get angry, but only that he re-

---

1 Cf. 4 Mach. 1.1–2. (Emmet's translation is cited in Introd. n. 4 above.)
2 Exod. 20.13; cf. 4 Mach. 2.5-6.
3 Cf. Plotinus, *Enneads* 3.2.10 and 6.8.6, cited by Courcelle, *Recherches*
100 n. 5. Ambrose discusses man's knowledge of good and evil and
of the natural law in general in several other places in his works;
see B. Maes, *La Loi naturelle selon Ambroise de Milan* (Analecta
Gregoriana 162; Rome 1967) 151 n. 50.
4 Cf. 4 Mach. 1.25

119

strain himself through reason, check his indignation, and withdraw from punitiveness,[5] as the psalmist teaches us when he says, "Be angry, and sin not."[6] He made concession to what is natural but forbade what is guilty.

(1.2) Therefore right reason proceeds entirely from other considerations, does not originate in itself, and thus is always a follower. For it has its beginnings either from what is natural or what is advantageous. Then it either restrains what is natural or champions what is advantageous. Further, it does not cut out concupiscence from the soul but brings it about that we are not subject to the concupiscence.[7] For who is so great that he can rid himself of bodily passion? Only the man who could say about the unfruitful fig tree—which is the wickedness of the Jews—"Behold, for three years now I have come seeking fruit on this fig tree and I find none. Cut it down, therefore." And his servant answered him, "Let it alone this year too, till I dig around it and manure it. Perhaps it will bear fruit; but if not, afterwards cut it down."[8] He acted properly in making his recommendation to his master, because he could not have claimed for himself the power to cut out fault in the body but reserved it to the master.

(1.3) Further, what man can we consider finer and stronger than the holy David? He had desired water from the cistern of Bethlehem, although it was cut off by a hostile army. That desire he was not able to remove, but he could mitigate it. For we do not find that the others lacked water, and the army was very large. And surely the king could have lacked water far less, in view of the other springs nearby. But he suffered a kind of irrational longing and wanted that water which was walled in and surrounded by the enemy, so that it could not have been readily brought without great risk.

---

5 Cf. 4 Mach. 3.2–5.
6 Ps. 4.5.
7 Cf. 4 Mach. 1.6.
8 Luke 13.7–9.

Thus he said, "Who will get me a drink from the cistern that is in Bethlehem by the gate?"[9] And when three men[10] were found to break down the enemy camp and bring the water which he had desired with a very great desire, he knew that he had obtained that water at the cost of danger to others. He poured it out to the Lord, so that he might not seem to be drinking the blood of those who had brought it.

This incident is evidence that concupiscence indeed comes before reason but that reason resists concupiscence.[11] David suffered what is human—an irrational longing—but it is praiseworthy that he cheated the irrational concupiscence in a rational manner with the remedy that was at hand. I praise the men who were ashamed at the desire of their king and preferred to bring his shameful action to an end even with danger to their own well-being. I praise the more him who was ashamed at the danger to others in his own desire, and who compared to blood the water sought at the price of hazardous chance. At once, like a conqueror who had checked his desire, David poured out the water to the Lord, to show that he quenched his concupiscence by the consolation found in His Word.[12]

(1.4) Therefore the prudent mind can restrain and keep in check the assaults of the passions, even the severe passions, and cool all the heat of the most burning concupiscence, channel the emotions elsewhere, and by the use of right reason scorn the passions.[13] For indeed, when God created man and implanted in him moral laws and feelings, at that time He established the royal rule of the mind over man's emotions,

---

9 2 Kings 23.15. Ambrose interprets this action of David allegorically in *De apologia prophetae David* 7.34–35; no translation of the latter is yet available in any modern language.
10 Ambrose follows the version in 2 Kings 23.16–17 here; in 4 Mach. 3.12 the number of men is given as two.
11 The story of David, with the same conclusion, appears at 4 Mach. 3.5–16.
12 Cf. 2 Kings 23.16–17.
13 Cf. 4 Mach. 3.17–18.

so that all his feelings and emotions would be governed by its strength and power.[14] God added this to His creature's beauty, that He would mold man's very mind with divine precepts and fashion it with the teachings of wisdom; with these, man would know what he must avoid and realize what he must choose.[15] The mind, then, holding to the teaching of wisdom by right reason, so as to know both the divine and the human, is instructed in the law, through which it learns which passions it ought to make subject to itself.[16]

(2.5) Standing as natural leaders, so to speak, among the passions are pleasure and pain, and the others follow these.[1] For these two embrace them all, and both of these are passions, not alone of the body, but also according to the soul. And because I have said that the other passions are subject to these, concupiscence comes before pleasure and rejoicing after pleasure; moreover, fear comes before pain and sadness after pain, whereas mental agitation is a passion common to pleasure and pain.[2] I will only mention the others, I mean pride, avarice, ambition, strife, and envy, which are passions according to the soul.[3] I will only mention, too, the insatiable desire for eating and the outpouring of excessive and wanton living, vices which are tied to the body and operate through it.

Temperance rightly quenches the ardor of such passions, insofar as possible. First it tempers the mind by moderation and control, it molds the mind, then tightens the reins placed on the violence of the body by its abstinence from pleasures.[4] Therefore the law curtails excess in regard to food and abundant banquets, not only to cut back on luxurious living but also to open a path for the use of reason through the con-

---

14 Cf. 4 Mach. 2.21–22.
15 Cf. 4 Mach. 1.15–17.
16 Cf. 4 Mach. 1.14.

---

1 Cf. 4 Mach. 1.20.
2 Cf. 4 Mach. 1.21-24.
3 Cf. 4 Mach. 1.26.
4 Cf. 4 Mach. 1.33–34.

sideration paid to the restricting precept.[5] Reason would then curtail the attractions of gluttony and the other excessive desires and would check the passions and emotions of the body.[6] Therefore temperance comes before correction and is the mistress of learning.

(2.6) Proceeding from it, holy Jacob received from his brother the primacy which he had not possessed;[7] by his agreement to that preference, Esau taught for the future that those who do not govern their own selves are worthless in judgment. Proceeding from temperance, Joseph mastered the heat of his young manhood and, through the application of right reason, strengthened his mind when it was tried by the enticements of adultery.[8] Indeed, although he was healthy and strong, still he preferred to support himself by the employment of reason and said to the wife of his master, "Seeing my lord, on account of his confidence in me, knows not anything in his house and has given into my hands all things whatsoever that he has, nor is anything withheld from me except yourself, because you are his wife, how then can I do this wicked act and commit sin in the presence of God?"[9] This is, then, the use of right reason that the Greeks call "reasoning,"[10] by which the mind that is directed toward wisdom becomes firm. For such reason is beautiful, because he ought not to have been ungrateful for the kindnesses of his master, nor could the sin have been hidden that he committed in the presence of God—and it could not have escaped God's notice.

(2.7) Good, therefore, is reason, for it generally divests a man of a disposition to hostility and sets aside the pain of an injury. Moreover, reason often pacifies the conqueror on the

---

5 Cf. Lev. 11.4–47.
6 Cf. 4 Mach. 1.35.
7 Cf. Gen. 25.31–32.
8 Cf. Gen. 39.1–20; 4 Mach. 2.1–3. A similar story in classical literature appears in the temptation of Bellerophon; see Homer, *Iliad* 6.155–202.
9 Gen. 39.8–9 (Septuagint).
10 The Greek word used by Ambrose is "logismos," the same word which appears in 4 Mach. in the sense of "reason."

battlefield, slows the sword of the man about to strike, and snatches away from death the one that makes entreaty, for reason, when it is just, urges us to spare the conquered.[11] In the matter of removing or alleviating the pain of an injury, who is a better teacher than the patriarch Jacob? He reproaches his own sons Simeon and Levi by saying, "You have made me an object of hatred, so as to be deemed a mortal enemy."[12] To be sure, they had avenged the wrong done their sister, for, contrary to the laws of their fathers, she had been defiled and her modesty violated.[13] Nor could Jacob, teacher of discipline and guardian of modesty, have approved of the defilement that had been committed, but he preferred that men of no restraint be checked by reason, for he knew that reason could moderate wrath.[14] (2.8) It is temperance, then, that cuts off desires. God commanded the first men to hold to it, for He said, "What is in the middle of the garden, you shall not eat, neither shall you touch it, lest you die."[15] And because they did not preserve temperance, the transgressors of this signal virtue were made exiles from paradise, with no share in immortality. For the law teaches temperance and pours it into the hearts of all men.

(3.9) Moreover, Scripture gives witness that temperance, wisdom, and discipline are taught—in the law as regards temperance, but as regards the other virtues, in the book of Job, in which it is written, "Is it not the Lord who teaches understanding and discipline?"[1] And in the Gospel the Lord Himself says, "Learn from me, for I am meek and humble of heart."[2] And elsewhere He says to the disciples, "Go, teach the nations, baptizing them in the name of the Father, and

---

11 Cf. Vergil, *Aeneid* 6.853.
12 Gen. 34.30; cf. 4 Mach. 2.19.
13 Cf. Gen. 34.1–31; 49.5–7.
14 Cf. 4 Mach. 2.20.
15 Gen. 3.3 (Septuagint).

---

1 Probably Job 33.16, in part from the Septuagint.
2 Matt. 11.29.

of the Son, and of the Holy Spirit."[3] On what account were the disciples so called, and what did they learn from Christ other than to practice the precepts of the virtues? Further, David says, "Come, children; hear me, I will teach you the fear of the Lord."[4] Surely the fear of God stands in the number of the virtues, because "the fear of God is the beginning of wisdom,"[5] and through it man receives the form of holy teaching of which Paul says, "But thanks be to God, because you were slaves of sin, but you have been obedient from the heart to that form of teaching in which you have been delivered, and having been set free from sin, you have become the slaves of justice."[6] Therefore teaching brings it about that we can come to justice; thus justice can be gained by learning. And so in our study let us direct our attention to the form of the Gospel's teaching. Even a little study often counts for a great deal. For everything depends on that study in which obedience is brought to bear, for obedience has weight on either side; it adds either guilt or grace. In the first Adam, it drew us to death; in the second Adam, it called us to life.[7]

(3.10) It is not that we can attribute our trouble to anything but our own will. No one is held to guilt unless he has gone astray by his own will. Actions which are imposed on those who resist contain no fault; the malevolence of sin follows only upon actions perpetrated voluntarily, and this fault we would divert to others. Christ chooses for Himself the volunteer soldier; the devil buys for himself at auction the volunteer slave. He holds no man bound to the yoke of slavery unless such a one has first sold himself to him at the purchase price of his sins.[8] Why do we blame the flesh, as if it

---

3 Matt. 28.19.
4 Ps. 33 (34).12.
5 Prov. 1.7 (Septuagint); 9.10; Ps. 110 (111).10; Sir. 1.16.
6 Rom. 6.17–18.
7 Cf. 1 Cor. 15.45, 47.
8 Ambrose's concept of redemption is heavily influenced by the notions of slavery and manumission. See C. Morino, *Church and State in the Teaching of St. Ambrose* 37–8 and 160 n. 64.

were weak? Our members are the tools of wrong and the tools of right.[9] You saw a poor man receiving injury; you protected him; your members are tools of benevolence, for with them you saved a poor man from injury. You saw a man in need; you presented him with gifts; with your hand you have driven death back from your heart. You saw a man who was being led to death; you delivered him, because it is written, "Deliver him who is being led to death";[10] your members are tools of right, if you have not permitted a man to die unjustly. You looked upon a woman, you chastised your body, you mortified your lusts, you turned away and forsook the harlot's wanton eyes; your members are tools of chastity.

But on the contrary, if your eye has looked upon a woman to covet her, you have opened a wound, you have driven a weapon into your body; your members are tools of sin.[11] You looked upon the property of orphans and drove them from the dwellings of their fathers,[12] you changed the landmarks that your forefathers set;[13] your members are tools of iniquity. And so the passions are the author of guilt, and not the flesh, for the flesh is the servant of the will.

(3.11) Therefore, let our will not put us up for sale. The Apostle cries out, "Don't you know that if you offer yourselves to anyone as obedient slaves, you are the slaves of him whom you obey, either slaves of sin to death or of obedience to justice?"[14] If, then, we are slaves either to sin or to justice, let us consider on which side the servitude is more endurable and the fruit richer. But what fruit can there be in death? "For the wages of sin is death";[15] so there is no fruit in it,

---

9 Cf. Rom. 6.13, 19.
10 Prov. 24.11; cf. Dan. 13.45–61.
11 Cf. Matt. 5.28.
12 Cf. 3 Kings 21, the story of Naboth, which also appears in Ambrose's work *On Naboth*, translated by M. R. P. McGuire in *S. Ambrosii De Nabuthae* (The Catholic University of America Patristic Studies 15; Washington 1927).
13 Cf. Deut. 27.17.
14 Rom. 6.16.
15 Rom. 6.23.

but only the loss of decency, since we blush at our deeds.[16] But to be a slave to justice is freedom; "for a slave who has been called in the Lord, is a freedman of the Lord; likewise, a free man who has been called is a slave of Christ."[17] Either status is excellent, that of being subject to Christ, for under His rule servitude is precious and freedom glorious. The servitude is precious, for it was bought at the price of blood of such worth; while the freedom is glorious, for no servitude to guilt, no bonds of sin restrain it, and no burden of guilty deeds, no traffic with crimes delivers it to the bondage of a servitude that is base.[18]

(3.12) Learn humility, O man, and recognize the power of the apostolic teaching. Should you say that you are a slave, you are a freedman; should you boast that you are free, you are a slave. For the man who has been redeemed as a slave has his freedom, and as for the man who has been called as a free man, it is good for him to know that he is a slave of Christ, under whom servitude is safe and freedom secure. Who claims that Paul is an illiterate, so to speak, in the law itself? He knew how to distinguish between a freedman and a free man, and so he did not speak carelessly but accurately: "For a slave who has been called in the Lord, is a freedman of the Lord; likewise a free man who has been called is a slave of Christ." For in truth we are all freedmen of Christ, but no one is a free man; we have all been procreated in servitude. Why do you adopt for your servile status the pride that comes with freedom? Why do you lay false claim to titles of nobility, when your inheritance is a slave's? Don't you know that the guilt of Adam and Eve

16 Cf. Rom. 6.21.
17 1 Cor. 7.22.
18 On the legal terminology involved here, see A. Berger, *Encyclopedic Dictionary of Roman Law* (Transactions of the American Philosophical Society 43.2; Philadelphia 1953), especially the entries "addicere" and "nexum"; see also, for a useful list of legal terms in Ambrose, *De Tobia*, the work of L. M. Zucker, *S. Ambrosii De Tobia* (The Catholic University of America Patristic Studies 35; Washington 1933) 19–21.

sold you into servitude? Don't you know that Christ did not buy you, but bought you back? "You were redeemed from the vain manner of life handed down from your fathers, not with gold and silver, but with the precious blood of the Lamb,"[19] the Apostle Peter cries out. Therefore you have been redeemed by the Lord; you who have been created are a slave, you who have been redeemed are a slave, and you owe servitude to Him as your Lord and Redeemer. And do not suppose that the status of a freedman under Christ is inferior to freedom. It is equal as regards dignity, superior as regards protection, the same in favor, safer against a fall, more protected against pride. You have received your freedom in such a way that you ought to remember your liberator, so as to realize that lawful obedience is due to Him, your patron; else freedom may be taken back from you on grounds of ingratitude. What is more fortunate than you are? You rule under the Lord and do service with Him as your patron.

(4.13) What do you possess, moreover, that the Lord has not given you?[1] He gave the law; He added His grace. The law denounced sin but in a hazardous situation could not entirely restrain it. For I became aware of sin that I did not know; I became aware that concupiscence was sin,[2] and from the opportunity afforded by this knowledge the wages of sin have piled up. Sin, which before seemed dead by reason of my ignorance, gained a new life in me; but I died under the wound of sin, because the very knowledge of guilt that would help me, so it seemed, did me harm—I knew sin, but could not avoid it. For the knowledge revealed the sin, and, through the good which was that proclamation, it multiplied the malevolence of sin itself. And so I committed sin beyond measure, because it was multiplied by the proclamation of the commandment; guilt grows when it is revealed and pre-

---

19 1 Peter 1.18–19.

---

1 Cf. 1 Cor. 4.7.
2 Cf. Rom. 7.7–8.

cautions are not taken against it. How then is the commandment good, which for me is death? And how is it not death
for me? For through the commandment's revealing the good
which it symbolizes, sin has worked death in me. Indeed, it is
certain that death came to me as long as I knew the sin that
I did, just as the Lord Himself says, "If I had not come and
spoken to them, they would have no sin."[3]

(4.14) Why then are you surprised if the law brings death
to certain men, when the saving advent of the Lord—our redemption—also brings death? For a man who does not believe seeks death for himself from grace, but the grace of the
commandment remains. Just as a knowledge of poisonous
potions is attained for training in medicine, so God's commandment is attained for eternal life. Now in the case of a
man who makes wicked use of harmful potions, his knowledge
of them is turned to a dangerously evil purpose, and the
greater his knowledge of poisons, the more his understanding
of the risk he runs. Just so, in the case of those who interpret
the law wickedly and cannot avoid the sins revealed and forbidden there, the very form of the commandment brings
about their death. Just as an antidote is good, although not
good for an unwise or immoderate man, so is the commandment good, although it is not good for the immoderate man.
Therefore the commandment, which for someone is death, is
a good. And so receive the answer to the first proposition,
namely that the commandment, which for me is death, can
be a good—a good through the nature of its salvific precept,
death through the lack of moderation of the flesh.

(4.15) Because we have learned that the commandment
which for me is death is a good, now let us examine how that
which works death for me, albeit through a good, is not
death for me. For the Apostle preached as follows: "Is then
that which is a good, death for me? By no means! But sin,
that it might be manifest as sin, worked death for me through

---

3 John 15.22.

that which is good."[4] And so let us consider each point. The commandment is indeed of the law, while the law is spiritual;[5] I see its grace, I praise its beauty, I proclaim its wording, I admire its teaching; but because "I am carnal, and sold under sin,"[6] I am drawn into guilt against my will. Sin indeed dominates, as if over a slave. Accordingly, I hate sin—and I commit it. The mind hates it, the flesh desires it, but I am in both; with my mind I consent to the law and with my flesh I do that which I do not want.[7] The commandment to which I consent is good, and the mind which chooses what is good, is good—good for judging, but often weak for making resistance, because the body's desire opposes it and leads it captive to the enticements of error.

(4.16) In this danger the one remedy is that the grace of God should free the man whom the law could not. For thus it is written, "Unhappy man that I am! Who will deliver me from the body of this death? The grace of God through Jesus Christ our Lord."[8] Thus it comes to pass that the sin which was hidden—I mean my concupiscence, which I did not suppose to be sin—worked death for me, until it was revealed, and the sin itself was committed beyond measure. For it was sin, even though it was not known to be so, but with knowledge it piled up, took on an increment of error, so to speak, and, by the wording of the commandment, fell into the order of a crime. Yet for me it is not death, for I readily flee to Christ, through whom we are freed from every danger of death. Therefore the second proposition has also been settled, because the commandment of the law is not death for me, even though it works death. For we are troubled by reason of frailty, but we escape by reason of Christ.

(5.17) And so, to return to the beginning of this discourse,

---

4 Rom. 7.13.
5 Cf. Rom. 7.14.
6 *Ibid.*
7 Cf. Rom. 7.14–23.
8 Rom. 7.24–25.

that mind is good which has the control of the reason and is directed toward the teachings of wisdom; but it endures a grievous strife with the body of death, and often the enticement, which is of the flesh, conquers the reason, which is of the mind. Accordingly, the Lord first gave the law; the mind of man devoted itself to the law by way of compliance and began to serve it so as to be subject to it. But the flesh was not subdued, because the wisdom of the flesh was not subject to the law and opposed its teachings.[1] For the flesh could not have been obedient to virtue, since it had been given over to its own desires and enveloped in its own panderings. Accordingly, we must work to keep the grace of God.

Therefore the mind is good if it is directed toward reason, but not at all perfect unless it enjoys the rule of Christ. The Lord Jesus comes to fix our passions to His cross and to forgive our sins. In His death we have been justified, so that the whole world might be made clean by His blood. Indeed, in His death we have been baptized.[2] (5.18) If, then, sins are forgiven us in His death, let the passions of our sins die in His death, let them be held fast by the nails of His cross. If we have died in His death, why are we called back again to worldly things as if we were alive to them? What have we to do with the elements of the world, with desires, with luxury and wanton behavior? We have died to these in Christ. But if we have died in Christ, we have arisen in Christ;[3] therefore let us dwell with Christ, let us seek with Christ the things that are above, not those that are earthly and corruptible.[4] Christ, rising from the dead, left the old man fixed to the cross, but He raised up the new man.

Therefore Christ died so that we also might die to sin and

---

1 Cf. Rom. 8.7.
2 Cf. Rom. 6.3.
3 Cf. Rom. 6.8.
4 Cf. Col. 3.1–2.

rise again to God.[5] Our flesh is dead; why does it live again
to sin? Why is it obedient to sin again? Why does sin rule
again among the dead, when death is the end of sin? We have
died in the flesh, we have been renewed in the spirit. Let us
walk in the spirit,[6] because we have received the spirit of
Christ. If then Christ is in us, let our flesh be dead by reason of
sin, but let our spirit live by reason of justification.[7] (5.19)
Thus what was impossible for the law has been settled if we
walk in the spirit. In so doing we bury the passions, if we do
not destroy the cross which is this body and do not write again
the handwriting of sin which has been erased in the cross of
Christ, and if we do not put on the clothing of the old man
which we have taken off.[8] For it is written in the Canticle,
"I have put off my garment, how shall I put it on? I have
washed my feet, how shall I defile them?"[9] Therefore we have
mortified the members of our body; why do its vices sprout
up again? The law did not prevail because it did not mortify
the flesh; it passed by like a shadow,[10] because it did not enlighten; it shaded us from the Sun of Justice,[11] because it piled
up offenses—therefore it was a hindrance.

(6.20) What need was there, then, that a law be proclaimed,
if it was not going to be of help? We already had the natural
law; each person was a law for himself and had the book of
the law written in his heart.[1] We did not keep it; why was
the other added to it, when the flesh could not have gained
justification in the works of that other? A bond was acquired,
not a release; there was added the recognition of sin, but not
the forgiveness of it. We all sinned; we were able to present

---

5 Cf. Rom. 6.11.
6 Cf. Gal. 5.16, 25.
7 Cf. Rom. 8.10.
8 Cf. Col. 3.9.
9 Cant. 5.3.
10 Cf. Heb. 10.1.
11 Cf. Mal. 3.20 (4.2).

---

1 Cf. Rom. 2.14–15.

an excuse by way of ignorance—everyone's mouth has been blocked up.[2]

(6.21) Nevertheless, the law was of help to me. I began to confess what I used to deny, I began to know my sin and not to cover over my injustice. I began to proclaim my injustice to the Lord against myself, and You forgave the impieties of my heart.[3] But this too is of help to me, that we are not justified by the works of the law.[4] Thus I do not have the wherewithal to enable me to glory in my own works, I do not have the wherewithal to boast of myself, and so I will glory in Christ.[5] I will not glory because I have been redeemed. I will not glory because I am free of sins, but because sins have been forgiven me. I will not glory because I am profitable or because anyone is profitable to me, but because Christ is an advocate in my behalf with the Father,[6] because the blood of Christ has been poured out in my behalf. My guilt became for me the price of redemption, through which Christ came to me. On account of me, Christ tasted death. Guilt is more fruitful than innocence; innocence had made me proud, guilt rendered me subject. (6.22) And so you see in what respects the giving of the law was of help to you.

But you say that sin was very abundant through the law. Now where sin was very abundant, grace also was very abundant.[7] You have died to sin, O man; thus the law is not a hindrance any more. You rise again through grace, and so the law was of help because it won grace. You have received also the pledge of the love of Christ, because Christ, who has died for you, is an advocate for you and is saving up the reward gained by His blood. He has reconciled the sinner to the Father; much more does He recommend the innocent man

---

2 Cf. Ps. 62 (63).12, Rom. 3.19.
3 Cf. Ps. 31 (32).5.
4 Cf. Rom. 3.20; Gal. 2.16.
5 Cf. Phil. 3.3.
6 Cf. 1 John 2.1.
7 Cf. Rom. 5.20.

and protect the humble one, because He has chosen the blameless man for Himself. (6.23) Therefore, as a debtor to so great a benefit, do you not make repayment with your obedience? He has made you an heir, a joint heir, an heir of God, a joint heir of Christ;[8] He has poured out on you the spirit of adoption.[9] Count these blessings, and associate them not so much with the bondage of debt as with the maintenance of the gift you have received. You are a joint heir of Christ, if you suffer and die and are buried with Christ.[10] Take on His passion, so that you may deserve to be with Him above the passions. See how He has forgiven you your earlier sins, in order that the fact of your having sinned might not prove a hindrance to you. See how He exhorts you not to lose what you have received.

The goal of such toil is quickly attained, and the crown is one of everlasting enjoyment, the suffering is endurable, the reward is beyond measure. What troubles you? Is it your humble and obscure position? But for the future you will possess the glory and fame that come from devotion and faith. Are your funds too little, and your livelihood too meager? But you will possess the riches of an eternal reward; with them, you can have no need of anything else. Is it the loss of your children? You had reared them in time; you will receive them in eternity. It will be said of you, "Happy he who has a seed in Sion and a family in Jerusalem."[11] "The sufferings of the present time are not worthy to be compared with the glory to come,"[12] the Scripture tells you.

(6.24) Further, the happy life is not diminished by such adversities as worldly troubles or sufferings of body but is confirmed by them. Further, the happy life does not feel sorrow at the loss of an inheritance, and it courageously hides the loss of dear ones and absorbs the grief. Further, the man

---

8 Cf. Rom. 8.17.
9 Cf. Rom. 8.15.
10 Cf. Rom. 6.4.
11 Isa. 31.9 (Septuagint).
12 Rom. 8.18.

who is always in the tranquil harbor does not know shipwreck.[13] What does it mean that you toil in common with
all creation? On account of you, the world itself endures the
servitude of corruption, and you along with the saints share
in common in this toil and expectation. The sun recognizes
its own setting,[14] the moon its waning, the bright stars their
wanderings, while we await the redemption of our whole
body.[15]

(6.25) But are you afraid of the uncertain twists of life
and the plots of the adversary? You have the help of God, you
have His great liberality, so great that He did not spare His
own Son on your behalf.[16] Scripture made use of a beautiful
expression to proclaim the holy purpose toward you of God
the Father, who offered His Son to death. The Son could not
feel death's bitterness, because He was in the Father; for Himself He gave up nothing, on your behalf He offered everything. In the fullness of His divinity[17] He lost nothing, while
He redeemed you. Think upon the Father's love. It is a matter
of His goodness that He accepted the danger, so to speak, to
His Son, who was going to die, and in a manner drained the
sorrowful cup of bereavement, so that the advantage of redemption would not be lost to you. The Lord had such
mighty zeal for your salvation that He came close to en-
dangering what was His, while He was gaining you. On account of you He took on our losses, to introduce you to things
divine, to consecrate you to the things of heaven. Scripture
said, too, in a marvelous fashion, "He has delivered him for

---

13 The imagery of the "tranquil harbor" here probably derives immediately from Apuleius, *Metamorphoses* 11, and ultimately from Cicero,
Tusculan Disputations 1.49.118; similar imagery appears at *Death as a
Good* 4.15; 8.31; 9.38 (translated in this volume). For a thorough
discussion of the matter, see P. Courcelle, "De Platon à saint Ambroise
par Apulée," *Revue de philologie* 35 (1961) 15–28, especially 22–23
and the references given there.
14 Cf. Ps. 103 (104).19.
15 Cf. Rom. 8.18–23; 2 Peter 3.13; Apoc. 21.1.
16 Cf. Rom. 8.32.
17 Cf. Col. 2.9.

us all,"[18] to show that God so loves all men that He delivered His most beloved Son for each one. For men, therefore, He has given the gift that is above all gifts; is it possible that He has not given all things in that gift? God, who has given the Author of all things,[19] has held back nothing.

(6.26) Therefore, let us not be afraid that anything can be denied us. We ought not have any distrust whatever over the continuance of God's generosity. So long and continuous has it been, and so abundant, that God first predestined us and then called us. Those whom He called, He also justified; those whom He justified, He also glorified.[20] Can He abandon those whom He has honored with His mighty benefits even to the point of their reward? Amid so many benefits from God, ought we to be afraid of certain plots of our accuser? But who would dare to accuse those who, as he sees, have been chosen by the judgment of God? God the Father Himself, who has bestowed His gifts—can He make them void? Can He exile from His paternal love and favor those whom He took up by way of adoption? But fear exists that the judge may be too harsh—think upon Him that you have as your judge. For the Father has given every judgment to Christ.[21] Can Christ then condemn you, when He redeemed you from death and offered Himself on your behalf, and when He knows that your life is what was gained by His death? Will He not say, " 'What profit is there in my blood,'[22] if I condemn the man whom I myself have saved?" Moreover, you are thinking of Him as a judge; you are not thinking of Him as an advocate. But can He give a sentence that is very harsh when He prays continually that the grace of reconciliation with the Father be granted us?

---

18 Rom. 8.32.
19 Cf. *ibid.*
20 Cf. Rom. 8.30.
21 Cf. John 5.22.
22 Ps. 29 (30).10.

(7.27) But even if any severities threaten us, they ought not at all to separate us from Christ. Why should we not endure hard and bitter sufferings for Christ, when He accepted such indignities for us? Love ought to exist in us in such a fashion that we are not called away from Christ by any dangers. For it is written, "Much water cannot shut out love, and floods will not confine it,"[1] because the soul of the lover passes through the torrent.[2] No storm, no profound danger, no fear of death or of punishment diminishes the strength of love; in such happenings we are tested, in them lies the happy life, even though it is deluged by many dangers. (7.28) For the wise man is not broken by bodily ills nor is he disturbed by misfortunes, but he remains happy even amid troubles. Bodily adversities do not diminish the gift of the happy life or take away anything from its sweetness. For the happiness of life does not lie in bodily pleasure, but in a conscience pure of every stain of sin, and in the mind of the man who knows that the good is also the pleasurable, even though it is harsh, and that what is shameful does not give delight, even though it is sweet.

Therefore, the motive for living well is not bodily pleasure, but the mind's sagacity. For it is not the flesh, which is subject to passion, that judges, but the mind, because nothing gives more pleasure than honorable counsels and noble deeds; that is why the mind is the interpreter of what constitutes the happy life. Now sagacity, or reason that has control over passion, is better than passion, and what judges is more excellent than what is subject to judgment. Nor is it possible that the nonrational be better than reason.[3] And so the man who follows Jesus has within himself his own recompense, and in his own love he has reward and grace. Even though he endures hardships, still he is happy in his way of life, happy

---

1 Cant. 8.7.
2 Cf. Ps. 123 (124).5.
3 On the passage from 7.28 to this point, cf. Plotinus, *Enneads* 1.4.2.

even amid dangers, as the Lord established when He said, "Blessed are they who suffer persecution for justice' sake."[4]

(7.29) The happy life, then, does exist among men, but I mean only among those in whom life has been made perfect. Now the perfect life is not that of the senses, but the life of reason, lived according to management exercised by the reason and natural vigor possessed by the mind. In this there is found, not a part of man, but his completion, which appears not so much in his status as in his actions, and these, after all, make a man happy. To such a man, what is good but he himself? This good he possesses, this good is with him, and it will be the source of future goods for him.[5] In regard to this good, Solomon said, "Drink water from your own vessels, and from the springs of your own wells. Let the waters from your own fountain overflow for you and run into your own streets. Let them be appointed for yourself alone, and let no stranger partake with you. Let the spring of your water be yours alone."[6]

Therefore, make use of the good that is within. (7.30) Now the best evidence of this good is that the man who possesses it does not have need of other things. Whatever would a man need who despises lesser things and cleaves to the best? For it is written, "Let the stag of friendship and the foal of graces converse with you."[7] Let friendship go before you and be together with you at all times, for friendship with the virtues and love of the highest good is good. And so the man who has been made perfect seeks nothing else but the only and admirable good. On this account the Scripture also says, "One thing I have asked of the Lord, this will I seek after, that I may dwell in the house of the Lord all the days of my life and may see the delight of the Lord."[8] And do not scorn such a man as one who is needy and in want, because he is

---

4 Matt. 5.10.
5 On the passage from 7.29 to this point, cf. Plotinus, *Enneads* 1.4.4.
6 Prov. 5.15–18 (Septuagint).
7 Prov. 5.19 (Septuagint).
8 Ps. 26 (27).4.

content with the solitary companionship of the one good, so
to speak. For he will be very much enveloped in the friendship of this good. For the friendship overflows into happiness
in the possession of the good, and so he desires nothing else.
The man who possesses all things does not seek anything as
if it were new. For there exists none of the good that he
does not possess, and he does not take pleasure in an over-
supply, but only in necessary supplies and in that specific
necessity which is necessary, not for himself, but for the flesh
that cleaves to himself. He yields only to what is not at variance with the purpose of the inner man, so that by this he
may make both one[9] and may reconcile the inner and the
outer man alike to God,[10] so that one spirit may be in both.[11]

(7.31) A man of such purpose is not diminished nor broken
by adversities, nor restrained by barriers, nor made sorrowful
by the loss of his dear ones. For his instruction the Apostle
says, "But we would not, brethren, have you ignorant concerning those who are asleep, lest you should grieve even as
others who have no hope."[12] He consoles himself with faith
in the resurrection and with the grace of the reward that is to
come and he does not admit sorrow, on account of the intent
with which he cleaves to God; rather, he rejoices in the
pleasure of God's presence. Now the man who is saddened by
such misfortunes is not saddened in conformity with God's
will, and what is not in conformity with God's will is filled
with folly. Therefore,[13] the sadness that is of this world and
is not in conformity with God's will[14] and every anxiety over
distress of the body are not found in the man who has been
perfected. In the case of such a man, the state of his body and
the use he makes of his outer nature, so to speak, do not

---

9 Cf. Eph. 2.14.
10 Cf. Eph. 2.16; 2 Cor. 4.16.
11 On the entire passage 7.30, cf. Plotinus, *Enneads* 1.4.4.
12 1 Thess. 4.13.
13 On the passage from this point to 7.32, cf. Plotinus, *Enneads* 1.4.5.
14 Cf. 2 Cor. 7.10.

count beside the intent of his mind and his essential nature. Unconquered, the soul ought to maintain an unvarying steadfastness against the pleasures of the body and the simple weakness of our nature, the bereavements and expenses and reproaches, so that it may rend the body and divest itself of fleshly feelings. For it desires to possess the palm of happiness, and its reward consists, not in sharing in a single virtue, but in the fellowship of many virtues, of all, if possible.

(7.32) Accordingly,[15] the man who has been perfected does not know the inconveniences of the body or the adversities of the world, nor does he feel them, for he has a mind foreign to fear of such kind, that such things may happen. It is not that a life is defined as more perfect if it is without such misfortunes, but a life is more perfect if it reflects contempt for them. For if the definition were such that the happy life was the one that could be found free and clear of unfortunate occurrences, surely someone could not be termed happy if such occurrences came to pass. And so such matters have been put aside, and in judging of the happy life only this is demanded, that the definition of it should consist in nothing else but the possession of the true and the good. For the man who has this despises all other things and has no need of them.

(8.33) I ask now whether the wise man is pleased with bodily health. We cannot deny that he is pleased in conformity with his nature and gladly accepts the absence of pain rather than its presence. But perhaps, if the occasion should demand, he would readily accept bodily weakness and offer his entire body to death for the sake of Christ. Also, apart from motives of faith and justice, that same man would not be affected in spirit or broken with bodily pain if his health should fail, for he can console himself with his perfection in the virtues. (8.34) I ask too whether he takes pleasure in his children. Who would deny it? The search is for a man who has been perfected, not one hard as iron. Still,

---

15 On the entire passage 7.32, cf. Plotinus, *Enneads* 1.4.6.

even if he should lose his children, he is not less happy on that account, for he is not less perfect on that account, and what has been perfected is happy. Yes, this sort of perfected man generally appears in the endurance of adversity more than in the enjoyment of prosperity. Although the presence or absence of external advantages and bodily joys usually does not take anything from virtue or add anything to it, for many men the brave endurance of adversity has been as much ground for congratulation as the absence of encounter with it. But this is to judge by the appearance of things and not by their importance.

(8.35) What[1] is important is this, that the just man wishes nothing but the only and excellent good, that he strives for it only, considers it unique among goods, and desires nothing else with it but itself alone always, and takes pleasure in it. If another good that may give him pleasure, such as the sweet gift of children, is added, the only good is not lost; the other good is merely added. For accidentals, which cannot increase happiness, do not lessen it, because the only good remains full and inviolable; the soul clothes itself for this good, is submissive to it, has poured itself into it. Virtue that has been perfected remains always amid adversities and pleasures; adversities do not take away anything from its perfection, nor do pleasures add anything. After all, for the man who has climbed to the summit, what feeling of gain or loss can there be in perishable things?

(8.36) He will not consider himself wretched either if he or his children fall into captivity, something that is reckoned a very grave misfortune by most men; rather, he will bear with patience what nature brings or what seems good to the Lord.[2] Therefore the just man has said, "Good is the word which the Lord has spoken. Let peace and trust be in my days."[3] Surely the just Ezechias did not rejoice that the disaster of

---

1 On the entire passage 8.35, cf. Plotinus, *Enneads* 1.4.7.
2 On the passage from 8.36 to this point, cf. Plotinus, *Enneads* 1.4.7.
3 4 Kings 20.19.

captivity had fallen upon his children,[4] but he could not oppose the will of the Lord and so he received the Lord's commands with patience like a humble servant. Thus it happens that one could judge that merit and virtue could be evident even in captivity. For Jeremia was not less happy in captivity,[5] nor was Daniel,[6] nor Esdras,[7] nor were Anania and Azaria and Misael less happy than if they had not fallen into captivity.[8] They entered into captivity in such a way that they brought to their people both present consolations in captivity and the hope of escaping from it.

It[9] falls to the man who has been perfected to sustain nature's common lot with courageous spirit, to bring it to better things, and not to give way before those experiences that most men consider fearful and frightening. Instead, like a brave soldier, he must withstand onslaughts of the most severe calamities and undergo conflicts; like a pilot of foresight, he must steer his ship in the storm, and as he meets the mounting waves, he must avoid shipwreck by plowing through such waters rather than by turning away from them. Such a man is not afraid in persecution nor too weak amid tortures, fearful that he may provoke the torturer. Rather, like a strong athlete, he matches blow for blow the man lashing him, if not with the scourge of deadly strife, at least with the lash of his speech. Such a man despises what most men fear and says, "The arrows of children are their wounds."[10] Although he fights with the most severe pain, he does not show himself wretched but reveals a strength of spirit that shines like a light in a lantern even amid rough storms and winds of the greatest severity, a strength that cannot be quenched.

---

4 Cf. 4 Kings 20.17–18.
5 Cf. Jer. 37–38.
6 Cf. Dan. 1.6.
7 Cf. 1 Esd. 7.6.
8 Cf. Dan. 3.19–96.
9 On the passage from this point to ". . . but like a stern judge he condemns the unbelief . . ." cf. Plotinus, *Enneads* 1.4.8, 7.
10 Ps. 63 (64).8.

He is not weak in regard to wrongs done to his own, nor anxious about the burial of his body, for he knows that heaven is its due. He is not too downcast over the captivity of his fellow citizens, but like a stern judge he condemns the unbelief of those who do not have faith, and their errors. So did Daniel act, for he disclosed the thievery of the priests and disproved their superstitions, which, as he showed, had no support in truth but were clouded with deceits.[11] To sum up, the man who has been perfected is such that he wishes to do good to all men and desires that no evil befall any man; but if something happens beyond his wish, he loses nothing of his own happiness.[12]

(8.37) But perhaps someone may suppose that illness and bodily weakness are a hindrance to fulfilling the work of perfection, in that the works and accomplishments of one's hands cannot continue. Now the just man will not consider such things a hindrance to himself; rather, he will reproach the man who weeps and is wretched over them, and he will charge him on grounds of cowardice. For such a man puts more value in the enjoyment of the body than in the strength of the spirit; he desires those things to which he is a slave, although he has the ability rather to exercise control over them; he groans in poverty when he has the power to be beyond worldly riches, for the man of faith has a whole world of riches;[13] he weeps over his lowly status, when he ought to look down upon the powers of princes and rule over the rich and powerful. For the life of the just man is such that he ought to reckon as wealth held in common the wealth that he has.[14] He ought, further, to share it with the needy, to distribute it to the poor, to retrench upon his own pleasures,

---

11 Cf. Dan. 14.9–22.
12 Cf. Plotinus, *Enneads* 1.4.11.
13 Cf. Prov. 17.6 (Septuagint).
14 For a discussion of the concept of private property, and the rejection of it, in Ambrose, cf. Dudden 2.545–550; a convenient citation of relevant passages appears in M. R. P. McGuire, *op. cit.* (above ch. 3 n. 12) 106–107.

to reduce his expenses, to exhibit frugality and moderation, to hold to a course of restraint in prosperity and patience in adversity, endurance amid pain and high courage amid dangers. He ought not to know the desire for everlasting bodily health, nor be shaken by fear of impending death; he ought not to suppose that the man who abounds in children and friends and good health and joy in conformity with the order of nature is better off than one who is without such things. He ought to judge merits not by the externals of the world but by the internal possession of virtue.

(8.38) The just man, too, is of such a nature—and who would deny this?—that he is afraid of nothing and stands in dread of nothing save the loss of virtue. He checks the idle fears of other men, which they manifest in their concern for dangers, their dread of death, and their bodily infirmity; he teaches them that it is far better to depart from the body and to be with Christ;[15] he shows them that good works are not hindered by bodily weaknesses but are increased. Such a man gains commendation, not by the glory of his ancestry or the wealth or assistance of his relatives, but by his good heart. For Elias was no less happy than Moses, and yet the one was in need of food and wearing cheap sheepskin,[16] without children or funds or companionship, while the other was the leader of peoples, rejoiced in offspring, and was girded with power. In different ways they secured equal merit, as it is revealed in the Gospel, when they shone with the Lord Jesus in the glory of the resurrection.[17] He seems to have given them an equal reward as equal witnesses of His glory. And Eliseus was no less happy than David, although the one was subject to kings while the other possesed royal power; yet they obtained equal grace in prophecy and holiness.

(8.39) What indeed is lacking to the man who possesses the good and has virtue always as his companion and ally? In what role of life is he not most powerful? In what poverty is

---

15 Cf. Phil. 1.23.   16 Cf. Heb. 11.37.   17 Cf. Matt. 17.3.

he not rich? In what lowly status is he not noble? In what leisure not industrious? In what weakness not vigorous? In what infirmity not strong? In what quiet of sleep not active? Even when he is asleep, his own virtue does not forsake him. In what solitude is he not in a crowd? The happy life surrounds him, grace clothes him, the garment of glory makes him radiant. He is no less happy when at leisure than when he works, no less filled with glory when he sleeps than when he is awake, because he is no less safe and sound when sleeping than when he is awake. Now when can he appear to be on holiday? His mind is always at work. When can he appear to be alone? He is always with that good of which the psalmist says, "We shall be filled with the good things of your house."[18] When can he appear to be downcast? "His citizenship is in heaven."[19] When can he appear not to be handsome? He conforms himself to the likeness of the beautiful and only good; although weak in his members, he is strong in his spirit.

If a man who has been accustomed to sing to the accompaniment of a harp should find the harp shattered and broken and its strings undone and the use of it interrupted, he would put it aside and not call for its measures but would delight himself with his own voice. Just so will such a man as we have here allow the harp that is his body to lie unused. He will find delight in his heart and solace in the recollection that his conscience is clear. He will sustain himself on God's words and the prophetic writings and will hold that sweet and pleasant good in his soul and embrace it in his mind. For nothing can happen to him, since the grace of God's presence always breathes with favor upon him and he is always present to himself as one filled with the utmost tranquillity of spirit.[20]

18 Ps. 64 (65).5.
19 Phil. 3.20.
20 The Fourth Tractate of the First Ennead also concludes with imagery of the cithara. Cf. Plotinus, *Enneads* 1.4.16. The same imagery occurs in Plato, *Phaedo* 85 E–86 D. The concept of the soul as a harmony, developed in *Phaedo* 86 B, may be derived from the later Pythagoreans; it was held by Aristoxenus, on the evidence of Cicero, *Tusculan Disputations* 1.9.19, and Lactantius, *Institutes* 7.13.9.

Book Two

IN THE PRECEDING BOOK I discussed the precepts of the virtues; in this following one permit me to employ examples of famous men who were placed in the greatest dangers and yet did not lose happiness of life but gained it instead. Wasn't Jacob happy although he left his native land?[1] Clearly he was, for he undertook the hardships of exile in order to lessen his brother's wrath. Now if the man who avoids sin is happy, it cannot be denied that the man who lightens the guilt of someone else and turns his offense aside is happy. And so by his voluntary exile he avoided the fratricidal murder that had been prepared for him;[2] by that action he sought deliverance for himself and conferred upon his brother freedom from guilt. God's grace accompanied him everywhere and rightly so; thus he would gain the gift of the happy life even when he was asleep. For he would see the mysteries of things that were to come and hear the prophecies of God.[3] In his sleep he was a good workman and in his poverty he was rich; in the work and life of a hired servant he won for himself by that same service both a marriage and an inheritance.[4] Likewise he is outstanding in his attempts to win back his brother's affection; he tried with gifts and services to banish every trace of wrath and to turn aside the hurt and offense he had given.[5] He showed that he was not diminished by exile, for he could bestow what he had not received.

---

1 Cf. Gen. 27.41–28.7.
2 Cf. Gen. 27.41.
3 Cf. Gen. 28.12.
4 Cf. Gen. 29.16–21.
5 Cf. Gen. 32.14–21.

(1.2) But I am hurrying on too quickly to later events and passing over useful matters, since I must first define what the happy man is. For it is written, "Happy is the man who has not walked in the counsel of the wicked nor stood in the way of sinners nor sat in the chair of pestilence."[6] The Scripture means that the man who has abstained from fellowship with unbelievers is happy, for it is wickedness not to acknowledge the Author of life, the Father of salvation as it were. It means too, that the man who has not continued in sin or persisted in extravagance and lust is happy; such a man, meditating on the law of the Lord day and night,[7] will be like a tree that will give fruit in due season.[8] What went before is meritorious of reward, whereas this last is the reward of meritorious actions.

(1.3) Which of those actions that are connected with the meriting of happiness was not found in holy Jacob? He kept so far off from the fellowship of the wicked that from him the faithful people received their name and were called Israel.[9] He contemplated God with the eyes of the spirit that is within and kept from sin; he abstained from the intoxication of every extravagance, so as to drain the cup of toils and hardships and care nothing for tranquillity and ease. Is it not aptly and truly said of him that he too will give fruit in due season? For of him it is written, "Behold, the smell of my son is as the smell of a plentiful field."[10] He had been made perfect in virtue's every flower and was fragrant with the grace of the holy blessing and of the happiness of heaven. He is indeed the field[11] which the Lord has blessed, not the earthly field with its rugged woods and crashing torrents, its swampy, sluggish waters and unproductive grainlands and barren vine-

---

6 Ps. 1.1.
7 Cf. Ps. 1.2.
8 Cf. Ps. 1.3.
9 Cf. Gen. 32.28–29.
10 Gen. 27.27.
11 The text from this point to 1.4 appears in slightly changed form in the *Commentary on the Canticle of Canticles* (2.27), for which see above, p. 5.

yards, filled with sterile rock and gravel, pockmarked and arid with drought or wet with blood, and choked over with brambles and thorns, but the field of which the Church speaks in the Canticle, "I have adjured you, O daughters of Jerusalem, by the powers and virtues of the field."[12] This is the field of which the Lord also says, "With me is the beauty of the field."[13] In this field the grape is found that was pressed and poured out blood and washed the world clean; in this field is the fig tree, and beneath it the saints will find rest and be renewed by a good and spiritual grace;[14] in this field is the olive tree fruitful in the overflowing ointment of the peace of the Lord; in this field flourish the pomegranate trees,[15] that shelter many fruits with the one bulwark of faith and nurture them with the warm embrace of love, so to speak.

(1.4) And so Jacob was fragrant with the fragrance of such fruits; he followed God amid dangers and believed that he was safe everywhere, led by the Lord. Although the fragrance of the field is pleasant and sweet because it is a natural fragrance, still there breathed in the holy patriarch the fragrance of grace and virtue. How moderate and restrained he was! He did not claim the food that had been prepared for him but yielded without delay to his brother's request for it and received from him the birthright of the firstborn.[16] How respectful he was toward his parents! Through his mother's love he earned the preference over his elder brother,[17] and through the gift of his father's blessing he was made holy.[18] How respectful of God's commands he was! He refused to do wrong to his brother. How honorable! He refused to practice deceit upon his father.[19] How respectful! He could not refuse his mother what she ordered.[20]

---

12 Cant. 2.7 (Septuagint).
13 Ps. 49 (50).11.
14 Cf. Mich. 4.4.
15 Cf. Cant. 8.2.
16 Cf. Gen. 25.29–34.   17 Cf. Gen. 27.1–17.
18 Cf. Gen. 27.18–29.   19 Cf. Gen. 27.12.   20 Cf. Gen. 27.13–14.

(2.5) But we ought not to leave his parents without excuse for having preferred their younger son to the elder. At the same time we must take care so that no one, in turning to their example, would make an unfair judgment between his sons or suppose that he should love the one and esteem the other less. From this line of conduct fraternal hatreds are aroused, and the crime of fratricide is contrived to gain a worthless sum of money. Let children be nurtured with a like measure of devotion. Granted that one's love may fasten more upon some trait in a child who is more agreeable or similar to oneself, the exercise of justice ought to be the same in regard to all. The more that is given to the child that is loved and who seeks his brothers' love, the more is taken away from the one who is burdened with jealousy at the unfair preferment. Esau threatened that he would kill his brother.[1] Neither the fact of brotherhood nor respect for their parents kept him from his fratricidal madness, and he grieved that the blessing had been snatched away from him, whereas he should have proved himself worthy of it by forbearance rather than by crime. (2.6) However, Rebecca did not prefer one son to another son but a just son to an unjust one. And indeed, with that pious mother, God's mysterious plan was more important than her offspring. She did not so much prefer Jacob to his brother; rather she offered him to the Lord, for she knew that he could protect the gift that the Lord had bestowed. In the Lord she took counsel also for her other son; she withdrew him from God's disfavor, lest he incur graver culpability if he lost the grace of the blessing he did receive.

(2.7) But take the lesson of the good rivalry that existed between the parents. The mother would contribute her affection, the father his faculty of judgment. With her tender love the mother would be more inclined toward the younger son, while the father would observe the honor due by nature

---

1 Cf. Gen. 27.41.

toward the older one. The father would give the greater honor, the mother the more affection, provided that each of them cherishes each of the children and they do not both combine in favor of one and deprive the other. Let there be an equality between the opposed and rival positions, and although the interests are unlike, let a like favor be shown to both children and the love of their parents be equal. Let the one parent make good what the other has diminished. Thus Isaac and Rebecca rivaled each other in loving affection so as to treat neither child as the lesser, but both as equal.[2]

(2.8) Nevertheless, the one who was given the preference by the prophecy[3] did overcome; activity overcame delay, mildness overcame severity. While the one son sought the game of the fields by the rough ways of hunting,[4] the other furnished his loving father with the food of a gentle manner, the grace acquired at home, and a feast of tenderness and mildness and of affection. In regard to the soul, whatever gift has presented itself is more pleasing than any choice gift one thinks one should bring. Jacob went to his sheep and brought blameless offspring, that is, the gifts foretold in holy prophecy;[5] for he believed that no food was sweeter to the patriarch than Christ, who was led like a sheep to the slaughter and like a lamb to be a victim.[6] He judged that this was a useful nourishment both for his relatives and for the people, of which he was a symbol, for through it there was to come the forgiveness of sins.

(2.9) Accordingly, Jacob received his brother's clothing, because he excelled the elder in wisdom.[7] Thus the younger brother took the clothing of the elder because he was conspicuous in the merit of his faith. Rebecca presented this clothing as a symbol of the Church; she gave to the younger

---

2 Cf. Gen. 25.28.
3 Cf. Gen. 25.23.
4 Cf. Gen. 25.27.
5 Cf. Gen. 27.9, 14, 17.
6 Cf. Jer. 11 (12).19.
7 Cf. Gen. 27.15.

son the clothing of the Old Testament, the prophetic and priestly clothing, the royal Davidic clothing, the clothing of the kings Solomon and Ezechias and Josias, and she gave it too to the Christian people, who would know how to use the garment they had received, since the Jewish people kept it without using it and did not know its proper adornments.[8] This clothing was lying in shadow, cast off and forgotten; it was tarnished by a dark haze of impiety and could not be unfolded farther in their confined hearts. The Christian people put it on, and it shone brightly. They made it bright with the splendor of their faith and the light of their holy works. Isaac recognized the familiar fragrance that attached to his people,[9] he recognized the clothing of the Old Testament, but the voice of the people of old he did not recognize; therefore he knew that it had been changed. For even today the same clothing remains, but the confession of a people of greater devotion begins to sound harmonious; Isaac was right to say, "The voice indeed is the voice of Jacob, but the hands are the hands of Esau."[10] And Isaac "smelled the fragrance of his garments."[11] And perhaps that means that we are not justified by works but by faith, because the weakness of the flesh is a hindrance to works but the brightness of faith puts the error that is in man's deeds in the shadow and merits for him the forgiveness of his sins.

(3.10) Afterward, when the blessing had been pronounced, the elder brother arrived.[1] By this it is revealed that the kingdom was predestined to be bestowed on the Church rather than on the synagogue, but had secretly entered the syna-

---

8 For further discussion of this passage, in which Jacob appears as a type of the Christian people, see Gryson, *Prêtre* 65 n. 7 and G. Figueroa, *The Church and the Synagogue in St. Ambrose* (The Catholic University of America Studies in Sacred Theology, Second series 25; Washington 1949) 10-11 and 10 nn. 25, 26.
9 Cf. Gen. 27.27.
10 Gen. 27.22.
11 Gen. 27.27.

---

1 Cf. Gen. 27.30.

gogue so that sin might abound and, when sin had abounded, that grace might also abound.[2] At the same time, it would be clear that the candidate for the kingdom of heaven must be quick to carry off the blessing and to appropriate the prerogative for which he has been recommended. On this account the younger son was not blamed by his father but praised, for Isaac says, "Your brother came deceitfully and received your blessing."[3] For deceit is good when the plunder is without reproach. Now the plunder of piety is without reproach, because "from the days of John the kingdom of heaven suffers violence and the violent bear it away."[4] Our fathers celebrated the Pasch in haste and ate the lamb in haste,[5] not making delay, and the holy Joseph summoned his brother Benjamin by a holy fabrication and deceit.[6]

(3.11) Nevertheless, Esau brought it about by his demands and entreaties that he did receive a blessing, but such a blessing as was in agreement and correspondence with the earlier one, namely that he should serve his brother.[7] Indeed, the one who could not command and rule the other ought to have served him, in order to be ruled by the one who was more wise. It was not the role of the holy patriarch to deliver his own son to the ignoble state of slavery. But since he had two sons, one without moderation and the other moderate and wise, in order to take care for both like a good father, he placed the moderate son over the son without moderation, and he ordered the foolish one to obey the one who was wise. For the foolish man cannot of his own accord be a disciple of virtue or persevere in his intent, because the fool changes like the moon.[8] Isaac was right to deny Esau freedom to make his own choices; else he might drift like a ship in the waves

---

2 Cf. Rom. 5.20.
3 Gen. 27.35.
4 Matt. 11.12.
5 Cf. Exod. 12.11.
6 Cf. Gen. 42.20.
7 Cf. Gen. 27.38–40.
8 Cf. Sir. 27.11–12.

without a helmsman. But Isaac made him subject to his brother according to that which is written, "The unwise man is the slave of the wise man."[9] Therefore the patriarch was right to make him subject, so that he might amend his dispositions under rule and guidance. And so Isaac says, "By your sword shall you live; you shall serve your brother,"[10] for holiness has mastery over cruelty and kindness excels over emotions that are harsh.

(3.12) Every man who does not possess the authority conferred by a clear conscience is a slave; whoever is crushed by fear or ensnared by pleasure or seduced by desires or provoked by wrath or felled by grief is a slave. In fact, every passion is servile, because "everyone who commits sin is a slave of sin,"[11] and, what is worse, he is the slave of many sins. The man who is subject to vices has sold himself to many masters, so that he is scarcely permitted to go out of servitude.[12] But take the man who is the master over his own will, judge over his counsels, agent of his judgment, the man who restrains the longing of his bodily passions and does well what he does. (Note that by acting well he acts rightly, and one who acts rightly acts without blame or reproach because he has power over his actions.) Such a man is assuredly a free man. For the man who does all things wisely and in complete accord with his will is the only free man. It is not accidental status that makes the slave, but shameful and foolish conduct. Indeed, the wise servant rules the foolish master, and "their own servants will lend to the masters."[13] What will they lend? Not money, surely, but wisdom, just as the law also says, "You will lend to many nations and will not borrow."[14] For the Jew lent to the proselyte the prophecies of God's law.

---

9 Prov. 11.29.
10 Gen. 27.40.
11 John 8.34.
12 Ambrose is here using a phrase in the Latin (*servitio ei exire vix liceat*) reminiscent of Vergil, *Eclogues* 1.40 (*servitio me exire licebat*). The similarity is one of language rather than of thought.
13 Prov. 22.7 (Septuagint).   14 Deut. 15.6.

But because he himself could not see the mysteries of the law and did not comprehend the prophecies which he possessed, he lent the Gentiles the letter and now borrows from them the grace of learning in the spirit. He has deservedly been made subject to servitude, because the borrower is a slave, as if sold for the profit of his creditor.[15] But the man who bestows the profit of a holy teaching is a prince, even as the law says, "You will be the prince over many nations, but you will not have princes from them."[16]

Surely the man who rules and possesses the principality of wisdom is a prince. This principality the Jewish people possessed, but because they could not keep its teachings, they must learn what it did not know how to teach. (3.13) This, then, is what the patriarch Isaac says, "You shall serve your brother. But the time will be, when you shall shake off and loose his yoke from your neck."[17] He means that there will be two peoples, one the son of the slave-girl, the other of the free woman[18]—for the letter is a slave, whereas grace is free[19]—and that the people that is attentive to the letter is going to be a slave as long as it needs to follow the expounder of learning in the spirit. Then that will also come to pass which the Apostle says, "that the remnant may be saved by reason of the election made by grace."[20] "You shall serve your brother," but then you will perceive your advancement in servitude only when you begin to obey your brother voluntarily and not under compulsion.

(4.14) Hereupon there arose enmity, and Esau threatened that after the death of their father he would kill his brother.[1] But if needs be, let us learn from Rebecca how to make pro-

---

15 Cf. Prov. 22.7.
16 Deut. 15.6.
17 Gen. 27.40.
18 Cf. Gal. 4.22–31.
19 Cf. 2 Cor. 3.6.
20 Rom. 9.27; cf. Isa. 10.22.

---

1 Cf. Gen. 27.41.

vision that enmity may not provoke wrath and wrath rush headlong into fratricide.[2] Let Rebecca come—that is, let us put on patience,[3] the good guardian of blamelessness—and let her persuade us to give place to the wrath.[4] Let us withdraw somewhat further, until the wrath is softened by time and we are taken by surprise at having forgotten the wrong done us. Therefore patience is not much afraid of exile but readily enters upon it, not so much to avoid the danger to salvation as to escape giving incitement to wrongdoing. The loving mother, too, endures the absence of her dearly beloved son and purposes to give more to the one whom she has harmed, while still consulting the interests of both, to render the one safe against fratricide and the other blameless of crime.

(4.15) We have heard the words of an intemperance that is drunk with bodily desires; let us consider the deeds of true virtue. It needs nothing but the grace of God; it pursues the only and supreme good, and it is content with that only good from which we receive all things, but on which we bestow nothing because it has no need of anything, just as David says, "I have said to the Lord, you are my Lord, for you have no need of my goods."[5] And what does the Lord need, when He abounds in all things and imparts everything to us, while providing all things without deficiency?

(4.16) Jacob set out and slept—evidence of tranquillity of spirit—and saw angels of God ascending and descending.[6] This means he foresaw Christ on earth; the band of angels was descending to Christ and ascending to Him,[7] so as to

---

2 Cf. Gen. 27.42–45.
3 Rebecca appears as a type of patience also at *Isaac, or the Soul* 1.1 and *Flight from the World* 4.21 (both translated in this volume). For a full listing of persons appearing as types in Ambrose, see W. Wilbrand, "Die Deutungen der biblischen Eigennamen beim hl. Ambrosius," *Biblische Zeitschrift* 10 (1912) 337–50.
4 Cf. Rom. 12.19.
5 Ps. 15 (16).2.
6 Cf. Gen. 28.10–12.
7 Cf. John 1.51.

render service to their rightful master in loving servitude. (4.17) And he came to a well[8] to drink from his own vessels and from the springs of his own wells, and that the waters from his own spring might be his in abundance,[9] for the spring of life is in the hands of the just man. (4.18) And he came to Laban and pastured Laban's sheep.[10] Wrongdoing remains unattended, whereas wisdom does not forgo its task of government. It does not know how to be unoccupied even among strangers, nor does it know how to be an exile even among foreigners. How can it be an exile, when it keeps its own law everywhere and has its possessions in itself? (4.19) The just man Jacob comes in like a hired hand and yet is the master who, in his ministry of preaching the Gospel, gathered together a flock that is resplendent in the brilliance of its many signal virtues.[11] Thus, when the flock came to drink, he would set before them in the troughs the bough of storax and walnut and that from the plane tree; those who felt desire for the mysteries of the most blessed Trinity that were prefigured there could engender offspring that were not at all discolored, by conceiving them in a devout mind.[12] Good were the sheep that produced the offspring that were good works and that were not degenerate in holy faith. By the storax is meant the incense and the evening sacrifice that is offered to God the Father in the psalm;[13] by the walnut bough, the priestly gift that is offered by Christ. For this is Aaron's bough, that blossomed when it was set down, and through it the grace of priestly holiness was manifested.[14] By the plane tree is meant an abundance of spiritual fruit,

---

8 Cf. Gen. 29.2.
9 Cf. Prov. 5.15–16.
10 Cf. Gen. 29.9–15.
11 Cf. Gen. 30.31–35.
12 Cf. Gen. 30.37–43.
13 Cf. Ps. 140 (141).2. The concepts of the psalm as an offering and of prayer as incense appear also in Ambrose in *Joseph* 3.17 (translated in this volume) and *Explanation of Psalm 118*, 22.44. See Gryson, *Prêtre* 72 and n. 17.
14 Cf. Num. 17.16–26.

because a vine attaches itself to this tree so that the tree may be fertile through the symbiosis and pour itself out into rich offspring. Even so, the addition of the grace of the Spirit has generally nurtured the gifts of the Lord's passion as well as the forgiveness of all sins.

(5.20) Accordingly, as Scripture says, Jacob became rich by such means and reared a very good flock for Christ.[1] He improved it with the title of faith and a diversity of virtues, the marks of a glorious name. And so he did not consider himself poor, for he was rich with the wealth of faith. He provoked the hostility of Laban's sons on grounds of his very great wealth, since he had increased his own flock by adding the other to it.[2] And God said to him, "Return to the land of your father and to your own kin, and I will be with you,"[3] showing that nothing is lacking to the man who has the fullness of all things. This alone is more than enough for the man who has been perfected, in it all things subsist, and to it all things are referred; nothing is strange to it, nothing further is necessary to it, peace and faith are sufficient for it, so that through them it might reconcile what at first had been in discord. And no wonder if Jacob possessed peace, for he had set up a column and anointed it to God,[4] and that column is the Church. Now the column has been called "the mainstay of the truth."[5] That man anoints it who pours the ointment of faith upon Christ and that of compassion upon the poor.

(5.21) Now let us consider how the just man ought to behave if enmity arises. First, let him avoid it; it is better to go away without strife than to settle down with contention. Next, let him possess a property that he can carry off with him so that he cannot be held under any obligation by the adversary but may say, "Identify whatever of yours I may

---

1 Cf. Gen. 30.43.
2 Cf. Gen. 31.1.
3 Gen. 31.3.
4 Cf. Gen. 35.20.   5 1 Tim. 3.15.

have."[6] And Laban searched and found nothing of his with Jacob.[7] He was a great man and truly happy who could lose nothing of his and possess nothing of another's, that is, possess nothing too little and nothing to excess. Therefore the man who has no lack of anything has been perfected; the man who has nothing to excess is just—this is to observe the proper mean of justice. How powerful virtue is! Alliance with it brought gain but did not inflict loss. This is what perfection is; it gives the greatest advantage to those who hold to it but brings them no disadvantage whatsoever.

(5.22) Accordingly, the man who desired to do harm to Jacob was not able to send him away empty. For the wise man is never empty but always has the garment of prudence on himself and is able to say, "I was clad with justice and I clothed myself with judgment,"[8] as Job said. Surely these are the inner veils of the spirit, and no one can take them away except when someone strips them off by his own guilty action. In fact Adam was found stripped so, and naked,[9] whereas Joseph was not naked even though he had thrown off[10] his external clothing, as he possessed the safe covering of virtue. Therefore the wise man is never empty. How could he be empty? He has taken from the fullness of Christ and keeps what he has received. How could he be empty? His soul is filled, for it guards the garments of grace it has received. We must be afraid that someone may lose the veil of blamelessness, and that ungodly men may transgress the bonds of justice with onslaughts of sacrilege and persecution and snatch away the garment of the soul and of the spirit. This does not readily happen unless a man has first been stripped of his clothing by the voice of his iniquity. On this account

---

6 Gen. 31.32.
7 Cf. Gen. 31.33.
8 Job 29.14.
9 Cf. Gen. 3.10–11.
10 "Abandoned" would better suggest the reality; cf. Gen. 39.12. The story is treated at greater length in *Joseph* 5.22–6.28 (translated in this volume).

David also says, "If there is iniquity in my hands, let me deservedly fall empty before my enemies. Let the enemy pursue my soul and take it."[11]

(5.23) Therefore none of the enemies can take your soul unless it has first been made empty. Do not be afraid of those who can plunder treasures of gold and silver; such men take nothing from you. They take away what you do not have, they take away what you are not able to possess, they take away, not an ornament to your soul, but a burden on it, they take away what does not enrich your heart but weighs it down; "for where your treasure is, there also will your heart be,"[12] as you have heard in today's reading. Many men shut in their gold with bars upon their gates, but they have no confidence in either their bolts or their barricades. Many men employ guards, but they too are generally more afraid of the guards. Many go to bed upon buried gold;[13] their gold is beneath the ground and so is their heart. Watch out, then, that you do not entrench your heart in the ground while you are still living. We have no need to be afraid of thieves who steal such gold; but you must watch out for the usurer who examines the wealth of your soul, if you have bargained for any coin of more serious sin. He confines your heart in the earth and buries your soul in the ground, where you have hidden your gold. He crushes your spirit with interest compounded a hundredfold and buries it in a heavy sepulcher, from which no man rises again. Follow the example of holy Jacob; he had no part in the vices of others, nor was he empty and devoid of his own virtues, but he was filled with the fruit of justice.

(5.24) But this pertains to the moral sense, whereas the mystical sense is that Laban, whose name means "he that has been purified"[14]—and even Satan transfigures himself into an

---

11 Ps. 7.4–6.
12 Matt. 6.21; cf. above, Intr. n. 3.
13 Cf. Vergil, *Georgics* 2.507.
14 The name Laban is interpreted as "radiant" in *Flight from the World* 5.26 (translated in this volume).

angel of light[15]—came to Jacob and began to demand his possessions from him.[16] Jacob answered him, "Identify whatever of yours I may have,"[17] that is, "I have nothing of yours. See if you recognize any of your vices and crimes. I have not carried off with me any of your deceits and I have no share in your guile; all that is yours I have shunned as a contagion." Laban searched and found nothing that was his.[18] How happy is the man in whom the enemy has found nothing that he could call his own, and in whom the devil has come upon nothing that he could call his own, and in whom the devil has come upon nothing that he would recognize as his own. That appeared to be impossible in the case of man, but Christ supplied the model of it when He said in the Gospel, "The prince of this world will come and in me he will find nothing."[19] Now whatever belongs to the devil is nothing, because he can have no lasting possession.

(5.25) Further, it is the Lord Jesus Himself who was prefigured in Jacob, a man of two marriages, that is, one who shares both in the law and in grace. He admired the virgin Rachel first; she was predetermined to marriage with him and he loved her with devoted affection.[20] But Lia, like the law, entered in secretly and took him by surprise,[21] and her eyes were somewhat weak,[22] like the synagogue, that could not see Christ from blindness of spirit. Holy Rachel possessed beauty in abundant measure, and Jacob sought her over and beyond the first marriage.[23] She was a sign even then by the interpretation of her name that the preference would belong to the Church. Happy was Rachel, who took away her reproach by bearing a child of her own;[24] happy was Rachel,

---

15 Cf. 2 Cor. 11.14.
16 Cf. Gen. 31.25–30.
17 Gen. 31.32.
18 Cf. Gen. 31.33–35.
19 John 14.30.
20 Cf. Gen. 29.18, 30.
21 Cf. Gen. 29.22–27.
22 Cf. Gen. 29.17.
23 Cf. Gen. 29.26–30.

24 Cf. Gen. 30.23.

who concealed the false idols of the Gentiles and declared that their images were full of uncleanness.[25] Let no one believe that she had betrayed the respect and devotion due her father because she sat while he stood,[26] for it is written, "He who loves father and mother more than me is not worthy of me."[27] When the cause of religion was at stake, faith had a just claim upon the judgment seat and unbelief like a defendant deserved to stand.

(6.26) These events have been examined to the point where the angels of God met holy Jacob on his journey.[1] Next he sees the camp of God nearby and says, "This is the encampment of God";[2] God's help is generally with men of faith and men who have been perfected. Moreover, as one who had been perfected, he thought of reconciliation with his brother.[3] Accordingly he thought to invite Esau with humility and to prevail on him with kindnesses and considered that he could be won over with gifts as well. Therefore Jacob went along with his wives and children to meet his brother, so that even if Esau was angry at him, he would relent out of allegiance to ties of kinship.[4] (6.27) "And he bowed down seven times on the ground."[5] What does that mean? The law says, "You will bow down before the Lord your God and you will worship him only."[6] Yet Jacob bows down before Esau, who is intemperate and wrathful and threatens to commit the crime of fratricide. Did he perhaps bow down on ground that was congealed with human gore, wet with the poisons of serpents or poor with barren gravel or appalling with its

---

25 Cf. Gen. 31.34–35.
26 Cf. Gen. 31.35.
27 Matt. 10.37.

---

1 Cf. Gen. 32.2.
2 Gen. 32.3.
3 Cf. Gen. 32.4–21.
4 Cf. Gen. 33.1–2.
5 Gen. 33.3.
6 Deut. 6.13.

hard, rough crags?[7] What does it mean, that he bowed down seven times? The answer would remain open if one did not remember Peter's question in the Gospel, "If my brother sins against me, how often shall I forgive him? Up to seven times?"[8] and the answer of the Lord Jesus, "not only seven times, but even seventy times seven."[9] And so the holy patriarch foreshadows this in prophetic spirit, since he is looking to Christ who is coming and who would command that pardon be extended to one's brother not only to seven times but even to seventy times seven. Thus, in view of this meeting, Esau would forgive his brother the injury he thought he had received; although the offended party, Esau would return to friendship, because the Lord Jesus was going to take flesh and come upon the earth for that very reason, to give us manifold pardon for our offenses.

(6.28) Then, intending to ask for peace from his brother, Jacob slept in the encampment.[10] Perfect virtue possesses tranquillity and a calm steadfastness; likewise the Lord has kept His gift for those who are more perfect and has said, "My peace I leave to you, my peace I give to you."[11] It is the part of those who have been perfected not to be easily influenced by worldly things or to be troubled with fear or tormented with suspicion or stunned with dread or distressed with pain. Rather, as if on a shore of total safety, they ought to calm their spirit, immovable as it is in the anchorage of faith, against the rising waves and tempests of the world. Christ brought this support to the spirits of Christians when He brought an inner peace to the souls of those who had proved themselves, so that our heart should not be troubled or our spirit be distressed. That this peace is beyond all understanding our apostolic teacher proclaimed when he said, "And the peace of God, which surpasses all understanding,

---

7 Cf. Vergil, *Georgics* 2.212; *Aeneid* 4.366.

8 Matt. 18.21.

9 Matt. 18.22.

10 Cf. Gen. 32.14.   11 John 14.27.

will guard your hearts and feelings in Christ Jesus."[12] And so the fruit of peace is the absence of disturbance in the heart. In short, the life of the just man is calm, but the unjust man is filled with disquiet and disturbance. Therefore the ungodly man is struck down more by his own suspicions than most men are by the blows of others, and the stripes of the wounds in his soul are greater than those in the bodies of men who are lashed by others.

(6.29) It is a sublime thing that someone is tranquil within himself and in agreement with himself. Externally, peace is sought through the anxious forethought of the emperor or the hands of the soldiers, or it results from the favorable outcome of wars or some massacre among the barbarians, if they turn their own weapons on one another in a hostile move. Such a peace comes to pass through no power of ours, but it is a stroke of good fortune. Surely the glory of that peace is assigned to the emperor, but we have in us the benefit of inward peace, which is in the spirit and is held in the heart of every one of us. The benefit of this peace is greater in that temptations coming from a spirit of wickedness,[13] rather than hostile arms, are repulsed. This peace that shuts out the enticements of the bodily passions and calms the disturbances arising from them is nobler than the peace that checks the attacks of barbarians; it is a greater thing to withstand the enemy shut up within oneself than the one that is far off.

(7.30) Therefore Jacob, who had purified his heart of all pretense and was manifesting a peaceable disposition, first cast off all that was his, then remained behind alone and wrestled with God.[1] For whoever forsakes worldly things comes nearer to the image and likeness of God. What is it to wrestle with God, other than to enter upon the struggle for virtue, to

---

12 Phil. 4.7.
13 Cf. Eph. 6.12.

---

1 Cf. Gen. 32.23–25.

contend with one who is stronger and to become a better imitator of God than the others are? Because Jacob's faith and devotion were unconquerable, the Lord revealed His hidden mysteries to him by touching the side of his thigh.[2] For it was by descent from him that the Lord Jesus was to be born of a virgin, and Jesus would be neither unlike nor unequal to God. The numbness in the side of Jacob's thigh foreshadowed the cross of Christ, who would bring salvation to all men by spreading the forgiveness of sins throughout the whole world and would give resurrection to the departed by the numbness and torpidity of His own body. On this account the sun rightly rose on holy Jacob,[3] for the saving cross of the Lord shone brightly on his lineage, and at the same time the Sun of Justice rises on the man who recognizes God,[4] because He is Himself the Everlasting Light. (7.31) But Jacob limped because of his thigh.[5] "On account of this the children of Israel do not eat the sinew even to the present day."[6] Would that they had eaten it and had believed! But because they were not about to do the will of God, therefore they did not eat. There are those, too, who take the passage in the following sense, that Jacob limped from one thigh. Two peoples flowed from his lineage, and there was then being revealed the numbness which one of them would presently exhibit toward the grace of faith. And so it is the people itself that limped by reason of the numbness of its unbelief.

(7.32) Indeed, not long after the preceding revelation, Dina, Jacob's daughter, was violated and deflowered of her modesty and virginity by the son of a stranger.[7] Her brothers, who did not understand the mystery, first offered the strangers an alliance in faith through intermarriage[8] and

---

2 Cf. Gen. 32.26.
3 Cf. Gen. 32.32.
4 Cf. Mal. 3.20 (4.2).
5 Cf. Gen. 32.32.
6 Gen. 32.33.
7 Cf. Gen. 34.1–5.
8 Cf. Gen. 34.13–17.

then killed them,[9] out of a zealous desire for vengeance. But Jacob esteemed compassion with a forbearance that was moral, or he foresaw, with an understanding that was mystical, the mystery of the Church that would be gathered together from the nations.[10] Therefore it was with reluctance and sorrow that he learned of that spectacle of the vengeance that had been taken.[11] On this account God's answer was given to Jacob, who prophesied the coming of the Lord Jesus: "Arise and go up to Bethel,"[12] that is, to the house of bread, where Christ was born, as the prophet Michea gives testimony when he says, "And you, Bethlehem, house of Ephrata, are not too little to be among the first of Juda. For out of you will come forth the ruler in Israel, and his going forth is from the beginning, from the days of eternity."[13] Truly that is the house of bread, which is the house of Christ, who came to us from heaven as the bread of salvation[14] so that now no one may be hungry, but each one may gain for himself the food of immortality. There the patriarch was commanded to dwell; there he was commanded to make an altar to God, who appeared to him.[15] There he took the strange gods and buried them under a turpentine tree;[16] there also Rachel was buried on the way to Ephrata, that is, Bethlehem;[17] and there Jacob set up a column over her grave.[18]

(7.33) What great mysteries these are! There, there is the Church of God, in which God appears and speaks with His humble servants. There the idols of the nations are taken away and buried, for the faith of the Church has destroyed every

---

9 Cf. Gen. 34.25–29.
10 Ambrose identifies this Church with the Christian Church. See G. Figueroa, *op. cit.* (cited above ch. 2 n. 8) 4–20.
11 Cf. Gen. 34.30.
12 Gen. 35.1.
13 Mich. 5.1 (2).
14 Cf. John 6.51.
15 Cf. Gen. 35.1.
16 Cf. Gen. 35.2–4.
17 Cf. Gen. 35.19.
18 Cf. Gen. 35.20.

practice of paganism. But why, I ask, did he bury them under a turpentine tree? Assuredly that is an unproductive species. And so the gods of the nations are there, where no fruit is. There the earrings of the pagans are buried, and they gave them to Jacob[19] so that now they could grow used to hearing a new language and could forget the old sleep of unbelief, and so that their ears could become deaf to sacrilege and be purified for grace. It was there, and rightly so, that Daniel detected the false testimony against Susanna.[20] For unbelief wanted still to plant its roots there, but it could not remain hidden because it was detected by the spirit of prophecy. The deceit practiced by the priest was consistent with the admission of the truth. It was there that he said that chastity had been corrupted, where the idols of the nations were buried.[21] But the truth of the Church did not shelter unbelief; rather it buried it and blocked the ears of the pagans. (7.34) It is appropriate, too, that the holy Rachel was buried there, for all those who are baptized in Christ are buried together with Him. So we are taught by the Apostle, who says, "For we were buried with him by means of baptism into death, in order that, just as he has arisen from the dead, raised up through his own power, so we also may rise up by his grace."[22] Every deceit of the pagans really is buried at the time when someone has been washed free of his vices, because our old man, fastened to the cross, now does not know how to be a slave to the old sin. It is appropriate as well that a column is set up over Rachel's grave, because the Church is the column and mainstay of the truth.[23]

(8.35) Now Jacob grew old, and he had already grown old previously by nature, but there struggled within him the energy and vitality of youth and the tranquillity of old age. For there is an old age that is vigorous in grace and a youth

---

19 Cf. Gen. 35.4.
20 Cf. Dan. 13.54.
21 Cf. Acts 15.20; Rom. 1.18–25.
22 Rom. 6.4.   23 Cf. 1 Tim. 3.15.

that is venerable in counsel, of which the Scripture says, "Old age is venerable, and a spotless life is old age."[1] Jacob led such a life; by his good works he anticipated the period of great old age, so that he could pluck his fruit before its season and not fear for the last things in their season. Happy indeed is the young man who leads a good life, but happy also is the old man who has led a good life. What the young man hopes for, the old man has obtained; what the old man was, this the man who is young desires to be. To be sure, the latter has a longer span of troublous sea still remaining to him and is being tossed about by the waves, while the old man is in the anchorage of old age as in a harbor. Therefore Jacob was of this sort; he possessed, shut up and sealed under the safe and sound key of grace, goods that young men could scarcely hope for. Now what you possess is better than what you still hope for. And so young men who had been overwhelmed at a certain season by the storms of adversity came to Jacob as if into a harbor, while he, as if he were in a watchtower looking over this life, kept watch with an anxious heart and provided remedies for precarious situations far in advance.

(8.36) There was hunger in the whole land,[2] and Jacob, now extremely advanced in age, was the first to learn of news that the active young men did not know, whether through hearing . . . I shall [later] see.[3] Meanwhile, he was the first to advise his sons that grain was abundant in Egypt.[4] They must travel there, to buy what would be necessary for their use. He willingly agreed to their plan to send his youngest son also at the same time.[5] And when they reported that his son

---

1 Wisd. 4.8–9.
2 Cf. Gen. 41.56.
3 The Latin text shows a gap at this point, and the meaning of the words that surround it is not clear. Schenkl (CSEL) suggests a restoration that would yield the following sense: ". . . and Jacob . . . was the first to learn of news that the active young men did not know—whether through hearing it or through discerning it in the spirit, I shall [later] see."
4 Cf. Gen. 42.1–2.   5 Cf. Gen. 43.13.

Joseph was living,[6] he did not wait for his son to come to
him—for although his body was broken, the power of his
spirit was vigorous[7]—but rather proceeded to meet his son;
mean and measure do not have preference over love. Accordingly, he was not aware of any of the hindrances of weariness
and old age when he was on his journey, for love lightens
toil. But after he had obtained the joy of regaining his son
and some short time had passed—seventeen years, to be exact,
but that is a small period of time in comparison with the long
lifespan of a patriarch[8]—he knew that he was nearing the
end of his life. He called his son Joseph and bound him by
the heir of his lineage who was to come, that he should not be
buried in Egypt.[9] A short time after he had received the
promise, when he was ill and his son Joseph had come to him,
he sat up on his bed as if he had regained his strength, blessed
the twelve patriarchs, and prophesied.[10]

(9.37) Now some may say that Jacob was not happy, since
he was in the very days of his death, when he was almost
speaking more with God than with men; and that he was
not happy, since his eyes were heavy in old age and he could
not see.[1] Indeed, some men consider blindness a severe hardship and a disaster. But even then Jacob was happy, since
he discerned in spirit what he could not discern with the
sight of his eyes. Although he was considered not to see present
events, he saw those that were to come. But even Joseph was
misled. He had brought his elder son to Jacob's right and
his younger son to the left, so that the order of blessing might
correspond to the order of age. But Jacob stretched out his
right hand over his younger grandson and his left over the
elder. Joseph wished to place his father's right hand over

---

6 Cf. Gen. 45.26–28.
7 Cf. Vergil, *Aeneid* 5.754; 11.386.
8 Cf. Gen. 47.28.
9 Cf. Gen. 47.29–31.
10 Cf. Gen. 48.1–49.28.

---

1 Cf. Gen. 48.10.

Manasse, the elder grandson,[2] but Jacob answered him, "I know, my son, I know; he too shall become a people, he too shall be exalted, but his younger brother shall be greater than he."[3] And he added the reason for his preference when he said, "His seed shall be a multitude of nations."[4] Thus he saw better when his bodily sight was impeded, so that he showed that the sighted Joseph had been misled. Who indeed sees better than the man who sees Christ? And who can say that he was suffering an impediment of vision when he saw the Church shining brightly in Christ? Is it not clear that a disability cannot be an impediment to happiness? Jacob suffered an impediment in the function of his eyes; yet, when his bodily strength was exhausted, he left his body in the bed as if it were in a grave, rose up in his own person, composed himself far away from others and within himself, withdrew from things present, and joined the age to come in the last days. For thus it is written, "I shall tell you the things that will befall you in the last days."[5]

(9.38) What then was lacking to Jacob, when God was present to him and had said to him as he was about to set out, "I will go down to Egypt with you and I will lead you forever"?[6] And God did not fail him, when the Holy Spirit spoke in him. Who is so powerful in his own dwelling as Jacob was in that of a stranger? Who is so rich amid plenty as he was amid hunger? Who is so strong in youth as he was in old age? Who is so active in business as he was in retirement? Who is so swift in the race as he was on his bed? Who is so joyful in the flowering of his youth as he was in proximity to death? Who is so wealthy in his kingdom as he was in a foreign place? Indeed, he gave his blessing to kings. He was not poor, and rightly so, for he did not have need for anything. He was not poor, for he did not think that he was

---

2 Cf. Gen. 48.17–18.
3 Gen. 48.19.
4 Gen. 48.19 (Septuagint).
5 Gen. 49.1.   6 Gen. 46.4.

poor. Who would say that he was poor, when the world was unworthy to have him as its citizen and therefore his citizenship was in heaven?[7] He was indeed exceedingly rich in the wealth of a pure and blameless life and handsome with a beauty of soul greater than bodily beauty, for it does not know a withering away. He was undaunted by age, and he could, when he wished, go out from this hovel of the body and enter into the realms of paradise that are above with vigor of mind, rejoicing in spirit as he gave the last instructions for his burial.[8] He did not suppose that he would be shut up in an earthly tomb, but that he would be received in a dwelling up above; therefore he gave instructions for his burial as if for that of someone else. Sure of himself, he considered his death as immortality. He appeared to be entangled in the body and hindered by it, but he anticipated the times to come with watchful concern. In regard to the persecutors of the Lord, the perpetrators of wrongdoing who were going to come from the tribe of Simeon and Levi, he said, "Let not my soul come into their council and in their conspiracy let not my passions be engaged."[9] Who is so healthy in strength as Jacob was strong in weakness? For he said, "Cursed be their fury, because it is proud and foolhardy, and their wrath, because it is hardened. Shall I divide them in Jacob and scatter them in Israel?"[10]

(9.39) Who then is so harmonious in song as he was in speech? He has been heard in all the world and is heard among all peoples and through all the ages. Who sang the distinctions among the seven notes in measures so sweet, the way he resounded with the sevenfold grace of the Holy Spirit?[11] Undone in his bodily members, he still lifted him-

---

7 Cf. Phil. 3.20.   8 Cf. Gen. 49.29–31.   9 Gen. 49.6 (Septuagint).
10 Gen. 49.7.
11 Cf. Vergil, *Aeneid* 6.646. Comparison of the seven notes of Orpheus' instrument to the seven gifts of the Holy Spirit occurs also in *The Prayer of Job and David* 4.10.36 (translated in this volume) and elsewhere in Ambrose. See P. Courcelle, "Les Pères devant les enfers Virgiliens," (cited in Select Bibliography) 32–33 and n. 8.

self up with his courage and raised himself with his spirit.
When the joining of his limbs was dissolved, the harmony of
his body was destroyed like that of a cithara. But he looked
out from the depth of his spirit and did not feel the loss of
it; rather, he permitted it to lie in disuse on the ground, while
he delighted himself with song from within and took pleasure
in a prophetic cadence. He said, "Juda, may your brothers
praise you; your hands will be on the back of your enemies;
the sons of your father will bow down to you. A lion's whelp
is Juda; from my seed you have sprung up to me. Resting,
you have slept as a lion and the whelp of a lion. Who will
rouse him?"[12] and later, "He will wash his robe in wine
and his mantle in the blood of the grape. His eyes are
joyful from wine and his teeth are whiter than milk."[13]

What song is more sweet, what sound more pleasant, than
the forgiveness of sins and the resurrection of the dead? This
is the song that holy David, the instrument of God's word
and interpreter of the Lord's speech, sang on a spiritual
cithara. With such measures of grace he calmed his noble
soul and spirit. With such song he smoothed the roughness of
this world, with such sound he softened its hardness, with
such a psaltery he crushed the dread fear of death, with such
sweet chords he trampled underfoot the regions that are below.

(9.40) But let us hear also the other sounds which the holy
patriarch Jacob produced with the wonderful instrument of
his spirit. "Nephthali is a spreading vine, putting forth beauty
in its shoot. My son Joseph is increased, my son is increased,
my son is jealously desired, my young son; return to me,"[14]
and later, "He has prevailed over the blessings of the enduring
mountains and over the desires of the everlasting hills."[15]
What is sweeter than a blessing? What is more pleasing than

---

12 Gen. 49.8–9 (Septuagint).
13 Gen. 49.11–12 (Septuagint).
14 Gen. 49.21–22.
15 Gen. 49.26.

eternity? The very words are songs, and in the words there appear the great rewards of prayer and the pinnacles of merit.

(9.41) What is more agreeable than the example of holy Joseph? He freed us from the reproach by the mystery of the Lord's cross. For just as Christ became a curse to destroy the curse of the law[16] and became sin[17] to take away the sin of the world,[18] so He became a reproach to remove the reproach of paganism, but that reproach that is Christ was considered more precious than the treasures of Egypt. Accordingly, Moses left the court of the king Pharao[19] and chose the reproach of faith, and before that reproach the seas divided.[20] Nephthali himself is a vine spread through the whole world, to dispense to all peoples the richness of a spiritual drink. He is increased, that is, having the name which is above every name,[21] who offered Himself to death on behalf of all men, and therefore He hears from the Father, "Return to me." Jacob spoke, and God was heard. Jacob gave a blessing and the Lord reechoed it, saying to His Son, "Return to me," that is, "Return after the passion. Return to your dwelling, return with the trophy,[22] return to me, so that the dead may follow you in your resurrection and may rise in like manner by your power and example, that you may become the firstborn from the dead,[23] that you may sit at the right hand of the Father." On this account the Son also said, "Hereafter you shall see the Son of Man sitting at the right hand of the Power."[24]

(9.42) Who would say that Jacob was not happy even in the last hour of his death, when he poured forth God's prophecies? Who would say that Joseph was not happy in

---

16 Cf. Gal. 3.13.
17 Cf. 2 Cor. 5.21.
18 Cf. John 1.29.
19 Cf. Exod. 2.15.
20 Cf. Exod. 14.21.
21 Cf. Phil. 2.9.
22 The trophy is probably the body of Christ. See C. Mohrmann, "À propos de deux mots controversés: tropaeum–nomen," *Vigiliae Christianae* 8 (1954) 154–73, especially 157–58.
23 Cf. Col. 1.18; Apoc. 1.5; 1 Cor. 15.20; Ps. 88 (89).28.   24 Matt. 26.64.

prison, where, with the spirit of wisdom, he interpreted the truth of the dreams he had heard and revealed the course of future events?[25] Who would say that Isaia was not happy, when he was being cut in two?[26] Or Jeremia, when he was being drowned? Or holy Daniel, when he stood fearlessly among the lions[27] and a prophet seized by an angel brought him his midday meal?[28] To be sure, he was not happy because he was eating the meal of a stranger but because he kept the mouths of the hungry lions shut by his own merits. Who would say, further, that the mother of the Machabees was not happy? After the death of her seven sons, she herself made the eighth, to the glory of a heavenly triumph.[29]

(10.43) I, who am a priest and will be helped by your prayers, O Eleazar,[1] will not omit to mention you, who are a priest. You were of a priestly family, and skilled in the law, and old in years when you were delivered up to the persecutor Antiochus.[2] You could not be overcome by temptations or bent by promise of reward or broken by bitter torments. Indeed, the persecutor began with flattery, because he judged that his tortures could be surmounted.[3] "I am ashamed before your gray hair," he said, "I reverence your old age, I marvel at your sagacity. Why do you think you should abstain from the good banquet that nature provides? Soften your obstinate attitude, wake up at last, while I still prefer to use persuasion on you rather than torture. Else you may be prevailed upon by torments to do what you refuse to do when you are asked in a reasonable way." To this the old man replied, "I am not led by my own will, Antiochus, but am bound by

---

25 Cf. Gen. 40.
26 Cf. Heb. 11.37.
27 Cf. Dan. 6.2–29.
28 Cf. Dan. 14.33–39.
29 Cf. 2 Mach. 7.41.

---

1 Cf. 2 Mach. 6.18–31.
2 Cf. 4 Mach. 5.4.
3 Cf. 4 Mach. 5.5–13.

respect for the law, which has taught that one must abstain from the flesh of the swine. You judge that that creature is very beautiful, yet you cannot deny that moderation is preferable to excessive pleasure, and obedience to the law to transgression of it. But if you consider this a slight matter, the eating of the swine's flesh, how will the man who has shown contempt for the law in the smallest matters keep it in great matters? And if a creature of that sort is valuable, you are compensated when we are cheated of that which is very beautiful. Moreover, our abstinence is a training in restraint. We learn to curb excess, to overcome the passions, to shut out concupiscence, to resist bodily delights. It is an exercise of fortitude to refuse to give way to punishments in defense of the law, and a mark of justice and prudence, to keep to the course we have chosen to follow out of fear of God, even under threat of death. Who would command food for free men? Who would show himself so laughable as to be a slave to this? But you will not laugh. I am not such an old man that fortitude of spirit is not young in me."[4]

(10.44) Accordingly, after he had been hung up, Eleazar was lashed severely on either side, and his aged limbs could no longer bear the punishing blows.[5] The torturers and the operators of the rack had grown weary, but he, though bent down to the ground, manifested an unbending spirit. And someone, whether out of pity for his great old age or from a desire to trick him with temptations, said, "Only answer that you will eat; we will vouch for you without your partaking of that food."[6] But he cried out, "Let it not befall me by any means, that I, an old man, should become an incentive for youth to go astray. Even to this point I was in conformity with the plan of salvation. Shall I gain a brief span of life by such mockeries and sell the efforts of an entire lifetime for

---

4 Cf. 4 Mach. 5.14–38.
5 Cf. 4 Mach. 6.1–10.
6 Cf. 4 Mach. 6.11–15.

provisions for a short old age? Old age ought to be the harbor after one's earlier life, not the shipwreck of it. I will not deny you, O law of my fathers, I will not abjure you, O hallowed customs of my ancestors, I will not stain you, O priestly headbands, I will not soil you publicly with the dust of unbelief, O my gray hair."[7] What more is there? By dying in torments Eleazar became an example of perseverance for others, whereas he had been chosen for an example of weakness.[8] Therefore the man is happy in whom torments cannot overcome the reason. Or was that man not happy, who could with strength of spirit be victorious over his punishments and amid such mighty waves could keep his suffering blameless with the oars[9] of love?

(11.45) After Eleazar, punishment was inflicted on the seven young men with their mother.[1] The tyrant was allowed to abuse them; while he supposed that it was crafty to begin with the old man, he had chosen a teacher who would give his followers greater strength. Antiochus, relying on their youth, summoned them to commit wrong with a promise of rewards,[2] and he threatened them with terrible punishments to arouse their fear.[3] But although he was a mighty general, the young men were not ignoble, and they answered him, "Why do you despise us and treat us condescendingly as if we were boys? Faith is old, its teachings sound. Proceed, put us to the test, make our youthful bodies subject to whatever punishments you wish, you will find that our hearts are not puerile, and your machines of torture will not be stronger than the observance of the precept of the law. Youth, emulat-

7 Cf. 4 Mach. 6.16–23.
8 Cf. 4 Mach. 6.24–30.
9 Cf. Vergil, *Aeneid* 1.301, 6.19. The image of rowing occurs frequently in Ambrose; see R. T. Otten, "Caritas" (cited above, *Isaac* ch. 4 n. 103) especially 446–47, 446 n. 6 and 447 n. 1.

1 Cf. 2 Mach. 7; 4 Mach. 8.3.
2 Cf. 4 Mach. 8.5–8.
3 Cf. 4 Mach. 8.9–15.

SAINT AMBROSE

ing old age, will overcome him whom old age overcame. We
follow, as sons follow their father or students their teacher.
Gather the intended instruments of torture; they offer a lesson
in patience until we see them, not the dread of the unknown."[4]

(11.46) Antiochus ordered the eldest son to be taken. But
the latter laughed and said, "You are right to keep to the
succession established by nature. But why do you think that
you should violate God's law? And as concerns our devotion,
we are all the eldest. But still I rejoice that you have begun
with me. What is your aim, tyrant? I confess that we are
servants of the Almighty God. And we are learning from
you what we must do. If you are so very obstinate in your
desire to wrench the truth away, why should we not think that
we should keep it with all our power?" What more is there?
Various kinds of punishments were employed, but love overcame the frenzy and savagery. His soul was driven from his
body but his sense of piety was not driven from him.[5]

(11.47) The second brother came; he was not unworthy of
his brother, but fulfilled his duty with a devout profession
of faith. Even when the skin was being drawn off his head,
he said in response, "You are taking the skin away, granted,
but I have a spiritual helmet that you cannot take away."
In truth, no one can take away this helmet, just as the Apostle
taught later in regard to the Church of the Lord, "that the
head of the man is Christ and we are his members."[6] The
young man correctly foresaw that teaching of the Apostle
through God's Spirit. Like savage beasts they stripped off
the skin of his head and they vented their rage with the
ferocity of leopards. But while he was dying, the young
man said, "How good it is to die for religion, how sweet is
all the bitterness of a death suffered out of pious devotion,
because the reward of these sufferings is enduring! Your torments, king, are very severe, but you yourself are being tor-

---

4 Cf. 4 Mach. 8.28–9.9.
5 Cf. 4 Mach. 9.10–25.
6 1 Cor. 11.3; Eph. 5.30.

mented more severely by hidden punishments, in that you perceive that your power is overcome."[7]

(11.48) When he was dead, the tyrant ordered the third brother to be brought. And while he was laying snares of temptation for him on the one hand, and, on the other, was anxious to strike fear into him, the brother replied to him, "I shall not do your will or surrender to your command. After the happy and noble suffering of my brothers, I will not deny the holy bond of brotherhood. Employ whatever torments you will; the more you oppress me with them, so much the more will you bring it to pass through your bitter punishments that you will receive stronger proofs of our bond of brotherhood." Therefore the tyrant ordered his tongue to be cut out. But the brother cried out, "You have been overcome, Antiochus, for you command that the instrument of my speech be cut out. You have admitted that you cannot reply to reason, and you are giving proof that the scourges inflicted by my tongue are greater than your lashes. For I am not afraid of your lashes, whereas you cannot endure the scourges of my voice. But these scourges are from holiness, while your lashes are from unbelief. But when my tongue has been removed, it will scourge you the more severely with its murmuring even as it falls. Do you think you can get away, Antiochus, if you snatch away my voice? God listens to those who do not speak also, and He listens to them more. See, I have opened my mouth, I have stretched out my tongue.[8] Cut off my tongue, but you will not cut off my constancy, you will not take away my courage, you will not blot out my reason, you will not snatch away my witness to the truth, you will not snatch away the cry that is in my heart. If my tongue should be cut off, my blood will cry out and it will be said to you, 'The voice of your brother's blood cries to me.'[9] For He hears the voice of blood, who hears your innermost thoughts. 'Although darkness covers me and the enclosures of the walls

---

7 Cf. 4 Mach. 9.26–31.   8 Cf. Job 33.2.   9 Gen. 4.10.

surround me,'[10] the ungodly man may say, because no witness stands near him; yet God searches out all things and sees all things, and there is no crime that can escape the notice of the judge of all, who knows all things before they take place. Why do I speak idly? My wounds are more eloquent; even though those wounds may be covered over, even though the scar may be hidden, faith is not hidden. And do not congratulate yourself that by taking away my tongue you may snatch away my avowal of praise to God. I have already praised God enough in words, now let me praise Him in suffering."[11]

(11.49) And when he had been killed, the tyrant ordered the fourth brother bound to the wheel so that all his limbs might be undone by its rotation. But amid his horrible torments the brother said, "You are putting asunder my bodily members, but you are adding grace to my suffering and not snatching away the consolation from my death." For his is a voice of thunder on the wheel, because heaven's prophecy reverberates in the good and blameless course of such a life, just as it reverberated in the case of John and James, the sons of thunder.[12] Accordingly, I now understand more plainly what I have read, that one wheel runs within another and is not impeded. For a life lived without any offense is a rounded life, whatever the sufferings in which it is lived, and even within such it runs like a wheel.[13] The law runs within grace, and the keeping of the law lies within the course of God's mercy; the more it rolls, the more it gains approval. "It is better to suffer adversities from the ungodly here, so that we may be able to find consolation from the Lord there." And fulfilling his course, he gave up the spirit and poured forth his soul in victory.[14]

(11.50) When the fifth brother was presented, the tyrant first had him beaten and then ordered that fire be applied to

---

10 Sir. 23.18 (26).
11 Cf. 4 Mach. 10.1–12.
12 Cf. Mark 3.17.
13 Cf. Ezech. 1.15–20.   14 Cf. 4 Mach. 10.12–11.1.

him and that he be put over the flames. The gore flowed out
from his wounds, and, from the sores that had been dug out,
the blood poured forth so that it quenched even the masses of
fire. Yet amid the crackling of the fires he was heard to say,
"Thanks be to you, O Lord, because you have permitted us
to say, "We have passed through fire,'[15] even as the psalmist
expresses the same thought in another passage, 'You have
tried us by fire, as silver is tried by fire.'[16] I will stand beside
you, cleansed by the fire like gold, and whatever guilt I had
the fire has burned away." Accordingly, he too was transformed from corruption to incorruption[17] and breathed forth
his life.[18]

(11.51) Torments were employed upon the sixth brother as
well. But he said, "Be not deceived without cause[19] and attribute it to your own power that you are practicing such
torments against us. This is the wages of our offenses, that
we may be punished for our sins, and thanks be to God, for
our sins are being punished twofold here so that consolation
may be afforded us there. Thanks be also to you, because you
are so hard and cruel that the Lord, against whom we have
sinned, may become merciful toward our people through such
punishments as ours. We are lightening our affliction, too,
while we take pleasure in sufferings endured for the faith."
He too was torn to pieces with bitter torments and joined
his brothers.[20]

(11.52) There remained the youngest of the brothers, and
by now Antiochus was ashamed that he had been an object
of mockery to one of tender years. Therefore he desired to
entrap the young man with deceits, by promising him honors,
riches, friendship with himself, and a part in his secret
counsels.[21] But the holy mother exhorted her son, and said

---

15 Ps. 65 (66).12.
16 Ps. 65 (66).10.
17 Cf. 1 Cor. 15.42.
18 Cf. 4 Mach. 11.1–13.
19 Cf. 2 Mach. 7.18.
20 Cf. 4 Mach. 11.13–12.1.   21 Cf. 2 Mach. 7.24.

to him as she had to the others, "I know not how you entered into my womb; I neither gave you breath nor formed your members, but these are the gifts of Almighty God."[22] Antiochus, upon seeing the anxious mother, supposed that she was afraid for her son's safety, and he began to urge her also that she should recall her son from his purpose.[23] But she said to her son in her native language, "You only are left, my son, the entirety of my prayers; you were the last, and concluded my bringing forth; now be the last, and conclude my rejoicing. Have pity on me, that bore you in the womb over the span of so many months, that you do not bring shame upon my old age in a single moment, nor stain the many trophies of your brothers, nor abandon their holy company. Their victories await you. Look upon heaven, from which you have drawn your spirit, to the Father of all; look upon earth, which previously furnished you with sustenance; look upon your brothers, who miss their companion; look upon me, your mother, who gave my milk to you. The Lord gave all of you to me as lights for my seven days; I have already closed the sixth day and the works of them all are very good. You owe it to me, my son, that I, who have toiled upon those six, should find rest in you, the seventh,[24] as if I were now at leisure from the works of the world."[25] Accordingly, the young man rushed forward, saying, "What are you waiting for?"[26] and giving expression to many cries. For he could not be torn from fellowship with his brothers, and their deaths were far more happy than the ruling might of the king. The youngest brother pressed upon the king with his loud reproaches,[27] and, after suffering torment through tortures of a bitter kind, he completed the service of this life.[28]

---

22 Cf. 2 Mach. 7.21–23.
23 Cf. 2 Mach. 7.25–26.
24 Cf. Gen. 2.2–3.
25 Cf. 2 Mach. 7.27–29.
26 Cf. 2 Mach. 7.30.
27 Cf. 2 Mach. 7.30–36; 39.
28 Cf. 4 Mach. 12.

(11.53) The mother was offered up to death last of all.[29] Who would say that she was not happy? As if fortified with seven walls, she stood among the bodies of her sons and felt no onslaught of death. Who, I ask, would be in doubt about her happiness? As if surrounded by seven turrets, she lifted up her head into the dwelling-place of paradise. Encircled by her seven sons, she brought to the heavenly altars a choir most holy to God, and melodious not alone with its voices but also with its sufferings, to sing the praises of the Lord. How good is the offspring of faith! How safe is that harbor of pious devotion! How bright is the lamp of the Church that shines with sevenfold light[30] and furnishes oil for all the lights from the eighth, which is her womb! It is aptly said of them, "Give a portion to those seven and also to those eight,"[31] because men who have been nurtured in the law and crowned through grace may obtain a share in grace through either number. They are seven as in the days of the week,[32] eight as in the Gospel, with the devout mother added for the increase in suffering, for in such sons she brought to birth and bore an unblemished model of holiness.

(12.54) There come back to mind the words of that holy woman as she said to her sons, "I bore you, I gave you milk to drink, do not lose your excellence."[1] That is the way other mothers often call their sons back from martyrdom, not to it. But she considered that her maternal love lay in this, if she could urge her sons to a life that is everlasting rather than a temporal one. Therefore, as a devout mother, she was looking to the struggles in which her sons were engaged. Although her mother's heart was shaken with compassion, out of zeal for holiness she checked her grief.[2] When Antiochus made his

---

29 Cf. 2 Mach. 7.41.
30 Cf. Exod. 25.37.
31 Cf. Eccles. 11.2.
32 Cf. 4 Mach. 14.7–8.

1 Cf. 2 Mach. 7.27.
2 Cf. 4 Mach. 14.20; 15.8, 11–12.

offer and she could have chosen safety for her sons, she preferred the peril.[3] Restraining her natural laments, she desired that her sons' punishment be increased, so that their death might come more quickly. We see that the mother's prayers were directed toward the sons, not that she might leave anyone of them behind as a survivor, but that she might gain them all as joint heirs of death.

(12.55) But the sons did not fall short of such a mother. They joined in giving encouragement to one another;[4] with a single desire and with their souls drawn up for battle, as it were, they said, "Let us trample down death's hostile onslaught. For we shall be alive even at the time when we shall have died. Let no one forsake the ranks of holiness, let no one withdraw from the triumphal battle. We have vowed our souls, not to a man, but to Almighty God, and we are in service, not to a man, but to the Creator of all. Such is the nature of this battle, that a man conquers with the more glory, the more cruel the manner of his death." Therefore no one was afraid, no one was agitated, none of the many brothers went to his death very slowly,[5] rather they all ran to death through bitter torments as if running to the road of immortality.[6] Their mother, perceiving that the ranks of her sons were in complete accord, like the devout soul that she was, offered in her sons the members of her own body, and it seemed to her that she was undergoing the desired torments through her own limbs.

(12.56) Her sons fell, all wounded by the torments; in death they rolled upon the dead, bodies rolled on bodies, heads were cut off above heads, the place was filled with the corpses of her sons.[7] Their mother did not weep or wail or close the eyes or mouths of any of them in death or wash

---

3 Cf. 4 Mach. 15.26–27.
4 Cf. 4 Mach. 13.11–18.
5 Cf. 4 Mach. 14.4.
6 Cf. 4 Mach. 14.5.
7 Cf. 4 Mach. 15.20.

their wounds.[8] She knew that her sons would be in greater glory, if they appeared torn to pieces and jumbled together with dust and blood. In such a condition, generally, are conquerors on their return from war, when they bring back the trophies taken from the enemy. The mother did not think that coverings should be put over her sons' bodies, or that their funeral rites should be accompanied except by the accompaniment of her own death. What cithara could produce sweeter songs than the sons did by their death amid such severe tortures?[9] Lamentations burst out even from those who did not wish to make them. One could look upon the bodies of the murdered brothers in a row like the strands of strings upon a musical instrument. One could hear the seven-stringed psaltery resound with lamentations of triumph. Not in such a fashion could those alluring songs of the Sirens—or so they were said to be—attract their listener,[10] for they were attracting him to shipwreck, but these songs were leading him to sacrificial victory. Not so could the songs of swans calm the hearing and the spirit,[11] for swans die in the natural order whereas the brothers died out of love for holiness. Neither does the deep cooing of doves in a secluded wood resound with such total sweetness as did the brothers' final dying words. Nor does the moon shine so brightly among the stars, as that mother did among her sons; she led them to martyrdom to give them light and embraced them as victors as she lay among them.[12]

(12.57) O mother truly harder than adamant,[13] sweeter than honey, more fragrant than flowers! O indissoluble bond of holiness! O love strong as death, zealous faith and devotion unyielding as hell![14] No deluge of mighty sufferings could

---

8 Cf. Vergil, *Aeneid* 9.486–87.
9 Cf. 4 Mach. 14.6–8.
10 Cf. 4 Mach. 15.21. The tempted sailor was Ulysses.
11 Cf. *ibid.*
12 Cf. 4 Mach. 17.5.
13 Cf. 4 Mach. 16.13.
14 Cf. Cant. 8.6.

banish your love, no flood of mighty anguish could drown it.[15]
Just as the ark rode unharmed in its course in the deluge that
inundated the whole world, so did you remain unmoved in
your holiness against a flood of mighty sufferings;[16] although
you could have chosen safety for your sons, you would not.
(12.58) With what love can I describe you, devout children
of a holy mother? With what style of discourse can I catch
the likeness of your figure and the likeness of your souls?
You have stood among the armies of the king, to which the
whole world was subject—even India turned aside and fled
from them into the remote parts of the farthest sea—and you
only, and without warlike combat, have achieved victory
over the proud king.[17] In you the weapons of holiness alone
won the victory; the tyrant paid his penalty, because he could
not conquer you and because he died a horrible death.[18]

---

15 Cf. Cant. 8.7.
16 Cf. 4 Mach. 15.31–32.
17 Cf. 4 Mach. 17.14–15.
18 Cf. 2 Mach. 9; 4 Mach. 18.5.

JOSEPH

(De Ioseph)

INTRODUCTION

OMPOSED AS A SERMON, *Joseph* has been variously dated from 387 to 389-390; a date in the autumn of 388 seems probable.[1] Ambrose refers in the text to his encounter with Calligonus, grand chamberlain of the Emperor Valentinian II, when the chamberlain attempted to seize a basilica in Milan for use of the Arians.[2] If this event took place in 386, granting Ambrose's allusion to the execution of Calligonus, which took place two years later, a date no later than 388 would seem necessary.

"The work fairly teems with scriptural allusions and hence there is a considerable diminution of Vergilian and other classic influences."[3] Indeed only three Vergilian reminiscences have been found in *Joseph*, while scriptural quotations are so numerous as almost to preclude any other major source of influence. References abound especially to Genesis and the Psalms and, in the New Testament, to Matthew, Luke, John and the Pauline Epistles. There are, however, occasional borrowings from Philo,[4] and the possibility of traces of other philosophical works should not be dismissed without investigation.

---

1 On the work in general, see Dudden 683–684 and Palanque 442, 522. A brief survey of the dates assigned by various scholars is given by Palanque (522 and n. 221), and further discussion by U. Moricca, *Storia della letteratura latina cristiana* 2.1 377–79, especially 377 n. 362. See also *Joseph*, ch. 6 n. 4 below.
2 See *Joseph* 6.30–35.
3 Sister Mary Dorothea Diederich, S.S.N.D., *Vergil in the Works of St. Ambrose* (The Catholic University of America Patristic Studies 29; Washington 1931) 48.
4 The references to Philo, not cited in this volume, appear in Schenkl's CSEL edition (32.2.72–122). See also P. Courcelle, "Traditions platonicienne et chrétienne du corps-prison," *Revue des études latines* 43 (1965) 406–43, especially 413 n. 4. For an excellent study of Philo, see CHP 137–57, and 674 (bibliography).

In this work Joseph appears as "a mirror of purity"[5] and a type-figure of Christ.[6] Each action or event of his history, however slight, is invested with allegorical meaning.

Apparently neither *Joseph* as a whole nor any substantial portion of it has ever before been translated into any language.[7]

---

5 *Joseph* 1.2.
6 See especially *Joseph* 2.8: "Who is he [Joseph] before whom parents and brothers bowed down to the ground but Jesus Christ?" But similar references are pervasive in the text.
7 There is a translation of 1.1–4 in *Liturgical Readings from the Fathers of the Church: the Lessons of the Temporal Cycle and the Principal Feasts of the Sanctoral Cycle According to the Monastic Breviary* (St. Meinrad, Ind. 1943) 99–100.

JOSEPH

THE LIVES OF THE SAINTS are for the rest of men a pattern of how to live; accordingly, we are interpreting more fully the order of events set out in the Scriptures. Thus, as we come to know Abraham, Isaac, and Jacob and the other just men by our reading, we may, as it were, follow in their shining footsteps along a kind of path of blamelessness opened up to us by their virtue. While I have often preached about these patriarchs, today the story of the holy Joseph comes up.[1] Although there were many kinds of virtue in him, there shone forth above all the mark of chastity. In Abraham you have learned the undaunted devotion of faith, in Isaac the purity of a sincere heart, in Jacob the spirit's signal endurance of toils. For it is right that after the treatment of the virtues in general you should give attention to moral principles in their specific kinds. Although the former have wider application, still the latter are more precise and enter the heart the more readily, the more they have been defined and delimited.

(1.2) Therefore, let the holy Joseph be set before us as a mirror of purity. For in his character and in his actions modesty shines forth, and the splendor of grace is bright like a companion to his chastity, as it were. On that account he was loved by his parents also more than their other sons. But that fact gave rise to enmity, and this was not to be passed over in silence. (1.3) From this, then, the theme of the entire

---

1 It would appear that one of the lessons had dealt with Joseph. In speaking of his treatment of the other patriarchs, Ambrose seems to have in mind the spoken sermons that lie behind his *Isaac* and *Jacob* (both translated earlier in this volume) and his *Abraham* (on which see *Isaac,* ch. 1 n. 1).

story has come, so that we may know forthwith that the man who has been perfected is not tempted to do the wrong of avenging his suffering and does not pay back evils in return. On this account also David says, "if I have rendered to them that repay me evils."[2] What reason would there be for Joseph to deserve preference over the others if he had harmed those who harmed him and loved those who loved him? For most men do just this. But it is remarkable if one loves his enemy, as the Savior teaches.[3] Therefore, one deserves to be noticed who did this before the Gospel, who showed compassion when harmed and forgiveness when attacked, who did not repay injury when put up for sale but paid out grace for insult—the conduct we have all learned after the Gospel yet cannot observe.[4] (1.4) Therefore let us learn envy of the saints, that we may imitate their forbearance, and let us come to know that they were superior, not in nature but in insight; they were not unaware of their faults but corrected them. But if envy consumed even the saints,[5] how much more must we take care that it may not inflame sinners?

(2.5) And so we are taught the proper nature of parental love and filial gratitude. It is pleasant to love one's children and very pleasant to love them exceedingly, but often even parental love does harm to the children unless it is practiced with restraint; for it may give the beloved child free rein out of excessive indulgence or, by preference shown to one child, may alienate the others from the spirit of brotherly love. That son gains more who gains the love of his brothers. This is a more splendid manifestation of generosity on the part of the parents and a richer inheritance for the sons. Let the children be joined in a like favor, who have been joined in a like nature. Love does not know monetary profit, in which there

---

2 Ps. 7.5.
3 Cf. Matt. 5.44.
4 Other examples in Ambrose of such conduct taken from the Old Testament include Moses (*Explanatio psalmorum duodecim* 43.63) and David (*Explanation of Psalm 118* 15.15).
5 Cf. Gen. 37.4.

is a loss of love. What wonder if quarrels arise among brothers over an estate or a house, when enmity blazed up among the sons of holy Jacob over a tunic?[1] (2.6) What then? Should we find fault with Jacob because he preferred the one son to the others? But we cannot take from parents their freedom to love the more those children whom they believe to be the more deserving, nor ought we to cut off the sons from their eager desire to be the more pleasing. To be sure, Jacob loved the more that son in whom he foresaw the greater marks of virtue; thus he would not appear to have shown preference so much as father to son, but rather as prophet to a sacred sign. And Jacob was right to make for his son a tunic of many colors, to indicate by it that Joseph was to be preferred to his brothers with his clothing of manifold virtues.

(2.7) Indeed, God's grace shone on Joseph even in his boyhood. For he had a dream that when he was binding sheaves with his brothers—so it appeared to him in the vision—his sheaf rose up and stood straight, while the sheaves of his brothers turned and bowed down to his sheaf.[2] Now in this the resurrection of the Lord Jesus that was to come was revealed. When they saw Him at Jerusalem, the eleven disciples and all the saints bowed down; when they rise, they will bow down bearing the fruits of their good works, just as it is written, "Coming they shall come with joyfulness, carrying their sheaves."[3] Although his brothers disparaged the reliability of the dream out of their envy, still they expressed his interpretation of it in their own words when they replied, "Are you to be our king? Are you to rule over us?"[4] For that vision indicated the King who was to come, and before Him all flesh of human kind would bow down with bended knee.[5] (2.8) Moreover, Joseph saw another dream and told it to his father and brothers, that the sun and moon and eleven stars

1 Cf. Gen. 37.3–4.
2 Cf. Gen. 37.5–8.
3 Ps. 125 (126).6.
4 Gen. 37.8.   5 Cf. Phil. 2.10.

were bowing down to him.[6] On this account his father reproved him and said, "What will be the meaning of this vision that you have dreamed? Can it be that I and your mother and your brothers will come and bow to the ground before you?"[7] Who is He before whom parents and brothers bowed down to the ground but Jesus Christ? Joseph and His mother with the disciples bowed down before Him and confessed the true God in that body, of whom alone it was said, "Praise him, sun and moon; praise him, all you stars and light."[8] Further, what is the meaning of the father's reproach but the hardness of the people of Israel? Christ comes from them according to the flesh, but today they do not believe that He is God and are not willing to bow down to Him as their Lord, because they know that He was born from among themselves. Accordingly, they hear His replies but they do not understand them. They themselves read that the sun and moon praise Him, but they are unwilling to believe this was said with reference to Christ. Therefore, Jacob is mistaken in regard to the symbol, which refers to another, but is not mistaken in the love, which is his own. In him paternal love did not go astray, but rather there is depicted an affection for a people that was going to go astray.

(3.9) Therefore the patriarch did not refuse to believe in a dream so mighty, for in a twofold prophecy he prophesied both together; that is, he represented and personified both the just man and the people, because the Son of God was going to come to earth to be loved by just men and denied by unbelievers. And so Jacob, in sending his son to his brothers to see if it was well with the sheep,[1] foresaw the mysteries of the Incarnation that was to come. What sheep was God searching for in the concern manifested even at that time

---

6 Cf. Gen. 37.9.
7 Gen. 37.10.
8 Ps. 148.3.

---

1 Cf. Gen. 37.11–14.

by the patriarch? The very ones of whom the Lord Jesus Himself said in the Gospel, "I did not come except to the lost sheep of the house of Israel."[2] "And he sent him to Sichem,"[3] which name is interpreted as "shoulder" or "back,"[4] that is, to those who did not turn to the Lord but fled from His face and turned away, an expression properly applied to the sinner, for "Cain went out from the face of the Lord,"[5] and the psalmist says, "You will make them turn their back."[6] Now the just man does not turn away from the Lord, but runs to meet Him and says, "My eyes are ever towards the Lord."[7] And when the Lord said, "Whom shall I send?" Isaia offered himself of his own accord and said, "Behold, here I am."[8] Simeon also waited to see Christ the Lord; after he saw Him, because he had seen the Pardoner of sins and Redeemer of the whole world, he asked to be freed from the use of this flesh, just as he had been relieved of his sin, and said, "Now dismiss your servant, Lord, because my eyes have seen your salvation."[9] Zacchaeus, too, first gained the special privilege of having the Lord's commendation bestowed on him for this, that he climbed a tree to see Christ.[10] Therefore, Joseph was sent by his father to his brothers, or rather by that Father "who has not spared his own Son but has delivered him for us all,"[11] by that Father of whom it is written, "God, sending his Son in the likeness of sinful flesh."[12]

---

2 Matt. 15.24.
3 Gen. 37.14.
4 Ambrose interprets Sichem as "shoulder" or "neck" in *Abraham* 1.2.5, 2.3.8; as "shoulder" in *The Patriarchs* 3.11; and as "coming up" in *The Prayer of Job and David* 4.4.16 (the latter two translated in this volume). The interpretation as "back" does not occur elsewhere in Ambrose.
5 Gen. 4.16.
6 Ps. 20 (21).13.
7 Ps. 24 (25).15.
8 Isa. 6.8.
9 Luke 2.29–31; cf. Luke 2.21–40.
10 Luke 19.4; cf. Luke 19.1–10.
11 Rom. 8.32.
12 Rom. 8.3.

(3.10) "And Joseph was wandering about,"[13] because he could not find his brothers. And it was right that he wandered about, for he was seeking those that were going astray. Yes, "the Lord knows who are his."[14] Indeed, Jesus also, when He was wearied from His journey, sat at the well.[15] He was wearied, for He was not finding the people of God whom He was seeking; they had gone out from the face of the Lord.[16] The man who follows sin goes out from Christ; the sinner goes out, the just man enters in. Indeed, Adam hid himself as a sinner,[17] but the just man says, "Let my prayer enter in in your sight."[18] (3.11) Now Joseph found his brothers in Dothain, which means "desertion."[19] And where is the man who deserts God but in desertion? No wonder if they deserted who did not hear Him saying, "Come to me, all you who labor and are burdened, and I will give you rest."[20] Therefore Joseph came to Dothain, "and they saw him coming from afar, before he drew near to them, and they raged that they might kill him."[21] It is right that they were far off who were in desertion, and so they were raging, because Christ had not drawn near to them. For if the model of Christ had drawn near to them, they would surely have loved their brother. But they could not be near, for they were plotting fratricide. "Behold, that dreamer is coming. Now therefore come, let us kill him."[22] Were not the men who were saying such words plotting a sacrilegious fratricide, as Solomon says of them,

---

13 Gen. 37.15.
14 2 Tim. 2.19; cf. John 10.14.
15 Cf. John 4.6.
16 Cf. Gen. 4.16.
17 Cf. Gen. 3.8.
18 Ps. 87 (88).3.
19 Ambrose here translates the name "Dothain" by the word *defectio* ("desertion"). In *Flight from the World* 8.47 (translated in this volume), he uses a similar word *defectus* in the sense of "failure." Cf. Gen. 37.18.
20 Matt. 11.28.
21 Gen. 37.18.
22 Gen. 37.19–20 (Septuagint).

"Let us remove the just one, because he is profitless to us"?[23] (3.12) And in Genesis they also said, "And we shall see what will become of his dreams."[24] This is written in regard to Joseph, but it is fulfilled in regard to Christ, when the Jews said in the course of His passion, "If he is the King of Israel, let him come down now from the cross, and we will believe him. He trusts in God; let him deliver him now, if he wants him."[25] But were those brothers so unholy as to kill their brother? And from what source do the merits of the mighty patriarchs derive, so that the law designates the tribes of the entire people by their names? How are names of holiness in accord with marks of crime? In this also they served as a model of the people; their own souls were not toiling under a burden of crime. This gave rise to all the enmity and the plotting of fratricide; the enmity is by way of figure, the holiness by way of love.

(3.13) Indeed, Ruben and Juda observed the holy bonds of brotherhood and desired to free Joseph from their hands.[26] Juda receives the preference by his father's blessing, and rightly so, when it is said to him, "The sons of your father shall bow down to you. A lion's whelp is Juda and he is the expectation of nations."[27] Surely this is appropriate to Christ alone, for whom it was in store that He should be worshiped by His brothers and awaited by the nations, and that He should wash His tunic in wine by the passion of His own body, because He did not stain His flesh with any spot of sin. Aser also surely did not believe this applied to him, "Aser, his bread shall be fat and Aser himself shall be with princes."[28] And what of Joseph himself, to whom it was said, "My son

---

23 Wisd. 2.12.
24 Gen. 37.20.
25 Matt. 27.42–43.
26 Cf. Gen. 37.21–22, 26–27.
27 Gen. 49.8–10.
28 Gen. 49.20.

Joseph is to be increased, my son is to be increased, my son is envied, my young son; return to me"?[29]

Conferring together against that counsel, the brothers abused him in whom "the blessing prevailed over the blessings of the enduring mountains and was stronger than the desires of the everlasting hills."[30] Who did he understand was being prefigured in himself? Only He who surpasses the merits of all men and possesses the summit of limitless power beyond the desires of all the saints, He whom no man matches in prayer. And so, in the case of the patriarchs, enmity is repaid through grace, for they are both excused from their guilt and made holy by the gift of revelation. For it is not so much a matter of blame in having said what refers to the people as it is a matter of happiness in having seen what refers to Christ. The people assumed the character of a sinner to receive the grace of their Lord and Redeemer. Assuredly grace destroyed guilt; guilt did not diminish grace.

(3.14) And so that we may recognize that all this is a mystery in reference to the people and to the Lord Jesus, "Come, let us sell Joseph to the Ismaelites."[31] What is the interpretation of the name Joseph? Only that it means "God's grace" and "expression of God the Highest."[32] And so who is being sold? Only that man who "since he was in the form of God, thought it not robbery to be equal with God, but emptied himself, taking the form of a servant."[33] And we would not have bought Him, unless His own people had sold Him. The sale was bad, the purchase worse. They sold him to traders; the latter bought a good fragrance from traitors. Juda sold him, the Ismaelites bought him,[34] and in our tongue their name means "holding their own God in hatred." Therefore we find that Joseph was bought for twenty gold

---

29 Gen. 49.22.
30 Gen. 49.26.
31 Gen. 37.27.
32 Cf. *Joseph* 14.84, where the name is interpreted as "the witness and interpreter of the Godhead."
33 Phil. 2.6–7.   34 Cf. Gen. 37.25–28; Matt. 26.14–15; 27.5–6.

pieces by one account, for twenty-five by another, and thirty
by another, because Christ is not valued at the same price
by all men.[35] To some He is worth less, to others more. The
faith of the buyer determines the increase in the price. To one
who is more pious, God is more valuable; to a sinner a Redeemer is more valuable. He is also more valuable to the man
who has more grace. But He is more valuable as well to the
man to whom many things have been given, because he loves
more to whom more has been forgiven. The Lord Himself
said just this in the Gospel in reference to the woman who
poured ointment over His feet and bathed them with her
tears and wiped them with her hair and dried them with her
kisses. Of her He says to Simon, "Wherefore I say to you,
her sins, many as they are, have been forgiven her, because
she has loved much. But he to whom less is forgiven, loves
less."[36]

Sometimes differences in price contain an expression not
only of amount but also of value, as you have in the case of
the ointment which the Lord said had been poured out for
His burial.[37] It is written that Judas said, "This could have
been sold for three hundred denarii,"[38] a number that seems
to have conveyed the meaning not of an amount, but of the
cross. Likewise, here too the difference as between twenty or
thirty pieces of gold or silver contains an indication of a fulfillment attained by doubling or tripling. For the twenty-five
gold pieces are [doubled] the years of jubilee, which is the
number [fifty] of forgiveness,[39] and they mean a very valuable
portion. Here too, so that you may note the symbolic repre-
sentation of the Lord's passion, the patriarch Juda says, "Let
us sell Joseph to the Ismaelites and let not our hands be laid

---

35 Cf. Gen. 37.28, where Septuagint and Vulgate agree on twenty pieces
   of silver as the price.
36 Luke 7.47.
37 Cf. Matt. 26.12.
38 Mark 14.5; John 12.5.
39 Cf. Lev. 25.10.

upon him,"[40] and earlier he had done well to say, "Do not lay hands upon him,"[41] which is what the Jews said in the Lord's passion, "It is not lawful for us to put anyone to death."[42] Thus the word of Jesus could be fulfilled, signifying by what death He was going to die.[43] (3.15) Accordingly, even at that time, the cross that was to come was prefigured in sign; and at the same time that He was stripped of His tunic,[44] that is, of the flesh He took on, He was stripped of the handsome diversity of colors that represented the virtues. Therefore His tunic, that is, His flesh, was stained with blood, but not His divinity; and His enemies were able to take from Him His covering of flesh, but not His immortal life. The wild beasts of Judea stained this tunic with blood,[45] those wild beasts of whom the Lord says, "Behold, I send you forth as lambs in the midst of wolves."[46] (3.16) As for the pit being dry,[47] what wonder if the pit of the Jews does not have water? For they abandoned the fountain of living water and made for themselves broken pits.[48] And so that you may know that this mystery is true, the Lord Himself says of Himself, "They have laid me in the lower pit, in the dark places and in the shadow of death."[49]

(3.17) Now they buy Christ who bring good fragrances,[50] the incense with which the altars of a devoted heart are ablaze (on this account David also says, in the Greek, "Let my prayer be directed as incense in your sight,"[51]) and cement,[52]

---

40 Gen. 37.27.   41 Gen. 37.22.   42 John 18.31.
43 Cf. John 18.32.
44 Cf. Gen. 37.23; John 19.23–24.
45 Cf. Gen. 37.31–33.
46 Luke 10.3.
47 Cf. Gen. 37.24.
48 Cf. Jer. 2.13.
49 Ps. 87 (88).7.
50 Cf. Gen. 37.25; 2 Cor. 2.15–16.
51 Ps. 140 (141).2; Ambrose actually presents the verse in Greek.
52 Throughout this passage Ambrose plays on the Latin word, *resina*, which can mean both "cement" and "balm." Cf. Gen. 37.25, and see ch. 9.46, below.

too, with which broken stones are joined together. It is a spiritual cement to make whole the break in your soul, to bind together what was torn apart, to make fast what was loosened. For this spiritual cement strengthens and adjusts the members of the soul that were broken up, in a sense, so that they may be joined together without harm. Indeed Jeremia seeks this, so that he may attempt to heal Babylon, if he can, for he says, "Take balm for her corruption, if in any way she will be healed. We have cared for Babylon, and she has not been healed."[53] The synagogue has not been healed, because that balm has passed to the Church. Therefore the traders came from Galaad,[54] that is, from their possession of or dwelling in the law, and brought their wares 'o the Church, so that that balm might heal the sins of the nations. Of them it is said, "Be strong, you hands that are feeble and you knees that are without strength."[55] The balm is unspoiled faith. Such a faith Peter exhibited, when he said to the lame man, "In the name of Jesus Christ of Nazareth arise and walk."[56] And he arose and walked, as was right. Such a faith Peter had when he said to the paralytic, "Aeneas, the Lord Jesus heals you; get up and make your bed."[57] And he got up and made his bed. Such a faith he had when he said to the dead woman, "Arise in the name of our Lord Jesus Christ."[58] And the departed woman arose. With the mortar made from this cement those stones are fastened together from which God is able to raise up children to Abraham.[59] With the medicine made from this balm the lame man is made straight, the paralytic is healed, the dead woman is revived.

---

53 Jer. 51.8–9.
54 Cf. Gen. 37.25.
55 Isa. 35.3 (Septuagint).
56 Acts 3.6; cf. Acts 3.1–11.
57 Acts 9.34.
58 Acts 9.40.
59 Cf. Matt. 3.9.

(3.18) Now the fact that they sprinkled his tunic with the blood of a goat[60] seems to have this meaning, that they attacked with false testimony[61] and brought into enmity for sin Him who forgives the sins of all men. For us there is a lamb, for them a goat.[62] For us the Lamb of God has been killed, who took from us the sins of the world, whereas for them a goat piled up sins and amassed offenses. Therefore, "fill up the measure of your fathers."[63] And Jacob rightly lamented the losses to his posterity; as a father he wept for his lost son[64] and as a prophet he mourned the destruction of the Jews. Indeed, he also tore his clothing, and we read that that was done in the passion of the Lord Jesus by the chief priest, who exercised not a private role but an office with a public function.[65] The curtain of the temple was also torn,[66] so that it might be made clear by such signs that the mysteries had been profaned, the people stripped of the garments of salvation, and that the kingdom had been divided and was to be destroyed, because every divided kingdom will easily be destroyed.[67] And it really was divided, when that which was Christ's began at that time to be the devil's. For those who separated the Son from the Father could not remain undivided.

(4.19) Accordingly, Joseph was sold, led into Egypt, and bought by the chief of the cooks.[1] The person who cooks the raw food so that souls may dine on the sweet taste of faith is not superfluous, for no food is more pleasant than knowledge and teaching. Previously there existed in Egypt a raw unbelief, and no flame of the awareness of God, no desire for

---

60 Cf. Gen. 37.31.
61 Cf. Matt. 26.59–61.
62 Cf. John 1.19; Exod. 12.4–5.
63 Matt. 23.32.
64 Cf. Gen. 37.34.
65 Cf. *ibid.;* Matt. 26.65.
66 Cf. Matt. 27.51.
67 Cf. Matt. 12.25.

---

1 Cf. Gen. 37.36; 39.1.

true knowledge, had made it tender, no fiery words of the Lord had cooked it.[2] Now Joseph was sold in Egypt because Christ was going to come to those to whom it was said, "It was for your sins that you were sold,"[3] and thus He redeemed with His own blood those that had been sold by their own sins. But Christ was sold because He took our condition upon Himself, not our fault; He is not held to the price of sin, because He Himself did not commit sin.[4] And so He made a contract at a price for our debt, not for money for Himself; He took away the debtor's bond,[5] set aside the moneylender, freed the debtor. He alone paid what was owed by all. It was not permitted us to go out from bondage.[6] He undertook this on our behalf, so that He might drive away the slavery of the world, restore the liberty of paradise, and grant new grace through the honor we received by His sharing of our nature. This is by way of mystery.

(4.20) But as for what pertains to the moral interpretation, because our God wishes all men to be saved,[7] through Joseph He also gave consolation to those who are in slavery, and He gave them instruction. Even in the lowliest status, men should learn that their character can be superior and that no state of life is devoid of virtue if the soul of the individual knows itself. The flesh is subject to slavery, not the spirit, and many humble servants are more free than their masters, if in their condition of slavery they consider that they should abstain from the works of a slave. Every sin is slavish, while blamelessness is free. On this account the Lord also says, "Everyone who commits sin is a slave of sin."[8] Indeed, how is each greedy man not a slave, seeing that he auctions himself off for a very tiny sum of money? The man who has

---

2 Cf. Ps. 17 (18).31; 118 (119).140.
3 Isa. 50.1.
4 Cf. 2 Cor. 5.21.
5 Cf. Col. 2.14.
6 Cf. Vergil, *Eclogues* 1.40 for similarity of wording.
7 Cf. 1 Tim. 2.4.
8 John 8.34.

piled up what he is not going to use is afraid that he may lose all that he has piled up; the more numerous his acquisitions, the greater the risk he will run in keeping them. How is he not a beggar who considers his possessions small? For although he seems rich to me, in his own view he is in want, and one who does not know how to trust that which he desires does not gain consolation for his wishes by proofs. Moreover, how is that man who is subject to lust not also a slave? First he blazes with his own fires, and he is burnt up by the torches within his own breast. To such men the prophet rightly says, "Walk in the light of your own fire and in the flame that you have kindled."[9] Fear takes hold of them all and lies in wait for each one when he is asleep; so that he may gain control over one object of desire, a man becomes the slave of them all. The man who makes his own masters is the slave to a wretched slavery indeed, for he wishes to have masters that he may fear; indeed, nothing is so characteristic of slavery as the constant fear. But that man, whatever his servile status, will always be free who is not seduced by love or held by the chains of greed or bound by fear of reproach, who looks to the present with tranquillity and is not afraid of the future. Doesn't it seem to you that a man of the latter kind is the master even in slavery, while one of the former kind is a slave even in liberty? Joseph was a slave, Pharao a ruler; the slavery of the one was happier than the sovereignty of the other. Indeed, all Egypt would have collapsed from famine unless Pharao had made his sovereignty subject to the counsel of a mere servant.[10]

(4.21) Therefore, lowly servants have grounds on which they may glory; Joseph also was a servant. Those who have passed from freedom into slavery through some exigency have a source of consolation. They have something to imitate, so that they may learn that their status can change,

---

9 Isa. 50.11.
10 Cf. Gen. 41.55–56.

but not their character; that among household servants there
is liberty and that in servitude there is constancy. Masters
have something to hope for through good and humble servants. Abraham found a wife for his son through a servant of
his household.[11] The Lord blessed the Egyptian's house on
account of Joseph, and the blessing of the Lord was granted
to all his property both in house and in fields.[12] "And he entrusted all things whatsoever were his into the hands of Joseph."[13] We note that what the masters could not govern,
mere servants governed.

(5.22) But why should I enlarge on arrangements that
pertained to a private house in the case of that slave who
ruled an empire? It counts for still more that he earlier
ruled himself; although he was comely to look upon and
very handsome in appearance, he did not direct the charm
of his countenance toward another's wrongdoing but kept it
to win grace for himself.[1] He thought that he would be the
more attractive, if he were proved more handsome not by
the loss of his chastity but by the cultivation of modesty. That
is the true beauty that does not seduce the eyes of others or
wound their fragile hearts but gains the approval of all men;
it will do harm to none but win praise for itself. Now if any
woman gazes with wanton eyes, the sin is attributable only
to her who cast the wicked glance, not to him who did not
wish to be looked upon with wicked intent, and there is
no guilt in the fact that he was looked upon. It was not
within the power of a mere servant not to be looked upon;
the husband should have been on his guard against the roving eyes of his wife. If the husband had no fear in regard
to his spouse, Joseph thought it to be evidence of her chastity,
not the permissiveness of neglect. Still, let men also learn to

---

11 Cf. Gen. 24.
12 Cf. Gen. 39.5.
13 Gen. 39.6.

1 Cf. Gen. 39.6–7.

guard against the roving eyes of women; even those men who do not wish to be loved are very much loved. Indeed, Joseph was very much loved, although he rejected the lover. And Scripture did well to absolve him, for it said, "The wife of his master cast eyes on Joseph";[2] that is, he did not show himself or take her unawares, but she cast her nets and was captured in her encircling of him, she spread her snares and stuck fast in her own bonds.

(5.23) Further, she said to him, "Lie with me."[3] The first weapons of the adulteress are those of the eyes, the second those of words, but one who is not seduced by the eyes can resist the word. A defense is at hand when the passions are still free. And so it is written that "he refused."[4] Therefore he first overcame her attack through a struggle in his heart and drove her back with the shield of his soul, so to speak; then he launched his word like a spear to force her retreat. "And he spoke to the wife of his master."[5] She is correctly called the wife of the master, and not the mistress of the house, for she could not extort what she wanted to obtain. For how was she the mistress? She did not have the power of one who rules, she did not observe the discipline of a mistress, she provided mere servants with enticements to lust. But he was a master who did not take up the torches of that lover, did not feel the bonds of that seducer, was not terrified by any fear of death, and preferred to die free of sin rather than to choose participation in guilty power. He was free who believed it shameful not to make recompense for favor. Indeed, he does not make his excuses as a frightened man nor is he on his guard as one fearful of danger. Rather, he flees the charge of ingratitude and the stain of sin as one who owes a debt to his master's kindness and his own blamelessness, and, as a just man, he is terrified of the con-

---

2 Gen. 39.7.
3 *Ibid.*
4 Gen. 39.8.
5 *Ibid.*

tagion of guilt. The adulteress threw her third dart by the persistency of her invitation, but Joseph did not listen to her.[6] After the first words, one has something to guard against. Lust is not only impure, but insolent, demanding, and wanton as well, and the adulteress has respect for nothing. She who felt no sorrow at her first loss of modesty lies in wait to perform her seduction.

(5.24) Finally, when Joseph went in by reason of his duty and the office entrusted to him, and the witnesses and household servants were far off,[7] she seized him and said, "Lie with me."[8] He is absolved by the testimony of Scripture, because he was unable to abandon the service entrusted to him by his master. Indeed, it is not enough that he entered the inside of his house without concern as one who could not be seduced; the just man had an obligation to take care not to give opportunity to a woman in a state of frenzy, else she might be undone by his sin. But while he perceived that the wife of his master was his adversary, still he had to guard against giving offense to his master by neglecting his duty. At the same time, he supposed her forwardness still consisted in speech, not in laying hands on him. (5.25) He is absolved for having entered in and praised for having slipped away; he did not value the clothing of his body higher than the chastity of his soul. He left the clothing, which the adulteress held back in her hands, as if it were not his,[9] and considered foreign to him the garments that the impure woman had been able to touch and seize. He was, after all, a great man; although sold, he did not know the nature of a slave; although much loved, he did not love in return; although asked, he did not acquiesce; although seized, he fled away. When he was approached by his master's wife, he could be held by his garment but not seduced in his soul. He did not endure even

---

6 Cf. Gen. 39.10.
7 Cf. Gen. 39.11–12.
8 Gen. 39.12.
9 Cf. ibid.

her words for long, either, because he judged it to be a contagion if he should delay very long; else the incentives to lust
might pass over to him through the hands of the adulteress.
Therefore he stripped off his garment and cast off the sin.
He left behind the clothing by which he was held, and fled
away, stripped to be sure, but not naked, because he was
covered better by the covering of modesty. Yes, a man is not
naked unless guilt has made him naked.

Indeed, we learn in earlier passages that Adam, after he
abandoned God's commandments through his transgression
and contracted the debts of a grievous sin, was naked.[10] On
this account he himself also says, "I heard your voice in the
garden, and I was afraid, because I was naked, and I hid myself."[11] For he knew that he was naked, seeing that he had
lost the marks of God's protection. Accordingly, he remained
in hiding because he did not have the garment of faith which
he had put aside by his transgression. You are looking at a
remarkable fact. The one man was naked, who did not lose
his tunic; the other, who stripped himself of his clothing
which he left in the hands of the adulteress, was not naked.
The same Scripture stated that the one was naked but denied
that the other was. And so, Joseph stripped himself but did
not make himself naked; he kept the uncorrupted garments
of virtue, but he stripped himself of the old man with his
actions so that he might put on the new, who is being renewed in perfect knowledge according to the image of his
Creator.[12] But Adam remained naked; he could not clothe
himself again, once he had been stripped of the unique clothing of virtue. On this account he received a tunic of skins,[13]
because a sinner could not possess a spiritual one. So, then,
Joseph left his clothing behind and laid bare the shameless-

---

10 Cf. Gen. 3.7.
11 Gen. 3.10.
12 Cf. Col. 3.9–10.
13 Cf. Gen. 3.21.

ness of the adulteress, which could not afterward be concealed.

(5.26) Indeed, he went out of doors while she spread the news of the temptation that arose from her own adultery; she said in a loud voice that the Hebrew had fled and left his garment behind.[14] Thus she revealed what she should have concealed, so as to do harm to an innocent man by inventing a crime. But the just man Joseph did not know how to make accusation, and so the impure woman accomplished this with impunity. Therefore I might say that she was the one who had really been stripped, although she was keeping the clothing of another. She had lost all the coverings of chastity, whereas he was sufficiently provided for and protected; his voice was not heard, and yet his blamelessness spoke for itself. So later, although silent at her trial, Susanna gave the better speech in prophecy and thus merited to be defended by the prophet, while she did not seek the help of her own voice.[15] Therefore I might say Joseph was happier, when he was put into prison, because he was giving witness on behalf of chastity. For modesty is a good gift, but one of lesser merit when it involves no risk; where, however, it is maintained at the risk of one's safety, there it wins a more abundant crown. With his case unheard, his truthfulness unexamined, Joseph is sent into prison as if guilty of a crime;[16] but the Lord did not abandon him even in prison. The innocent should not be troubled when they are attacked on false charges, when justice is overcome and they are shoved into prison. God visits His own even in prison, and so there is more help for them there, where there is more danger.

(5.27) But what wonder if Christ visits those that lie in prison? He reminds us that He Himself was shut up in prison in His followers, as you find it written, "I was in prison, and

---

14 Cf. Gen. 39.12–18.
15 Cf. Dan. 13.
16 Cf. Gen. 39.19–20.

you did not come to me."[17] Where does God's mercy not enter in? Joseph found favor of this sort; he that had been shut up in the prison kept the locks of the prison, while the jailer withdrew from his post and entrusted all the prisoners to his power.[18] Consequently Joseph did not suffer from prison but even gave relief to others as well from the calamity of imprisonment.

(6.28) The initiator of this injustice is a woman, and eunuchs appear.[1] But the woman is one of the Egyptian women, who are accustomed to banter wanton words with their men, to arouse men who are modest, to pursue those who flee, to be very insistent with those who have a sense of shame. When she could not protect her own vices, she accused the innocent; she joined deceit to deceit, held on to the possessions of others, herself condemned others, and set no limit to her fury. Whatever was the reason for her cruelty? Only that she saw that her cravings were meeting with resistance and her forbidden desires were being frustrated of receiving consent. See the reason why the prison opens—to admit the innocent; why criminals are freed of their chains—that these may be put on the faithful; why falsifiers of the truth are let go—that one who refused to falsify his trust may be locked in.

(6.29) What can I say in regard to those eunuchs? They ought to serve as an example to other eunuchs that their standing is fragile and weak and all their hope lies in the will of the king; for them a slight offense is a very great danger, while prosperity is a paltry condition of service. One boasted because he was the chief butler, the other because he was the chief baker. Both committed offenses, were put into prison, and were entrusted to the holy Joseph by the jailer of the prison.[2] When they were there several days, they saw a

---

17 Matt. 25.43.
18 Cf. Gen. 39.21–23.

1 Cf. Gen. 40.1.
2 Cf. Gen. 40.1–4.

dream. When Joseph went to see them again, he found them downcast and troubled in spirit, because they were troubled by the dream and could not discover anyone to interpret it. But he said, "Is not the interpretation of a dream through God? Therefore tell it to me." "And the chief butler told his dream: 'There was a vine in my sight, and on the vine there were three branches; it blossomed and sent out buds, and the clusters of grapes were ripe and the cup of Pharao was in my hand. And I took the grapes and squeezed them into the cup and gave the cup into the hands of Pharao.' And Joseph said to him, 'The three branches are three days. Three days still, and Pharao will remember your service and restore you to your former office and you will give the cup into Pharao's hands. But remember me by your own case, when it shall be well with you, and you will do me a kindness and remember me to Pharao and take me from this prison, because I was stolen from the land of the Hebrews and here I have done nothing evil, but still they have cast me into the dungeon of this prison.' "[3]

(6.30) I do not choose to speak of the dream of the other man. You surely remember my words, that even then I avoided its interpretation in the case of one from whose end I shy away, at whose death I shudder.[4] Rather, let us speak of him who thought he was happy since he was chief butler and believed that this was the summit and crown of all power, that he would give the cup to the king. This was his glory, this was his grandeur in this world; when he was deprived of this he felt sorrow, and when he was restored to it he re-

---

3 Gen. 40.8–15.
4 The allusion here is to the eunuch Calligonus, a Syrian and grand chamberlain to the Emperor Valentinian II. Calligonus had threatened Ambrose with death in 385 or 386 in the course of the dispute over the Arian attempt to gain possession of Ambrose's basilica in Milan, but after two years he himself had fallen into disfavor and was executed. See the letter of Ambrose to his sister Marcellina, translated as No. 60 by Sister M. Melchior Beyenka, *Saint Ambrose: Letters* (FOTC 26). See also Augustine, *Contra Iulianum Pelagianum* 6.14.41 and, for a brief account, Dudden 683 and nn. 13, 14.

joiced. But this is a dream, and all worldly power is a dream, not a reality. To be sure, he saw by way of a dream that his preeminent position was restored to him. Isaia also says that men of this kind are such as take delight in prosperity in this world.[5] A man who eats and drinks in his sleep thinks he is filled with food and drink, but when he awakens, he begins to be more hungry; then he understands how insubstantial were that dreamer's food and drink. Just so, a man who is asleep in this world and does not open his eyes to the mysteries of God, as long as he is in a deep corporeal sleep, supposes that such worldly power is of some importance, seeing it, as it were, in his dreams. But when he has awakened, he discovers how insubstantial the pleasure of this world is.

(6.31) Look now upon that true Hebrew, the interpreter not of a dream but of reality and of a signal vision. He came from the fullness of divinity and the liberty of heavenly grace into this prison of the body.[6] The allurement of this world could work no change in Him, no corrupt and worldly pleasure could subvert Him, and although tempted He did not fall. Although attacked, He did not attack; at the last, when He was grasped by His bodily garment by the adulterous hand of the synogogue, as it were, He stripped off the flesh and ascended free of death. The harlot made false accusation when she could not hold Him; but the prison did not frighten Him and hell did not hold Him. Yes, He delivered others even from that place where He had descended as if for punishment. Where the bonds of death were drawn tight for Him, even there He loosened the bonds of the dead.

(6.32) Look, therefore, on that Hebrew as he says to the chief of the eunuchs, who had incurred the displeasure of the king but had been restored to his post, "Remember me by

---

5 Cf. Isa. 29.8.
6 Cf. Col. 2.9, and, for the influential concept of the body as a prison of the soul, P. Courcelle, "Traditions platonicienne et chrétienne du corps-prison," *Revue des études latines* 43 (1965) 406–43, especially 426 and n. 6.

your own case, when it shall be well with you, and you will
do me a kindness and remember me."[7] He made his request
a second time for this reason, because he knew that the
other would not remember what harm he had escaped, when
he had regained power. And so Joseph reminded him a second time, because he freed him a second time. Thus, if the
recollection of the earlier kindness did not have a hold on
him, at least the remembrance of the later one would present
itself, and that man would not scorn the author of his deliverance or do violence to him out of treacherous deceit. But
what is worse, forgetfulness of the kindness swiftly stole in
in time of prosperity. The butler, once restored to his post,
did not remember the interpreter of his dream but forgot
about him.[8] But even though he forgot, Christ did not
forget but spoke to the butler, yes, spoke to him through a
mere servant and said, "Remember me by your own case,"
that is, "Remember what you have heard in regard to your
office. But even though you have forgotten now, you will remember me to get out of a danger, while you forgot a kindness." Nevertheless, when he was raised up in power, he did
not remember. Yet how important was this power, the charge
of the wine? See the basis of all his boasting—that he was
chief of the eunuchs who supplied the wine for the cups
of the king!

(6.33) "And it happened after two years."[9] Unless I am mistaken about this period of time involving our enunch, it
was two years even to the day. After the two years he had
regained his office, but he did not remember, even though
he had been reminded. For he came to know that the kingdom itself, even, was a dream in this world, whereas he had
not believed his own dream. He learned also that kings have
dreams and that not even their powers are universal.[10] But let

---

7 Gen. 40.14.   8 Cf. Gen. 40.23.   9 Gen. 41.1 (Septuagint).
10 Schenkl sees a lacuna here and suggests "that the gifts (or benefactions) of kings are mere dreams." No lacuna appears in the PL text,
   however.

me pass over this subject in sorrow, lest it grow worse with the mere mention of it; it does not please me to recall that discourse of mine which I poured forth in my sorrow at that time and which was forced from me by the outrage done upon the church.

(6.34) Now then, the butler was reminded of his own dream through the dream of the king and said, "I remember my sin."[11] That confession was late indeed, but would it were true. After committing sin, you confess what you should have avoided before you committed sin. How swiftly you had forgotten, "Remember me."[12] Of course you know that this word was spoken at that time, but you had ears blunted by the arrogance of power, and being drunk with wine, you did not hear the words of sobriety. Even now, "remember me," you that confess your sin late. You that inquire of the mere servant, why do you deny the Master? Now be drunk, not with wine, but with the Holy Spirit. Remember what he suffered, with whom you slept your sleep and dreamed your dream.[13] He too was a chief, and chief over the royal banquets, which were part of the work of the bakers.[14] He believed that he was exalted because he had in his power the king's bread; he did not know that such power took many turns. He threatened others, although he was shortly to be given over to the extreme penalty himself, and he did not listen to Joseph, who spoke prophecy even though he was only a humble servant of the Lord. The prophecy was that he was going to lose his head at the command of that king in whose regard he flattered himself so very much, and he was to be left as food for the birds.[15] At least this example should restrain you from giving credence to unbelief.

(6.35) There are also other examples of the arrogance and

---

11 Gen. 41.9.
12 Gen. 40.14.
13 Cf. Ps. 75 (76).6.
14 Cf. Gen. 40.16.
15 Cf. Gen. 40.16–19.

weakness of the servants of kings which are exhibited in the history of later times. Doeg too was a chief, and chief over the king's animals for the training of the mules, that is, the impotent animals.[16] He also accused the priest of the Lord and roused the king by treachery to the peril of the priest— and he was a Syrian.[17] Am I in error, when his birthplace accords with his deeds? Aman also was himself a chamberlain of the king, while he strove with unbounded audacity to invade the churches of the Lord and to plunder and persecute a faithful people, but he paid for his sacrilegious acts with severe punishments.[18]

(7.36) But let us return to the chief butler. Like one drunk with much wine, he forgot his benefactor for a long time, but finally he disclosed the sequence of events, not out of gratitude, but out of calculation, so that he might furnish the king with an interpreter.[1] When he learned of this, the king also ordered Joseph to be summoned; when the latter had been brought out of prison, Pharao asked if he could interpret a dream for him.[2] Pleased with his explanation, the king undid the injustice and conferred office upon him. See then whether those events are not in accord with present occurrences. Injustice was committed before it could be recognized by the king, whereas favor was restored when Joseph was recognized by the king. Thus the king is free of guilt, because the injury which that holy man suffered was done by another, while the favor he received belonged to the king.[3] (7.37) Now the dream and its interpretation are as follows, "God has revealed to Pharao whatsover he is doing. The seven good cows are seven

---

16 Cf. 1 Kings 21.7.
17 Cf. 1 Kings 22.18, and, for the allusion to Calligonus, n. 4, above.
18 Cf. Esth. 3.1, 8, 9; 7.10, and also n. 4, above.

1 Cf. Gen. 41.9–13.
2 Cf. Gen. 41.14–15.
3 Dudden, p. 683, suggests that ". . . in the passage where Pharaoh is exculpated of blame for the persecution of Joseph, we may detect a politic allusion to Valentinian II. . ." See ch. 6 n. 4, above.

years, and the seven good ears are seven years. The dream of Pharao is one. And the seven lean cows, which came up after them, are seven years, and the seven lean ears destroyed by the wind are seven years. There will be famine in seven years. This is the thing which I have said, 'God has revealed to Pharao whatsoever he is doing,' behold seven years are coming of great plenty for the whole land of Egypt; but after these there will come seven years of famine and they will forget the plenty in all Egypt. And the famine will consume the whole land and the plenty of the land will not be known by reason of the famine which is going to come after these things; for it will be very great. And inasmuch as Pharao repeated the dream a second time, it is because the thing from God will be true and God will hasten to do it."[4]

(7.38) The dream is old, the events are fresh.[5] The earlier stores were consumed by the later years; where before there was abundance and plenty, in that place there developed a lack of all supplies. Had anyone given the king counsel of this sort, that he should keep some of the earlier plenty for the later years of his reign, a liberal and profuse quantity of supplies would have overflowed for distribution in the time that awaited. But even the limitless outpouring of the earlier period left the later years destitute, and men who were plundering all things did not desire to have recourse to a certain Joseph. And yet did not I, Joseph—for who is the speaker?— shout still that those fat cows were a sign, not only of wantonness, but, as well, of neglect of the reverence due God? For in regard to unbelievers it is said, "Fat bulls have besieged me,"[6] and in regard to the people of the Jews it is written, "He grew fat and gross and corpulent and forsook God who made him."[7] Therefore that dream of worldly

4 Gen. 41.25–32.
5 Another allusion to Calligonus and the Arian attempt to gain control of Ambrose's basilica. See ch. 6 n. 4, above.
6 Ps. 21 (22).13.
7 Deut. 32.15.

superabundance could not last forever; there would be a time
when severe famine would come upon them.

(7.39) And yet I judge that this dream was not revealed
only to one or two but was set out before all men for this
reason, because the seven years of this world that are fat and
sleek with worldly plenty are swallowed up by those ages to
come in which there will be everlasting repose and the observance of the spiritual law. Among the fathers, that tribe
of Ephraim, rich in God, keeps such observance like a good
heifer, not taut in the udder of the body but abundant in
spiritual milk[8] and grace. God says that He sits upon her
beautiful neck, as is written, "Ephraim is a heifer taught to
love victory, but I passed over upon her beautiful neck."[9]
Accordingly, let not the oil of the sinner anoint our head,[10]
and false fruits ought not to delight us; else it may be said
also of us, "You have planted wickedness and gathered in its
iniquities. You have eaten false fruit because you have trusted
in your chariots."[11] And it does not trouble me that such a one
has lean ears and ears destroyed by the wind, because David
also was a better man at the time when he was wasting away
like a spider,[12] and a sacrifice to God is an afflicted spirit.[13]
Those men turn out better whom the wicked spirit has tried in
this world with severe wrongs.

(7.40) On this account I think that Joseph merited rewards that were more mystical, because he spoke concerning
mystical things. For what is the meaning of the ring that was
put upon his finger?[14] Only this, that we may understand that
the pontificate of faith was bestowed on him so that he could
himself seal others. What of the robe, which is the garment
of wisdom?[15] Only this, that preeminence in wisdom was

---

8 Cf. Vergil, *Eclogues* 4.21.
9 Osee 10.11.
10 Cf. Ps. 140 (141).5; 22 (23).5.
11 Osee 10.13.
12 Cf. Ps. 38 (39).12.
13 Cf. Ps. 50 (51).9.
14 Cf. Gen. 41.42.   15 Cf. *ibid.*

granted to him by the King of Heaven. The chain of gold[16] appears to represent good understanding; the chariot[17] too signifies the exalted height of merit. Now who is he who took a wife from the Gentiles but He who gathered a Church for Himself from the nations? And from her He received His son Manasse, through whom He forgot all His sufferings,[18] which He experienced from the sacrileges of the Jews. He received also another son, Ephraim, through whose growth[19] it became clear that the reception of a lowly condition in the flesh did not lower divinity but made an increase in glory.

(7.41) Indeed, anyone who was suffering from famine was sent to Joseph.[20] Who are these people? Those of whom it is said, "They shall return at evening, and shall suffer hunger like dogs."[21] Now there was famine, not in one locality alone, but over the whole land, because there was no one to do good. Therefore the Lord Jesus, taking pity on the hungers of the world, opened His granaries[22] and disclosed the hidden treasures of the heavenly mysteries, of wisdom and of knowledge, so that none would lack for nourishment. For Wisdom said, "Come, eat my bread,"[23] and only the man who is filled with Christ can say, "The Lord feeds me, and I shall want nothing."[24] Therefore Christ opened His granaries and sold, while asking not monetary payments but the price of faith and the recompense of devotion. He sold, moreover, not to a few men in Judea, but sold to all men so that He might be believed by all peoples.

(7.42) "And all countries came into Egypt to buy of Joseph."[25] Yes, the famine had taken hold of them. For all men

---

16 Cf. *ibid.*
17 Cf. Gen. 41.43.
18 Cf. Gen. 41.51.
19 Cf. Gen. 41.52.
20 Cf. Gen. 41.55.
21 Ps. 58 (59).7.
22 Cf. Gen. 41.56.
23 Prov. 9.5.
24 Ps. 22 (23).1.
25 Gen. 41.57.

that have not been fed by Christ are hungry. And so let us
buy the nourishment with which we can avert famine. Let no
one hold back out of consideration of his poverty, let no
one who does not have money be afraid. Christ does not ask
money, but faith, which is more valuable than money. Indeed Peter, who did not have money, bought Him. "Silver
and gold I do not have," he said, "but what I have I give you.
In the name of Jesus Christ arise and walk."[26] And the
prophet Isaia says, "All you who are thirsty, come to the
water, and you that have no money come, buy, and drink and
eat without money and without the price of the wine."[27] For
He who paid the price of His blood for us did not ask a price
from us, because He redeemed us not with gold or silver but
with His precious blood.[28] Therefore you owe that price with
which you have been bought. Even though He does not always
demand it, you still owe it. Buy Christ for yourself, then,
not with what few men possess, but with what all men
possess by nature but few offer on account of fear. What
Christ claims from you is His own. He gave His life for all
men, He offered His death for all men. Pay on behalf of your
Creator what you are going to pay by law. He is not bargained for at a slight price, and not all men see Him readily.
Indeed, those virgins in the Gospel whom the bridegroom kept
out upon his coming, were left out of doors exactly because
they did not buy the oil that was for sale.[29] On this account
it is said to them, "Go rather to those who sell it and buy
some for yourselves."[30] Likewise that merchant deserves praise
who sold all his goods and bought the pearl.[31]

(8.43) And Jacob said to his sons, "Why are you idle? Behold, I have heard that there is grain in Egypt. Go down

---

26 Acts 3.6.
27 Isa. 55.1.
28 Cf. 1 Peter 1.18–19. References to man as purchased by Christ occur
   elsewhere in the New Testament; cf. 1 Cor. 6.19–20, 7.23, and Acts
   20.28 (of the Church).
29 Cf. Matt. 25.1–13.
30 Matt. 25.9.
31 Cf. Matt. 13.45–46.

there and buy food for us."[1] This is not something Jacob said
one time; he says it daily to his sons who come to Christ's
grace too late, "Why are you idle? Behold, I have heard that
there is grain in Egypt." From this grain there comes the grain
that rises again.[2] And so whoever suffers famine ought to
attribute it to his own sloth. "Behold, I have heard that there
is grain in Egypt." Generally, indeed, younger men hear of
something more quickly than their elders, for many of the
former travel about and are engaged out of doors. But an old
man is the first to hear of *this* business matter, yet an old man
who has lived to a great age in faith, an old man whose old
age is worthy of respect, and the time of his old age is a
spotless life.[3] (8.44) Nor does everyone undertake this business matter, but only the sons of Jacob and only those sons
of more mature age. Thus ten sons go, whereas the youngest
son does not go.[4] The father did not send him; else "infirmity may befall him."[5] Benjamin, the youngest, was still
subject to infirmity. Granted, the name Benjamin the
patriarch is read, but Paul, who was of the tribe of Benjamin,[6]
was being prefigured. Jacob was right to hesitate over his infirmity. Indeed he was made infirm so that he could be healed.
He suffered blindness, but this was an infirmity unto salvation.[7]

(8.45) Yes, that blindness brought him light. We have received the story; let us come to know the mystery. The patriarchs had gone at first without Benjamin, and the Apostles
without Paul. Each came, not as the first, but was summoned
by those who were the first, and by his arrival he made the
goods of those who were first more plenteous. "There is grain

---

1 Gen. 42.1–2.
2 Cf. John 12.24–25.
3 Cf. Wisd. 4.8–9.
4 Cf. Gen. 42.3.
5 Gen. 42.4.
6 Cf. Rom. 11.1.
7 Cf. Acts 9.8–9.

in Egypt"; that is, where the famine is greater, the plenty is greater. There is much grain in Egypt. Surely, and God the Father says, "Out of Egypt I called my son!"[8] Such is the fecundity of that grain; for there could not have been a harvest unless the Egyptians had sown the grain earlier. There is, then, grain which no one earlier believed to exist; the patriarchs engage in negotiations in regard to this grain. And they indeed brought money, but the good Joseph gave them the grain and gave them back the money.[9] For Christ is not bought with money but with grace; your payment is faith, and with it are bought God's mysteries. Moreover, this grain is carried by the ass,[10] that before was unclean according to the law but now is clean in grace.[11]

(9.46) Nevertheless Benjamin, the youngest, was kept back and still stayed close to his loving father. The bonds of the law held him back, and ancestral custom. The famine was increasing because he was coming late.[1] Two brothers, Ruben and Juda—that is, humility and confession[2]—make intercession on his behalf. He has them as sureties with his father, to them he is entrusted; one of them is the firstborn, the other restored to life. The firstborn represents the law; the one restored to life, the Gospel. The young Benjamin is led down by them and arrives, accompanied by good fragrances and carrying with him the cement[3] with which stones of marble are fastened together; thus, by his own preaching as by a spiritual cement he might fasten together living stones. He also carries honey, which destroys the harmful effects of an

---

8 Osee 11.1; Matt. 2.15.
9 Cf. Gen. 42.25–28.
10 Cf. Gen. 44.3.
11 Cf. John 12.14–15; Zach. 9.9.

1 Cf. Gen. 43.1–14.
2 Juda appears as "confession of sin" in 14.84 below; the name Ruben does not seem to appear in an allegorical interpretation elsewhere in Ambrose. Cf. Gen. 29.32 (Ruben) and 29.35 (Juda).
3 Cf. Gen. 43.11. For the two senses of the Latin word (*resina*) see ch. 3 n. 52, above.

internal wound, without the bitter pain of any cutting. Such indeed was the preaching of Paul that it destroyed the festering infection and drained off the tainted fluid with the sting of its argument, for it sought rather to cauterize the sick vitals of the heart than to cut them. That the incense is a sign of prayer,[4] and the cassia and aloes are signs of burial, David the psalmist taught us when he said, "myrrh and aloes and cassia from your garments."[5] For Paul came to preach the cross of the Lord, an oak that is always verdant. And almonds appear, which are rather hard in the shell but more tender in the meat—it was right that Aaron's priestly rod was of the almond tree,[6] and Jeremia's staff as well[7]— and double money too.[8] Who would doubt that these gifts were useful? For the life of the patriarch and the preaching of the Apostle are always verdant in the heart of each man, and the speech of the saints shines brightly with the splendor of the precept of salvation, like silver tried by the fire.[9] And it is with reason that they carry double money, for in them there is prefigured the coming of Paul, who presented presbyters who labor in the word and in the teaching with a double honor.[10]

(9.47) Moreover, "Joseph saw them and Benjamin his brother by the same mother."[11] The Hebrews are seen now and they are seen by Christ, who is the true Joseph, when they come with the figure who symbolizes Paul. And Joseph speaks to them gently and mildly, inviting them to take food together. Earlier, however, when they came without Benjamin, he did not even recognize them but turned away from them, as it is written, "and he spoke harshly to them."[12] For

---

4 Cf. Ps. 140 (141).2.
5 Ps. 44 (45).9.
6 Cf. Num. 17.23 (8).
7 Cf. Jer. 1.11–12.
8 Cf. Gen. 43.12, 15.
9 Cf. Ps. 11 (12).7.
10 Cf. 1 Tim. 5.17.
11 Gen. 43.29.
12 Gen. 42.7.

they did not recognize him by whom they were recognized. They advance, then, by the merit of Paul, whom the Lord Jesus loved more than the other brothers, as being a younger brother begotten from the same mother. Let the Jews turn to Him whom they have denied to be their Lord. Even though He was crucified from their synogogue, yet He loves them more as born of the same parent, if only they come to know, even late, the Author of their salvation. But being aware of their own offenses, they do not believe that Christ is so very merciful as to forgive their sin and pardon their wrongdoing. And thus their future line of conduct was prefigured in the patriarchs. They were invited to grace, were summoned to the banquet of the table of salvation, and suspected that a false accusation was being readied against them and an ambush was being laid.

(9.48) And they began to desire to plead their case to the man who was steward of the house at the door of the house.[13] They still hesitate to enter in and prefer to be justified from their works,[14] for they desire to prove a case rather than to receive grace and so they are refuted at the gates. But the man who awaits the fruit of the virgin's womb and the inheritance of the Lord is dealing in the goods of the Son and is not ashamed at the gate. Rather, at the end of this life he drives back the enemy so that the latter, who is aware of his quite serious guilt, may not hinder him as he hastens to higher things. (9.49) On this account, the steward answered them in a mystical sense. And know who this is, when you read that Moses was faithful in all his house. For Moses and Peter and Paul and the other saints are the stewards, but Christ alone is the master. It is written, "Moses was faithful in all his house as a servant for a testimony of those things which had been said, but Christ as the Son in his own house, which house we are, if we hold fast liberty and the glory of the hope."[15]

---

13 Cf. Gen. 43.19–24.   14 Cf. Gal. 2.16.   15 Heb. 3.5–6.

(9.50) This steward, then, answered them, "Peace be to you, have no fear. Your God and the God of your fathers has given you treasures in your sacks. I have received your good money."[16] They indeed had said to him, "We found the money of each one of us in our sacks. We have brought back our money in full weight."[17] O mighty mysteries, and mysteries clearly portrayed! This is to say: Why are you puffed up? Do you assume too often that the money you have in your sacks is your own? What indeed do you have which you have not received? But if you have received it, why do you boast as if you have not received it? Now you have been satisfied, you have become rich;[18] you believe that you possess the money, but the God of your fathers has given the money to you. He is your God, He is the God of your fathers, and you have denied Him. But He grants pardon and forgiveness and receives you back if you should return. He is the one who does not ask your money but gives His own. He has given you money in your sacks. Now your sacks hold money, that used to hold mire; and therefore he is your companion who says, "You have cut off my sackcloth and have clothed me with gladness."[19] The gift of gladness is Christ, He is your money, He is your price. The Lord Jesus does not demand from you the price of His grain, does not ask the weight of your money. Your money is unsound, the money in your purse is not good. (9.51) "I have received your good money";[20] that is, it is not your material money but your spiritual money that is good. You have brought it down out of faith and devotion like the sons of Jacob; it is expended without loss and is counted out without any deficit, seeing that for such a price the loss that is death is avoided and the profit that is life is gained.

---

16 Gen. 43.23.
17 Gen. 43.21.
18 Cf. 1. Cor. 4.7–8.
19 Ps. 29 (30).12.
20 Gen. 43.23.

(10.52) "And they made ready the presents, until Joseph came at noon."[1] Paul's faith hastened the coming of noon. Before, Paul was blind; afterward he began to see the light of justice, because if anyone opens his way to the Lord and hopes in Him, the Lord will also bring forth his justice as the light and his judgment as the noon.[2] And when God appeared to Abraham by the oak of Mamre, it was noon, and the everlasting light from the Lord's presence shone on him.[3] It is noon when the real Joseph enters into His house to dine. The day shines more at that time, when we celebrate the sacred mysteries. (10.53) "And they brought him the presents."[4] We bring the presents; He renews the banquet.[5] He says, "Serve the bread,"[6] which the Hebrews take by themselves, but the Egyptians cannot eat it.[7] But how generous was his kindness before the banquet! What a moral lesson in his practice of consideration and courtesy! The brothers were still suspicious concerning the false accusation which they thought was being prepared against them by Joseph. He invited them to dinner. Their inclination wavered; his kindness persevered. He is the first to speak, the first to ask, "How are you?" (10.54) And again he says, "Is the old man your father well?"[8] It is the part of a superior to invite the inferior to conversation, to inspire confidence in his discourse, to ask not only after them but also after their parents. (10.55) They answer him, "Your servant, our father, is well."[9] He said "the old man" so as to do him honor; they called him "servant" so as to offer the service of their humility. "Old age" suggests honor and dignity,

---

1 Gen. 43.25.
2 Cf. Ps. 36 (37).5–6; Wisd. 5.6.
3 Cf. Gen. 18.1. The Septuagint text speaks of an oak; the Vulgate does not.
4 Gen. 43.26.
5 As Joseph is a type-figure of Christ, the reference is probably to the eucharistic meal; the presents then are the offerings of the faithful. See R. Gryson, *Prêtre* 74–75.
6 Gen. 43.31.
7 Cf. Gen. 43.32–34.
8 Gen. 43.27.
9 Gen. 43.28.

whereas "servitude" appears submissive and more closely related to modesty than to pride.

(10.56) Now "raising his eyes he saw Benjamin, his brother by the same mother."[10] The moral sense is, that we see those we love before others and the gaze of our eyes lights first on those whom we consider first in our mind's eye. And for the most part, when we are busy all around with another mental employment, we do not see those whom we find before our eyes. Thus our sight is directed by the guidance of our mind. And so, holy Joseph saw Benjamin his brother; he remembered him, he looked for him, he almost had not seen his brothers in Benjamin's absence because the sight of them was of no help whatsoever. Neither was he satisfied only to have seen him; as if not knowing him, Joseph asked, "Is this your youngest brother?"[11] It is the way and the favor of love, that we should possess those we love not only with our eyes but also by our conversation. Joseph had recognized his beloved brother, but he asked for this reason, that he might speak the name of him that he had in his heart. (10.57) Indeed, he did not wait for a reply but at once blessed him and was troubled at the attainment of his wish. Now "his heart was tormented,"[12] because his freedom to embrace the brother he longed for was postponed. Thereupon, "entering into his chamber he wept and washed his face and restrained himself."[13] The stings of a great love swiftly prick the heart, unless the reins of desire are relaxed. Joseph was being overcome by feeling but put off by deliberation; reason was in contest with love. He wept, so that he could moderate the surges of his holy love.

(10.58) The foregoing is in the moral sense. In the mystical sense, however, the Lord Jesus saw Paul—for "the eyes of the Lord are upon the just"[14]—and said, "Is this your youngest

---

10 Gen. 43.29.
11 *Ibid.*
12 Gen. 43.30.
13 Gen. 43.30–31.
14 Ps. 33 (34).16.

brother?"[15] He is still called the youngest, for he did not yet
exhibit a venerable faith of mature age,[16] and he had not yet
grown into the perfect man, "into that measure of the age
of the fulness of Christ,"[17] as Paul himself says. Indeed, he is
called a young man only in that passage where he kept the
garments of those who were stoning Stephen.[18] And on that
account he desired that Philemon imitate not his youth but
his old age, as he wrote, "I rather beseech, since you are such
a one as Paul, an old man."[19] On that account he preaches
that younger widows are to be refused, not by reason of their
age, but on account of a kind of wantonness in offenses that
are reaching full growth and an immaturity in virtue.[20] But
chastity merits greater praise in a young man than in one
who is old. Moreover, I think it is not far from the truth if
we adopt the following interpretation. Although Paul was
struck and taken up and was terrified because blindness had
befallen him, still he began to come near when he said, "Lord,
what will you have me do?"[21] For that reason he is called the
youngest by Christ, so that he who was called to grace could
be excused from the guilt of his hazardous years. Yes, Christ
saw him when the light shone round him;[22] because young
men are recalled from sin more by fear than by reason, Christ
applied the goad and mercifully admonished him not to kick
against it.[23]

(10.59) Moreover, he was troubled, just as you find in the
Gospel that Christ was troubled in spirit when He raised
Lazarus[24] and wept there[25] so that He might first wash away

15 Gen. 43.29.
16 Cf. Vergil, *Aeneid* 1.292 ("venerable faith") and 12.438 ("mature age").
17 Eph. 4.13.
18 Cf. Acts 7.58.
19 Philemon 9.
20 Cf. 1 Tim. 5.11.
21 Acts 9.6.
22 Cf. Acts 9.3.
23 Cf. Acts 9.5.
24 Cf. John 11.33.
25 Cf. John 11.35.

the sins of the dead man by His tears. But now He wept and washed His face inwardly. The blindness of Paul is the weeping of Christ; he washes his face when his lost sight is restored to him.[26] Christ washed His own face when Paul was baptized,[27] so that through him the Lord Jesus might be seen by many men. And for that reason his share in the banquet was made fivefold greater,[28] because he was to be preferred to his elders, not only as regards sagacity of mind, but also in the warfare of the body and the grace of chastity.

(11.60) Moreover, "they drank and were merry together with him."[1] The greater prerogative is given to Paul from the beginning of his faith; of him it is said to Ananias, "Go, because he is to me a vessel of election to carry my name among the Gentiles."[2] From the beginning he is inebriated with an inebriation, but a sober one, so that he also might say with the saints, "And your cup which inebriates, how goodly it is!"[3] (11.61) And the silver cup is put in his sack alone.[4] Benjamin did not know this; Paul was in error, but he was called. They sent after him in the morning; indeed, the night of blindness had advanced and the day of faith was near at hand.[5] (11.62) The sacks of the brothers are first examined according to the order of age of each brother.[6] God's Scripture is teaching you a moral lesson. Previously, they sat at the banquet in Joseph's presence in order of age from the firstborn.[7] You see that the place of honor is to be given to the eldest. On the other hand, the sacks of each are searched in order of age[8] so that you may know that Paul has been

---

26 Cf. Acts 9.18.
27 Cf. *ibid.*
28 Cf. Gen. 43.34.

---

1 Gen. 43.34.
2 Acts 9.15.
3 Ps. 22 (23).5.
4 Cf. Gen. 44.2.
5 Cf. Rom. 13.12.
6 Cf. Gen. 44.12.
7 Cf. Gen. 43.33.
8 Cf. Gen. 44.11–12.

chosen by the judgment of heaven. The rest were examined, but this man was given the preference. The silver cup was not found in the sack of anyone else, only in his sack. What is the meaning of its being put in his humble sack? Joseph indeed was merry[9] so that he might practice deception, and he sent the cup so that he might by a holy trick recall the brother whom he loved; yet the light of God's mysterious plans is clearly reflected.

(11.63) Christ finds this money in us, which He has Himself given us. We possess the money of nature, we also possess the money of grace. Nature is the work of the Creator, grace the gift of the Redeemer. Even though we are unable to see Christ's gifts, nevertheless He is giving them; He is working in a hidden way and is giving them to all men, but there are few who are able to keep them and not lose them. Yet He does not give all things to all men. Wheat is given to many, but the cup to one, who is presented with the prophetic and priestly function. For it is not everyone but only the prophet who says, "The cup of salvation I will take up and I will call upon the name of the Lord."[10] (11.64) Therefore the word of heavenly teaching already shone in Paul's body, since he was instructed in the law. But because he was still not subject to the justice of God, the cup was within the sack, the teaching within the law, the lamp within the bushel.[11] Nevertheless, Ananias was sent to give a blessing and to lay on his hand and open the sack.[12] When the sack was opened, the money shone forth, and when the scales fell, in a way like fastenings on the sack, Paul saw straightway.[13] His bond was unbelief; the loosening of it became faith. And for that reason, when the veil which is set over the heart of the Jews was set aside[14]—

---

9 Cf. Gen. 43.34.
10 Ps. 115 (116B).4 (13).
11 Cf. Rom. 6.20; Matt. 5.15; Mark 4.21; Luke 11.33.
12 Cf. Acts 9.12, 17.
13 Cf. Acts 9.18.
14 Cf. 2 Cor. 3.13–18.

like the opening of the sack—he turned to the Lord. Free of
the bond, he obtained the grace of liberty and said, "But we
all, beholding the glory of God with faces unveiled, are transformed into the same image."[15] For when his shoe was undone, he preached the Gospel with the bare feet of free
speech. The Jews held him back and desired to hinder him,
but when the money glittered in his sack, they tore their
garments and returned back.[16] For the free preaching of Paul
on behalf of Christ laid bare the people of the Jews and tore
away all their grace, (11.65) and so they, who could not see
ahead of themselves, went back. Those who lose Christ do
return back. Indeed, in the Gospel too, when they were seizing
the Lord Jesus for death, they drew back and fell upon the
ground.[17] It was appropriate that they went back, for they
fell from heavenly grace to earthly defilement. And so, by an
interpretation in the moral sense, they did not wish to return
without their brother; in the mystical sense, they were unwilling to return without Paul. With the loss of him, they
claimed that the old age of the father of the people would
be brought down into sorrow. (11.66) And so Juda desired
to remain with Joseph so as not to see the evils which came
upon his father;[18] that is, he foresaw and desired to guard
against the evils which were going to come to the people of
the Jews. But since this very preaching was still not unimpeded
in the case of that figure who was symbolic of the chiefs of the
Jewish people, Joseph wept,[19] that is, Jesus wept in him.

(12.67) And he ordered all to withdraw so that he could
be recognized by his brothers. For, even as He said, He had
not come except to the sheep which were lost of the house
of Israel.[1] And lifting up his voice with weeping he said, "I

---

15 2 Cor. 3.18.
16 Cf. Gen. 44.12–13.
17 Cf. John 18.6.
18 Cf. Gen. 44.33–34.
19 Cf. Gen. 45.2.

---

1 Cf. Matt. 15.24.

am Joseph. Is my father still alive?"[2] This means, He stretched out His hands to an unbelieving and contradicting people, for He did not seek an envoy or messenger but, as their very Lord, desired to save His own people.[3] "I myself who spoke, I am here,"[4] and "I was made manifest to those who sought me not, I appear to those who asked me not."[5] What else did He cry out at that time but "I am Jesus"?[6] When the chiefs of the Jews tempted Him and asked, "Are you the Son of God?" He answered, "You say that I am," and to Pilate He said, "You say that I am a king; in this I was born."[7] And when the chief priest said, "I adjure you by the living God, that you tell us whether you are Christ, the Son of God,"[8] He responded, "You have said it. Nevertheless I say to you, hereafter you shall see the Son of Man sitting at the right hand of the Power and coming upon the clouds of heaven."[9] This is what he means when he says, "I am Joseph" —I am in God's power. "Is my father still alive?"—that is, "I do not deny my father, I know my brothers, if you recognize your brother or a father recognizes his son. Is my people still alive then? From a family of that people I have chosen a brother for myself."

(12.68) "Come to me,"[10] because I have come near to you, yes, even so far that I made myself a sharer in your nature by taking on flesh. At least do not flee a partaker of your fellowship, if you do not know the Author of your salvation. (12.69) "And they came to him and he said, 'I am Joseph your brother whom you sold into Egypt. Now therefore be not grieved, and let it not seem to you a hard case, that you

---

2 Gen. 45.3.
3 Cf. Isa. 65.2; Ps. 27 (28).9.
4 Isa. 52.6.
5 Isa. 65.1.
6 John 18.5, 8.
7 John 18.37. For the translation "in this," rather than "for this," see above *Isaac* ch. 5 n. 49.
8 Matt. 26.63.
9 Matt. 26.64.
10 Gen. 45.4.

sold me here; for God sent me before you for life.' "[11] What fraternal devotion! What a good brotherly relation! He would even excuse His brothers' crime and say that it was God's providence and not man's unholiness, since He was not offered up to death by men but was sent by the Lord to life. What else is the meaning of that intervention made by our Lord Jesus Christ, who excelled all His brothers in holiness? When He was on the cross, He said in behalf of the people, "Father, forgive them; for they do not know what they are doing."[12] What other meaning is there either in that holy appeal made in the midst of the disciples? For He said, "Peace to you! It is I, do not be afraid."[13] And when they were startled and panic-stricken and thought they saw a spirit, again He said to them, "Why are you disturbed and why do doubts arise in your hearts? See my hands and feet, that it is I myself. Feel and see, for a spirit does not have flesh and bones, as you see I have."[14] And so, even then these future mysteries were revealed to later times.

(12.70) Indeed they are expressed in the same words, so that we may know that He is the same who spoke before in Joseph and afterward in His own body, seeing that He did not change even the words. For at that time He said, "Be not grieved,"[15] and later, "Go up to my father and say to him, 'Thus says your son Joseph: God has made me master of the whole land of Egypt.' "[16] And in the Gospel Christ says, "Do not be afraid. Go, tell my brothers to go into Galilee, and there they shall see me."[17] And later He says, "All power in heaven and on earth has been given to me,"[18] which is to say, "This was the doing of God's design in order that I might re-

---

11 Gen. 45.4–5.
12 Luke 23.34.
13 Luke 24.36; John 20.19.
14 Luke 24.38–39.
15 Gen. 45.5.
16 Gen. 45.9.
17 Matt. 28.10.
18 Matt. 28.18.

ceive power, and not the work of human cruelty." He who is counting out the reward does not reproach the crime. (12.71) Now as to what appears in Genesis, "for God sent me before you to life,"[19] Christ repeats this in the Gospel when He says, "Teach all nations, baptizing them in the name of the Father, and of the Son, and of the Holy Spirit."[20] For this is the recompense and the life of the saints, that they have also brought about the redemption of others. (12.72) And notice that the following, too, was not written without purpose in Genesis, "And you will be near me, you and your sons and your sons' sons."[21] For this is what Christ said in the Gospel, "Behold, I am with you all days, even unto the consummation of the world."[22] (12.73) How clear also is that mystery! For when every commandment had been fulfilled, so to speak, Joseph embraced his brother Benjamin and fell upon his neck.[23] Likewise, when the Gospel is brought to completion, Christ embraces Paul in the arms of His mercy, as it were, so as to lift him up into heaven once the latter has shown submission by inner belief as if by bending his neck. On this account also, when he was lifted up by Christ, he said, "But our citizenship is in heaven."[24]

(13.74) And Pharao rejoiced because Joseph had known his brothers. From there the news spread in Pharao's house, and he urged the holy Joseph to invite his brothers to come with their father. He also gives orders that their packs be filled with grain and loaded onto wagons.[1] What can account for such consideration shown to a stranger? Only that a great mystery was being revealed, a mystery the Church today does not deny. The Jews will be redeemed; the Christian people will

---

19 Gen. 45.5.
20 Matt. 28.19.
21 Gen. 45.10.
22 Matt. 28.20.
23 Cf. Gen. 45.14.
24 Phil. 3.20.

---

1 Cf. Gen. 45.16–20.

rejoice at this union, give aid to the limit of its resources, and send men to preach the good news of the kingdom of God,[2] so that their call may come sooner. To each of the brothers two garments are given.[3]

(13.75) And it is Paul who is dispatched when his words are published; to him Christ gives three hundred pieces of gold and five garments of various colors.[4] A man who preaches the cross of Christ has three hundred pieces of gold, and so he says, "For I determined not to know anything among you, except Jesus Christ and him crucified."[5] And it is appropriate that he receives the gold pieces, because he preached not in the persuasive words of wisdom but in the demonstration of the Spirit.[6] Moreover, he receives five robes, either as the manifold teachings of wisdom or because he was not seduced by any enticements of the bodily passions. Where there was danger for others, he maintained the victory. He overcame all the pleasures of the flesh by a signal self-control and exercise of virtue; no bodily infirmity blunted his character or his zeal. When he was in the body, he did not know that he had a body. Indeed, when he was caught up into paradise, whether in the body or out of the body he did not know, he heard secret words that a man may not repeat;[7] at the last, he had no earthly fragrance at all on earth, as he teaches when he says, "For we are the fragrance of Christ for God as regards those who are saved."[8]

(13.76) Therefore Paul excels and his portion is superabundant, but still the other preachers have their own gift; they each receive two garments. What are these garments? You should have no hesitancy about identifying them, because you have read what was said of Wisdom, "She made

---

2 Cf. Luke 8.1.
3 Cf. Gen. 45.22.
4 Cf. *ibid.*
5 1 Cor. 2.2.
6 Cf. 1 Cor. 2.4.
7 Cf. 2 Cor. 12.2–4.
8 2 Cor. 2.15.

for her husband double garments."[9] One is mystical, the other moral. But not all the Apostles or prophets or pastors or powers have the grace of healing, nor do all speak in tongues. Where there are diverse rewards, there are diverse merits.

(13.77) And presents are also sent on ahead to the father.[10] The son does honor to the father; so Christ invites His people with promises and invites them with presents. The presents are carried on asses that before were profitless and fit only for toil but now are profitable;[11] they carry in a figurative way the presents of Christ, and in the Gospel they are going to carry the Giver of the presents.[12]

(13.78) Now "he sent away his brothers, and they departed. And Joseph said to them, 'Be not angry on the way.' "[13] How well he teaches us to guard against anger, for that can separate even brothers who love one another. We must above all guard against discord on the way, where the very accompaniment involved in travel ought to partake in the gift of inviolability. Is this not what our Lord Jesus said when He was about to depart from this body, when He was sending away His disciples, that they should not be angry on the way? For He says, "Peace I leave with you, my peace I give to you."[14] For where there is peace, wrath does not have place, discord is removed, dissension routed. And so this is what He is saying, "My peace I give to you," that is, "Be not angry on the way." And consider whether He isn't saying that one must guard against indignation on this way, that is, in the entire course of this life, because anger often leads even the blameless into sin. For as we rightly grow more angry and desire to restrain the sin of another, we commit sins of greater severity. And so the Apostle says, "Do not

9 Prov. 31.22 (Septuagint).
10 Cf. Gen. 45.23.
11 Cf. *ibid.*; Philemon 11.
12 Cf. Matt. 21.7.
13 Gen. 45.24.
14 John 14.27.

avenge yourselves, but give place to the wrath,"[15] which is, let us turn aside from the wrath, else it may snatch us up. On this account also, when the Lord Jesus sent away His disciples to preach the Gospel, He sent them without gold, without silver, without money, without a staff,[16] and He did it so that He might remove incentives to quarreling and the tools of vengeance.

(13.79) "And they went up from Egypt and came into the land of Chanaan to their father Jacob, and they told him, saying, 'Joseph your son is living and he is ruler of all the land of Egypt.' "[17] What is the land of Chanaan? A land that was faltering. Is it not clear that the time of the Apostles is being described? They entered the faltering synagogues of the Jews and preached the power of the Lord Jesus, as we find in the Acts of the Apostles when Peter says, "This Jesus God has raised up, and we are all witnesses of it. Therefore, exalted by the right hand of God and receiving from the Father the promise of the Holy Spirit, he has poured forth this gift which you see."[18] We surely notice how the Scripture says that He is alive and ruler of the whole land, for He opened His storehouses of spiritual grace and gave the abundance to all men.[19] The Apostles spoke thus, but the Jews did not believe them; rather they laid hands on them and thrust the preachers of salvation into prison.[20] (13.80) On this account also it is written of Jacob, "He was greatly frightened in heart,"[21] for he did not believe his sons. He was greatly frightened from love of an unbelieving people, but afterward he came to recognize Christ's deeds; won over by the mighty benefactions and mighty works, he revived and said, "It is a great thing for me, if my son Joseph is still alive.

---

15 Rom. 12.19.
16 Cf. Matt. 10.9–10; Mark 6.8; Luke 9.3, 22.35.
17 Gen. 45.25–26.
18 Acts 2.32–33.
19 Cf. Gen. 41.56.
20 Cf. Acts 5.17–18.
21 Gen. 45.26.

I will go and see him, before I die."[22] The first and greatest
foundation of faith is belief in the resurrection of Christ.[23]
For whosoever believes Christ has been restored to life,
quickly searches for Him, comes to Him with devotion, and
worships God with his inmost heart. Indeed, he believes that
he himself will not die if he has belief in the Source of his
resurrection.

(14.81) "And Israel, rising up, came to the well of the
oath and sacrificed a victim to the God of his father Isaac."[1]
It is appropriate, for that man rises up who is hastening to
Christ. Faith precedes devotion. First he rose up, later he sacrificed. The man who has searched out the knowledge of God
offers a good sacrifice. (14.82) Now "at night in a vision God
spoke to Israel, saying, 'Jacob, Jacob.' He said, 'What is it?'
God said, 'I am the God of your fathers, do not fear, go down
into Egypt; for there I will make you into a great people and I
will lead you forever.' "[2] But the Jews do not understand
what they themselves read and they deny Moses, whom they
praise, when they are unwilling to believe his writings! They
are invited from this place to pass over to the Church of God—
what could be clearer? Before, they were confined within the
narrow limits of Judea; they are invited to pass to the people
of God that was gathered together from the whole world,
from all tribes and peoples, and was made into a great people—what could be clearer? Indeed, "their sound has gone
forth into all the earth."[3] Thus Jacob is called by his sons,
that is, the people of the Jews is invited to grace by Peter
and John and Paul.

(14.83) Our God Himself also exhorts that people with His
own prophecy and promises them advancement in the faith,

---

22 Gen. 45.28.
23 Cf. 1 Cor. 15.12–19.

---

1 Gen. 46.1.
2 Gen. 46.2–4.
3 Ps. 18 (19).5; Rom. 10.18.

the fruit of His gift, for He says to them, "Joseph shall put his hand on your eyes."[4] It was not that the holy patriarch was troubled as to who should close his eyes, although in the clear understanding of it a natural love is also being expressed. For we often desire to embrace those whom we love; how much more, when we are about to depart from this body, do we take delight in the last touch of our beloved children and find consolation in such a provision for our journey. Yet in a mystical sense we may take it to mean that afterward the people of the Jews is going to know its God. For this is a mystery, that the true Joseph places His hands over the eyes of another, so that he who before did not see may now see.[5] Come to the Gospel, read how the blind man was healed, when Jesus put His hand on him and took away his blindness. Indeed, Christ does not put His hand on those who are going to die but on those who are going to live or, if on those who are going to die, rightly so, because we first die in order that we may live again.[6] For we cannot see God unless we die to sin previously.

(14.84) Therefore seventy-five souls go down into Egypt, just as it is written,[7] and this in the mystical sense is the number of forgiveness. For after such great hardness, after such great sins, they would be considered unworthy unless there were granted them the forgiveness of sins. Juda—that is, the confession of sin[8]—goes to meet Joseph. The people of the Jews that is to come sends him ahead as a forerunner of itself. So also the true Joseph, that is, "the witness and interpreter of the Godhead,"[9] comes to meet those who before were the possession of unbelief, because now their confession

---

4 Gen. 46.4.
5 Cf. John 9.6–7.
6 Cf. Rom. 6.1–11.
7 Cf. Gen. 46.27. The Septuagint gives the number as seventy-five; the Vulgate, as seventy.
8 Above, 9.46 (see ch. 9 n. 2), the name Juda is given the meaning "confession."
9 Above, in 3.14, the name Joseph is differently interpreted.

precedes them. For Christ is the interpreter of the Godhead, because "no one has at any time seen God, except the only-begotten Son, who is in the bosom of the Father, he has revealed him."[10] It is He who in the last times will receive the people of the Jews, by then in an advanced age and grown weary, and do so, not according to its merits, but according to the election of His grace; and He will put His hand on its eyes to take away its blindness. And so He postponed its healing, so that the people that earlier did not think it should believe might be the last to believe and might lose the prerogative of earlier election. On this account also the Apostle says, "that a partial blindness has befallen Israel, until the full number of the Gentiles should enter, and thus all Israel should be saved."[11] (14.85) And thus it is that the deeds of the patriarchs are symbols of events to come. Indeed, Jacob himself speaks to this effect to his sons: "Gather yourselves together, that I may tell you the things that shall befall you in the last days. Gather yourselves together and hear Israel your father."[12]

---

10 John 1.18.
11 Rom. 11.25–26.
12 Gen. 49.1–2.

THE PATRIARCHS

(De patriarchis)

INTRODUCTION

MBROSE COMPOSED *The Patriarchs* as a written commentary rather than a sermon or a treatise developed from a sermon. It has often been joined in the manuscript tradition with *Joseph,* but existence of an intrinsic relationship between the two works is very doubtful.[1] Since there is reference in the present work to Ambrose's *Explanation of the Gospel According to Luke,* itself dated *ca.* 390, *The Patriarchs* must be placed in the same period, most likely in 390 or 391.[2]

Exegesis of the scriptural blessings of the patriarchs and the symbolic or typological interpretation of them has a long history in Christian literature from Tertullian on.[3] *The Patriarchs,* a typical example of the genre, is derived from Hippolytus.[4] One of a number of such works which enjoyed popularity in the fourth century,[5] it relies heavily on Jacob's

---

1 On this point, and on the work in general, see Dudden 684; Palanque 442–43, 540.

2 See Palanque 540 (with a date after 390); Dudden 684 *(ca.* 390); Paredi 439 (about 391); U. Moricca, *Storia della letteratura latina cristiana* 2.1, 380 n. 372 *(ca.* 389).

3 See M. Simonetti, *Note su antichi commenti alle Benedizioni dei Patriarchi* (Annali delle Facoltà di Lettere, Filosofia e Magistero 28, Università di Cagliari, Cagliari 1960) and the brief but useful review by J. Smit Sibinga in *Vigiliae Christianae* 18 (1964) 238–39.

4 See Simonetti, n. 3 above. For specific examples, see W. Wilbrand in *Biblische Zeitschrift* 10 (1912) 338 n. 2 and O. Bardenhewer in *Literarische Rundschau* 24 (1898) 201. The text of Hippolytus, i.e., his commentaries on the blessings of Isaac, Jacob, and Moses, appeared in 1953 as volume 27 of the *Patrologia Orientalis,* with a translation in French. The original Greek text of his *Blessing of Jacob* is extant, but only fragments of the *Isaac* and *Moses. Jacob* and *Moses* exist in both Armenian and Georgian versions. See J. Quasten, *Patrology* 2 (Westminster, Md. 1953) 165–66, 174–76.

5 For the popularity enjoyed by works of this kind, and discussion of specific works, including *The Patriarchs,* see H. Moretus, "Les Béné-

blessings, or prophecies, imparted in Genesis 49; there is also frequent reference to Moses' blessing of the tribes of Israel in Deuteronomy 33. Many of the patriarchs are taken to represent Christ in one respect or another; Benjamin is a figure of the Apostle Paul. The work is marred by occasional references of an anti-Semitic tenor, notably in one passage.[6]

No translation of *The Patriarchs* has apparently been published.

---

dictions des patriarchs dans la littérature du ive au viiie siècle," *Bulletin de littérature ecclésiastique* 3rd ser. (1909) 398–411; (1910) 28–40, 83–100.
6 Viz., 2.9.

THE PATRIARCHS

WHEN WE READ that he was blessed who was blessed by his father, and that he was cursed who was cursed by his father,[1] we learn above all else what great reverence to show our parents. And God gave this privilege to parents so as to arouse respect in the children. The formation of the children is, then, the prerogative of the parents. Therefore honor your father, that he may bless you.[2] Let the godly man honor his father out of gratitude, and the ingrate do so on account of fear. Even if the father is poor and does not have plenteous resources to leave to his sons, still he has the heritage of his final blessing with which he may bestow the wealth of sanctification on his descendants. And it is a far greater thing to be blessed than it is to be rich. (1.2) Joseph hurried to receive a blessing.[3] Indeed, he presented his sons Manasse and Ephraim, and Jacob blessed them.[4] Because Jacob had twelve sons, and Paul, as one chosen later, was going to be the thirteenth Apostle, a thirteenth tribe would thus be sanctified from the descendants of Manasse and Ephraim and divided between them both. Thus Paul would not appear outside the enumeration of the tribes of the fathers; as an outstanding preacher of both the Old and the New Testaments, he would readily confirm that the inheritance of a father's blessing was of help to himself as well.

(1.3) What signal mysteries there are in this! Joseph took his sons, who were born to him in Egypt, and brought them

---

1 Cf. Gen. 9.25–26.
2 Cf. Exod. 20.12.
3 Cf. Gen. 48.1.
4 Cf. Gen. 48.8–20.

before his father. He placed Ephraim at his right, but at the
left of his father Israel, and Manasse at his left, but at Israel's
right. But Israel, stretching out his right hand, put it on
Ephraim's head, although he was the younger son and stood at
his grandfather's left. And he put his left hand on Manasse,
who was at his right, and, with his hands crossed so, he blessed
them.[5] In this Joseph observed the order of nature, to grant
more to the elder son. Likewise, Isaac also desired to give his
blessing to Esau, the first son, but Jacob believed the younger
son was to be preferred as a symbol of the younger people,
just as he himself had been preferred by his mother.[6] (1.4)
Indeed, in our tongue, Manasse signifies "out of forgetfulness,"[7] because the people of the Jews forgot their God, who
made them,[8] and whoever from out of that people believes is
called back, as it were, from forgetfulness. Moreover, Ephraim
promises fruitfulness in faith by the meaning of his name,
"who made his father to grow," just as Joseph himself says,
"because God has made me to grow in the land of my humilia-
tion."[9] This refers especially to the younger people, which is
the body of Christ, making its Father to grow and not for-
saking its own God.

(1.5) Indeed, the old man Jacob stated that this mystery
referred in a spiritual sense to the peoples. For since his son
Joseph thought that he had made a mistake from a defect
in his vision, which was a bit dim, he wanted to change
the position of his hands, saying " 'Not so, father, for this is
the firstborn; put your right hand on his head.' But he refused
and said, 'I know, son, I know. He too shall become a people,
he too shall be exalted, but his younger brother shall be

---

5 Cf. Gen. 48.13–20.

6 Cf. Gen. 27.1–40.

7 Cf. Gen. 41.51. The same story appears also in Ambrose's *Explanation
of Psalm 118* 14.32, where the name Manasse is interpreted as "forgetfulness."

8 Cf. Deut. 32.18.

9 Gen. 41.52. See *Explanation of Psalm 118* 14.32, where, however,
Ephraim means "consolation."

greater than he, and his seed will be a multitude of nations.' "[10] Yes, by the order also in which he gave his blessing, he prophesied that Ephraim was to be preferred to the elder brother, for he said, "In you Israel will be blessed and it will be said, 'May God do to you as to Ephraim and Manasse.' "[11] And so, although they were grandsons, they were adopted into the place of sons, so that they would not be deprived of their grandfather's blessing.

(2.6) After the joyous conferral of this blessing, Jacob called his sons as well.[1] Whereas before he had preferred the younger to the elder, he begins with the eldest. In the former case he preferred the symbolic gift; in this one he maintains the order of age. Likewise, earlier he had blessed all men with all their posterity and offspring of times to come in the persons of the two brothers; a repetition of that blessing of the people might seem superfluous, or the earlier blessing might be considered invalid. And so it is with reason that Jacob says he is presenting anew his announcement of events which were to come in later ages, rather than a blessing. (2.7) Indeed, he begins like this, "Ruben, my firstborn, you are my strength and the beginning of my children, hard to be endured and very insolent, you have acted with outrage. You should not have burst forth like water; for you went up into your father's bed, you defiled the couch where you went up."[2] Doesn't this seem to be a reproach rather than a blessing? Thus it really is more a prophecy than a blessing. For a prophecy is an announcement of events to come, whereas a blessing is the longed-for bestowal of sanctification and of graces.

(2.8) The Jews suppose that the old man is saying these things to his son Ruben on this account, because the latter lay with Bala, his father's concubine, and polluted his father's

---

10 Gen. 48.18–19.
11 Gen. 48.20.

---

1 Cf. Gen. 49.1–2.
2 Gen. 49.3–4.

bed. But they are easily refuted; this had already taken place. Now Jacob is promising that he will speak of events to come in the last days, not what took place before. Therefore, the meaning is consistent and in accord with the thought of the patriarch himself; he sees the future passion of the Lord under persecution from the Jews and execrates the boundless audacity of that firstborn people. It is unbelieving and not subject to God's law; it does not know how to carry Christ's yoke on its stiff neck,[3] and it inflicts on the Author of life, not only the crime of murder, but the wrong of sacrilegious insult as well. (2.9) "You should not have burst forth like water"; else it may burst out into greater insanity, and a demented and frenzied passion may not permit sinners to come to their senses. Rather, let them do penance for their offenses, for it was a hard people that went up to its father's bed and polluted a holy couch. That is, it fastened the flesh of our Lord Jesus, our Creator, to the gibbet of the cross, on which His saints rest with the refreshment of salvation as if on a kind of bed and paternal couch. Therefore, who would deny that this was spoken in reference to that people, when all these details fit that people? For Israel itself was called the firstborn and said to be stiff-necked, and of it Moses said, "You are a stiff-necked people."[4] And really, who is so stiff and insolent and abusive as the people of the Jews? Through the Lord Jesus they had seen the dead raised up, the blind given sight; when they could not deny His godlike works, they lashed Him with scourges and fastened Him with nails. The Gospel text declared this was done at the instigation of the scribes and priests, Caiphas the chief priest venting his rage as well. And so the holy prophet shunned participation in that great crime; else, since the race proceeded from him, they might dare to claim for themselves a fellowship with the great patriarch.[5]

---

3 Cf. Exod. 33.3.
4 *Ibid.*
5 The tenor of this entire passage (2.9) is regrettable. Some might undertake a defense of Ambrose's attitude here by pointing out that the

(3.10) That just man calls his posterity to witness and dis-inherits it, for it did not keep its father's dispositions. Because Jacob foresaw the crime, he shrank in horror from being in-fected by that counsel. He says, "Let not my soul come into their counsel nor my heart be engaged in their assembly, because in their fury they slew a man and in their willfulness they hamstrung a bull."[1] What he is saying concerning his sons, he is indeed saying concerning Simeon and Levi.[2] But by their names he means the tribes of like name. This is the very attractive interpretation deduced by the Jews. They suppose that Jacob is reproving his sons for this reason, because those two, more than their other brothers, desired to take vengeance on the Sichemites on account of the outrage committed on their sister. They pretended that they wanted to enter into the good graces of the men of Sichem, and so they persuaded the latter that they should be circumcised. Thus, with religious harmony, peace would be strengthened between them and there would be strong bonds of intermarriage. But Jacob's sons attacked the circumcised men, who were weakened by their fresh wounds and the loss of their strength, which was impaired by the pain; when the third day came, they killed them.[3] And so perhaps those two are avengers more than the others, because they are the progenitors of the scribes and priests. For no one ought to uphold chastity more than wise men and priests.

(3.11) But in this also the Jews are mistaken. For the brothers supplied the reasons for their own misfortune when

---

saint was a man of his time, and by citing the existence of similar passages in other Fathers; the present translator will not. Contrast the clear repudiation of any notion of a collective guilt of the Jewish people for Christ's death, as found in the Second Vatican Council's *Declaration on the Relationship of the Church to Non-Christian Religions*, section 4. See W. M. Abbott, S.J., and J. Gallagher, *The Documents of Vatican II* (Baltimore 1966) 663–67 and the notes thereto.

1 Gen. 49.6.
2 Cf. Gen. 49.5.
3 Cf. Gen. 34.13–31.

they claimed to their father that they, although young in years, were vindicators and avengers of a wrong done to the sense of respect and of a violation of chastity. Surely, the holy Jacob could not have condemned the fact that they did not permit their sister to be unavenged, in the position of a harlot, who had lost her virginity and did not have the consolation of a vindication. This is especially the case, seeing that Jacob himself approved the deed; for when he had possession of Sichem, he gave it at his death to his most beloved son Joseph and said to him, "I give to you above all your brothers Sichem in particular, which I took from the hands of the Amorrites with my sword and bow."[4] The act is undeniable; still, we can interpret that by "Sichem" are meant "shoulders,"[5] and by "shoulders" are meant "works." Therefore, Jacob chose the holy Joseph before the others as heir to his good works, for the other brothers could not match his works. Who indeed could match Christ's deeds? (3.12) Moreover Christ, being unspotted and chaste, has carried back the spoils of victory from this earthly sojourn and from the instigators of impurity. With heavenly words and the sword of the spirit He has taken a place that was free of debaucheries and outrages, for a dwelling of the saints. Where before there were men who dwelt in licentiousness and were the foremost in riotous living, where there had been incentives to lust and the kindling to wickedness, there holy ministers now give the teachings of chastity, and many virgins, as models of virtue, are radiant with the splendor of the light that is above.

(3.13) It is the tribes, then, that are meant by the names of the patriarchs. From the tribe of Simeon come the scribes, from that of Levi the chief priests, who brought their wickedness to completion and filled up the entire measure of their fathers' unholiness[6] in the passion of the Lord. They took

---

4 Gen. 48.22 (Septuagint).
5 For the interpretation of Sichem, cf. *Joseph* ch. 3 n. 4.
6 Cf. Matt. 23.32.

counsel against the Lord Jesus, to kill Him, even as Isaia says, "Alas for their souls! Because they have counselled an evil counsel against themselves, saying, 'Let us bind the just one, for he is profitless to us.' "[7] They killed the prophets and Apostles who announced the coming of the Lord of salvation and preached His glorious passion and resurrection. Thereafter, in their greed and out of their desire for earthly wickedness, they fled from sharing in the divine, from chastity of body and moderation of spirit, contempt for money, and profit in grace. "They hamstrung a bull," clearly that bull that brings forth horns and hooves; the poor see him and rejoice,[8] because with the word of God he has raised up the horn of his people,[9] whereby it drove back its enemies and won the prize of a heavenly crown. This is the bull by which the Church is represented in the moon; for she is waxing at that time when she strives, as it were, with the horns of a bull to encompass the whole world.

(3.14) Nevertheless, Jacob seems to attach the gift of a blessing even to this prophecy. For when he said to Ruben his firstborn, "You should not have burst forth like water,"[10] he set a limit to the sin, because water generally purifies us of offenses and summons our hearts back from all their frenzied vices. Likewise, when he said to Simeon and Levi, "I will divide you in Jacob and scatter you in Israel,"[11] he revealed that they were to be redeemed in the gathering together of the nations. For when the shepherd has been struck down, the flock that was previously brought together is scattered;[12] thus, one who did not belong could enter in and all Israel could be saved.[13] And we ought in particular to assume this as regards the tribe of Levi, for it appears that the Lord Jesus traced His

---

7 Isa. 3.9–10 (Septuagint).
8 Cf. Ps. 68 (69).32–33.
9 Cf. Ps. 148.14.
10 Gen. 49.4.
11 Gen. 49.7.
12 Cf. Matt. 26.31.
13 Cf. Rom. 11.26.

origin from that tribe, as concerns His taking on of the body. Of that tribe are the priests Levi and Nathan, and, in the Gospel which he wrote, Saint Luke counted them among the ancestors of the Lord.[14] For the Priest of the Father and Chief of all priests, even as it is written, "You are a priest forever,"[15] should have laid claim to succession from a priestly line. (3.15) On this account also Moses blessed this tribe and said, "Give to Levi the lot of his own approbation, and to the holy man his truth."[16] Moses also blessed the tribe of Ruben, as you find written, "Let Ruben live and not die, and let him be many in number."[17] For he would not have blessed them if he had known that they were undeserving of a blessing according to the thought of the patriarch. Assuredly the one filled out what the other had touched upon in passing.

(4.16) The tribes of Juda and Levi were united by a fusion of their lines of descent, and that is why Matthew assigns Christ's family to the tribe of Juda.[1] And the Apostle says, "for our Lord has sprung out of Juda."[2] Thus, from the tribe of Levi may be counted a heritage that is priestly and filled with holiness, while from the tribe of Juda—to which David and Solomon and the rest of the kings belonged—there shines forth the splendor of a royal descent. And so, by the testimony of the Scriptures, Christ is shown to be at once both king and priest. And the holy Jacob had good reason to express himself fully as regards the grace bestowed on Juda, for he said, "Juda, your brothers shall praise you; your hands shall be on the back of your enemies; the sons of your father shall bow down to you. A lion's whelp is Juda; from my seed, my son, you have come up to me. Resting, you have slept like a lion and like a whelp; who will arouse him? A judge shall not fail

---

14 Cf. Luke 3.29, 31.
15 Ps. 109 (110).4.
16 Deut. 33.8 (Septuagint).
17 Deut. 33.6 (Septuagint).

1 Cf. Matt. 1.3.
2 Heb. 7.14.

from Juda nor a chief from his loins, until he comes for whom it has been reserved, and he is the expectation of the nations. Binding his ass to a vine and his ass's colt with sackcloth, he will wash his robe in wine and his mantle in the blood of the grape. His eyes are joyful from wine, and his teeth are whiter than milk."[3]

(4.17) This address appears to be directed to the patriarch Juda, indeed, but that later Juda is meant, the true Confessor who was born of that tribe and who alone is praised by His brothers; of them He says, "I will declare your name to my brothers."[4] He is the Lord by nature, but a brother by grace; His hands, which He stretched out to an unbelieving people,[5] are on the back of His enemies. For with those same hands and by that same passion He protected His own, subjugated hostile powers, and made subject to Himself all men who were without faith and devotion. Of these the Father says to His Son, "And you will rule in the midst of your enemies."[6] Their own wickedness made them enemies, not Christ's will. In this there is a great gift of the Lord. Before, spiritual wickedness[7] used generally to make our neck bend to the yoke of captivity. Thus, even David wrote that he felt in a way the hands of those who triumphed over him, for he said, "Upon my back sinners have wrought."[8] But now spiritual wickedness is subject to the triumph of Christ, and to His hands, as it were; that is, it undergoes the affliction of captivity, being subject forever in deeds and in works. And it is He indeed to whom the sons of His Father bow down, when we bow down to Him; for He has permitted us to call upon the Father, and to be subject to the Father is to be subject to virtue.

---

3 Gen. 49.8–12 (Septuagint).
4 Ps. 21 (22).23.
5 Cf. Isa. 65.2; Rom. 10.11.
6 Ps. 109 (110).2
7 Cf. Eph. 6.12.
8 Ps. 128 (129).3.

(4.18) "A lion's whelp is Juda." Isn't it clear that he both represented the Father and manifested the Son? Is there any clearer way to teach that God the Son is of one nature with the Father? The one is the lion, the other the lion's whelp. By this paltry comparison, their unity in the same nature and power is perceived. King proceeds from king, a strong one from one who is strong. Because Jacob foresaw that there would be those to claim that the Son was younger in age, he replied to them by adding, "From my seed you have come up to me. Resting you have slept like a lion and like a whelp." And in a different passage you find that the whelp is Himself "the lion of the tribe of Juda."[9] Therefore, seeing that he had said "whelp," it was good that Jacob at once put "lion"; this is to say: Do not let your ears be deceived, because they heard "whelp"; I described that Son, I did not say He was younger. He also is a lion just as the Father is. Let men hear that Jacob called him both "lion" and "whelp"—"lion," as one possessing full and perfect power, "whelp" as the Son. Otherwise, when anyone heard, he might not think that the Son was equal to the Father. But the Son is not being named in such a way as to be separated from the Father. Jacob, who confesses the Son, also esteems Him equal.

(4.19) Moreover, he represented the Son's incarnation in a wonderful fashion when he said, "From my seed you have come up to me." For Christ sprouted in the womb of the virgin like a shrub upon the earth; like a flower of good fragrance, He was sent forth in the splendor of new light and came up from His mother's vitals for the redemption of the entire world. Just so, Isaia says, "There shall come forth a rod out of the root of Jesse and a flower shall come up out of the root."[10] The root is the household of the Jews, the rod is Mary, the flower of Mary is Christ. She is rightly called a rod, for she is of royal lineage, of the house and family of

---

9 Apoc. 5.5.
10 Isa. 11.1.

David.[11] Her flower is Christ, who destroyed the stench of worldly pollution and poured out the fragrance of eternal life.

(4.20) Therefore you have become acquainted with the incarnation; learn of the passion. "Resting, you have slept like a lion." When Christ lay at rest in the tomb as if in a kind of bodily sleep, as He Himself says, "I have slept and have taken my rest and have risen up, because the Lord will sustain me."[12] On this account also Jacob says, "Who will arouse him?" that is, Him whom the Lord will take up. Who else is there to rouse Him again, unless He rouses Himself by His own power and the power of the Father? I see that He was born by His own authority, I see that He died by His own will, I see that He sleeps by His own power. He did all things by His own dominion; will He need the help of someone else to rise again? Therefore He is the Author of His own resurrection, He is the Judge of His death, He is expected by the nations. (4.21) For that reason, "until he comes, a leader shall not fail from Juda,"[13] so that confidence in the royal line of succession may be kept unimpaired even to His birth. For afterward, as I taught in the homily I delivered upon the Gospel,[14] the line of succession was corrupted through Herod and lost its prerogative of rank. Yes, because they denied the true king, they began to have false kings. And so the patriarch is saying this: The inheritance of an unblemished line of succession, traced through the kings, will be kept among the judges and kings of the Jews, "until he come for whom it has been reserved," reserved that He may gather together the Church of God out of the assembly of all the nations and the devotion of the Gentile peoples. That is, this awaits Him, this is kept for Him as His due—the prerogative of such great grace is given to Him.

---

11 Cf. Luke 1.27.
12 Ps. 3.6.
13 Gen. 49.10.
14 In his *Explanation of the Gospel According to Luke* 3.41 (no English translation available).

(4.22) "And he is the expectation of the nations." Jacob spoke more meaningfully than if he had said, "The nations are expecting him," for in Christ lies the entire hope of the Church. Therefore it is said to Moses, "Remove the sandals from your feet."[15] Otherwise Moses, who was chosen as leader of the people, might be thought to be the bridegroom of the Church. It was for that reason that Josue, son of Nun, removed his sandals,[16] in order that he also could preserve the gift of so great a function for Him who was to come. It is for that reason that John says, "A man is coming after me, the strap of whose sandal I am not worthy to loose,"[17] and he also says, "He who has the bride is the bridegroom; but the friend of the bridegroom, who stands and hears him, rejoices with joy."[18] This means: He alone is the husband of the Church, He is the expectation of the nations, and the prophets removed their sandals while offering to Him a union of nuptial grace. He is the bridegroom; I am the friend of the bridegroom. I rejoice because He is coming, because I hear the nuptial chant, because now we do not hear the harsh penalties for sinners, the harsh torments of the law, but the forgiveness of offenses, the cry of joy, the sound of cheerfulness, the rejoicing of the nuptial feast.

(4.23) He is the one "binding his ass to a vine and his ass's colt with sackcloth," so that the assembly of the nations may possess the fervor of the Holy Spirit.[19] Before, it was slack and neglectful, but now it is devoted through Christ. Let us be bound with bonds of a faith that is like a fruitful branch and cannot be undone, as it were, to that everlasting vine, that is, to the Lord Jesus, who says, "I am the vine, my Father is the

---

15 Exod. 3.5.
16 Cf. Josue 5.15 (16).
17 John 1.27.
18 John 3.29.
19 A similar implied comparison of the Church to a colt occurs in *Cain and Abel* 2.3.11 (translated by J. J. Savage in FOTC 42); and other comparisons to animals occur in *The Holy Spirit* 2.10.109 (wild animals—lion, leopard, fox, wolf; translated by R. J. Deferrari in FOTC 44) and *Abraham* 1.9.93 (camel).

husbandman."[20] This explains the mystery that the Lord Jesus in the Gospel ordered an ass's colt to be loosed and Himself sat upon it;[21] thus, like one that was bound to a vine, he could find rest in the everlasting goodness of the saints.

(4.24) "He will wash his robe in wine." The good robe is the flesh of Christ, which has covered the sins of all men, taken up the offenses of all, concealed the misdeeds of all—the good robe which has clothed all men with the garment of rejoicing. He washed this robe in wine at His baptism in the Jordan, when the Holy Spirit came down like a dove and remained upon Him.[22] By this, it is indicated that the fullness of the Holy Spirit will be indivisible in Him and will not depart. On this account also the evangelist says, "The Lord Jesus, full of the Holy Spirit, returned from the Jordan."[23] Therefore Jesus washed His robe, not to wash away His stain, for He had none, but to wash away the stain which was ours. Then Jacob continued, "and his mantle in the blood of the grape." This means that in the passion of His body He washed the nations with His blood. Truly the mantle represents the nations, as it is written, "As I live, says the Lord, unless I shall clothe myself with them all, as with a garment,"[24] and in another passage, "Like clothing you will change them, and they will be changed."[25] And so with His own blood He cleansed, not His own sins, for there were none, but the offenses which we committed. It was appropriate that Jacob spoke of a grape, because Christ hung on the wood like a grape. He is the vine, He is the grape; He is the vine because He cleaves to the wood and the grape because, when His side was opened by the soldier's lance, He sent forth water and blood. For thus John said that "there came out from him blood and water,"[26] water

20 John 15.1.
21 Cf. Matt. 21.1–7; Zach. 9.9; Isa. 62.11.
22 Cf. John 1.32.
23 Luke 4.1.
24 Isa. 49.18.
25 Ps. 101 (102).27.
26 John 19.34.

for baptism, blood for redemption.[27] The water washed us, the blood redeemed us.

(4.25) And therefore the prophet says, "His eyes are joyful from wine and his teeth are whiter than milk," for he means the prophets and the Apostles. For some, like eyes of Christ, have foreseen and announced His coming, and of them Christ Himself says, "Abraham saw my day and he rejoiced,"[28] and one of the prophets says, "I saw the Lord of hosts."[29] Seeing Him, they were filled with a spiritual joy. Others, however, that is, the Apostles, whom the Lord cleansed from every stain of sin, were made whiter than milk, for no blemish darkened them afterward. Indeed, milk is a temporal thing, but the grace of the Apostles remains forever; they provided us with that spiritual sustenance which is of heaven, and they nourished the vitals of the spirit which is within. There are also those who think that the commandments of the Lord, which were revealed from the mouth of God, being clear, have become to us like milk. Nourished upon them, we come to the sustenance of the bread of heaven. On this account also Paul says, "I gave you milk to drink, not solid food; for you were not yet ready."[30] The Corinthian in the beginning of faith is initiated with milk to drink, whereas those saints whose faith is proclaimed in the whole world[31] are strengthened with more solid food, as if they had been weaned.

(5.26) "Zabulon shall dwell by the sea, and he will be by the passages of ships, and will extend as far as Sidon."[1] The very interpretation of his name gives promise of better things,

---

27 See Ambrose, *On the Sacraments* 5.1.4: ". . . then one of the soldiers touched his side with a lance, and from his side water flowed and blood. Why water? Why blood? Water to cleanse, blood to redeem" (translated by T. Thompson, *St. Ambrose, On the Sacraments and On the Mysteries* 96; see *ibid.* n. 1).
28 John 8.56.
29 Isa. 6.1.
30 1 Cor. 3.2.
31 Cf. Rom. 1.8.

---

1 Gen. 49.13.

since in our tongue it means "freedom from the things of night," which is surely a good, and appropriate to one who trusts in the wings of the Lord. For the truth of the Lord encompasses him, so that he is not afraid of the terror of the night or of the thing that walks about in darkness.[2] (5.27) Therefore, "Zabulon shall dwell by the sea." Thus he may look upon the shipwrecks of others while himself free from danger; he may behold others driven here and there on the sea of this world, those who are borne about by every wind of doctrine, while himself persevering on the ground of an immovable faith.[3] Just so, the most holy Church is grounded and founded in faith, as she beholds the tempests of heretics and the shipwrecks of the Jews, because they refused the pilot whom they had had. Therefore she dwells beside the waters, but she is not disturbed by the waters. She is ready to give help rather than being herself subject to danger; even so, if any men have been driven by severe storms and want to take refuge in the harbor, the Church is at hand like a harbor of salvation. Opening her arms, she calls into the lap of her tranquillity those who are in danger and shows them a trusty place of anchorage. Therefore the churches in this world are scattered over the coasts like seaports; they stand to meet the afflicted, and say to them that a refuge has been prepared for believers, where they can beach their wind-battered vessels.[4]

(5.28) Over these churches are the princes of Zabulon and the princes of Nephthali, as Psalm 67 teaches.[5] Some of them are liberators from the time of night, for they cry out, "Let us therefore lay aside the works of darkness, and put on the armor of light."[6] Others are of an apostolic breadth, for they

---

2 Cf. Ps. 90 (91).4–6.
3 Cf. 1 Tim. 1.19.
4 Cf. Vergil, *Aeneid* 1.551. Passages of a Vergilian tenor in language and imagery are frequent in Ambrose's metaphors of the sea. For the harbor as a place of rest and security, see C. Bonner, "Desired Haven," *Harvard Theological Review* 34 (1941) 49–67. See also *Death as a Good*, ch. 4 n. 9 above.
5 Cf. Ps. 67 (68).28.
6 Rom. 13.12.

can say, "Our mouth is open to you, O Corinthians, our heart is enlarged."[7] They are those who, when they were in darkness, saw a great light, as the prophet bears witness when he says, "The land of Zabulon and the land of Nephthali, the way of the sea beyond the Jordan. The people who dwelt in darkness have seen a great light; upon those who dwelt in the land of the shadow of death a light has arisen."[8] (5.29) Therefore our Lord God set the descendants of the former patriarch as watchmen along the approaches of shipping. His watchful care and spiritual line of descent extend even to Sidon; that is, he reaches even to the Gentiles, so that the mercy of the Lord may lighten the sins of the nations. The original Sidon is the son of Ham,[9] the very same who was condemned by his father's curse for his total lack of filial respect.[10] And so deliverance from the night depends on keeping watches at a spiritual bulwark, as it were; else someone may fall upon the crags of this life. Deliverance extends even to sinners who have committed the most serious offenses, even to the Sidonians themselves. Before, because of their strong superstition, they were called "hunters of offenses," as the interpretation of the name shows. But Christ forgave them, freed them from the inheritance of the curse and presented them with the inheritance of the blessing, so that where sin was greater, there grace may now be more abundant.[11]

(6.30) "Issachar desired the good, and rested in the midst of lots. And seeing the place of rest that it is good, and the land that it is rich, he bowed his shoulder to labor and became a husbandman."[1] Issachar is called "reward," and therefore he represents Christ, who is our reward, because we

---

7 2 Cor. 6.11.
8 Isa. 9.1–2.
9 Cf. Gen. 10.15. Actually, he is Ham's grandson; his father was Chanaan.
10 Cf. Gen. 9.18–27.
11 Cf. Rom 5.20.

---

1 Gen. 49.14–15 (Septuagint).

buy Him for ourselves for the hope of everlasting salvation, not with gold and silver but with faith and devotion. On this account also David says of Him, "Behold, the inheritance of the Lord are children; the fruit of the womb is a reward."[2] And Moses says of Him, "a reward of those dwelling around the sea."[3] He is the one who desired the good from the beginning and did not know how to desire what is evil. Of Him also Isaia says, "Before the child knows how to call his father or mother, he does not trust evil, choosing what is good."[4] He rested among the lots of the Old Testament and the New, and in the midst of the prophets. And, therefore, He appeared in the middle between Moses and Elias,[5] to show us that He had rest through discourse with them, through whom many renounce their sins and believe in the living God, and that they themselves are witnesses of His resurrection and blessed repose. (6.31) Accordingly, to call the nations to the grace of His resurrection—which is the rich and fertile land that bears everlasting fruits, fruits a hundredfold and sixtyfold[6]—He bowed His shoulder to labor, bowed Himself to the cross, to carry our sins. For that reason the prophet says, "whose government is on his shoulder."[7] This means, above the passion of His body is the power of His divinity, or it refers to the cross that towers above His body. Therefore He bowed His shoulder, applying Himself to the plow—patient in the endurance of all insults, and so subject to affliction that He was wounded on account of our iniquities and weakened on account of our sins.[8] "And he became a husbandman," for He knew how to sow His own land with good grain and to plant fruitful trees with deep roots.

---

2 Ps. 126 (127).3.
3 Deut. 33.19 (Septuagint).
4 Isa. 8.4; 7.16.
5 Cf. Matt. 17.3.
6 Cf. Matt. 13.8; Mark 4.8.
7 Isa. 9.6.
8 Cf. Isa. 53.3–5.

(7.32) "Dan shall judge his people like one tribe of Israel. And Dan became a serpent sitting in the way and biting the horse's heel in the path, and the horseman will fall backward, awaiting salvation from the Lord."[1] The simple interpretation is this, that the tribe of Dan also supplied the judge in Israel. Granted, after Josue the son of Nun, the judges of the people were from various tribes. However, Samson was from the tribe of Dan[2] and he judged for twenty years.[3] But the prophecy does not mean him, but the Antichrist, a cruel judge and savage tyrant who will come from the tribe of Dan and will judge the people. Like a serpent sitting in the way, he will try to throw down those who walk in the way of truth, for he desires to overthrow the truth. Indeed, this is to bite the horse's heel, so that the horse, injured by the infusion of poison and wounded by the serpent's tooth, lifts up his heel. Just so the betrayer Judas, when tempted by the devil, lifted up his heel[4] upon the Lord Jesus to throw down the rider who threw Himself down to lift up all men. He fell, then, not thrown forward on His face as if sleeping, but backward, so that He might reach out from higher things to those which were before and might await salvation from God. For He knew that He was to be raised up and therefore He expected Adam, who lay dead, to rise up.

(7.33) On this account, when we run well[5] in the way, let us beware that the serpent may not lie hid anywhere in the path and undermine the footstep of the horse—that is, of our body—and suddenly throw the sleeping rider. For if we are vigilant, we ought to be on our guard in some measure and shun the bites of the serpent. Therefore, let the sleep of neglect, the sleep of the world, not overwhelm us, let the sleep of wealth not overwhelm us, lest it be said of us also,

---

1 Gen. 49.16–17.
2 Cf. Judges 13.2.
3 Cf. Judges 15.20.
4 Cf. Ps. 40 (41).10; John 13.18.
5 Cf. Gal. 5.7.

"They have slept their sleep, and all the men of riches have found nothing."[6] But there are indeed riders who sleep, of whom it is written, "They have slumbered who mounted on horses."[7] Should avarice wound your heart, should lust inflame it, you are a sleeping rider, and on that account you are not able to restrain your body, that is, your horse. Keep watch then, so that even though you will be thrown, that is, even though you will die, you do not sleep. For those who sleep their sleep find nothing; but do you await salvation from the Lord, look for it to come, so that you may find the grace of the resurrection. Judas was sleeping; therefore he did not hear the words of Christ. Judas was sleeping, yes, sleeping the sleep of wealth, for he sought recompense from his betrayal.[8] The devil saw that he was sleeping, yes, buried in the deep sleep of avarice; he let himself into his heart,[9] wounded the horse, and threw the rider, whom he separated from Christ.

(7.34) Moses blessed this tribe, saying, "Dan is a lion's whelp and he shall flee away from Basan,"[10] that is, from confusion. For this reason we ought rather to interpret according to the Greek, from which our translation comes, that Dan himself became a serpent sitting in the way. Dan expounds judgment, and therefore that tribe has entered into a severe danger of judgment, for the serpent, the Antichrist, has slipped into it to injure it with his poisons as it runs. But nonetheless that tribe will be freed from confusion when it has acknowledged the rider who rises again and says, "Whoever is ashamed of me before men, I in turn will be ashamed of him before my Father in heaven. But whoever acknowledges me before men, I also will acknowledge him before my Father, who is in heaven."[11]

---

6 Ps. 75 (76).6.
7 Ps. 75 (76).7.
8 Cf. Matt. 26.15.
9 Cf. Luke 22.3.
10 Deut. 33.22.
11 Cf. Matt. 10.33, 32; Mark 8.38; Luke 9.26.

(8.35) "Gad, trial shall try him, and he shall try them at their heels."[1] The trial is the cunning assembly of scribes and priests who tried the Lord Jesus about Caesar's tribute[2] and John's baptism,[3] as Scripture teaches. In His holiness, Jesus turned the trial back upon them. "At their heels," that is, replying immediately without any deliberation, so that He might rather corner those trying Him. For when they said, "By what authority do you do these things?" Christ did not respond to their inquiries, but rather He Himself inquired, saying, "I also will ask you one question, and if you answer me this, I in turn will tell you by what authority I do these things."[4] Again, when they said, "Is it lawful to give tribute to Caesar, or not?" He said, "Why do you try me, you hypocrites? Show me the coin of the tribute." And when they offered it, again He asked, "Whose are the image and inscription?" They say to Him, "Caesar's." And thereupon He bound them in their own words and tied them in their own entanglement. For then He said to them, "Render to Caesar the things that are Caesar's and to God the things that are God's,"[5] so that they could not contradict their own words. Indeed they marveled and went off from Him. But it is not cause for marvel, if Christ, who saw before their heels, answered at their heels. (8.36) Moses explained clearly that this prophecy of holy Jacob was in reference to Christ, for he spoke thus: "Blessed is he who enlarged Gad. He has rested like a lion, breaking arms and chiefs. And he saw from his beginning that the land of the chiefs assembled with the leaders of the tribes was there divided; the Lord executed justice and judgment for Israel."[6] (8.37) Consequently, we recognize Him who rested like a lion, when He broke the arms of the powerful, because He saw from the beginning the divisions among those who

---

1 Gen. 49.19.
2 Cf. Matt. 22.15–22.
3 Cf. Matt. 21.25.
4 Matt. 21.23–24.
5 Matt. 22.17–21.
6 Deut. 33.20–21 (Septuagint).

were trying Him. Therefore, there is an opening in the earth to swallow up calumniators at the point where trial is made by unbelievers.[7]

(9.38) "Aser, his bread is rich, and he will furnish food to princes."[1] Aser in our tongue means "riches." Who then is rich except where there is the depth of the riches of the wisdom and knowledge of God?[2] Who is rich but the Lord Jesus, who always abounds and never fails? He came into this world a poor man and abounds in all things; He has filled all men. How mighty He is in riches, for He has made all men rich by His poverty! But He was poor for our sakes, and rich with the Father. He was poor to deliver us from want, as the Apostle teaches when he says, "Being rich, he became poor for your sakes, that by his poverty you might become rich."[3] His poverty enriches, the fringe of His garment heals,[4] His hunger satisfies, His death gives life, His burial gives resurrection. Therefore He is a rich treasure, for His bread is rich. And "rich" is apt, for one who has eaten this bread will be unable to feel hunger.[5] He gave it to the Apostles to distribute to a believing people,[6] and today He gives it to us, for He, as a priest, daily[7] consecrates it with His own words. Therefore this bread has become the food of the saints.

(9.39) Likewise we can take the Lord Himself, who has given us His own flesh, just as He said, "I am the bread of life. Your fathers ate the manna in the desert, and have died. But this is the bread that comes down from heaven, so that if anyone

---

7 Cf. Deut. 11.6.

---

1 Gen. 49.20.
2 Cf. Rom. 11.33.
3 2 Cor. 8.9.
4 Cf. Matt. 9.20–22; 14.34–36.
5 Cf. John 6.35.
6 Cf. Matt. 15.36.
7 This passage, along with others, apparently indicates that the Eucharist was celebrated on weekdays as well as on Sundays at Milan in the time of Ambrose. See Gryson 275 and n. 76, and especially V. Monachino, *La cura pastorale a Milano, Cartagine e Roma nel secolo IV* (Analecta Gregoriana 41; Rome 1947) 52-54.

eat of it he will not die."[8] And so that no one might suppose
that He is speaking of this death that comes through the
separation of soul and body,[9] and have reason to doubt, since
it is known that the holy Apostles died this death, He continued, "I am the living bread that has come down from
heaven. If anyone eat of this, he shall live forever."[10] This
means: I did not speak before concerning temporal life or the
death of that life; even if anyone dies by such a death, still,
if he has taken my bread, he will live forever. For he who
proves himself, takes it;[11] but he who takes it will not die by
the death of a sinner, because this bread is the forgiveness of
sins. (9.40) Moses, too, delivered a very appropriate prophecy
when he said, in his blessings, "Aser is blessed with children,
and will be acceptable to his brothers, and he shall dip his foot
in oil. His shoe shall be iron and brass, and as your days are,
so will your powers be. There is not anyone as is your God
in heaven, your helper and the mighty Lord of the firmament,
and the God of the highest, protecting you, and through the
strength of his powerful arms he casts out your enemy from
your presence, saying, 'Let him perish.' And Israel shall dwell
securely alone upon the land, Jacob in grain and wine, and
heaven shall be misty with dew for you."[12]

(10.41) "Nephthali[1] is a spreading vine, putting forth beauty
in its shoot."[2] One branch of the vine is cut off, because it

---

8 John 6.48–50.
9 The concept of death as a separation of soul and body, or a departure
  of the soul from the body, is found also in Origen and Macrobius,
  among others, and it appears in *Death as a Good* 2.3, 8.31. Cf. *Death*
  ch. 2 n. 5.
10 John 6.51.
11 Cf. 1 Cor. 11.28.
12 Deut. 33.24–28. The translation of this passage is based on the text
  of Migne, PL 14.686–687, which at this point gives a clearer reading
  than the CSEL text.

---

1 The text from this point to 10.44 appears also in the *Commentary on
  the Canticle of Canticles* 3.26 (PL 15.1898), for which see above,
  p. 5.
2 Gen. 49.21 (Septuagint).

seems useless, so that the vine may not run wild in the profusion of its branches and be unfruitful. Another is cut back only for a little while and is permitted to grow so that it may produce fruit. Its beauty is in its product. While it rises to things which are above, it embraces the vine; mounting to the top, it clothes the necks of the crossbeam, as it were, with a necklace of precious vine shoots. There is also such beauty in its product, because it pours forth many fruits from full shoots. (10.42) This branch is beautiful, but it is a far fairer thing that the reference is to a shoot clinging to a spiritual vine, of which we are the branch and can bear fruit, if we remain on the vine; but otherwise we are cut off. (10.43) The holy patriarch Nephthali was an abundant shoot. For this reason Moses says, "Nephthali is the abundance of those that receive; he shall be filled with a blessing from the Lord, he shall possess the sea and the south."[3] This is in explanation of that which Jacob had said, that he is a spreading vine. That is, through the grace of faith he was stripped of the bonds of death, and in him there is foreshadowed the people of God, called to the liberty of faith and to the fullness of grace and spread over the whole world. It clothes the crossbeam of Christ with good fruit and encompasses the wood of that true vine, that is, the mysteries of the Lord's cross; it does not fear the danger of acknowledging Him, but rather, even amid persecutions, it glories in the name of Christ.

(10.44) That man is truly set free from bonds who is not bound by any bond of fear. (For this reason the prophet says, "They shall go forth and leap for joy like young bullocks loosened from bonds."[4]) And on that account the people of God puts forth beauty in its shoot, because it has been set in a place of pasture and led out beside the water of refreshment;[5] through the sacraments of its regeneration it produces the

---

3 Deut. 33.23.
4 Mal. 4.2 (Septuagint; = 3.20 Confraternity).
5 Cf. Ps. 22 (23).2.

good beauty of the Word, and it is taken up into that most fair grace of Christ, who is able to increase the attraction of your beauty. (10.45) Indeed, since it is beautiful above all men, it gives that which it has—for no one can give what he does not have—and so it is said, "The Lord has reigned, he is clothed with beauty."[6] For He is clothed with beauty in the grace of the Church; in baptism, she has set aside all offenses and their defilements and has shone with the splendor of a heavenly grace. And so the bridegroom says of her, "Who is she that looks forth like the dawn, beautiful as the moon, choice as the sun, marvelous in splendid array?"[7]

(11.46) Now, to conclude the narrative with a kind of epilogue, just as God's Scripture also is concluded, let us relate the prophecy of holy Jacob in regard to the holy Joseph. "My son Joseph is to be increased, my son is to be increased, is to be envied, my young son; return to me. Bringing counsel against him, they spoke wickedly and the masters drew their bow against him. And their bows were broken with their power, and the sinewy hands of their arms were unloosed through the hands of the mighty one of Jacob, and from there Israel was strengthened by the God of your father. And my God has helped you and blessed you with the blessing of heaven from above, and with the blessing of a land having all things by reason of the blessings of breasts and womb, the blessings of your father and mother. He prevailed over the blessings of the enduring mountains and was stronger than the desires of the everlasting hills. They shall be on the head of Joseph and on the crown of the head of the brothers of whom he was the leader."[1] (11.47) What is the reason why the father honored his son Joseph more abundantly than all his sons? Only because he saw in him the mysteries prefiguring Christ.

---

6 Ps. 92 (93).1.
7 Cant. 6.10 (9).

---

1 Gen. 49.22–26.

On this account he blessed Him who was awaited, rather than him who was seen, and said, "My son Joseph is to be increased." Who is to be increased but Christ, whose grace is always increased, for His glory does not have an end to its advance? Of Him also John says, "He must increase, but I must decrease,"[2] because, through that perfect and saving name of His, grace was piled up and abounded in this world—"My son is to be increased." And so, because his brothers saw that he was growing, they began to envy him; moreover, He whom Joseph prefigured also met with envy from those whom He loved more. In fact He said, "I have not come except to the lost sheep of the house of Israel."[3] And they said, "We do not know where he is from."[4] He had care for them and they denied Him.

(11.48) "My young son"—in truth he was young, for he was almost the last to be born. Indeed, Scripture also says, "Jacob loved him, because he was the son of his old age."[5] This has reference likewise to Christ. For the Son of God, rising like the dawn through His birth from the virgin Mary, came late to a world that was growing old and on the point of perishing. As a son of old age, He took on a body according to the mystery, while before the ages He was always with His Father. (11.49) For this reason the Father says to Him, "Return to me," calling forth from earth to heaven the one whom He had sent for our salvation. And so, raising up His only-begotten Son, He made vain the counsel of those who spoke evil—on this account Isaia also says, "Vain is the counsel of your spirit"[6]—and He abolished all the reproaches which they directed as if they were shooting arrows. He destroyed the power of those who were trusting in their own strength and

---

2 John 3.30.
3 Matt. 15.24.
4 John 9.29.
5 Gen. 37.3.
6 Isa. 19.11.

not in God. "From there Israel was strengthened by the God of your father, and my God has helped you." Who is he who strengthened Israel and helped a son, but God the Father only? For He said, "Jacob is my servant, I will uphold him; Israel is my chosen one, let my soul uphold him."[7] (11.50) "And he blessed him with the blessing of heaven from above, and with the blessing of a land having all things." For He made all things subject to the Son,[8] those of heaven according to the blessing of heaven and those of earth according to the blessing of the land, so that He might have dominion over both men and angels.

(11.51) And therefore, in that contemptible body, so to speak, "You prevailed by reason of the blessing of breasts and womb, the blessings of your father and mother." Jacob said the breasts, or the two Testaments, in one of which Christ was foretold and in the other revealed. And he did well to say "breasts," because the Son nurtured us and offered us to the Father as men nourished on a kind of spiritual milk. Or else he is speaking of Mary's breasts, which were truly blessed, for with them the holy virgin gave milk to drink to the people of the Lord. This is the reason the woman in the Gospel says, "Blessed is the womb that bore you and the breasts that nursed you."[9] But as to what Jacob says, "the blessing of the womb, the blessing of your father and mother," if we should choose to interpret it as the womb only of Mary, the reason why he coupled the two blessings will escape our notice, for he could have spoken of the womb only of the mother. But I think it more appropriate that we should take it, according to the spiritual mystery, as the two begettings of the Lord Jesus, that according to the divinity and that according to the flesh, because He was begotten from the Father before all ages. For this reason also the Father says, "My heart has uttered a good Word,"[10] because the Son has proceeded from the most pro-

---

7 Isa. 42.1 (Septuagint).
8 Cf. Ps. 8.7; 1 Cor. 15.27.
9 Luke 11.27.   10 Ps. 44 (45).2; cf. Ps. 109 (110).3.

found and incomprehensible substance of the Father and is always in Him. For this reason also the evangelist says, "No one has at any time seen God, except the only-begotten Son, who is in the bosom of the Father, he has revealed him."[11] "The bosom of the Father," then, is to be understood in a spiritual sense, as a kind of innermost dwelling of the Father's love and of His nature, in which the Son always dwells. Even so, the Father's womb is the spiritual womb of an inner sanctuary, from which the Son has proceeded just as from a generative womb. To be sure, we read in different versions, now that it was the Father's womb, again that it was His heart, with which He uttered the Word, and again that it was His mouth from which justice proceeded and from which wisdom came forth, as wisdom herself says, "From the mouth of the Most High I came forth."[12] Thus, since the One is not limited and all things declare the One, the blessing refers rather to the spiritual mystery of generation from the Father than to some part of the body. But just as we interpret it to mean that generation from the Father, likewise let us interpret it to mean the generation from Mary unto the completion of faith, when the mother's womb is blessed, that virginal womb of Mary which brought forth for us the Lord Jesus. The Father speaks of that womb through the prophet Jeremia, "Before I formed you in the womb, I knew you, and before you came forth from your mother's womb, I sanctified you."[13] Therefore the prophet showed that there was a twofold nature in Christ, the divine and the fleshly, the former from the Father, the latter from a virgin, but in such a way that Christ was not deprived of His divinity when He was born from a virgin and was in the body.

(11.52) From here "he grew strong over all the mountains and the desires of the everlasting hills." For He shone forth

---

11 John 1.18.
12 Sir. 24.3 (5).
13 Jer. 1.5.

like a heavenly light above all those men of exalted merit,
patriarchs and prophets and apostles, and beyond the sun
and moon and archangels as well, even as He says, "No disciple
is above his teacher, nor is the servant above his master."[14]
Who indeed among them was there to whom all things were
subject? Rather, Christ gave to them their nature. In Him all
His saints are blessed, because He is the head of all, above
the heads of all[15]—for "the head of the woman is the man, the
head of the man is Christ"[16]—and above the crowns of the
heads of all men, because He is the surpassing crown of the
whole of mankind. But the highest crown belongs to the just,
because He won them through grace and through a sharing of
His resurrection, as it were, and calls them brothers.[17] On
this account also we understand by the brothers of Joseph
those brothers, rather, of whom the psalmist says, "I will proclaim your name to my brothers, in the midst of the assembly
I will sing your praises."[18]

(11.53) Yes, and when Moses was about to finish the course
of his life, and he blessed the tribe of Joseph, he was surely
not giving the blessing to that Joseph who was already
deceased, but to Christ, as you find it written in regard to
Joseph, "Of the blessing of the Lord be his land, of the ends
of heaven and of the dew, and of the abysses of fountains from
beneath and of the fruits of the sun's revolution according to
the season, and of the coming together of the months, and of
the summit of the mountains from the beginning, and of the
summit of the everlasting hills and at the season of the fullness
of the earth, and may it come upon the head of Joseph and
upon his crown from him who was seen in the bush. He is
honored among his brothers. His beauty is that of the firstborn of a bull, his horns are those of a unicorn. With them
he will push the nations at once even to the end of the earth.

---

14 Matt. 10.24.
15 Cf. Eph. 1.22; 4.15.
16 1 Cor. 11.3; cf. Eph. 5.23.
17 Cf. Matt. 12.49–50.   18 Ps. 21 (22).23.

These are the myriads of Ephraim and these the thousands of Manasse."[19] (11.54) It is the same blessing, which contains all the fullness of the things of heaven and of the earth and the special grace of Christ; when He was seen in the bush, He said even to Moses, "Loose the sandals from your feet,"[20] and He is God over all men, because "he is the head of the body, the Church; he, who is the beginning, the firstborn from the dead, that in all things he may have the first place, for in him all fullness was pleased to dwell."[21] And so the prerogative conferred on Him alone by this blessing reaches from the summit of heaven even to the end of earth. For "he is before all creatures, and in him all things hold together,"[22] and He also "made all things peaceful through the blood of his cross, both as to the things that are on the earth and the things that are in heaven."[23] The holy Joseph, who is His prefiguration, receives a choice blessing so that he may be held in honor among his brothers.

(11.55) "His beauty is that of the firstborn of a bull, his horns are those of a unicorn, with them he will push the nations." Yes, a good bull, like a sacrificial victim[24] for the offenses of the whole world, to make all things peaceful. His beauty is holy, for everything firstborn is holy, as I have shown elsewhere;[25] for that reason Levi deserved to be called the firstborn, not by order of age but by the prerogative conferred by a holy line of descendants. And Christ's beauty is truly holy, for it is written in reference to Him as arisen, "fair in beauty above the sons of men,"[26] because He is the firstborn

---

19 Deut. 33.13–17. The translation is based on the text of the Roman edition, as reported in Migne, PL 14.690 note d. The exact sense of the passage is obscure.
20 Exod. 3.5.
21 Col. 1.18–19.
22 Col. 1.17.
23 Col. 1.20.
24 Cf. Vergil, *Georgics* 2.146.
25 *Cain and Abel* 2.2.7, 4.13 (English translation by J. J. Savage, FOTC 42).
26 Ps. 44 (45).3.

from the dead[27] and has the horns of the unicorn. But we
should inquire how Moses, when he spoke of horns, chose
those of the unicorn, since the unicorn itself does not appear
among the generations of wild animals, so the experts say.
And so we ought rather to judge that the Word is unique,
because the substantial Word of God is one Word, and not
many. For this reason also Anna says, "The Lord shall judge
the ends of the earth, and he shall exalt the horn of his
Christ,"[28] and Isaia says, "My beloved had a vineyard on the
horn of a hill in a fertile place."[29] For in the only-begotten
Son of God the Church flourishes, keeping the unique Word
of God, in whom there is the fullness of power and of wisdom,
and from whose abundance there has sprouted a crop of faith.
This is the Word the saints follow.

(11.56) "The[30] ten thousands of Ephraim and the thousands
of Manasse,"[31] that is, let Him rule over both the Jews and
the Gentiles and acquire the fullness of the Church for Himself from both peoples. And therefore holy Jacob put his
right hand upon Ephraim because, as you read that the bride
says in the Canticle of Canticles, "My beloved is white and
ruddy, chosen out of ten thousands."[32] Indeed, when the young
women of the chorus praised David, Mary's ancestor, from
whose line of descent Christ was born through the parturition
of a virgin, they did so in terms of ten thousands, but they
praised Saul in terms of thousands,[33] although the latter should
have had the preference out of respect toward the king. Therefore He who has exalted the horn of Christ and proclaimed
His glory Himself also receives the horns. On this account, like-

27 Cf. Col. 1.18.
28 1 Kings 2.10.
29 Isa. 5.1.
30 The text from this point, to and including ". . . although the latter
   should have had the preference out of respect toward the king"
   appears in the *Commentary on the Canticle of Canticles* 5.60 (Migne,
   PL 15.1934). See above ch. 10 n. 1.
31 Deut. 33.17 (Septuagint).
32 Cant. 5.10.
33 Cf. 1 Kings 18.7.

wise, the saints are called unicorns in a psalm verse, "and as the beloved son of unicorns."[34] For in an animal of this sort the appearance of horns indicates the advent of a more mature age. Just so, when horns begin to grow from the head of our soul, as it were, they seem to indicate the advent of a more perfect virtue, and they grow until they are filled out. With this horn the Lord Jesus crushed the nations, to trample on superstition and impart salvation, just as He Himself says, "I will strike and I will heal."[35] And therefore, like an imitator of this bull, the psalmist says, "In you we will push down our enemies,"[36] that is, "destroying every lofty thing that exalts itself against the knowledge of God."[37] And therefore the animals that are clean according to the law[38] have horns, for the law is spiritual. Those who can repel the enticements of this world through the word of God and the observance of virtue seem to be protected by horns upon their heads, so to speak, as if by weapons. And with good reason the wonderful power of discourse that incites the good soldiers of Christ to battle, so that we may carry back the spoils from our enemy the devil, is called a horn [trumpet].[39] Therefore we are in a battle, and we perceive that many of us are captives in the camp of our enemy. Them we must deliver from a very heavy yoke of slavery.

(12.57) The devil has very many wolves that he sends against the sheep of Christ. And therefore He whom Joseph prefigured, in order to protect His own sheep, seized the very enemy that was coming to plunder the sheep, the wolf Paul, and from a persecutor turned him into a teacher. Of him Jacob says, just as it is written, "Benjamin is a ravenous wolf, in the morning he shall still be eating and for the evening he

---

34 Ps. 28 (29).6.
35 Deut. 32.39.
36 Ps. 43 (44).6.
37 2 Cor. 10.5.
38 Cf. Deut. 14.3–21.
39 Cf. Ps. 97 (98).6.

shall distribute food among chiefs."[1] He was a wolf when he scattered and devoured the sheep of the Church; but he who had been a wolf became a shepherd. He was a wolf when he was Saul, when he would go into houses and drag men and women off to prison. He was a wolf when he breathed threats of murder against the disciples of the Lord and asked for letters from the chief priests to seize the humble servants of Christ.[2] Jesus blinded him with an outpouring of light,[3] as if he were a wolf roaming abroad in the darkness of night. And so, when Rachel gave birth to Benjamin, she called his name "son of my sorrow,"[4] as a prophecy that from that tribe Paul would come, to afflict the sons of the Church in the time of his persecution and to trouble their mother with a grievous sorrow. But nonetheless, at a later time, the same Paul distributed food among chiefs, when he preached the word of God to the Gentiles and stirred very many to faith, for they received the grace of the Lord through his preaching, as did the deputy of the proconsul Paulus,[5] and the chief Publius.[6] (12.58) Moreover, when Moses blessed the tribe of Benjamin, he also said aptly, "The beloved of the Lord shall dwell confidently, and God shall overshadow him all the days, and the beloved of the Lord shall rest between his shoulders."[7] Paul was also made a vessel of election,[8] for he was converted only through the Lord's compassionate love. For this reason he attributes nothing to his own merit but assigns everything to Christ and says, "For I am the least of the apostles, and am not worthy to be called an apostle, because I persecuted the Church of God. But by the grace of God I am what I am, and

---

1 Gen. 49.27. For Benjamin as a figure of the Apostle Paul, cf. *Joseph* 8.44–9.47.
2 Cf. Acts 9.1–2.
3 Cf. Acts 9.3–9.
4 Cf. Gen. 35.18.
5 Cf. Acts 13.7–12. In most versions it is the proconsul Paulus himself who is converted, not a deputy.
6 Cf. Acts 28.7–10.
7 Deut. 33.12.
8 Cf. Acts 9.15.

his grace in me has not been poor."[9] He dwelt confidently in the house which he used to empty of its inhabitants, he dwelt in the habitations of Christ, whereas before he used to roam in the woods like a wolf. And God overshadowed him when Christ appeared to him. Although he saw nothing when his eyes were opened,[10] still he saw Christ. And it was fitting that he saw Christ present and also heard Him speaking. That overshadowing is not the overshadowing of blindness but of grace. Indeed, it is said to Mary: "The Holy Spirit shall come upon you and the power of the Most High shall overshadow you."[11]

(12.59) "And he shall rest between his shoulders," that is, between good actions and works of great value. For you also find above that "Issachar bowed his shoulder to labor and became a husbandman." Imitating him, Paul planted new gardens of faith and then said, like a good husbandman, "I have planted, Apollo has watered."[12]

---

9 1 Cor. 15.9–10.
10 Cf. Acts 9.8.
11 Luke 1.35.
12 1 Cor. 3.6.

FLIGHT FROM THE WORLD

(De fuga saeculi)

INTRODUCTION

HE WORK *Flight from the World*,[1] delivered as a sermon,[2] may be dated, from a passing reference involving a phrase book of the grammarian Arusianus Messius, to *ca.* 391–394 A.D.[3]

The work itself is almost as much moral-ascetical as exegetical. As its title indicates, it sounds the theme of the necessity of flight from the world for the Christian. The various changes are rung on this central theme with numerous examples, mostly from the Old Testament—Jacob, Moses, David, Lot, among others—but a few from the New—Paul and, in a minor reference, John the Baptist. Throughout, there is heavy reliance on the work of Philo, *On Flight and Finding.*[4]

---

1 On the work in general see Dudden 684–85; Palanque 441, 444, 549–50.
2 That the work was so delivered is reasonably clear from the concluding doxology at 9.58. See Palanque 441. The tone of the opening of the work also suggests pulpit delivery, as does the reference (3.16) to a gospel reading that included John 1.29. This lection is noted (under Eastertide) by G. G. Willis, *St. Augustine's Lectionary* (Alcuin Club Collections 44; London 1962) 15; a table (pp. 14-17) purports to give us "St. Ambrose's lectionary."
3 Cf. 3.16. Some uncertainty remains, since the date of Messius' book is not firm. See Dudden 684 (with a date after 391, before 394); Palanque 549 (autumn 394); Paredi 437 (about 394); U. Moricca, *Storia della letteratura latina cristiana* 2.1 371–73, especially 371 n. 334 (*ca.* 391). The history of scholarly work on the problem reflects a tendency to advance the date.
4 This work, titled in Latin *De fuga et inventione,* appears in English translation as part of the fifth volume of the Loeb Classical Library Philo. The parallels, set out in the CSEL text, have not been repeated in the notes to this volume. The discussion by M. Ihm, "Philo und Ambrosius," *Neue Jahrbücher für Philologie und Paedagogik* (1890) 282–88, sets out the texts of Philo and Ambrose in parallel columns. Ihm cites, in order, *Flight from the World* 5.26; 4.20; 2.5, 6, 7, 9, 13; 8.47, 48, 49, 45.

In the course of his controversy with the followers of Pelagius, Augustine had occasion to quote several passages from *Flight from the World*.[5] Apparently, no English translation of Ambrose's work has been published; there are, however, published translations into German and Italian.[6]

5 The citations appear in Augustine, *Contra duas epistulas Pelagianorum*, a work in four books published in 421; they are noted at the appropriate points in the notes to the translation which follows.

6 The German version, by F. X. Schulte, appeared in 1877 in volume 2 of the *Ausgewählte Schriften des heiligen Ambrosius*, pp. 425–71; this work contains also Schulte's German translation of *Death as a Good*. The Italian translation, by F. Portalupi, appeared under the title *De fuga saeculi* at Turin in 1959.

FLIGHT FROM THE WORLD

I HAVE OFTEN PREACHED[1] on flight from this world—
and would the preaching were so easy as the disposition to flee is wary and cautious! But, what is worse,
often the enticements of earthly desires steal in and blinding
vanities take possession of the mind. Thus you think upon that
which you desire to avoid, and you ponder it in spirit. It is
hard for a man to guard against this and impossible to rid
himself of it. Indeed, the psalmist bears witness that the matter
is more one of wish than of actualization when he says, "Incline my heart to your testimonies and not to covetousness."[2]
For[3] our heart and our thoughts are not in our power. When
suddenly blinded, they put mind and spirit into confusion
and lead them elsewhere than you had intended, call them
back to worldliness, introduce earthly things, bring in pleasures, and interweave enticements. At the very time when we
are making ready to lift up our minds, idle thoughts intrude
and we are cast down the more to things of earth.

(1.2) Who,[4] then, is so blessed as always to be ascending in
his heart? Yet how is this possible without God's help? In no

---

1 The text to and including ". . . ascent is in his heart" in 1.2 appears
in Augustine, *Contra duas epistulas Pelagianorum* 4.11.30 (CSEL 60.
561.19 ff.). The text of 1.1 appears also in Augustine, *Contra Iulianum
Pelagianum* 2.8.23 (Migne, PL 44) and *De dono perseverantiae* 8.20;
the latter text is available in English translation by Sister M. Alphonsine Lesousky, O.S.U., *The De dono perseverantiae of Saint Augustine*
(Catholic University of America Patristic Studies 91; Washington 1956).
2 Ps. 118 (119).36.
3 This sentence is cited twice in Augustine, *De dono perseverantiae*, at
8.19 and 19.48, in addition to its inclusion in the longer citation men-
tioned in n. 1, above.
4 The text from this point to and including ". . . ascent is in his heart"
is cited in *Contra duas epistulas Pelagianorum* 4.1 and *De dono
perseverantiae* 13.33.

way at all. Indeed, Scripture says on this point, "Blessed is
the man whose help is from you, O Lord; ascent is in his
heart."[5] Blessed indeed is the man who is not called back by
enjoyment or led away by pleasure, and who does not look to
lower things, something not even Lot's wife could avoid.[6]
Warned by that example, the Apostle, forgetting what was
behind and seeking for what is before, hastened on to the
prize[7] and deserved to attain it. For he saw Christ before him,
and he was called by Christ to the crown of justice;[8] but he
who attained it denied himself to himself in order to gain
Christ.[9] Indeed, he did not live, but Christ lived in him.[10]

(1.3) Amid so many passions of this body of ours, amid so
many enticements of this world, who indeed can keep his
footstep safe and undefiled? The eye looks back and leads the
mind's perception astray, the ear hears and turns one's attention away, a whiff of fragrance hinders thought, a kiss of the
mouth introduces guilt, a touch kindles the fire of passion.
"Death has entered in through the window,"[11] the prophet
said. Your eye is your window. If you look at a woman to lust
after her, death has entered in;[12] if you listen to the harlot's
words, death has entered in; if licentiousness takes hold of your
senses, death has gone in. And so, if anyone wants to ascend,
let him seek, not the joys of the world or the pleasant things or
the delights, but whatever is filled with pain and weeping;
for it is better to go into a house of sorrow than into a house
of rejoicing.[13] Indeed, Adam would not have come down from
paradise unless he had been beguiled by pleasure.

(1.4) Therefore David, who had experienced those very
glances which are dangerous for a man, aptly says that the

---

5 Ps. 83 (84).6.
6 Cf. Gen. 19.26.
7 Cf. Phil. 3.14.
8 Cf. 2 Tim. 4.8.
9 Cf. Phil. 3.8.
10 Cf. Gal. 2.20.
11 Jer. 9.20 (21).
12 Cf. Matt. 5.28.
13 Cf. Eccles. 7.2 (3).

man is blessed whose every hope is in the name of God.[14] For such a man does not have regard to vanities and follies if he always strives toward Christ and always looks upon Christ with his inner eyes. For this reason David turned to God again and said, "Turn away my eyes, that they may not see vanity."[15] The circus is vanity, because it is totally without profit; horse racing is vanity, because it is counterfeit as regards salvation;[16] the theater is vanity, every game is vanity. "All things are vanity!"[17] as Ecclesiastes said, all things which are in this world. Accordingly, let the man who wishes to be saved ascend above the world, let him seek the Word who is with God, let him flee from this world and depart from the earth. For a man cannot comprehend that which exists and exists always, unless he has first fled from here. On this account also, the Lord, wishing to approach God the Father, said to the Apostles, "Arise, let us go from here."[18]

(2.5) The law also teaches you the necessity of a flight from the world and of a pursuit of God. For it teaches precisely this when it says, "You will set apart for yourselves cities for refuge, and they shall be your places of refuge, to which the homicide may flee, everyone who has killed a soul unintentionally,"[1] and later, "Six cities shall serve you as places of refuge. Three cities you shall give beyond the Jordan and three cities you shall give in the land of Chanaan."[2] It is quite clear that the places of refuge were set up for those who were fleeing from this charge of homicide, but let us consider the matter in a more profound sense. There are four considerations which suggest that we must look more deeply into the mysteries involved in that passage. First, why were the six cities, which

---

14 Cf. Ps. 39 (40).5.
15 Ps. 118 (119).37.
16 Cf. Ps. 32 (33).17.
17 Eccles. 1.2.
18 John 14.31.

---

1 Num. 35.11.
2 Num. 35.13–14.

were given for a place of refuge to those laboring under the charge of homicide, given from among those cities which had fallen by lot to the Levites for their portion,[3] and why weren't the cities of other tribes also assigned to serve this function? Second, why were the cities six in number? Surely this number, neither more cities nor fewer, doesn't seem to have been prescribed without reason. Third, why were three cities appointed beyond the Jordan and three in the territory of Chanaan, to serve as a place of refuge for sinners? Fourth, why is a computation and precise indication of the time within which the homicide should dwell in the city of refuge included? That is, until the high priest dies, and after the death of the high priest the homicide may return to the city of his own dwelling.[4] Therefore it is appropriate to speak of each of these considerations, and to treat of the questions in the order in which I have proposed them.

(2.6) Thus I must first explain properly the fact that it was the cities of the Levites that were given for a place of refuge.[5] However, it is clear that the provision was a fitting one, because the Levites are those fleeing from this world to please God; they leave country, parents, children, and all their kin,[6] to cleave to God alone. Indeed, it was said also to Abraham, "Go out from your land and from your kin and from the house of your father."[7] But perhaps you may say, "He was not a Levite." But he had Levi in his loins, as we read in the Letter to the Hebrews.[8] And the Lord speaks to the Levites when He says to His disciples, that is, to the Apostles, "If anyone wishes to come after me, let him deny himself and take up his cross and follow me."[9] And yet it was then said to all, "You, however, are a chosen race, a royal priesthood, a holy nation,

---

3 Cf. Num. 35.6.
4 Cf. Num. 35.25.
5 Cf. Num. 35.6.
6 Cf. Luke 18.29.
7 Gen. 12.1.
8 Cf. Heb. 7.9–10.
9 Luke 9.23.

a people unto adoption."[10] The fullness has come,[11] the remnant has departed.[12] For Christ has called all men, the way of departure is open to all, that all may follow, and there has been set before all men a kingdom and life everlasting.

(2.7) Therefore one who has God as his portion should care for nothing except God; else he may be hindered by the duty of providing for the other need. For what is bestowed on other duties is snatched from the cultivation of religion and this, our proper duty. For the flight of the priest is really the renunciation of family, and a kind of alienation from dear ones, so that one who longs to serve God denies himself with regard to his own. Therefore it was right that a decree of the eternal law entrusted fugitives to fugitives; thus, those who have forgotten this world may receive those who condemn their own sinful works, seek forgetfulness of their earlier life, and desire to efface the worldly deeds they have performed. Therefore the minister of God's holy altar is one who is in flight from his own. For this reason the Lord, like a chief priest, gave an example for the Levites in His Gospel, when He said, "Who is my mother and who are my brothers?"[13] This means: I do not know my mother, I do not recognize my brothers, I am unacquainted with my near ones. "My mother and my brothers are they who hear the word of God and do it."[14] Therefore the minister knows the word of God only when he knows those in whom the word of God is at work. And so he is an exile from the world; fleeing from the body, fleeing from the passions, he deprives himself of all men to remain alone, even as Elias said, "And I alone am left."[15] But he was not alone, for he had Christ with him. And even the Lord was

10 1 Peter 2.9. The quotation appears in the same form in Ambrose, *On the Sacraments* 4.1.3, translated by T. Thompson in *On the Sacraments and On the Mysteries.*
11 Cf. Gal. 4.4.
12 Cf. Rom. 11.5.
13 Matt. 12.48.
14 Luke 8.21.
15 3 Kings 19.14.

left alone; "but I am not alone," He says, "because the Father is with me."[16]

(2.8) It is for that reason also that the Levites are ministers of God. And it is their cities that are appointed by the law for fugitive homicides, because it is their right to carry out God's commandments in regard to those who have committed a deadly crime. The Church does not know how to promulgate laws of her own; she knows that the priest should be obedient to the Lord's command. Hear the Levite as he says, "I have made delivery of such a one over to Satan for the destruction of the flesh, that his spirit may be saved in the day of our Lord Jesus Christ."[17] Therefore let fleshly affection be struck by the Levite's sword and die in us, so that our soul may live. For unless fleshly affection has perished, there can exist no fruit of eternal life.

(2.9) Moreover, the places of refuge consist of six cities for this reason, so that the first city may serve as knowledge of the Word and a model of living according to His image. For whoever has entered upon the way of such knowledge is safe from punishment, according to that which the Lord also said, "You are already clean because of the word that I have spoken to you,"[18] and in another passage, "Now this is everlasting life, that they may know you, the only true God, and him whom you have sent, Jesus Christ."[19] And so this city is like a metropolis and the five other cities of the Levites are near it. The second city is the consideration of the working of God, by which the world was created. The third city is the contemplation of His royal power and eternal majesty. The fourth city is reflection on God's clemency. The fifth city is the contemplation of God's law, that which commands what should be done. The sixth city, too, is a portion of the law, that which commands what should not be done. How great is the abundance of God's mercy! How great are the riches of His love! He has regard

16 John 16.32.
17 1 Cor. 5.5.
18 John 15.3.　　　　　　　19 John 17.3.

to the desires of each man and the frailties of the human condition, through which we are led unwillingly and reluctantly into guilt, and, overcome by enticements, often commit offenses which are not voluntary. Thus, God established for us various places of refuge, namely in six cities; in that number of days the world was fashioned, and in that same number, six, a remedy is afforded against worldly vices and the catastrophes of this age.

(2.10) The first remedy is as follows: If guilt has entered stealthily into any man of good intention, and if he desires to have perfect safety, such a one should hasten without any delay to the very summit of all things, where the Word of God is in the bosom of His Father, that is, in the hidden and secret place of God. The fountain of wisdom is there, and from it one may drink the everlasting drink of eternal life in place of death. The second remedy is this: A certain man cannot have a foretaste of the knowledge of that good because he is somewhat slow in ability or in understanding of the faith, whereas one must strive for the heights of knowledge with quick and vigorous mind and keen ability. At least, such a one should meditate on the works of the Lord, and from created things he should contemplate the Creator of so mighty a work. For from the goods which inhere in the nature of that creation—they are indeed very good, even as the Lord said[20]—one can apprehend the supreme and everlasting good.[21] The order of the universe, its arrangement and its beauty—isn't a man moved by this to love his Creator, even if he is slow in ability? For if we love our parents because they have produced us, how much more ought we to love the Creator of our parents and our own Creator! Therefore the power of God is a creating power. Even if God is not seen, He is judged from His works, and His works betray the workman, so that He who is not comprehended may be perceived. On

---

20 Cf. Gen. 1.31.
21 Cf. Rom. 1.20.

this account also the Lord says, "If you do not believe me, at least believe the works."[22] Therefore this city, too, is good for a place of refuge, because it bears witness to the favor of its builder and arouses our love. Thus we are the more desirous of Him who is seen to have bestowed on us this very beautiful construction. The third classification is the contemplation of royal power, so that we may be made subject to the king if we do not show deference to him as to a parent. Often, indeed, a man who is ungrateful for his salvation[23] becomes obedient to authority out of fear of him who wields command. Thus one who was unwilling and unable to recognize the gift of love may recognize a compulsion to moderate conduct. Then the compulsion makes that man good who should have been stirred by love.

(2.11) Such are the three cities across the Jordan, given for a place of refuge for a more perfect wisdom, that we may first flee from guilt, in resolution of spirit conformed to the image of God.[24] For so we have been created, as God says, "Let us make man to our image and likeness."[25] This, then, is the law of that first city. Thereafter, if we cannot form our heart in that way by reason of the frailty of the flesh and the entice-ments of the world, let us lighten the sin out of respect for our creation by the Father and out of zeal for His offspring, "for charity covers a multitude of sins."[26] Thus, let the man who cannot be according to the image of God be according to the fullness of charity. The one city excludes guilt; the other dissolves it. In short, this is the law of the second city, "You shall love the Lord, your God, with all your heart, and with all your soul, and with all your strength."[27] But if, on the other hand, there are cramped and tiny souls that are not able to admit the abundant gift of love, you have a third city,

---

22 John 10.38.
23 Cf. Vergil, *Aeneid* 10.666.
24 Cf. Rom. 8.29.
25 Gen. 1.26.
26 1 Peter 4.8.
27 Deut. 6.5.

so that the fear of God's power may make you careful, and the dread of it may make you bend. And the third law is this: "The Lord your God shall you worship and him only shall you serve."[28] These, therefore, are signal virtues, and they are placed beyond the Jordan as belonging to few men, and not to many. Thus you may represent your model, yourself an image; love your father, yourself a son; and worship your king, yourself a subject.

(2.12) However, there are those who have crossed over the Jordan—the name Jordan refers to their descent of it[29]—and who, then, have descended from those higher virtues to these lower ones, I mean the ones in which integrity and charity and humility are unsure. They have places of refuge to seek that are nearer to men. Thus, men who are subject to offenses and bent by vices that are not of their own choosing may hope that they can be reconciled to the Lord, if they seek forgiveness, and may hope that they can improve if they follow the commands of heaven's testaments, by which we are either fashioned to blamelessness or recalled from guilt. Therefore these cities of lesser rank are within the limits of the Jordan, so that we may gain God's favor for ourselves and may follow what He commands and avoid what He forbids. And so let us seek to gain God's favor, let us obey the precept we ought to follow and beware of the transgression that is forbidden. By observance of what is commanded and refusal of what is forbidden, let us show reverence for God's reconciling mercy and His law-giving providence.

(2.13) There remains the fourth consideration, what Scripture says concerning the death of the chief priest, "that the homicide shall be in the city of refuge even to that time, until the high priest dies."[30] In this passage the literal interpreta-

---

28 Matt. 4.10.
29 The name "Jordan" appears in Ambrose with a similar meaning in *The Prayer of Job and David* 4.4.14 (translated in this volume); *Abraham* 2.6.34; and *Commentary on Psalm 37*, 10.
30 Josue 20.6.

tion causes difficulty. First, the period of flight is limited by chance rather than by any consideration of fairness; further, in like cases the result is unlike. For it could happen that the high priest might die on the day after the homicide took refuge. However, what is the meaning beneath the uncertainty? And so, because the letter causes difficulty, let us search for spiritual meanings.[31] Who is that high priest but the Son of God, the Word of God? We enjoy His advocacy in our behalf before the Father,[32] for He is free from every offense, both willed and unintentional, and in Him subsist all things which are on earth and which are in heaven. For all things have been bound by the bond of the Word and are held together by His power and subsist in Him, because in Him they have been created and in Him all God's fullness dwells. And so all things endure, because He does not allow what things He has bound to be loosened, since they subsist in His will. Indeed, so long as He wills, He keeps all things in check by His command and rules them and binds them by a harmony of nature.[33] Therefore the Word of God lives, and He lives most of all in the souls of the holy, and the fullness of the Godhead never dies. For God's everlasting divinity and eternal power never die. To be sure, He dies to us if He is separated from our soul, not that our spirit is destroyed by death, but that it is loosened and stripped from union with Him. Yes, true death is the separation of the Word from the soul. Thereupon, the soul begins at once to be open to sins of volition.

(3.14) We find these kinds of virtues, not merely foreshadowed, but clearly portrayed, in the Apostle, who says, "So, for my part, I am ready to preach the gospel to you also who are at Rome. For I am not ashamed of the gospel, for it is the power of God unto salvation to everyone who believes, to Jew

---

31 Cf. 2 Cor. 3.6.
32 The figure of Christ as advocate is derived from 1 John 2.1–2. A convenient collection of passages touching on this theme in the works of Ambrose is found in Gryson, *Prêtre* 61 n. 5.
33 Cf. Col. 1.16–20.

first and to Greek. For in him the justice of God is revealed,"[1] that is, in him who believes. Then he continued, "from faith unto faith, as it is written, 'He who is just lives by faith.' "[2] In whom, then, is the justice of God revealed but in him who is like the image of the Son of God? You have the first precept with reference to the image of God. You have the second, because God's invisible attributes are understood through the things which have been made;[3] that is, His everlasting power and divinity are known by His works. This is the creative power. The third concerns the authority to rule, because the Word of God is that of a king and of a judge and filled with priestly justice. He reserves for those that are to come to His judgment both a reward for good acts and a punishment for wicked ones; of those men the Apostle says, "And we know that the judgment of God is according to truth against those who do such things."[4] Accordingly, a man who has known the truth and the justice of God ought not to do things that are deserving of death. God's reconciling goodness follows without fail, and concerning it the Apostle says, "Or do you despise the riches of his goodness and patience and long-suffering? Do you not know that the goodness of God leads you to repentance?"[5] That is, it ought to lead you to repentance. God calls you because He is good, so that you may be able to hope for pardon of your sins; for He that is ready to forgive does not wish to take vengeance. He arranged also for legislation, that is, for the giving of the law. Thus, whoever becomes lax through contemplation of God's goodness and is moved more to negligence than to repentance, may follow the law. "For whoever have sinned without the law, will perish also without the law; and whoever have sinned under the law, will be judged by the law."[6]

---

1 Rom. 1.15–17.
2 Rom. 1.17.
3 Cf. Rom. 1.20.
4 Rom. 2.2.
5 Rom. 2.4.
6 Rom. 2.12.

(3.15) Now the law is twofold, being both a natural law and a written law. The natural law is in the heart, the written law on tablets.[7] Therefore all are under the law, the natural law, but it does not belong to all men that each should be a law unto himself. However, that man is a law unto himself who does the commandments of the law of his own accord and manifests the work of the law written in his own heart. You possess the commandments to good in the law; still, we ought not merely to know them and listen to them in a careless fashion, but to do them as well. "For it is not they who hear the law that are just in the sight of God, but it is they who follow the law that will be justified."[8] You have come to know also the prohibitions of evil. First, nature herself is the teacher of good conduct. You know that one must not steal, and if your servant has stolen from you, you beat him, while if someone has lusted after your wife, you think he should be punished. Now, what you condemn in others you perpetrate yourself. You proclaim that one should not steal, but you steal; you say that one should not commit adultery, but you commit adultery. The law also followed, which was given through Moses, while through the law there followed recognition of sin.[9] You have learned what you should avoid, and yet you do what you know is forbidden. But what is the work of the law? Only that the whole world should be made subject to God, since it was not given only to the Hebrew but invited the stranger as well and did not exclude the proselyte. But because the[10] law was able to block up the mouth of all men,[11] yet could not change the heart, there was due the final remedy afforded by that last city. In this there was to be a refuge of

---

7 Cf. 2 Cor. 3.3. A good discussion of the two types of law, with special reference to this passage, occurs in B. Maes, *La Loi naturelle selon Ambroise de Milan* (Analecta Gregoriana 162; Rome 1967) 169–73.

8 Rom. 2.13.

9 Cf. Rom. 3.20.

10 The passage from this point to and including ". . . change the heart" appears in Augustine, *Contra duas epistulas Pelagianorum* 4.11.30 (CSEL 60.563.12).

11 Cf. Rom. 3.19.

salvation, that the death of the chief priest might free us from all fear of death and divest us of all dread of it.

(3.16) Who is he, but He of whom it was read, "Behold the lamb of God, behold him who takes away the sin of the world"?[12] "God has set him forth as a propitiation by his blood through faith, to manifest his justice."[13] Be satisfied now that He is the great high priest.[14] The Father swore an oath in His regard, saying, "You are a priest forever."[15] He said "forever," rightly, because other, temporal priests are all subject to sin, whereas He possesses an inviolable priesthood.[16] All are subject to death, but He is always living;[17] for how could He perish who Himself is able to save others? "For such a one was fitting for us."[18] The expression is correct, since among those who have had a love of words and of language, something of this sort is found, when someone says, "a higher place than was fitting for conquerors."[19] And I have not omitted this, so that we may know that the Apostle employs words that are natural to him rather than those in widespread circulation or those that are artfully contrived. "For such a high priest was fitting for us, one just, holy, innocent, undefiled, set apart from sinners and become higher than the heavens."[20]

---

12 John 1.29.
13 Rom. 3.25.
14 Cf. Heb. 4.14.
15 Ps. 109 (110).4; Heb. 7.21.
16 Cf. Heb. 7.23–24.
17 Cf. Heb. 7.25.
18 Heb. 7.26.
19 Sallust, *Historiae,* fragment 1.40. The quotation is not cited directly from Sallust, however, but from the *Exempla* of the Latin grammarian Arusianus Messius (text in Keil, *Grammatici Latini* 7.465). That the citation was from Arusianus was first established by Buecheler in his article "Coniectanea," *Rheinisches Museum* 43 (1888) 293–94. A handy discussion and restatement of the situation at this point in the text appears in Sister Charles, S.N.D., "The Classical Latin Quotations in the Letters of St. Ambrose," *Greece and Rome,* 2nd series 15 (1968) 186–97, especially p. 196 and n. 2. On the relationship of this citation to the date of *Flight from the World,* see the introduction to this work.
20 Heb. 7.26.

This, then, is the Word that dwells above the heavens and gives light to all things. For this reason, He has been anointed and chosen conformably to nature by God the Father,[21] because the Word is the light that has enlightened every man coming into this world.[22] This is the Word of God, in whom there inheres the high priesthood. In the account of the clothing of the chief priest, Moses describes the garments symbolically,[23] because the Word put on the world by His own power and is resplendent among all men as if He were clothed with it.[24] He also put on kinship with the human race through the taking on of this body, while saying to the Lord . . .[25] and pouring forth Himself, an ineffable love, upon all men out of the spirit and the fullness of His Godhead,[26] of whose fullness we have all received,[27] that we may know Christ's love which surpasses knowledge and may be filled unto all the fullness of God.[28] For Christ is the head of all, and from Him the whole body extends and is joined by a mutual joining of its parts to one another, while receiving its increase in the building up of itself in love.[29] Therefore this is the Word that surpasses, and that says to Moses in the building of the ark of the testimony, "And in the ark, you will put the testimonies which I will give you, and you will make to be put down a mercy seat,"[30] and later, "You will place the mercy seat on top of the ark and you will put in the testimonies which I will give, and I will make myself known to you from there and will speak to you from above."[31] This means, from there

---

21 Cf. Luke 4.18–19; Acts 10.38; Heb. 1.1–9.
22 Cf. John 1.9.
23 Cf. Exod. 25.5–9.
24 Cf. Ps. 92 (93).1.
25 That a lacuna appeared in the text at this point was suggested (rightly) by the CSEL editor, Schenkl; earlier editions do not show it. A part of it on which he ventures a conjecture would mean, "A body you have fitted to me" (cf. Heb. 10.5; Ps. 39[40].7).
26 Cf. Col. 2.9.
27 Cf. John 1.16.
28 Cf. Eph. 3.19.
29 Cf. Eph. 4.15–16.
30 Exod. 25.16–17.   31 Exod. 25.20–21.

where He is above the heavens, where He is with the Father, "from there I will speak to you."

(4.17) And so let us approach, relying on the assistance of faith and lifted up on its wings to the dwelling of grace, while fleeing this world and its contagion. Moreover, the flight consists in this: to keep away from sins, to take up the rule of the virtues unto the likeness and image of God, to enlarge our strength unto the imitation of God according to the limit of our potentiality. For the perfect man is the image and glory of God. For this reason also the Lord says, "Be you perfect even as your Father, who is in heaven, is perfect."[1] This, therefore, is to be like to God, to possess justice, to possess wisdom, and to be perfect in virtue. For God is without sin, and so the man who flees from sin is like to the image of God. There is no doubt, then, that one who keeps away from sin flees from it. For this reason also the Apostle cries out, "Flee immorality."[2] For the enticements of sin pursue us and lust pursues us. But flee from it as if from a frenzied mistress,[3] for if it lays hold on you, it gives you no rest day or night but troubles you, consumes you, and sets you ablaze. Flee from avarice; else it may lay hold of you from within. Flee from unbelief; else it may wrap you in its nets. For this reason also the Lord says, "And when they shall persecute you in this town, flee into another. Amen I say to you, you will not finish the towns of Israel before the Son of Man comes."[4] Granted, He seems to be urging us to flight on account of the weakness of the flesh. Still, that man makes a better flight who flees from worldly enticement, so as not to be held back by concern for his riches or consideration of treasure or by the cupidity of such a life.

---

1 Matt. 5.48.
2 1 Cor. 6.18.
3 A passage of similar tone, in which lust appears as a harsh, angry master, occurs in Cicero, *On Old Age* 47 (a convenient translation is that of H. G. Edinger, *Cicero: On Old Age; On Friendship* [The Library of Liberal Arts; Indianapolis 1968]). The thought goes back to Plato, *Republic* 329 C.
4 Matt. 10.23.

Rather, he hastens with straightforward purpose of soul to the glory of the heavenly kingdom, hurries on to the crown, and is not restrained from bodily suffering by contemplation of earthly things.

(4.18) Flight, then, is a death that has been either solemnized or foreshadowed. And perhaps the Lord portrays those cities of lawful refuge so that we may flee to the heights of those virtues which He dispenses in another passage as rewards to the good servant, when He says, "Because you have been faithful in a very little, you shall have authority over ten towns."[5] The law knew six cities, but because the Lord fulfilled the law—for He could say, "I have not come to destroy the law, but to fulfill it,"[6]—He bestows the more perfect number of forgiveness. (4.19) Therefore let us not be ashamed to flee, for this flight is a glorious one, to flee from the face of sin. Thus did Jacob flee at his mother's urging, for Rebecca said, "Arise and flee into Mesopotamia."[7] Thus did Moses flee from the face of King Pharao, so that the royal palace would not defile him or royal power ensnare him.[8] Indeed, he valued reproach for Christ as more precious than the riches of Egypt. Thus did David, too, flee from the face of King Saul,[9] and from the face of Absalom.[10] Indeed, in his flight he brought about an increase of holiness, for he spared a treacherous assailant and sought safety for a parricide. Thus did the Hebrew people flee, so that their faith and life might open a way for them amid the waves.[11] That flight was the path of guiltlessness, the way of virtue, the taking up of holiness. I dare to say it, thus did Jona also flee into Tharsis,[12] not by a bodily flight, but by an ascent of spirit, for he ascended even to the

---

5 Luke 19.17.
6 Matt. 5.17.
7 Gen. 27.43 (Septuagint).
8 Cf. Exod. 2.11–15; the occasion of Moses' flight was his killing of an Egyptian.
9 Cf. 1 Kings 19.18.
10 Cf. 2 Kings 15.14.
11 Cf. Exod. 14.
12 Cf. Jona 1.3.

likeness of Christ so as to become a symbol of Christ. "For even as Jona was in the belly of the fish three days and three nights, so will the Son of Man be three days and three nights in the heart of the earth."[13] For if he had not fled thus, never would he have been heard of in regard to the belly of the fish.

(4.20) But if you are hesitant, let Rebecca teach you how blessed the flight is that Jacob undertook. Rebecca urged, "Flee into Mesopotamia,"[14] and Isaac says, "Arise and go into Mesopotamia to the house of Bathuel."[15] In hymns and prophecies Bathuel is put by many for "wisdom"[16] as we find written before us, but upon interpretation in our tongue it means "daughter of God." Therefore Jacob is sent into the house of wisdom and is admonished to take a wife from the daughters of Laban, who dwelt in Charrah,[17] which means "caves."[18] In "caves" there is an image of the senses, which are, as it were, in caves of the body—sight in the eyes, hearing in the ears, smell in the nostrils, taste in the mouth. For one who takes delight in this world and rejoices in bodily pleasures is subject to the passions of the senses and has his dwelling and lodging in them. For this reason also Rebecca says that he should dwell for a few days with Laban,[19] but not over a long time; else he might be imbued with bodily pleasures and seduced by worldly enticements.

(4.21) Moreover, he is persuaded to dwell there in order to learn the powers of the senses—for he is desirous of knowledge —and the sites and regions of the flesh, as it were. Thus he may know himself and be aware of the vehemence of the flesh, the nature and reason of its creation, and the manner

---

13 Matt. 12.40.
14 Gen. 27.43 (Septuagint).
15 Gen. 28.2 (Septuagint).
16 The name "Bathuel" occurs with the meaning "wisdom" also in Ambrose, *Letter* 19.2, translated into English as Letter 37 by Sister M. Melchior Beyenka, O.P., *Saint Ambrose: Letters* (FOTC 26), p. 174.
17 Cf. Gen. 27.43; 28.2.
18 This interpretation occurs also in Ambrose, *Abraham* 1.2.4; 2.1.2; and 2.2.6.
19 Cf. Gen. 27.44.

of operation of each of the senses. "Who looks with lust at a woman"[20]—his eye is to that extent functioning wickedly. Therefore let the eye function in the discharge of its proper duty and not be led into sin at the command of a lustful mind, so as to render vice in place of service. And so a short time is granted for knowing the senses, or rather, experiencing them, perhaps the early beginnings of tender youth. But it is at once withdrawn, so that one does not totter overlong in a slippery place and the soul's inner footprints are not buried under a double inundation, from the body and from the world. But when Jacob has gained experience and has stood on ground that is unstable and unsure and moist, he is called back by his mother, who represents patience[21] and perseverance, for she says, "I will send for you and bring you back from there."[22] Thus, in a hazardous situation, you will find in that quarter a safe harbor of wisdom, which does not permit you to be tossed on the waves as if in shipwreck. Upon your return, you will know how to persevere as regards the worship of God, and you will be in the assembly of the nations as a sign of the Church that is to be gathered from the nations by faith.

(4.22) Therefore, formed by these teachings of patience and of perseverance, Jacob set out and gained for himself a bond of union with wisdom as a sharer of his intent.[23] That union was rich in the dowry of prudence, with which he could pass through his lifetime without any mishap. Then, once he had been increased with wisdom's treasury, he established a flock of sheep of varied colors,[24] but a mystical flock, shining in the diversity of many virtues. For this reason he retrenched upon boasting of the flesh, and this is the meaning of the

---

20 Matt. 5.28.
21 The name "Rebecca" frequently appears in the works of Ambrose in this sense, e.g., in *Isaac, or the Soul* 1.1 and *Jacob and the Happy Life* 2.4.14 (both translated in this volume).
22 Gen. 27.45.
23 Cf. Gen. 29.28–30. The reference is more specifically to his marriage to Rachel.
24 Cf. Gen. 30.25–43.

numbness of his thigh,[25] for this interpretation of the holy mystery is sound. Thus his spirit ascends into heaven by these virtues as if by a kind of steps;[26] he comes to know the mysteries of God and is strengthened and filled with them. So, when Laban examined Jacob's dwelling, he found nothing useless or purposeless there, no representations or likeness of vain idols.[27] For in his dwelling there was no image, but the reality, no likeness of ignorance, but the solid figure of justice and the symbolic expression of living virtue. And thus Laban searched through Jacob's spiritual dwelling and found no likenesses, for it was filled, not with representations but with realities.

(4.23) Moreover, Laban could have discovered the foundations and the supports of the virtues, had he not brought blindness in his heart and sightlessness in his unbelieving mind. In truth, when the minds of the Sodomites were overcome by such a blindness of depravity, they were unable even to find the door of holy Lot.[28] For on what account could an unholy mind have seen the going in or coming out of a holy man? The Lord Himself says in the Gospel, "For the prince of this world is coming and in me he finds nothing."[29] How could he have found nothing in Christ, in whom the fullness of the Godhead dwelt, and dwelt bodily,[30] and from whom power went forth and healed all men?[31] How could he have found nothing in completeness of power and richness of wisdom, understanding, and justice? You Yourself have said, O Lord, "I am full,"[32] and You Yourself have said, "Put your hand into my side and be not unbelieving, but believing."[33] He who did

---

25 Cf. Gen. 32.22–33.
26 Cf. Gen. 28.12.
27 Cf. Gen. 31.33–35.
28 Cf. Gen. 19.1–11.
29 John 14.30.
30 Cf. Col. 2.9.
31 Cf. Luke 6.19.
32 Isa. 1.11.
33 John 20.27.

not believe put in his hand and found You, Lord and God. Therefore the prince of this world, while not idle, yet is blind and empty. He only knows how to discern what is his, he only knows how to discover that, he does not know how to recognize the things of Christ.

(4.24) Or if the reading is as many texts have it, "In me he *does not find* nothing," this means: Satan will not find evil in Me, because evil is nothing; he will not find a dead man, because Christ is not dead. Further, how will he find a dead man in Christ, "who gives life to the dead and calls things that are not as though they were"?[34] The meaning is: He will not find sin in Me, who have taken away the sin of the world.[35] For how does He possess nothing who possesses all things, and, what is more, possesses all things that the Father possesses? Even so, Christ says, "All things that the Father has are mine."[36]

(5.25) Therefore let us flee from here, where there is nothing, where all that is reckoned noble is empty, and where the one who thinks himself to be something is nothing, yes, nothing at all. "I have seen the wicked man highly exalted and lifted up beyond the cedars of Libanus, and I passed by, and behold, he was not."[1] And do you pass by like David, pass by like the good servant, that it may be said to you, "Pass by and recline at table."[2] Pass by like Moses, that you may see the God of Abraham and of Isaac and of Jacob[3] and that you may see a great vision. This is a great vision, but if you wish to see it, remove the sandals from your feet,[4] remove every bond of iniquity, remove the bonds of the world, leave behind the sandals which are earthly. Likewise, Jesus sent the Apostles

---

34 Rom. 4.17.
35 Cf. John 1.29.
36 John 16.15.

---

1 Ps. 36 (37).35–36.
2 Luke 17.7.
3 Cf. Exod. 3.6; Matt. 22.32.
4 Cf. Exod. 3.5.

without sandals, without money, gold and silver,[5] so that they would not carry earthly things with them. For the man who seeks the good is praised, not for his sandals, but for the swiftness and grace of his feet, as Scripture says, "How beautiful are the feet of those who preach the gospel of peace, of those who bring glad tidings of good things!"[6] Therefore remove the sandals from your feet, that they may be beautiful for preaching the Gospel. "Remove,"[7] the text says, not "bind." "Remove," so that you may pass by and may find that the unholy man whom you admired on earth is nothing and can be nothing. Pass by, therefore, that is, flee from earth, where there is evil and where there is avarice. Likewise, David says to you, "Turn away from evil and do good."[8] To turn away is assuredly to flee; moreover, evil is on earth and good is in heaven. For this reason also he continues, "Seek after peace and pursue it."[9] Peace is in heaven. Indeed, He who came from heaven said, "Peace I give to you, my peace I leave to you."[10] And so, because we are to flee and turn away from evils, whereas evils are on earth and iniquities are on earth, let us flee from earthly things, so that iniquities may not overtake us, for they overtook even holy David, just as he himself bears witness, saying, "My iniquities have overtaken me, and I was not able to see."[11] For the eye of the soul is blinded by the smoke of iniquity, so that it does not see things that are clear. Thus indeed Laban was unable to see Jacob's goods,[12] and the prince of the world could not see the glory of Christ.[13]

(5.26) But perhaps you may say, "Why then was Jacob sent to Laban, if Laban was reprehensible?" If we think upon the

---

5 Cf. Mark 6.8–9 (where the Apostles are, however, told to retain their sandals); Matt. 10.9–10; Luke 9.3.
6 Rom. 10.15; Isa. 52.7.
7 Exod. 3.5.
8 Ps. 33 (34).15.
9 *Ibid.*
10 John 14.27.
11 Ps. 39 (40).13.
12 Cf. Gen. 31.33–35.
13 Cf. John 12.31.

latter's name, it means "radiant"[14] in our tongue. Thus Jacob is being bid to go forth to things of a greater splendor. But because he was fleshly, we do better to understand the things of a greater splendor as pertaining to this life. As one who had not yet been made perfect, he first went to Laban to rejoice with him in his light for the moment. But Laban had sons that were worse[15]—this means his name was more congenial than his works. And thus, by a mother's plan and God's word and the wish of Jacob himself, for he was a lover of obedience, the other is forsaken and abandoned.

(5.27) Moreover, holy Rachel—that is, the Church, or prudence—hid the idols,[16] because the Church does not know representations and figures of idols that are totally devoid of reality, but she knows the real existence of the Trinity. Indeed, she has destroyed darkness and revealed the splendor of glory. Let us then abandon the darkness, for we seek the sun; let us forsake the smoke, for we strive after the light. The smoke is iniquity; as smoke is to the eyes,[17] so is iniquity to those who practice it. The shadow is life; "for this our life on earth is a shadow,"[18] just as Job said. And what is here but trials? All time is spent in anxiety, all life in afflictions. "You will walk in the midst of snares."[19] And someone else complained of snares that were stretched out for him in the way in which he walked, but they were hidden snares.[20] That he might not fall and be captured, he desired to flee like a sparrow, but thus far the net was not broken.[21] "Flight has failed me."[22] He had wings made heavy through the dark water in the clouds of the sky, and perhaps he was unable to fly. Ac-

---

14 The name "Laban" appears with a somewhat different meaning in *Jacob and the Happy Life* 2.5.24 (translated in this volume).
15 Cf. Gen. 31.1.
16 Cf. Gen. 31.34.
17 Cf. Prov. 10.26.
18 Job 8.9 (Septuagint).
19 Sir. 9.13 (20).
20 Cf. Ps. 141 (142).4. The complainant is David.
21 Cf. Ps. 123 (124).7.
22 Ps. 141 (142).5.

cordingly, he sought to receive those wings that would enable him to fly away and rest, just as it is written, "Who will give me wings like a dove, and I will fly and be at rest?"[23] For where there is flight, there is rest. Indeed, he says in another passage, "If you sleep among the midst of lots, [you shall be as] the wings of a dove covered with silver."[24]

(5.28) But perhaps you may say, "How then does this man say that flight has failed him, when he had said previously, 'If I take my wings before the dawn'?[25] Is this not the opposite?" By no means. For the just engage in many struggles. Does an athlete contend only once? How often, after he has won many victor's crowns, is he overcome in another contest! How often it happens that one who has frequently gained the victory sometimes hesitates and is held fast in uncertainty! And it frequently comes to pass that a brave man is contending with brave men, and greater struggles arise, where proofs of strength are greater. Thus, when David sought to flee to avoid the adversary, he also did not find his wings. He was driven here and there in an uncertain struggle, seeing that, where he has his wings in his possession, the title of the psalm is "unto the end,"[26] that is, to the achievement and accomplishment of victory. Indeed he says, like a victor, "Lord, you have proved me and you know me. You know my sitting down and my rising up."[27] He deservedly possessed the power to fly, for he had received the wings to rise up. But David is still in the cave[28]—that is, in the flesh—in the cavern of this body, as it were, as he fights with King Saul, the son of hardness, and with the power of that spiritual prince who is not visible but is comprehensible. For this reason that psalm is entitled

23 Ps. 54 (55).7. This verse, with its imagery of flight, is a favorite with Ambrose; compare, e.g., *The Prayer of Job and David* 4.1.5–2.6 (in this volume). For a full discussion, see R. T. Otten, "Caritas," 442–48, especially 446.
24 Ps. 67 (68).14.
25 Ps. 138 (139).9.
26 Ps. 138 (139).1.
27 Ps. 138 (139).1–2.
28 Cf. 1 Kings 22.1.

"Understanding,"[29] which David brought to the end while he was in the flesh, but he merited by prayer to bring it to the end. Indeed, he began with a cry of prayer.[30]

(5.29) Consider too that this latter psalm is spoken in the voice of the Savior, whereas the former was in the voice of David, who did not have victory in his power but had hope of it from Christ. And yet afterward he stretched forth his hands to God like wings of his soul,[31] took refuge in the Lord, and sought the safe conduct of the Holy Spirit so as to know the way along which he could ascend. He saw that the heavens were bowed down that Christ might descend[32] and asked that the Lord might lift him up with His hand.[33] Or perhaps it was for this reason that he did not seek for his own wings then, because he had become more perfect and wanted the hand of Christ.

(5.30) As for the man who wishes to be lifted up by the hand of Christ, let him first fly away himself, let him have his own wings, for one who flees from the world has wings. And if he does not have wings of his own—and perhaps only the man who is able to fly has them—if then he does not have his own, let him get them from the one who has them. Thus a man who flees from the world does fly. "Behold, I have gone far off flying away, and I remained in the wilderness."[34] Thus, David flew away like the night raven in the dwelling, like the lone sparrow in the house.[35] Now if you apply this to Christ, He flew away in the passion of His body, so that He could protect the peoples of the nations under the shadow of His wings.[36] He flew away from the Godhead; He remained in the body and dwelt in the desert, so that the children of the

---

29 Ps. 54 (55).1.
30 Cf. Ps. 54 (55).2.
31 Cf. Ps. 54 (55).7.
32 Cf. Ps. 143 (144).5.
33 Cf. Ps. 143 (144).7.
34 Ps. 54 (55).8.
35 Cf. Ps. 101 (102).7–8.
36 Cf. Ps. 16 (17).8.

deserted wife might be more than those of her who had a husband.[37] Therefore let us seek after His body that we also may rise again; for where the body is, there also will the eagles be.[38]

(5.31) Let him who cannot fly like an eagle fly like a sparrow; and let him who cannot fly to heaven fly to the mountains; let him flee before the valleys which are quickly destroyed by water, and let him pass over to the mountains. Abraham's nephew passed over to the mountain of Segor and was saved;[39] but his wife could not climb it, for she looked back in womanly fashion and lost her salvation.[40] "Draw near the everlasting mountains," the Lord says through the prophet Michea, "arise from here, for this is not a rest for you by reason of uncleanness. You have been corrupted with corruption, you have suffered pursuit."[41] And the Lord says, "Then let those who are in Judea flee to the mountains."[42] Mount Sion is there, and so is the city of peace,[43] Jerusalem, built not of earthly stones but of living stones, with ten thousand angels and the Church of the firstborn and the spirits of those made perfect and the God of the just, who spoke better with His blood than Abel.[44] For the one cried out for vengeance,[45] but the other for pardon; the one was a reproach to his brother's sin, the other forgave the world's sin; the one was the revelation of a crime, the other covered a crime according to what is written, "Blessed are they whose sins are covered."[46]

---

37 Cf. Isa. 54.1; Gal. 4.27.
38 Cf. Matt. 24.28.
39 Cf. Gen. 19.12–29.
40 Cf. Gen. 19.26.
41 Mich. 2.9–11 (Septuagint).
42 Matt. 24.16.
43 Ambrose is quite eloquent in the titles he gives to the city of God, e.g., "heavenly Jerusalem," "heavenly kingdom," "eternal city," "heavenly city." See C. Morino, *Church and State in the Teaching of St. Ambrose* 31–33, especially p. 32 and nn. 19–27.
44 Cf. Heb. 12.22–24.
45 Cf. Gen. 4.10.
46 Ps. 31 (32).1.

(6.32) But let him who flees flee swiftly, so that he may not be overtaken; let him swiftly despoil this world, as the Hebrew did Egypt.[1] Let one who is in labor bring forth; else such a one may not be able to flee with the womb of the spirit heavily burdened by iniquities. Let that one flee, not as if bringing an infant at the breast, but as if bringing one that can walk; not carrying a little child, but presenting one who has been perfected in Christ.[2] Let that one flee, not as if on holiday on the sabbath,[3] but like a workman at his employment; not like one that is unproductive from the cold, but like one rich with the harvest. Yes, for that reason it is said, "Pray that your flight may not be in the winter, or on the sabbath."[4] The flight, then, is productive of virtues and not barren of merits. Such a flight does not know the chill of fear, the dread of death, the despondency of anxiety, the idle life of debauchery, the festivals of licentiousness, the stupefaction of insensibility. Rather, it calls for the relentless wayfarer of heavenly life, the vigorous seeker after the kingdom that is above, the rich farmer who forces his crops and plunders them by force.[5]

(6.33) For what is asked of you, O man? Only that you fear God, seek for Him, walk after Him, follow in His ways.[6] "With what shall I win over the Lord? Shall I win him over with holocausts?"[7] The Lord is not reconciled, nor are sins redeemed, with tens of thousands of young goats or thousands of rams,[8] or with the fruits of unholiness, but the grace of the Lord is won with a good life. "You have been told, O man, what is good. And what does the Lord require of you but to do justice and to love mercy and to be prepared to walk with your Lord?"[9] Accordingly, the Gospel says to you, "Arise, let

---

1 Cf. Exod. 12.35–36.
2 Cf. Luke 21.23; Matt. 24.19.
3 Cf. Matt. 24.20.
4 *Ibid.*
5 Cf. Matt. 11.12.
6 Cf. Deut. 10.12; 13.4.
7 Mich. 6.6 (Septuagint).
8 Cf. Mich. 6.7.
9 Mich. 6.8 (Septuagint); cf. Prov. 14.21.

us go from here,"[10] while the law says to you, "You shall walk after the Lord your God."[11] You have learned the method of your flight from here—why do you delay? Again the Gospel says to you, "Brood of vipers! Who has shown you how to flee from the wrath to come?"[12] And it says this to those who were coming to the baptism of repentance.

(6.34) Therefore repentance is a good flight; the grace of God is a good flight, for in it is the salvation of the fugitive; the desert is a good flight, for Elias fled there[13] and Eliseus and John the Baptist.[14] Elias fled the woman Jezabel,[15] that is, the outpouring of vanity,[16] and fled to Mount Choreb,[17] which means "a drying up," so that the outflow of fleshly vanity might be dried up in him and he might come to know God more fully. For he was by the torrent Chorrad, which means "knowledge," where he could drink in the abundant overflow of God's knowledge.[18] He fled from the world in such a way that he did not even seek out food for this body, except only what the servant birds had brought,[19] although his food for the most part was not of earth.[20] Indeed, he walked forty days in the strength of the food which he had received.[21] To be sure, it was not a woman that such a great prophet was fleeing, but it was this world. And it was not death that he feared, for he offered himself to the one that

---

10 John 14.31.
11 Deut. 13.4 (Septuagint).
12 Matt. 3.7.
13 Cf. 3 Kings 19.4.
14 Cf. Matt. 3.1; Luke 3.2.
15 Cf. 3 Kings 19.2.
16 The name "Jezabel" appears with similar meanings in Ambrose, *Exhortatio virginitatis* 5.30 (Migne, PL 16.344–45); *Letters* 30.10; 63.79 (translated as Letters 80 and 59, respectively, by Sister M. Melchior Beyenka, O.P., in *St. Ambrose: Letters* [FOTC 26]); and *On Naboth* 9.41–42 (translated by M. R. P. McGuire, *S. Ambrosii De Nabuthae* [The Catholic University of America Patristic Studies 15; Washington 1927]).
17 Cf. 3 Kings 19.8.
18 Cf. 3 Kings 17.5.
19 Cf. 3 Kings 17.6.
20 Cf. 3 Kings 19.5–7.
21 Cf. 3 Kings 19.8.

searched for him and said to the Lord, "Take my soul."[22]
He endured a weariness of this life, not a desire for it, but he
was fleeing worldly enticement and the contagion of filthy
conduct and the impious acts of an unholy and sinful generation.

(6.35) Solomon also explained the corruption of this world
under the guise of such a woman and taught avoidance of
the harlot's wiles.[23] This is the adulterous woman that is
another's, and he is exhorting you to guard yourself from her
and not to turn your heart aside to the ways of the world, but
to place it in the hand of the Lord, in which is the heart of
the king.[24] For when a man rules his own self—and that counts
for more than to govern others—his heart is in the hand of
God, and God turns it where He wills. No wonder if He turns
it to the good; perfect goodness is His. And so let us be in the
hand of God that we may seek the good, that incorruptible
and immutable good of which the prophet Amos says, "Seek
good and not evil, that you may live, and so the Lord God
almighty will be with you, as you have said, 'We have hated
evil and loved good.' "[25] And so, where the good God is, there
are the good things that David desired to see and believed
that he would see, even as he says, "I believe I shall see the
good things of the Lord in the land of the living."[26] They
indeed are the good things that endure always, that cannot
be destroyed by change of time or of age.

(6.36) One who has sought God and has found Him exists
among those good things. For where a man's heart is, there
also is his treasure;[27] the Lord is not accustomed to deny His
good gift to those who pray. And so, because the Lord is good
and especially good to those who await Him, let us cleave to
Him and be with Him with our whole soul, our whole heart,

22 3 Kings 19.4.
23 Cf. Prov. 7.5.
24 Cf. Prov. 21.1.
25 Amos 5.14–15 (Septuagint).
26 Ps. 26 (27).13.
27 Cf. Matt. 6.21.

and our whole strength,[28] that we may be in His light and
see His glory and enjoy the gift of heavenly joy. Accordingly,
let us lift up our spirits to that good and be in it and live in
it; let us cleave to it, for it is above every thought and every
reflection and enjoys an everlasting peace and tranquillity, and
that peace, moreover, is beyond every thought and every
understanding.[29] This is the good that enters into all things;
in it we all live and on it we all depend;[30] moreover, it possesses nothing beyond itself but is of God, for "no one is good
but only God."[31] Therefore, what is good is of God, and what
is of God is good. And for that reason it is said, "When you
open your hand, all things shall be filled with goodness."[32]
For, through God's goodness, all good things are deservedly
granted to us, and in them there is no admixture of evil.[33]
Scripture promised these good things to the faithful when it
said, "You shall eat the good things of the land."[34] That we
may obtain the good things, let us be like that good, the good
that is without iniquity and without deceit and without
severity but is with grace and holiness and purity and benevolence and love and justice. Thus goodness, like a prolific
mother, embraces all the virtues.

(7.37) There is, then, a reason of some importance why we
ought to flee from here, namely, that we may come from evil
to good, from uncertainty to trust, and a trust filled with the
truth, and from death to life. The Lord Himself also showed
that life—eternal life—is a good, when He said, "I have
set before you good and evil, life and death."[1] For if this life
is subject to the world and its wickedness, that other is surely
good, for it is not corrupted and changed, it does not deteri-

---

28 Cf. Deut. 6.5; Matt. 22.37.
29 Cf. Phil. 4.7.
30 Cf. Acts 17.28.
31 Mark 10.18.
32 Ps. 103 (104).28.
33 Cf. James 1.17.
34 Isa. 1.19.

1 Deut. 30.15 (Septuagint).

orate from any vice, and it is gained through virtue. Then let us flee the wickedness of this world, in which "the very days are evil,"[2] and flee it relentlessly. On that account Isaia cries out, "Be strong, you hands which are feeble and you knees which are without strength."[3] This means: Be strong, you knees, not of the body, but of the soul, so that the footstep of the spirit can rise up straightway to the heights of heaven. Thus conduct will be more stable, life more mature, grace more abundant, and discretion more guarded.

(7.38) For this is the meaning of flight—to know your goal, to unburden oneself of the world, to unburden oneself of the body. Otherwise someone may, on the contrary, rise up to no purpose; with their fleshly spirit puffed up, they may not keep their head, and it may be said of them, "They have fled and have not seen."[4] But this is the meaning of flight from here—to die to the elements of this world, to hide one's life in God,[5] to turn aside from corruptions, not to defile oneself with objects of desire, and to be ignorant of the things of this world. For the world lays sorrows of various kinds upon us, it empties when it has filled, and it fills when it has emptied. And all such proceedings are empty and vain, and there is no profit in them. The rich man is dead and possesses nothing because he is not rich as regards God, and therefore he is foolish,[6] because the worship of God is wisdom, while abstinence from evils is learning.

(7.39) Who, therefore, would not flee a place of wickedness, a workshop of depravity that does not know how to perish? Indeed, it was not without reason that the mark was set upon Cain, that no one might kill him.[7] Thus it was indicated that evil is not destroyed or removed from the earth. Cain was

---

2 Eph. 5.16.
3 Isa. 35.3 (Septuagint).
4 Job 9.25.
5 Cf. Col. 3.3.
6 Cf. Luke 12.20–21.
7 Cf. Gen. 4.15.

afraid that he might be killed,[8] because he did not know how to flee. For evil is augmented and amassed by the practice of evil, and it exists without moderation or limit, fights through guile and deceit, and is revealed by its deeds and by the blood of the slain, even as Cain also was revealed. And so, evil dwells on the earth and roams about here, and for that reason we ask that the will of God be done on earth just as it is also in heaven,[9] so that innocence may exist here also. Accordingly, because evil does not have a place there, it goes about here, vents its rage and pours itself forth here. It was not sunk in that flood that encompassed the world, nor was it burned in the fire of Sodom. In fact, later it sprouted in its nurseries with greater severity, and it even laid murderous, sacrilegious hands on the very Author of the salvation of all men. The law condemns the deed, but it does not take away the evil.[10] The Lord Jesus Himself condemned sin but preserved its author so that there might be one through whom the just could be proved. In very truth, because God did not make evil, and the devil's villainy introduced it, God postponed vengeance so that the devil could be overcome by those very persons whom he had deceived.

(7.40) And so, those who were deceived are being tried, that they may both pay the price of their hasty assent and assume a zeal for virtue and a diligent watchfulness. For this reason Scripture says, "Be wise as serpents."[11] Why as serpents? That he who wanted to strip others may be deprived of what is his and lose his own possessions, not the poisons, but the merits of his nature. In truth, he is cast down when you have ascended. For it is written, "I was watching Satan fall as lightning from heaven."[12] The text does not say "lightning,"

---

8 Cf. Gen. 4.14.
9 Cf. Matt. 6.10.
10 This sentence is cited by Augustine, *Contra duas epistulas Pelagianorum* 4.11.30 (CSEL 60. 563.14).
11 Matt. 10.16.
12 Luke 10.18.

but "as lightning," because he lost his own light, which he possessed before he wished to carry off your light from you. But perhaps you may cite what we read in reference to the Savior, that "as the lightning that flashes from under heaven, so also will be the coming of the Son of Man."[13] Here too "as lightning" is appropriate, because He is above the lightning. Indeed, lightning is "from under heaven," but the true light is above heaven. Therefore Satan is "as lightning" because he lost what he possessed, whereas you have regained what you had lost.

(7.41) The sentence was not relaxed in his regard as it was in yours. The grace of Christ, which has freed you, has bound him, and the curse directed against the serpent by reason of his deception of you endures. For thus it was said to him, "Cursed are you from all the beasts of the earth."[14] For he who was the enemy of the good is the common foe of all, and he is condemned on behalf of those that he still has not harmed, since he who has harmed man has harmed all things, for they are all subject to man. In truth, he broke the general law, because he is subject to man with the rest. Accordingly, his curse is made heavier by the general hatred and malediction of all. Further, the manner of his condemnation is not death, but a punishment of long duration. "Upon your breast and belly you shall go."[15] For the knowledge of sin had to be brought low, and wickedness trampled down, and the mystery of deceit banished from the face of God, as it were. At the same time, it is demonstrated that the wickedness of earth bends back upon the earth. Indeed, the Scripture continued, "and earth you will eat all the days of your life."[16]

(7.42) It appears that the serpent's nature is being delineated in the foregoing, but, rather, every vessel of evil is being delineated, and every serpent of depravity who casts him-

---

13 Cf. Matt. 24.27; Luke 17.24.
14 Gen. 3.14 (Septuagint).
15 *Ibid.*
16 *Ibid.*

self down on the belly and hides his poison inside himself and ponders it inwardly in his breast. He is slippery in his thoughts, he advances over his deceits and wraps himself in his deceptions; he is always moving and stirring his poisons by thought, and treading on his belly as well, that is, the seedbed of his heart. For this reason, David fittingly says, "Sinners are alienated from the womb, they have gone astray from the womb, they have spoken false things. Their madness is according to the likeness of a serpent, like the deaf asp that stops her ears, which will not hear the voice of the charmers nor of the wizard that are invoked by the wise man."[17] For this reason, the statement that we read in the prophetic book also seems fitting, "My bowels, my bowels are in pain!"[18] For wickedness exists there, where there ought to be guiltlessness; what should be the more calm in us experiences the greater suffering. It is trodden down by the footsteps of evil, pricked by its claws, and agitated by a kind of advance and increase of depravity where there exists the procreative seed of an everlasting posterity. It appears that the Scripture passage is to be interpreted to mean that the prophet felt pain that his children, whom he had begotten and reared, had perished,[19] but more that he did not possess the seedbed of the word in his bowels. And so he says his bowels, as if they were most precious. Indeed, the womb of the spirit is precious; in it there generally sprouts up from the seed of the word a fruitful crop of counsels, and in it the members that constitute all life —the members that are the virtues and the teachings, as it were—are used to be fashioned.

(7.43) But to return to the point, that God judged that evil was to be held in check for a time rather than to be destroyed, He says to the serpent, "I will put enmities between you and the woman, and between your seed and the seed of the woman.

---

17 Ps. 57 (58).4–6.
18 Jer. 4.19.
19 Cf. Jer. 16.1–4. In that passage, however, the Lord forbids Jeremia to marry and beget children to suffer this fate.

She shall watch for your head and you for her heel."[20] Where
there are enmities, there are discord and the desire to do harm;
where there is the desire to do harm, there evil is established.
Therefore, there is discord between the serpent and the
woman. Evil is at the base of discord; thus evil has not been
taken away. Indeed, it has been reserved for the serpent, that
he might watch for the woman's heel and the heel of her
seed, so as to do harm and infuse his poison. Therefore, let
us not walk in earthly things, and the serpent will not be able
to harm us. Let us take up the sandals[21] of the Gospel that
shut out the serpent's poison and blunt his bites, that we
may be provided with covering on our feet unto the Gospel.
And perhaps it is for that reason that Moses is bidden to
remove the sandals from his feet,[22] that he may take up the
sandals of the Gospel;[23] else it is because the preaching of the
Gospel is appointed, not for Moses, that is, not for the
prophets, but for the Apostles. As we have said above, such is
the sentence spoken against the serpent; let us consider what
sort of sentence has been directed against man.

(7.44) He that was the instigator of guilt is cursed, but he
that was deceived by the trickery of another is not cursed.
Still, because he did not keep the commandment of God, he is
condemned to the toil of his works—the earth indeed is cursed,
but in the works of the sinner—and he is cursed until he is returned into earth.[24] And so then, Jesus took flesh that He
might destroy the curse of sinful flesh, and He became for us
a curse[25] that a blessing might overwhelm a curse, uprightness
might overwhelm sin, forgiveness might overwhelm the sentence, and life might overwhelm death. He also took up death

---

20 Gen. 3.15.
21 Cf. Matt. 10.10; Luke 10.4. In both of these passages, however, the
    sandals are to be left behind.
22 Cf. Exod. 3.5.
23 Cf. Matt. 10.10; Luke 10.4.
24 Cf. Gen. 3.17–19.
25 Cf. Gal. 3.13.

that the sentence might be fulfilled and satisfaction might be given for the judgment, the curse placed on sinful flesh even to death.[26] Therefore, nothing was done contrary to God's sentence when the terms of that sentence were fulfilled, for the curse was unto death but grace is after death. And so we are dead to the world; why do we still struggle in regard to the world? We are dead with Christ; why do we still seek after the activities of this life? We bear about in our body the death of Christ, so that the life also of Christ may be made manifest in us.[27] Therefore it is not now our life that we live, but Christ's life,[28] the life of blamelessness, the life of chastity, the life of integrity and of all the virtues. We have risen with Christ; let us live in Him and ascend in Him so that the serpent may not be able to find our heel to wound on earth.[29]

(8.45) Let us flee from here. You can flee in spirit, even though you are kept back in body. You can both be here and be in the presence of the Lord, if your soul cleaves to Him and you walk after Him in your thoughts, if you follow His ways, not in pretense but in faith, and take refuge in Him. For He is a refuge and a power, and David says to Him, "I fled to you for refuge and I was not deceived."[1] And so, because God is a refuge, and because He is, moreover, in heaven and above the heavens, surely we must flee from here to there, where there is peace and rest from labors and where we can feast upon the great sabbath, even as Moses said, "And the sabbaths of the land shall be food for you."[2] For it is a banquet, and one filled with enjoyment and serenity, to rest in God and to look upon His delight. We have taken refuge with God; shall we return to the world? We have died to sin;

---

26 Cf. Gen. 3.17–19.
27 Cf. 2 Cor. 4.10.
28 Cf. Gal. 2.20.
29 Cf. Col. 3.1–2.

---

1 Ps. 76 (77).3.
2 Lev. 25.6 (Septuagint).

shall we seek sins again? We have renounced the world and the use of it; shall we stick fast again in its mire?

(8.46) Let us flee from here, because the time is short. Hear how you may flee, "And let those who have wives be as if they had none, and those who weep as though not weeping, and those who rejoice as though not rejoicing, and those who buy as though not possessing, and those who use this world as though not using it, for this world as we see it is passing away."[3] And so, let our works not pass away with the passing of this world as we see it, else we also may pass away; but let us endure in the truth. If we endure in Christ, we endure in the truth, and we will endure with Him and will not pass away. Rather, we will say, "The blessing of the Lord be upon you, we bless you in the name of the Lord."[4] For those who pass away cannot speak, because they have not said when passing by the way, "The blessing of the Lord be upon you," as the psalmist said. Consequently, if we wish that our works not pass away, let us not pass by the commandment of God, let us not pass by the careful search for the Lord Jesus and the grace that comes from meriting Him. The woman who entered even into the house of the pharisee, where Christ was at table, and poured ointment over His feet, did not pass Him by.[5]

(8.47) Let us not pass by the opportunity to advance in some teaching, just as the youthful Joseph did not pass it by. For he sought after his brothers and hastened to that place where they were pasturing the sheep, and, when he had learned that they were in Dothain, he went on there.[6] Moreover the meaning of the word Dothain is "a fitting failure,"[7] that is, a failure of idle conjectures which is not trivial but full and complete; in this there is an advance of the soul. When the wise man diminishes, he gives increase; the conjectures of the

---

3 1 Cor. 7.29–31.
4 Ps. 128 (129).8.
5 Cf. Luke 7.36–38.
6 Cf. Gen. 37.17–18.
7 The name "Dothain" appears with a slightly different interpretation in *Joseph* 3.11 (translated in this volume).

world fail, for they are compared to weak women. In order to show that Sara had come to such an advance that she brought forth laughter and joy, the Scripture fittingly says, "It had failed to be with Sara after the manner of women."[8] Good is the failing of desires, the failing of vanity, because it is an adding of truth. For this reason also a holy man says, "My soul has failed for your salvation."[9] Indeed, Sara was going to bring to birth the child that God had granted and, therefore, also had promised; she was going to give birth to joy and the sober intoxication of delight; she was about to bring forth offspring earlier than the expectation[10] by reason of a natural disposition to a quick labor, and she was delivered of wisdom. Indeed, in regard to other Hebrew women you find it written that the Hebrew women give birth before the midwives arrive.[11] This is so, because the souls of the just do not wait upon branches of learning arranged according to kinds of knowledge, nor do they require assistance in parturition, but they bring forth their offspring spontaneously and anticipate the expected time.

(8.48) Jacob was no less indefatigable at discovery than at execution.[12] When his mother said to him that he should bring in food for his father,[13] we perceive that different kinds of terms were involved. For he made his discovery quickly and bore witness that the Author of what he had discovered was God, who foreshadows both the prize of attentive care and the fecundity of natural ability. Thus the first term, attentive care, occurs in the act of discovery. What is discovered, is sought, and what is sought belongs to time, and what belongs to time is indeed a matter of attentive care. But as for what anticipates the usage of time, it is God who infuses that, God who gives it, and what God gives is a matter of nature and not of atten-

---

8 Gen. 18.11.
9 Ps. 118 (119).81.
10 Cf. Vergil, *Georgics* 3.348.
11 Cf. Exod. 1.19.
12 Cf. Gen. 27.1–14 (discovery), 15–29 (execution).
13 Cf. Gen. 27.10.

tive care. Therefore, natural ability is a gift of God, while that which is a gift of God belongs to nature. Therefore, ability belongs to nature, whereas discovery is a matter of attentive care. The former is timeless, the latter has need of time. And thus the former is ready to hand in time, while the latter is searched out over a span of time; the former is above us, but the latter is ascribed to us.

(8.49) Accordingly, Jacob's father sought the food of the word, for man does not live by bread alone but by every word of God.[14] Such was the food Isaac sought,[15] such the food Peter hungered for when he saw the mysterious signs of the future belief of the Gentiles.[16] Esau did not have at hand the food of a spiritual and more ready ability. And so he hunted[17] and searched and prepared to deliver a very rough and rustic speech. But Jacob anticipated him by a swift discovery and he spoke in the gentle and pleasant way of one who mostly stayed at home, so as to soothe and delight his father.[18] For this reason the father wondered and said, "What is this, my son, which you have found so quickly?" Jacob replied, "It is what the Lord your God gave into my hands."[19] The first term occurs in the question and the second in the reply. Therefore the father, finding all things complete that belonged either to the term natural ability or to the term attentive care, concluded with a summing up when he said, "Behold the fragrance of my son is like the fragrance of a full field which the Lord has blessed."[20] For a field possesses an ability of nature, which is its fertility, and an attentive care, which is the time bestowed on its cultivation. Consequently, in the field which is not lacking in either element, there is a fullness. At the same time, since he continued, "which the Lord has blessed,"

---

14 Cf. Matt. 4.4; Luke 4.4.
15 Cf. Gen. 27.4.
16 Cf. Acts 10.10–16.
17 Cf. Gen. 27.5.
18 Cf. Gen. 25.27; 27.22.
19 Gen. 27.20 (Septuagint).
20 Gen. 27.27.

Isaac appears to have given the preference to nature's gift over the toil involved in cultivation. Esau also confirmed this when he said, "Rightly is his name called Jacob, for he has now supplanted me a second time and has taken my rights of primogeniture."[21]

(8.50) But perhaps you may say, "Wherein did the son who was sent by his father to the hunt make delay?" Yet consider that the father was making a declaration that the son was unable to have ready what was desired in a spiritual way. And it was so, because he was in want as regards the ability or else required additional help as regards attentive care. Isaac also admonishes to swiftness, for he says, "Take bow and arrow."[22] He knows that the gift of ability is superior; still, he accepts also the fruit of an attentive care. (8.51) And there was reason for Jacob to offer food that was from the household,[23] for he won for himself a union with wisdom from the household of his own kindred.[24] Moreover, attentive care joined with wisdom is good, as is discovery joined with the ability bestowed by nature. Indeed, when holy Isaac had the union with wisdom in his view, he was walking about in a field, or rather, he was wandering apart.[25] Let us also first be joined with wisdom and go forth so into the field, desiring to seek and to find. For many seek poorly without wisdom. Accordingly, because Cain had not received the gift of discretion from God, he sought poorly, he went out into the field poorly.[26] But Abel sought well, for he fulfilled perfectly the duty of sacrifice;[27] good is the sacrifice of wisdom, good is the sacrificial victim, faith, and good is every virtue. In truth, wisdom has killed her own victims and mixed her own wine in the bowl.[28] And therefore, in order to give the drink of faith to the unwise

21 Gen. 27.36.
22 Gen. 27.3.
23 Cf. Gen. 27.9.
24 Cf. Gen. 28.1–4. The reference is to Jacob's marriage with Rachel; cf. ch. 4 n. 23, above.
25 Cf. Gen. 24.63.
26 Cf. Gen. 4.1–16.   27 Cf. Gen. 4.4.   28 Cf. Prov. 9.2.

pagans, she called them to her mixing bowl and said, "Let him who is unwise turn in to me,"[29] and to those without understanding she said, "Come and eat of my bread and drink the wine which I have mixed for you."[30] Plato judged that the discourse over this bowl should be copied into his books;[31] he summoned forth souls to drink of it, but did not know how to fill them, for he provided not the drink of faith but that of unbelief.

(9.52) Therefore, let us flee from here, even as holy Jacob fled from his native land,[1] for he knew that his true fatherland was above. Let us flee like harts to fountains of water, let our soul also thirst for those fountains for which David thirsted.[2] Who is that fountain? Hear him as he says, "For with you is the fountain of life."[3] May my soul say to this fountain, "When shall I come and appear before your face?"[4] God is indeed the fountain; let the man who longs for this fountain pour out his soul over himself,[5] that he may leave nothing to the possession of the flesh, but that his soul may overflow everywhere.

(9.53) Susanna did well to pour forth her soul, so that the fires of the body and the fears of death and the desires of life could not evaporate into it. Her soul, once poured forth over her, extinguished every fleshly desire, every worldly inclination. She would have been able also to extinguish the fires of the unnatural old men, the impure priests, had the outpouring of lust not overflowed in them. When they threatened to make a false accusation, should she deny consent to adultery,

---

29 Prov. 9.4.
30 Prov. 9.5.
31 Cf. Plato, *Symposium* 213 E. Ambrose cites Plato elsewhere in his works; see especially *Isaac, or the Soul* 8.78, and *Death as a Good* 5.19–21 (both in this volume).

---

1 Cf. Gen. 27.41–28.5.
2 Cf. Ps. 41 (42).2–3.
3 Ps. 35 (36).10.
4 Ps. 41 (42).3.
5 Cf. Ps. 41 (42).5.

Susanna groaned and said, "I am completely trapped. For if I do this thing, I shall perish in eternal death; but if I refuse, I shall not escape your hands."[6] Nevertheless, she judged it better to flee from the crime rather than from the danger. And so, she wept when accusation was made against her.[7] She wept when they demanded for themselves the judgment of adultery in regard to one that was chaste and pure. She was not lamenting her death but wept for the false accusation against chastity and the harm done religion. She poured forth over herself, not her body, but her soul; in fact, she would have poured forth her body, had she given consent to fleshly desires. Indeed, when she was condemned to death, she cried out as if she were the judge of the culprits who made false accusations,[8] and by the weight of her guiltless conscience she summoned God's knowledge into judgment on her own behalf.[9] She was not much troubled by the fear of death but was exalted by the power of him who denounced the judgment. Susanna, then, fled from the world, and she entrusted herself to God while in flight to the summit of the eternal city which embraces the entire universe, because all things are under God.

(9.54) Paul fled too, that he might pass out through a window and be lowered in a basket.[10] Yes, he knew that the triple-stranded rope could not break, but he fled so that he might preach the Gospel of the Lord in the entire world,[11] and consequently he was taken up into paradise.[12] Let us also flee through the window while heeding the Lord's precepts and keeping them with steady vision and chaste eyes.

(9.55) Let us flee like Lot,[13] who feared the crimes of the men of Sodom more than their punishments. A holy man

---

6 Dan. 13.22.
7 Cf. Dan. 13.34–35.
8 Cf. Dan. 13.42–43.
9 Cf. Dan. 13.44–62.
10 Cf. 2 Cor. 11.32–33.
11 Cf. 1 Cor. 9.16–18. For the "threefold rope," cf. Eccles. 4.12.
12 Cf. 2 Cor. 12.2–4.
13 Cf. Gen. 19.12–22.

surely, he chose to shut his house to the men of Sodom and flee the contagion of their offenses. When he dwelt with them, he did not come to know them, for he did not know their outrages and turned away from their disgraces. When he fled, he did not look back on them, for he did not desire to associate with them. The man who renounces the vices and rejects the way of life of his countrymen is in flight like Lot. Such a one does not look behind himself but enters that city which is. above by the passageway of his thoughts, and he does not withdraw from it until the death of the chief priest who bore the sin of the world.[14] He indeed died once, but He dies for each person who is baptized in Christ's death, that we may be buried together with Him and rise with Him and walk in the newness of His life.[15] (9.56) Your flight is a good one if your heart does not act out the counsels of sinners and their designs. Your flight is a good one if your eye flees the sight of cups and drinking vessels, so that it may not become envious as it lingers over the wine. Your flight is good if your eye turns away from the woman stranger, so that your tongue may keep the truth. Your flight is a good one if you do not answer the fool according to his folly.[16] Your flight is good if you direct your footsteps away from the countenance of fools. Indeed, one swiftly goes astray with bad guides; but if you wish your flight to be a good one, remove your ways far from their words.[17]

(9.57) The chief priest died for you and was crucified for you, so that you may cleave to His nails.[18] For in that flesh He took you up with your sins, and the debtor's bond of your offenses was fastened to that cross,[19] so that now you may

---

14 Cf. Num. 35.25, 32; John 1.29.
15 Cf. Col. 2.12; Rom. 6.4.
16 Cf. Prov. 23.33 (Septuagint); 26.4.
17 Cf. Prov. 5.8.
18 The figure of the nail is derived ultimately from a Platonic motif. For discussion of the use of the figure by Ambrose, with special reference to this passage, see R. T. Otten, "Caritas" 442–48, especially 447–48.
19 Cf. Col. 2.14.

have no debt to the world, which you have renounced once and for all. And it is right that you have no debt, for it is enough that you say, "For the world is crucified to me, and I to the world."[20] Thus you need not be afraid of death now if you carry Christ, in whom you can say, "O death, where is your victory? O death, where is your sting?"[21] In truth, when that old man of ours was fastened to the cross, the sin was destroyed,[22] the sting blunted, the guilt annihilated, that we may cease to be subject any more to shameful actions. The old man indeed has gone away.[23] But now there is in us, not the old man, but a new creation having in itself the likeness of Christ. We were buried together to the likeness of His death, and we have taken up the image of His life[24] and received the wings of a spiritual grace.

(9.58) Therefore, fly in such a way that it may be said of you, "Who are these that fly like clouds and like doves with their young?"[25] Thus, your clouds may drop down justice like dew[26] and your doves beget guilelessness.[27] Sail in such a way as if you were passing through the world, not roaming over it like the ships of Tharsis;[28] thus you may direct your course into spiritual havens and convey there the riches of the sea. Hasten in such a way that it may be said of you, "They have become swifter than eagles."[29] You see the necessity of fleeing from the wrath that is to come.[30] Those will be able to turn away from it who have placed their hope of escape in repentance and have imbibed a faith in the reconciliation that is to come through our Lord Jesus Christ. His reign is from the ages and now and always and forever and ever. Amen.

---

20 Gal. 6.14.
21 1 Cor. 15.55.
22 Cf. Rom. 6.6.
23 Cf. Eph. 4.22.
24 Cf. Rom. 6.4–5.
25 Isa. 60.8 (Septuagint).
26 Cf. Isa. 45.8.
27 Cf. Matt. 10.16.
28 Cf. Isa. 60.9. Ambrose discusses the ships of Tharsis more fully in *The Prayer of Job and David* 1.5.15.
29 Lam. 4.19.   30 Cf. Matt. 3.7; Luke 3.7.

THE PRAYER OF JOB AND DAVID

(De interpellatione Job et David)

INTRODUCTION

MBROSE'S SERIES OF SERMONS *The Prayer of Job and David*[1] exhibits considerable uncertainty both as to date and internal arrangement. References to the destruction of the statues of an emperor[2] and to an unidentified heretic[3] are too general to aid in the dating, but the period 387–389 seems probable.[4] The problem of determining the proper order of the four individual books is still more complex.[5] Manuscripts are in disagreement; many editions print that part of the work designated here as Book IV in the second position, and place Books II and III in third and fourth place, respectively. The arrangement followed in this book is that of Karl Schenkl in the *Corpus scriptorum ecclesiasticorum latinorum* (CSEL) text,[6] the text on which the translation is based. In any case, there does not seem to be any doubt that these sermons were in fact preached.

Both the absolute number and the proportion of biblical quotations throughout the work are so large as almost to preclude any other major source, although a very few Vergilian

---

1 On the work in general, see Dudden 687; Palanque 446, 520–22.
2 Cf. 3.8.24.
3 Cf. 2.4.16.
4 Dudden (687) suggests 388–389, which is accepted most recently by Paredi (438). Palanque (520–22) supplies a fine discussion of the problem, with stress on the uncertainties involved; he is inclined to a very tentative date of 387, on the basis of resemblances between this work and another sermon of Ambrose.
5 See the introductions of Schenkl, CSEL 32.2, pp. III–V, and of Migne, PL 14.793–98. See also U. Moricca, *Storia della letteratura latina cristiana* 2.1 pp. 393–94, for a well-reasoned defense of the order followed in PL (*viz.* I, IV, II, III), as opposed to Schenkl's order, followed here.
6 Volume 32.2, pp. 209–296.

reminiscences appear,[7] and Ambrose relies, as so often, on Philo for the interpretation of both personal and geographical names. Books I and II are based on the book of Job; Book III is in effect a commentary on Psalm 72 (73), while Book IV relies most heavily on Psalms 41 (42) and 42 (43). Consideration of the problem of evil appears as a prominent theme throughout. Ambrose's own penchant for textual analysis is occasionally revealed.[8]

Erasmus denied the authenticity of Book IV on stylistic grounds, but his view has not met with acceptance.[9] *The Prayer of Job and David,* not one of Ambrose's more influential works, has apparently not received published translation into any language.

---

7 At 2.4.15; 4.9.32; 4.10.36, all noted also at their appropriate positions in the notes to the text. The first two cases involve minor verbal resemblances; there is more substance to the parallel at 4.10.36.

8 Cf. especially 4.6.24.

9 See Schenkl, CSEL 32.2, p. III.

BOOK ONE

THE PRAYER OF JOB AND THE WEAKNESS OF MAN

OD'S SCRIPTURE GIVES PROOF in numerous passages that man must undergo many disturbances in this life and also that many consolations are at hand. With these, a spirit of sufficient vigor and awareness of the right should overcome present discomforts and look to those things that promise everlasting joy. The consolations do indeed outweigh the discomforts, because they impart calm in present difficulties and the hope of things to come. For this reason also the Apostle Paul says, "The sufferings of the present time are not worthy to be compared with the glory to come."[1] They are indeed unworthy of comparison with the consolation, not to speak of the fruit of the redemption. (1.2) For how is anyone's life on earth so fine that it could equal such heavenly glory? Is anything more sublime than the life of Paul? He endured so many dangers and overcame such great trouble and so many weaknesses. In those sufferings which he endured for the name of Christ, he died daily, as he himself says,[2] and he judged that in this time he was bearing nothing unworthy in view of his hope and expectation of such great glory. Elias suffered hunger and treachery and fears of death and bitter toil. Yet he alone was conveyed from heaven to earth in a fiery chariot by fiery horses and brought back so from earth to heaven.[3] He hid every merit that arose from this service

---

1 Rom. 8.18.
2 Cf. 1 Cor. 15.31.
3 Cf. 4 Kings 2.11—12. The Scripture passage mentions only Elias' departure from earth, however.

and brought forth the grace bestowed on a holy rider beyond
all the things of man. What can I say in reference to Peter?
He considered his cross unworthy of the future reward and
demanded that he be hung upside down to make some increment to his suffering, for he was not afraid to amass its torments upon his own self.

(1.3) On this account, holy David gave witness with reason,
both in the rest of his work and especially in the forty-first
psalm, that he was hastening to that glory, for he said, "When
shall I come and appear before the face of God?"[4] In this
psalm he portrayed clearly both the disturbances that arise
from human frailty and the consolations that are from the
Lord. In it, also, he prays to God on our behalf, on the
grounds that God was forgetful of His own work and of the
generosity and the grace that He had bestowed on man; He
abandoned man, whom He had undertaken to protect and
honor, and cast him out to destruction, feeble and wrecked by
various weaknesses.[5] Holy Job had done the same before David,
but the latter more from the viewpoint of the moral lesson,
and the former with greater vehemence. And so I have it at
heart to meditate upon the prayers of both, for in them the
nature of human life is portrayed, its case is pleaded, and
its privileged position is given form. Therefore we must consider these prayers in order.

(2.4) Job had lost his children and all that was his except
his wife,[1] who alone had been kept for him for a temptation.[2]
At that time he was covered all over with a grievous sore,[3]
and he perceived that his friends had come not to give consolation but to increase and magnify his pain. He noted that

---

4 Ps. 41 (42).3.
5 Cf. Ps. 41 (42).10–11.

---

1 Cf. Job 1.13–19.
2 Cf. Job 2.9–10.
3 Cf. Job 2.7.

the power to try him had been given to the adversary by the Lord.[4] Even though he felt that the arrows of the Lord were in his body and said that he was pierced by them,[5] yet, like the good athlete who does not give way to pain or refuse the hardships of the contest, he continued, "Let the Lord, having begun, wound me but not destroy me in the end. For what is my strength, that I hold out? And what is my time, that my soul should endure? Is my strength the strength of stones or this flesh of mine made of brass? And did I not have confidence in him? But help has departed from me, his visitation has despised me.[6] (2.5) Is not the life of man on earth a state of trial and his life like the days of a hireling? Like the servant who conceals himself in the shade in fear of his master or like the hireling waiting for his pay? So also have I waited empty months, and wearisome nights have been doled out to me. If I go to rest, I say, 'When will it be day?' If I rise, I again say, 'When will it be evening?' I am full of pains from evening until morning. My body is corrupted with the putrefaction of worms and I moisten the clods of earth with scrapings of bloody matter from my sores. My life is lighter than idle talk, and it perishes in empty hope. I shall say, 'My bed will comfort me.' You terrify me in dreams and frighten me in visions."[7]

(3.6) How wretched is man's condition! Like the hireling, he toils for others and is in want for himself, and he cannot sustain himself except by the compassion of another. Each day he endures a grievous slavery under fear and under dread. So as not to be caught by his master, he supposes that he can skulk in the roving, fugitive shadow of this world, as it were. Think upon him of whom Sirach speaks in Ecclesiasticus,

4 Cf. Job 2.1–6.
5 Cf. Job 6.4.
6 Job 6.9, 11–14 (Septuagint).
7 Job 7.1–6, 13–14 (Septuagint).

"Every man transgressing in his own bed, disdainful, and saying in his soul, 'Who sees me? Darkness and walls surround me. Whom do I fear?' "[1] Don't you think that that man is truly a hireling who squandered . . . ,[2] like the young man in the Gospel who, as we read, . . . the share of the inheritance received from his father, and when he was in need and in want, began to feed other men's herds as a way of relieving his hunger, meeting his expenses with his pay?[3] But he at least was finally converted, for he returned to his father and did not keep back his sins but revealed them. But the man who thinks that he is not seen by Him who sees all things and that his offenses can be concealed by darkness dwells in the shade; but in vain does he suppose that he is escaping notice, since the eye of the Lord, being brighter than the sun, uncovers all secrets, gives light to all darkness, enters into the knowledge of the inmost heart, and penetrates into the heights and the depths.[4] And so, the man who supposes that he is protected by the darkness is vain, since he cannot escape the light that shines in the darkness, and the darkness grasped it not.[5] Accordingly, he is discovered like a fugitive and a wicked hireling and is recognized before he can conceal himself. For all things are known to the Lord before He seeks them out, not only past events but also those which are to come. (3.7) Therefore, he who thinks that he is concealing his crime is lost in an empty hope, for that is idle talk and not the truth. Indeed, "the idle talk of sinners is hateful,"[6] not producing fruit but only lamentation. For "the talking of a fool is like

---

1 Sir. 23.18 (25–26).
2 In this single sentence the two groups of dots represent the two lacunae noted by Schenkl. For the first of these, Schenkl proposes, "[who] toils for others when he has [squandered]." A word like "wasted" would neatly fit the second gap.
3 Cf. Luke 15.11–16.
4 Cf. John 3.19–20; Sir. 23.19 (28).
5 Cf. John 1.5.
6 Sir. 27.13 (14).

a burden on a journey."[7] And what else is sin but a burden? It burdens the wayfarer in this world so that he is weighed down by a heavy load of crime. If he did not want to be subject to the burden, he should have heeded the Lord, who said, "Come to me, all you who labor and are burdened, and I will give you rest."[8]

(3.8) Now what could be more wretched? Even the bed, given for the repose of all men, inflicts its grievous wound. At that time, indeed, we are wont to remember what we have done, and our inner conscience is pricked by the goads of its own actions. For what reason does the Scripture say to such men, "What you say in your hearts, be sorry for on your beds"?[9] That is indeed a remedy for sin, but still the conscience has been wounded. Granted that at length sleep steals upon the weary; still we are terrified by sleepless nights and tormented by visions so that it comes now, not as a rest, but as a punishment. For so do the riches of the world depart, as a dream departs from one on awakening.[10] Someone awakens from a dream of such content, and he possesses nothing and loses that very possession which he believed he had.

(3.9) Imagine for me now that rich man, who was heaping up profits every day and gains of various sorts and was being tormented by his greedy desires. Suddenly he regains his senses, and he considers within himself that "when he dies, he shall take nothing away, and the glory of his house shall not descend with him,"[11] and that his possessions give some pleasure in this life, but not for the future. Thus he opens up his eyes to heavenly things. Don't you think he drank like one who was drinking in his dreams and feasted like one who was feasting in his dreams, but he opened his eyes and recog-

---

7 Sir. 21.16 (19).
8 Matt. 11.28.
9 Ps. 4.5.
10 Cf. Isa. 29.7 (Septuagint); Ps. 72 (73).20.
11 Ps. 48 (49).18.

nized that his soul had hoped in nothing and was still hungry and thirsty?[12] Greed has no limit and is not fulfilled with plundering but spurred on by it, for it is the more in want, the more it has sought to acquire. And therefore this man arose, and the dream is empty.

(4.10) But let us listen again as Job speaks. His friends were pressing upon him; they had come to give consolation, and like enemies they were distressing him with bitter words. Now one kind of consolation for those who find themselves in wretchedness and sorrow is to be free from guilt, so that they may not appear to be bearing their sufferings and adversities as a punishment for sin. But his friends desired to take even this from the holy man Job, so that he might appear as the instigator of his own wretchedness, as one who had contracted the Lord's displeasure by grievous offenses and was enduring such afflictions in return for his wicked deeds. They described the punishments of the wicked,[1] who sowed vices and reaped sorrows for themselves. These perished by God's decree, for they were consumed by the breath of His wrath that blew upon those dwelling in houses of clay, and they withered;[2] God forsook the designs of the clever and blocked up the mouth of him that was unjust.[3] What the friends claimed was true indeed as regards the power of the Lord but not appropriate to the just deserts of that great man. (4.11) And so, Job replied to them, "In truth I know that it is so. For how can a mortal be just before the Lord? For if one should wish to come to trial with him, he will not hear him, so that one may not set a thousand words in opposition to his one word. For he is wise in understanding and strong and great. Who is hardy enough that he can

---

12 Cf. Isa. 29.8.

1 Cf. Job 4.8–9.
2 Cf. Job 4.19, 21 (Septuagint).
3 Cf. Job 5.13, 16 (Septuagint).

stand in his sight? He makes mountains to grow old, and they know it not, and he overturns them in his wrath. He shakes the earth from the foundations, and its pillars are moved. He speaks to the sun, and it does not rise, and places his seal against the stars. He alone has spread out the heaven and walks upon the sea as on a pavement. He makes the Pleiades and the Evening Star and the Great Bear and the constellation of the south. He does things great and unsearchable, glorious and immeasurable, of which there is no number. If he passes over me, I shall not see him, and if he passes by me, neither shall I know how."[4] How much stronger was his trumpet, when he made it resound concerning the power of the Lord! But in that power the just receive help and not destruction. Indeed, while it seems the Lord's power is being described, in fact it is the mysteries of our redemption that are being made manifest.

(5.12) What are the mountains which God made to grow old? Moses, Aaron, Josue the son of Nun, Gideon, the prophets, all the books of the Old Testament. Jesus the Lord came; He brought the New Testament, and that which was, was made old. The Christian was brought in new, the Jew grew old; grace was renewed, the letter grew old. God overturned the mountains and altered them. Yes, He overturned and subverted the understanding according to the letter and established the comprehension that is of the spirit. Therefore, that understanding of the law that is according to the flesh has passed away, and the law has become spiritual. For this reason the Apostle says, "We know that the law is spiritual, but I am carnal."[1] But he also, who was carnal, was made spiritual, just as he affirmed, saying, "I think that I also have the spirit of God."[2] And so Jesus made these

---

4 Job 9.2–11 (Septuagint).

1 Rom. 7.14.
2 1 Cor. 7.40.

mountains grow old, and the Jews know it not. Indeed, had they known it, they would never have crucified the Lord of majesty and would never still be pursuing their Jewish follies.[3] They, then, are the ones who know not. For this reason also the Lord Jesus says in the Gospel, "Father, forgive them, for they do not know what they are doing."[4] (5.13) But they are not excused because of their lack of knowledge, since they do not wish to know what they should have known. Surely we do not envy them if they are subject to the judgment of the Lord, for judgment generally grants absolution for previous offenses, not future ones. And one who crucified the Author of his salvation and afterward did not beg forgiveness, is not free of sin. Granted, he did not know previously whom he was persecuting. Nevertheless, he should have recognized that the one placed on the cross was the Lord of all the elements. For all the elements trembled beneath Him, the sky was darkened, the sun fled away, the earth split apart, the tombs of the departed lay open, and the dead regained the company of the living.[5] For this reason also the centurion said, "Truly this man was the Son of God."[6] The centurion recognizes a stranger, whereas the Levite does not know his own; the Gentile worships Him, the Hebrew denies Him. Therefore, it was not unreasonable that the pillars of the world were moved[7] when the chief priests did not believe.[8] But old pillars were moved that new ones might be established, just as God Himself thought it proper to say, "I have established the pillars thereof."[9] Learn what pillars He has established: "Peter and James and John, who were considered

---

3 On the regrettable tone of the passage which follows, see *The Patriarchs* ch. 2 n. 5.
4 Luke 23.34.
5 Cf. Matt. 27.51–53; Luke 23.44–45.
6 Matt. 27.54.
7 Cf. Job 9.6.
8 Cf. Matt. 26.60–68.
9 Ps. 74 (75).4.

the pillars, gave to me and to Barnabas the right hand of fellowship."[10]

(5.14) How then do they make the excuse that they did not know? Some of them saw, and others learned, that the sun had retired without completing its daily round, and, on the other hand, that it had gone forth before night's span had been accomplished and had turned night into day and day into night. Surely they should have understood that the sun was ordered to retire and ordered to go forth. For the Lord had ordained that He would be three days in the heart of the earth, and three nights.[11] The sun learned this and was keeping His precept. Therefore it was in hesitation, saying: "What am I to do? I rise and it is day, I set and it is night. If I keep to my course, I shall delay the salvation of the world. Let us hasten to our redemption also. I ought to hasten also to the new life; in truth, by the help of the cross, whereby all things are renewed, there will be both a new sun and a new heaven.[12] I hasten, therefore, that I may be able to see the Sun of Justice who gives light to the souls of all men.[13] But what am I to do? He wishes the resurrection to take place after three days. I have discovered what I am to do, so as not to make delay and to observe the number of the days. I shall not make full day and full night. I shall shorten the hours, so that the Lord Jesus may indeed be among the dead three days and nights, yet rise again from the dead more quickly than is allowed by the intervals between three days and nights. And so I shall shorten the hours when He has mounted the cross. From the sixth hour let there be night forthwith, that I may not see the passion of the Lord but may flee from the sight of a murderous persecution. I shall set and there will be a night of three hours; I shall go forth and

10 Gal. 2.9.
11 Cf. Matt. 12.40.
12 Cf. Apoc. 21.1; 2 Peter 3.13.
13 Cf. Mal. 3.20 (4.2); John 1.9.

shall renew the day, that it may be of three hours. The
first day has been traversed, the second night will follow
in its span, and likewise a day will follow. The third night
will begin, the Lord will rise in the night, and there will be
day in the light of Him that is rising, that the Scripture may be
fulfilled, 'And night shall be light as the day.'[14] This is that
great day which Abraham saw and he was glad,[15] that day
of which David also said, 'This is the day which the Lord
has made; let us be glad and rejoice therein.'[16] I shall be
present to it, not with a toilsome service but with the fruit
of rejoicing."

(5.15) Therefore the Lord Himself shall make the day
advance, and before the completion of the world there will
appear the Light of the world, that gives light to every man
coming into this world.[17] He is the Lord who seals and numbers the multitude of stars;[18] it is He who alone has spread
out the heaven, and who walked upon the sea as on a pavement,[19] when Peter saw Him walking and said, "Lord, bid me
to come to you over the water."[20] And the Lord commanded,
but he faltered and would have sunk and perished in the
waves, had the Lord not stretched forth His right hand to
him.[21] It was the flesh that faltered and the right hand that
saved. And the Lord said to him, "You of little faith, why did
you doubt?"[22] It was faith, therefore, that walked in the person
of the Apostle, and not the flesh. Indeed, faith faltered and
the flesh began to experience shipwreck. And this is not
said incorrectly, because the flesh is the ship of the soul, even
as it is written, "They that go down to the sea in ships,"[23]

---

14 Ps. 138 (139).12.
15 Cf. John 8.56.
16 Ps. 117 (118).24.
17 Cf. John 1.9.
18 Cf. Job 9.6; Ps. 146 (147A).4.
19 Cf. Job 9.8; Matt. 14.25.
20 Matt. 14.28.
21 Cf. Matt. 14.29–31.
22 Matt. 14.31.
23 Ps. 106 (107).23.

and in another passage, "There were pains as of a woman
in labor. With a vehement wind you shall break in pieces the
ships of Tharsis."[24] Yes, when our souls are in labor with the
Word, they give forth pains. But the soul that has brought
forth no longer remembers the anguish, for joy that the man
who redeemed the world has been born to it.[25] "The ships of
Tharsis," then, that is, spiritual[26] ships, which carried the
gold and silver of Solomon,[27] that is, our bodies, which contain a treasure in vessels of clay, as the Apostle said.[28] Or else
the meaning is that, even in this case, births are racked with
uncertainty, according to what is written, "Woe to those who
are with child or who have offspring at the breast!"[29] (For
when the soul is struck, the flesh does not know where to
turn.) Or else, the souls will be stirred up by the onrush of a
vehement wind, when the time will have been completed for
the resurrection to take place, according to what is written,
"Come, spirit, and blow on these dead and they will live."[30]
For this reason also Job himself says in a later passage, "For
I know that he is eternal and powerful, who is about to dissolve me on earth, to raise anew my skin which has suffered."[31]
Moreover, they are broken to pieces because they are raised
again unto judgment. Further, the breaking is good, for "God
does not despise a broken and humbled heart,"[32] and, in
another passage, "Heal the breaks thereof."[33] But it is also
said to Josaphat, "they are broken . . . go to Tharsis,"[34]

---

24 Ps. 47 (48).7–8.
25 Cf. John 16.21.
26 "Tharsis" also appears with somewhat different interpretations in
    Flight from the World 9.58 (translated in this volume) and *Letters*
    16.3; 71.5 (translated by Sister M. Melchior Beyenka as Letters 12
    and 46, respectively, in *Saint Ambrose: Letters* [FOTC 26]).
27 Cf. 3 Kings 10.22.
28 Cf. 2 Cor. 4.7.
29 Luke 21.23.
30 Ezech. 37.9.
31 Job 19.25–26 (Septuagint).
32 Ps. 50 (51).19.
33 Ps. 59 (60).4.
34 2 Par. 20.37. Very likely the lacuna in the text can be supplied
    in the manner proposed by Schenkl, so that the English translation

because he had associated himself with one who was wicked.[35] Therefore the breaking is in both senses, because each sense appears on the day of judgment, when "all who are in the tombs shall hear the voice of the Son of God and shall come forth, they who have done good unto resurrection of life, they who have done evil unto resurrection of judgment."[36] David the psalmist also conveys this meaning when he says, "There were pains of a woman in labor. As we have heard, so also we have seen in the city of the Lord of hosts, in the city of our God."[37] In truth he includes both the future sorrow and the joy, the sorrow from judgment and the joy from pardon.

(6.16) But let us return to the prayer as set out in order before us. "He has broken me many times. He does not suffer me to take breath, he has filled me with bitterness. And because he is powerful in strength, no one is able to withstand his judgment. If I am just in heart, my tongue goes astray. Wrath destroys one that is great and powerful. The wicked [fall] in grievous death, but the just are laughed to scorn, for they have been delivered into the hands of him that is unholy."[1] Look to each point. The powerful suffer grievously from their wrath, the wicked from their wrongdoing, the just from the weakness of their condition. Thus, nothing is without danger. In any man, fortitude and greatness are beguiled by their very power, wickedness is subject to torment, strength is mocked. One man falls because he has the more power, another is tormented because he has none. The fault lies in our condition, because "our life is swifter than a runner; it has passed away and has seen nothing. Like the

---

would read: "And your ships are broken. And they could not go to Tharsis."
35　Viz., Ochozias, king of Israel. Cf. 2 Par. 20.35–37.
36　John 5.28–29.
37　Ps. 47 (48).7, 9.

1　Job 9.17–20, 22–24 (Septuagint).

path of a ship or of an eagle in flight seeking food,"[2] so also
the life of man passes by. What we speak, we forget, and no
sign of our passage is detected, save that it is filled with grief
and lamentation. "I am struck in all my limbs. Would that
there were a mediator between us, to reprove and determine
between us both."[3]

(6.17) "I shall say to the Lord, 'Why do you judge me so?
Or is it good to you that I should be unjust, because you have
rejected the works of your hands and have favored the counsel of the wicked? Would you see as a mortal man sees? And
is your life as the life of a man, and are your years as the
years of a man, that you have sought out my iniquities and
diligently traced my sins? For you know that I have not acted
impiously; but who can deliver out of your hands?' "[4] Great
is the faith, great the power of conscience, to summon God as
a witness to its intent. Job does not deny what comes from the
human condition; he rejects what comes from unholiness and
confesses what comes from weakness. To have sinned is part
of the human condition, because no one is immune from
falling; to act in an unholy way is not part of the human
condition but is the poison of an unbelieving and thoroughly
wicked heart. The just man does not have to do with this,
but the pardon of man lies in the mercy of God and not in the
power of man. (6.18) "Your hands have formed me; afterwards you have turned and struck me down. Remember that
you have made me of clay and will return me into dust. Have
you not poured me out as milk and made me as cheese?
You have clothed me with skin and flesh, with bones and
sinews you have knit me together. You have put life and mercy
into me, and your visitation has preserved my spirit."[5] How
strong was the lamentation of that holy man for the weakness

---

2 Job 9.25–26 (Septuagint).
3 Job 9.28, 33 (Septuagint).
4 Job 10.2–7 (Septuagint).
5 Job 10.8–12 (Septuagint).

that is common to all men! How strong was the weight of
the charge that God made man with His own hands! Guilt is
excused under pretext of weakness, and grace is made manifest by the favor of an eternal work in us and by the kindness
of a heavenly protection. On this point David also spoke most
excellently, saying, "What is man that you are mindful of
him, or the son of man, that you visit him?"[6]

(6.19) "As you have these things in yourself, I know that
you can do all things, and that with you nothing is impossible.
If indeed I sin, you will keep a watch on me, but from iniquity you have not made me clean. If I am unholy, woe is
me! If I be just, I cannot rise up, for I am full of shame. I
am hunted as a lion for slaughter."[7] Consider the three points:
"If I sin, you will keep a watch on me." And therefore, O
man, confess your sin that you may obtain forgiveness. "State
your iniquities that you may be justified."[8] Why are you
ashamed to confess them, when you were born in them?[9] One
who denies his guilt and does not confess it, is in effect denying
his birth. But would you might keep what you have received!
Why do you suppose you are in possession of something that
you have not received? And so, let the sinner confess, the
unholy man lament, and the just one not raise himself up and
extol himself; else he may lose the reward of his justice
through pride. (6.20) And Job appropriately says, "If I am
just, I cannot rise up, for I am full of shame." For the just
man takes note of his own weakness more than . . ., the wise
man recognizes it, the foolish one does not.[10] Indeed, the wise
man is moved to repentance by his own faults, while the

---

6 Ps. 8.5.
7 Job 10.13–16 (Septuagint).
8 Isa. 43.26 (Septuagint).
9 Cf. Ps. 50 (51).7.
10 The CSEL text indicates a lacuna at this point. A number of restora-
tions are suggested; Schenkl gives conditional approval to the conjecture of Gelenius of Prague, or Siegmund Ghelen (1497-1554), which
would yield the sense: "For the just man takes note of his own
weakness more than the unjust one, and the wise man recognizes
his faults whereas the foolish one does not."

foolish one takes pleasure in his. "The just man is the accuser of himself,"[11] while the unjust one is his own apologist. The just man wishes to anticipate his accuser in the admission of his sin, while the unjust one desires to conceal his. The one rushes on in the beginning of his speech to reveal his wrongdoing, the other attempts to lay the accusation to rest by the garrulousness of his speech, so as not to reveal his wrongdoing.

(7.21) Again Job says, along the same line, "Why have you written evil things against me and laid to my charge the sins of my youth?"[1] He aptly seized on that period of life as cause for his complaint, for it is generally more unsteady as regards sin. Childhood, indeed, possesses innocence; and old age, prudence; and young manhood, that is so close to youth, a regard for one's good reputation and a sense of shame at committing sin. But youth alone is weak in strength, feeble in counsels, ardent in sin, scornful of those who give counsel, and ready to be seduced by pleasures. And so, amid the very rough and very tempestuous storms of this world, why is it that such frequent shipwrecks are attributed to that heedless time of life? For this reason David acted admirably in asking pardon for himself from the Lord for that entire time, when he said, "The sin of my youth and of my ignorance, do not remember."[2] For it is at that time most of all that bodily passion is inflamed and burns with the heat of warm blood.

(7.22) But let us give heed again to Job. "The mortal son of a woman has a short life and is filled with wrath. He bloomed like a flower and fell, he departs like a shadow and makes no stay. And is not an accounting demanded from him, and have you not made him to enter into judgment under your sight? Who is clean from stain? Surely no one, even

---

11 Prov. 18.17.

---

1 Job 13.26 (Septuagint).
2 Ps. 24 (25).7.

if his life upon earth is a single day."[3] Truly his condition is wretched! He is forced to give an accounting of his sin and yet cannot avoid sin. He is compelled to enter into judgment, to go into the sight of the Lord almighty to declare the reasons for his actions; yet these have taken place over the entire span of his life, when no one could be clean of sin. For guilt steals in from the very beginning of infancy, before there can be any perception of wrongdoing. And what a wretched situation, that his life is short, allurement is sweet, distress manifold, and wrath a matter of daily occurrence. Accordingly, amid a minute amount of enjoyment, there exists a constant bitterness. (7.23) "There is hope for a tree; for if it is cut, it will grow green, and if its branch dies in a rock, it will blossom by the scent of water, it will produce a crop like a tree lately planted. But a man that has died has departed; when a mortal falls, he is no more. For a time [only] the sea rages."[4] We have observed that the prophet's statement deals with the two lesser elements, earth and sea, which are subject to every form of damage and to repeated storms. How powerful was the proof Job gave of our distress! For the shady branches of trees, being earthly, rise unto the uses of life even when they have died, as he says. The sea, too, generally rages [only] for a time. But in truth, our flesh is always at a boil and is a storm unto itself, nor does it ever enjoy a holiday from the agitation of tempests or from pitiable shipwrecks.

(7.24) "When he has gone to sleep, he will not rise again even until the heaven is unstitched."[5] This appears to mean, until heaven is made new. "For there will be a new heaven and a new earth,"[6] just as it is written. For what is stitched up is old, and what is old will be changed.[7] Then listen as

---

3 Job 14.1–5 (Septuagint).
4 Job 14.7–11 (Septuagint).
5 Job 14.12.
6 Isa. 65.17 (Septuagint).
7 Cf. Matt. 9.16.

the psalmist says, "In the beginning, O Lord, you founded the earth, and the heavens are the works of your hands. They shall perish, but you remain; and all of them shall grow old like a garment, and you shall change them like a garment and they shall be changed."[8] We are able also to weave on the garment, because what is old is stitched upon, whereas what is new suffers force. "From the days of John the Baptist the kingdom of heaven suffers force, and those forcing it snatch it away."[9] The synagogue stitched upon it in the case of a few; the Church forces it in the case of thousands. Or else the meaning is, that heaven now appears to be stitched upon, being often interwoven with clouds and mist and the darkness of night and the golden redness of the rising day, a various and multicolored sight. Then "night shall be no more and they shall have no need of light of lamp and light of sun, because the Lord will shed light upon them,"[10] even as John said. Or else, "Woe to those who sew pillows to overthrow the souls of the people."[11] (7.25) The prophet was lamenting the wretched frailty of our condition, that has no rest in this life and loses everything by death's sudden onset. For the Holy Spirit revealed to him that man would not arise for so long a time, until He should come who would not stitch the old to the new nor join new material to old material[12] but would make all things new, even as He said, "Behold, I make all things new!"[13] For He is the resurrection,[14] the firstborn from the dead,[15] in whom we have all indeed received the prerogative of a future resurrection; yet till now He alone has risen in a perpetual resurrection.

---

8 Ps. 101 (102).26–27.
9 Matt. 11.12.
10 Apoc. 22.5.
11 Ezech. 13.18 (Septuagint).
12 Cf. Matt. 9.16.
13 Apoc. 21.5.
14 Cf. John 11.25.
15 Cf. Col. 1.18; Apoc. 1.5.

(8.26) And so, Job heeded what God had spoken in him and knew through the Holy Spirit that the Son of God not only would come to earth but was going to descend also into hell to raise up the dead—as indeed was done at that time as a testimony of present things and a model of future ones. He turned to the Lord and said, "Would you had kept me in hell and hidden me until your anger should cease and you would set a time for me when you would remember me. For if a man has died, he shall live, after finishing the days of his life. I will bear up, until I come again into existence. Then you shall call me, and I will obey you, but do not reject the works of your hands. Now you have numbered my devices, nor will any of my sins escape you. You have sealed up my iniquities in a bag and have set a mark, if I have omitted anything by inadvertence."[1] What a fine passage, for it strengthens us in regard to the resurrection! How it seems to accord with the Lord's words that we read in the Gospel! There He says, "Then they will begin to say to the mountains, 'Fall upon us,' and to the hills, 'Cover us.'"[2] For the wrath of the Lord will appear in the end of the world. Therefore holy Job rightly preferred to rise to the judgment rather than to the time of God's wrath, which is terrible even to the innocent. (8.27) At the same time, in saying "You will set a time for me, when you would remember me," Job is understood to be prophesying that he was going to be raised up in the passion of the Lord, as is shown clearly in the conclusion of that book.[3] Yet he does not cease to lament, and the more he understands that a resurrection awaits him, the greater his desire to flee from this life. For he sees that he has been given over into the hands of his adversaries and cast down into the power of the unholy. Even his friends have

---

1 Job 14.13–17 (Septuagint).
2 Luke 23.30.
3 Cf. Job 42.17. The Septuagint text reads: "And it is written that he will rise again with those whom the Lord raises up."

turned into enemies; although they should have consoled him, they bring in ruin upon ruin. Yet, mindful of his own clear conscience and unblemished prayer, he says, "Earth, do not cover over the blood of my flesh,"[4] so that his prayer may be directed as incense to the Lord[5] and may not lodge in the earth. For the prayer of the holy man pierces the clouds;[6] but the earth, opening its mouth, hides the prayer of the sinner in the blood of the flesh, just as was said by God to the murderer Cain. "You are cursed from the earth which has opened its mouth to receive the blood of your brother from your hand, when you will till the earth."[7]

(9.28) And so, the holy man tearfully laments the circumstances of such a life. "I am dying with a tortured spirit, I pray for burial and I do not obtain it. I am supplicating in distress. And what am I to do? My days have passed in horror, the strings of my heart have been broken."[1] Nevertheless, he does not detract from God's judgment at any point, for he knows that the depth of the wisdom and of the knowledge of God is profound and that His judgments are incomprehensible and His ways unsearchable.[2] (9.29) "The children of boasters have not trodden them, nor has the lion passed through them."[3] For who could comprehend His ways, who has penetrated His secret places deeply hidden?[4] "Where has wisdom been found, and what is the place of discipline? A mortal man does not know its way, nor has it been found among men. The abyss said, 'It is not in me' and the sea said, 'It is not with me.' "[5] O man, it is not permitted you to know

---

4 Job 16.18 (Septuagint).
5 Cf. Ps. 140 (141).2.
6 Cf. Sir. 35.17 (21).
7 Gen. 4.11–12.

1 Job 17.1–2, 11 (Septuagint).
2 Cf. Rom. 11.33; Job 5.9.
3 Job 28.8 (Septuagint).
4 Cf. Job 11.7.
5 Job 28.12–14 (Septuagint).

the heights of wisdom, and so it is written for you, "Be not high-minded, but fear."[6] Why do you wish to search with care into something which is not advantageous for you to know, nor is it given to you to be acquainted with it? Paul heard certain secrets of wisdom which he was forbidden to make known to others, and so he was caught up into paradise, caught up even to the third heaven, to hear things which he was not able to hear when he was on earth.[7] If it was not permitted to man to speak what he heard, how does he search out that which he has not heard? It is not permitted you to know the counsels of your emperor on earth, and do you wish to know God's counsels? It is not permitted you to search out with too much curiosity what takes place on earth, and do you seek out with too much curiosity what is done above heaven? Why do you hold discussion over wisdom's origin? Man does not know its way, nor has perfect wisdom been found among men. It was not in Moses nor in Aaron nor in Josue the son of Nun, it was not in David himself who says, "The uncertain and hidden things of your wisdom you have made manifest to me,"[8] because he also said in a later passage, "I became like a brute beast in your presence."[9] O man, it is beyond you to know the depth of wisdom; it is sufficient for you that you believe. "For if you do not believe, neither will you understand."[10] You cannot know the abyss, you cannot comprehend the abyss; how will you comprehend wisdom's depth? "The abyss said, 'It is not in me,'" and can you say that wisdom is in you?

(9.30) Therefore "the abyss said, 'It is not in me,'" because the Lord Himself said, "You will not leave my soul in hell."[11] The Apostle also said, "Who shall descend into the abyss?"

---

6 Rom. 11.20.
7 Cf. 2 Cor. 12.2–4.
8 Ps. 50 (51).8.
9 Ps. 72 (73).22 (23).
10 Isa. 7.9.
11 Ps. 15 (16).10.

(that is, to bring up Christ from the dead).[12] And so if the abyss is asked: Where is wisdom? it replies: "It is not in me," because it has risen. If the sea is asked: Where is wisdom? it says, "It is not with me," because it trod upon me and my waves could not disturb it.[13] And therefore, since you find yourself on this sea of that age, do not seek the perfect wisdom of God in this world, because the world has not known it. But if you wish to find it, tread upon the waves of that world, even as Peter did,[14] and walk upon the waters of that age. Wisdom will stretch forth its hand to you, just as it did to Peter also,[15] because the waters of that age left no one untroubled. They troubled Abraham, they troubled Moses, they troubled Peter. Moses passed through the sea, and through the sea he led his host on foot, but he was troubled beforehand.[16] Peter trod upon the waters, but his body would have sunk because he limped as he walked in the weakness of his faith.[17] And, therefore, do not seek wisdom in the sea, because the Lord Jesus did not say that He would be with the sea but with His Apostles, so that they might come to know Him in some measure. For He says to them, "Behold, I am with you even unto the consummation of the world."[18] Happy are they who enjoy His company; would He were also with us, but the sea is with us. Peter is with Christ, because he also trod upon the sea, while to us gold and silver are dear. But wisdom is above gold, it is not in gold.[19] And so he that desired to possess wisdom says, "Silver and gold I have not, but what I have, I give to you. In the name of Jesus Christ of Nazareth, arise and walk."[20] Because he did not

---

12 Rom. 10.7.
13 Cf. Matt. 14.25–26.
14 Cf. Matt. 14.29.
15 Cf. Matt. 14.31.
16 Cf. Exod. 14.10–22.
17 Cf. Matt. 14.28-33.
18 Matt. 28.20.
19 Cf. Wisd. 7.9.
20 Acts 3.6.

possess gold, he possessed the gift of a charitable work in the name of Christ. And so, it is said to you also, "Draw wisdom into the inner places.[21] It has escaped the notice of every man and was hidden from the birds of the air."[22] Men did not know where it was, nor did angels, for they are the birds of the air, of whom it is said, "And I saw an angel flying through the air."[23]

(9.31) No one could have known wisdom, because "no one knows the Son except the Father and no one knows the Father except the Son and him to whom the Son chooses to reveal him."[24] Therefore He revealed Him to John, since wisdom was with the Apostle, and so he spoke not his own thought, but that which wisdom poured into him: "In the beginning was the Word, and the Word was with God."[25] Death does not know wisdom, wickedness does not know it. Death indeed could not hold it, for wisdom said, "O death, where is your victory? O death, where is your sting?"[26] Wickedness does not know it, for wisdom said, "The wicked will seek me and they will not find me."[27] These can say, "We have heard the fame of it."[28] But it is only God who knows it, because "God has established well its way and knows its place."[29] Listen to the disciple as he tells what wisdom's receptacle is: "The only-begotten Son, who is in the bosom of the Father, he has revealed him."[30] For the Son knew the Father, because He says, "even as the Father knows me, and I know the Father."[31] There is a like measure of knowledge where there is unity of power. And so the Father, who knows

---

21 Job 28.18.
22 Job 28.21.
23 Apoc. 14.6.
24 Matt. 11.27.
25 John 1.1.
26 1 Cor. 15.55; cf. Osee 13.14.
27 Prov. 1.28 (Septuagint).
28 Job 28.22.
29 Job 28.23.
30 John 1.18.
31 John 10.15.

all things, the balance of the winds and the measure of the waters,[32] He has seen wisdom and has revealed it through His prophets.[33] For the Father has revealed wisdom and has searched it out, even as the Son also has revealed the Father; nothing escapes the knowledge of the Father, and He has said: "O man, why do you wish to know the depths of wisdom, which are over you? 'The fear of God is wisdom and to abstain from evil is knowledge.' "[34]

---

32 Cf. Job 28.24–25.
33 Cf. Job 28.27.
34 Job 28.28.

BOOK TWO

THE PRAYER OF HOLY JOB

OUR PREVIOUS DISCUSSION had to do with the prayer of holy men, for the condition of man is frail and weak, and nowhere does he have a firm hold upon himself save under the protection of heaven. Today we must take up the following topic, that the generality of men—yes, even many of the wise—are much affected when they perceive that the unjust abound in prosperity, whereas the just often suffer affliction in this life. And truly this is a perilous point, on which even holy men have scarcely been able to keep to the track of sound belief. Indeed, David also was troubled, for he had said in an earlier passage, "The hidden things of your wisdom you have made manifest to me."[1] But still, he later strengthened himself and searched out the way of perfect reason. The holy Job also struggled in dialogue over this point of belief with those three old friends who had come to give him consolation.[2] Let us then bring forward into view the discussions conducted by each man. For both are worthy to give us instruction on life, seeing that, when they were in adversity, they merited to be the more pleasing to God. And so let us listen to each in order.

(1.2) Eliphaz the king of the Temanites and Baldad the tyrant of the Shuhites and Sophar the king of the Mineans[3]

---

1 Ps. 50 (51).8.
2 Cf. Job 4–37.
3 Cf. Job 2.11. The designations "king" and "tyrant" come from the Septuagint.

reproached Job forcefully, on the ground that he was enduring such great punishments by reason of his sins. With their
feeble insight, they did not perceive that the Lord had given
him over to be tempted so that, like an athlete of Christ, he
might be fashioned by the temptations and attain to the
crown of a greater glory. Accordingly, they did not see
that great mystery of wisdom; their cramped hearts were
afraid that they might appear to be accusing God of injustice
in permitting punishments to be inflicted on a guiltless man.
They cast the onus for his punishments back upon holy
Job and said, "The whole life of the wicked is spent in
anxiety,"[4] and "Riches collected unjustly shall be vomited
up."[5] They claimed that he was suffering all the afflictions
that a man suffers on earth, by reason of his sins. For even
though a man is in prosperity, his prosperity cannot be made
perpetual, and it vanishes as swiftly as a dream, so that the
place of it is not found.[6] "But the mirth of the wicked is a
more severe ruin,"[7] they said, and so it was that even holy
Job had been changed from prosperity to adversity and had
fallen down from the highest to the lowest, as the price of his
offenses. Although he claimed that he was guiltless, they said
that he fell since the wicked man's portion is such that wrath,
coming upon him from the Lord, snows down sorrows on
him[8] and destruction envelopes his house.[9]

(2.3) Holy Job heard all this. He was seated in the dung,
with so many bruises and painfully cruel wounds, for his
body was covered all over with horrible sores.[1] As a brave
athlete, he spoke in mysteries and devoted himself, not to

---

4 Job 15.20 (Septuagint).
5 Job 20.15 (Septuagint).
6 Cf. Job 20.7–9.
7 Job 20.5 (Septuagint).
8 Cf. Job 20.23 (Septuagint).
9 For the sentence as a whole, cf. Job 20.28–29 (Septuagint).

---

1 Cf. Job 2.7–8.

seeking out remedies for his own illness, but to discourse
on holy topics. And so, the discourses of the sick man were
stronger than the discussions of those who were not sick. They
indeed spoke of injustices, but not according to knowledge;
they preached God's judgments, the punishments of the guilty
and the rewards of the saints, but they did not know how to
distinguish the guilty man from the just one. Indeed, him
that the Lord God proclaimed just, they charged with injustice
and accused of iniquity. They did not know, therefore, what
was appropriate to each person. But the holy man Job made
distinction in spirit as to how he should speak to each
one; therefore he was stronger than those who appeared
healthy and sound. And why do I say that he was found
stronger than the others? He was found stronger than himself. [He was stronger when sick than when he was healthy.]
For Job was stronger when sick than he had been when
healthy, according to that which is written, that "strength
is made perfect in weakness."[2] And so, when Job was suffering
weakness, then he had the greater strength. Indeed, he was
not sick in spirit, even though he was suffering bodily pain,
because his soul was not in the flesh, nor did it cleave to
the passions of the flesh; rather, it was in the spirit and had
covered itself with the strength of the spirit.

(2.4) And so it was that he voiced not the groanings of the
flesh and the weaknesses of the body but the words of the
spirit, words of exhortation and not of concession. And first,
indeed, he spoke more mildly, so as to produce in his friends
a sense of shame. For they were besetting a just man and
saying unjustly that he was enduring punishments that were
less than his sins; being sinners themselves, they were not
ashamed to make false accusations against a guiltless man.
Job says: "Take it for granted that I have erred, and that
the wayward one dwells with me, who pours out errors

---

2 2 Cor. 12.9.

over the minds of men, so that I speak words which I ought not, even as you say, and my words are erroneous and my speech inopportunely expressed.[3] Why do you make attack on me and reproach me, while not considering that that trial has come to me from the Lord, who has judged that I should be enclosed by a rampart of afflictions, as it were?[4] I am tried by adversities, I am surrounded on every side by toils and dangers.[5] Yet you revile, and still desire to overwhelm, one whom you should have helped. See, I laugh amid reproaches, and I shall not speak[6] nor reply to your insults. For you are not my judges, but it is the Lord who judges me, and nevertheless the time of his judgment has not yet come." What need is there to cry out before the judgment? It is good to keep silent while the judge is awaited, it is good not to repay insult with insult; else we also might be counted among the detractors.

(2.5) And so, let us imitate this man, who disproved his revilers by his silence. He indeed revealed the strength of his spirit, for insults did not affect it; and he made plain the guiltlessness of his conscience, for he did not give recognition to accusations but laughed at them as if they were foreign to him. But in truth, just as if some reproach were being cast against us, while we wish to justify, we embitter; while we desire to avenge, we make avowal, since the Scripture says that "you should turn aside the insult[7] and take away your garment, for a hurtful man is passing by."[8] And so let us keep silent, that he may pass by and not be provoked to burn our garment, for it is written, "Kindle not the coals of a sinner, lest perhaps you be consumed in his flaming fire."[9]

---

3 Cf. Job 19.4 (Septuagint).
4 Cf. Job 19.5–6 (Septuagint).
5 Cf. Job 19.8.
6 Cf. Job 19.7 (Septuagint).
7 Prov. 27.11 (Septuagint).
8 Cf. Prov. 27.13 (Septuagint).
9 Sir. 8.10 (13).

For that reason, then, the holy man is silent, even if a servant abuses him; even if a poor man insults him, the just man is silent; even if a sinner casts his reproaches, the just man laughs; even if one that is weak gives a curse, the just man gives a blessing. (2.6) David kept silent when Semei the son of Gera cursed him,[10] Job laughed,[11] Paul gave a blessing, even as he says, "We are cursed and we bless."[12] In truth, human virtue enjoyed its increase and advance from God's teaching, because by then He had come who would make men stronger that had been weak, and Paul had heeded Him when He said, "Bless those who curse you and pray for those who calumniate you."[13] What Christ said in word, He proved also by example. Indeed, when He was on the cross, He said in reference to His persecutors who were calumniating Him, "Father, forgive them, for they do not know what they are doing,"[14] so that He might pray for His calumniators, although He could have forgiven them Himself. And so Job laughed; for Christ had not yet come, and the prerogative of practicing mighty virtues was reserved to Him alone, because He is the beginning of the virtues, even as He said, "The Lord has created me, the beginning of his ways."[15]

(3.7) Job laughed and kept silent. He tells us the reason that silence is necessary: "I will cry out, and judgment is not yet."[1] He is saying: "The Lord has willed me to suffer these things. I am shut in by trials as if by walls, and I am not able to flee, until it shall please God to destroy the depths of my trials. Now, even if I cry out, judgment is not yet. I am still in the contest, I am still struggling, the combat

10 Cf. 2 Kings 16.5–14.
11 Cf. Job 19.7 (Septuagint).
12 1 Cor. 4.12.
13 Luke 6.28.
14 Luke 23.34.
15 Prov. 8.22 (Septuagint).

1 Cf. Job 19.7.

still awaits me, for the victor's crown has not yet come forth."
Further, no one receives the crown except him who has con-
tested lawfully.[2] (3.8) A third contest was in store for Job.
He had lost all that was his, that is, his inheritance along
with his children, and his flesh was suffering wounds; it remained for him to overcome the trials posed by words. The
combat was not a trivial one. Adam was beguiled by speech,[3]
and Samson was overcome by a word;[4] in truth, nothing penetrates the soul so much as polished discourse and, on the
other hand, nothing is so biting as discourse of a harsher
tenor.[5] Although they have overcome the torments that were
brought to bear against them, many persons have not withstood harsh discourse. Job suffered distress, but he withstood
and carried the burden of the words next to that of the
wounds. The president of the contest saw him; from out of
the cloud and the storm,[6] He gave His hand to him as he
struggled, declared that Job's opponents had suffered a grievous fall,[7] proclaimed him the victor, and gave him the crown.

(3.9) What is more appropriate than to laugh when we are
cursed? Indeed, we ought to rejoice if hostile statements are
made. First, because our enemy, although wishing to say something against us to fasten guilt on us, has found nothing which
is true but has made up falsehoods in place of the truth.
Then, because the Lord Himself said in the Gospel, in
reference to an accusation of this sort which was falsely
inflicted on the guiltless for justice' sake, "Rejoice and exult,
because your reward is great in heaven."[8] And so, one who
acknowledges an accusation ought to keep silent so as not to
irritate the wound and tear the scar. Likewise, one who does

---

2 Cf. 2 Tim. 2.5.
3 Cf. Gen. 3.6.
4 Cf. Judges 16.4–22.
5 Cf. Prov. 15.1.
6 Cf. Job 38.1.
7 Cf. Job 42.7.
8 Matt. 5.12.

not acknowledge it ought also to keep silent, for he is hearing of the misdeed of another and not his own. But if he replies, he makes it his own. If he is silent, he casts it back and wounds the calumniator. He ought also to keep silent who is confident of the aforesaid reward, for one who has not a judgment does not suffer prejudgment. And if there is prejudgment in the world, there will not be in the judgment of God. Indeed, so that you may know that insult is not prejudicial to a good conscience, listen to the saying of holy Job, who is a more substantial witness than if he had been ruler of the Roman world: "Now I shall be silent and I shall leave off; if now there is prejudgment unto me, then I shall not be hidden from your face."[9]

(3.10) And so, he gave these replies with a certain restraint at the beginning, so that he could warn his friends of the judgment of God, recall them from their arrogance and frenzy, and, like the good physician, make them recover. But after he observed that they persisted in their insults, he repeated himself more forcefully and struck them a stronger blow, so to speak, for they were stoning a guiltless man with the rocks of their words. "Hear, hear my words, let it not be mine to seek consolation from you; bear with me,"[10] for I shall speak more forcefully. The weight of my words will be heavy. I too shall speak along the lines of your belief, namely, that many men enjoy abundant prosperity and success in this world, while others are oppressed and find themselves in hardship, and that this latter condition appears to be inflicted as a punishment for sins. Even though I say this, do not laugh, as if I were in agreement with you. Even though I am a sinner, I am not answerable to man, because he is subject to sin, both he who judges and he who claims power for himself over me. And if I am judged as simply man, that

9 Cf. Job 13.19–20.
10 Job 21.2–3 (Septuagint).

judgment is common to all men. I ought not to be rebuked, for weakness is part of the human condition, even though a particular wickedness is not.

(4.11) But tell me, if I am suffering this by reason of my sin, as you charge against me, "why do the wicked live?"[1] And not only do they live, but they are filled with riches as well and their profits are multiplied; what is more, they have their children, and their households are abundant.[2] Such a way of life is, at first sight, clearly a good, but, in a more profound and mysterious sense, you will discover that what is considered good is not good, and what is considered evil, they reckon preferable. (4.12) "They have grown old in wealth."[3] The Greek text reads *pepalaiōntai* [they have grown old], so that it appears to refer, not to a lengthy continuance in the possession of riches so much as to a long-standing burden implicit in wealth. Just so, Ecclesiastes sees that riches are kept for ill by him who possesses them, for their loss causes a very great anxiety and disquiet.[4] Indeed they are lost, for they are left here and can be of no advantage to one who is dead. And so, the dead man felt anxiety in regard to them and could not find rest; he left what would bring him shame and did not take with himself what he could keep.[5] He was far different from him of whom it is written, "Blessed is the man that has filled his desire with them; he shall not be confounded, when he speaks to his enemies in the gate."[6] His inheritance is the Lord, his reward is from the offspring of the virgin Mary, and he is extolled with praises in the going forth of wisdom. For he had no cause for shame, since he had no desire for worldly things; rather, he put off the skin of the old man[7] and wounded the adversary with the

---

1 Job 21.7 (Septuagint).
2 Cf. Job 21.7–9 (Septuagint).
3 Job 21.7 (Septuagint).
4 Cf. Eccles. 5.12–13.
5 Cf. Luke 12.20–21, 33.
6 Ps. 126 (127).5.
7 Cf. Eph. 4.22; Col. 3.9.

dart of continence. Thus the foe, lame by reason of his own wound and confounded by admiration of his opponent's virtues, could not attack him at the end of his life. You find, therefore, that a man who has grown old in the desire for money, and has not been renewed in the receiving of grace, is not praiseworthy.

(4.13) Let us look to another point. "Their seed is according to their desire,"[8] that is, they are not reckoned among the just. For the just sow in the spirit and from the spirit they will reap everlasting life,[9] but those who sow according to their desire are not able to reap spiritual crops,[10] because material man does not perceive the things that are of the Spirit of God. For it is foolishness to him and he cannot know spiritual things,[11] and so he is not filled with spiritual goods but is called to judgment. (4.14) "Their children are before their eyes";[12] that is, they do what they do on this account, that they may be seen by men; it is not that they, as good men, take counsel to choose a course that may be sanctioned by the future judgment. Scripture, then, often puts "children" for "works," because our posterity is richer in its good deeds than in its children. For this reason, when Ezechia was delivered from a severe illness, he said, "From this day I shall beget children, who will proclaim your justice, O Lord of my salvation, and I will not cease praising you with the psaltery all the days of my life."[13] For the posterity of faith and devotion was good, and it did not know submission to the captivity which Ezechia's children endured.

(4.15) And Job continued, saying that "they have no dread, a scourge from the Lord is not upon them."[14] Moreover, the

---

8 Job 21.8 (Septuagint).
9 Cf. Gal. 6.8.
10 Cf. 1 Cor. 9.11.
11 Cf. 1 Cor. 2.14.
12 Job 21.8 (Septuagint).
13 Isa. 38.19–20 (Septuagint).
14 Job 21.9 (Septuagint).

just man says, "I have been scourged all the day."[15] He desires
to be scourged that he may be received by the Lord, and he
wishes to fear God, because "the fear of the Lord is the beginning of wisdom."[16] And he does not think it happiness
if "their cow does not miscarry,"[17] even as fools think. For
by the cow what is meant but the toil of cultivating the land?
This always recurs in a cycle and never ceases,[18] but when
it appears to be completed, it returns to its beginning. Such
are those who cultivate Sodom and Gomorra. And so those who
cultivate Egypt and turn over its clods of earth with the
plow of a determined heart, as it were, bring forth toil for
themselves and reap sorrows.[19] And so their cow does not
miscarry but brings forth, that their toil may be increased;
all things which they have conceived, they produce without
the fear of God. But the glory of the just is far different,
for they glory, not in abundance of riches nor in the offspring
of their cattle, but in the Lord, and they say, "On account
of the fear of you, we conceived in the womb and brought
forth the spirit of salvation."[20] In regard to the just, then,
it is said that they produced the spirit of salvation, which
they conceived on account of fear of God, and not from the
wickedness of this world, concerning which we read, "Behold,
he has been in labor with injustice and has conceived toil
and brought forth iniquity."[21] Therefore the miscarriage of
worldly things is better than their birth. Indeed, in regard to
the man who has come into this life and has endured the
vanity and darkness of this world over an extended longevity,
Ecclesiastes declared that "the miscarriage is better than he."[22]

---

15 Ps. 72 (73).14.
16 Ps. 110 (111).10.
17 Job 21.10.
18 Cf. Vergil, *Georgics* 2.401.
19 Cf. Job 4.8.
20 Isa. 26.17–18 (Septuagint).
21 Ps. 7.15.
22 Eccles. 6.3.

For the one enjoys rest rather than the other, because the former has not experienced the inconstancy of life, wherein even a man who lived a thousand years could not have seen the good. It is more of a grace to have avoided such things, then, than to have suffered them.

(4.16) But perhaps one would be moved by what Job added, that "they remain like everlasting sheep, while their little ones play, taking up the psaltery and the cithara, and they delight in the sound of the psalm. They have completed their life among good things, they have slept in the repose of hell."[23] Distinguish these matters, and, because you are spiritual, judge between them.[24] The unholy are like the everlasting, but they are not everlasting, because they cannot receive eternity from one who is not eternal. And so, he cannot give what he does not have; nor can one who does not possess the light give light, but he transforms himself into an angel of light[25] to deceive the unbelieving. He transforms himself, moreover, under the pretense of a false light, and not in the splendor of a perpetual brightness. For this reason also the Savior says, "I was watching Satan fall as lightning from heaven."[26] He is not lightning, but he is as lightning. Think upon some heretic who is devoted to bodily abstinence and the knowledge of the heavenly mysteries.[27] He is accounted like one who is everlasting, but he does not possess the recompense of eternal life, for one who does not possess the truth of faith possesses a false likeness. His little ones play like a woman who wishes to marry when she has been wanton.[28] She has been wanton on the psaltery and the cithara, that is, in the sound of her voice, but not in the depth of the

---

23 Job 21.11–13 (Septuagint).
24 Cf. 1 Cor. 2.15.
25 Cf. 2 Cor. 11.14.
26 Luke 10.18.
27 This is perhaps an allusion to Priscillian and his followers. See Dudden 687.
28 Cf. 1 Tim. 5.11.

mysteries, so that she echoes them with the lips but does not bring them into the heart.

(5.17) And so, men of this sort have completed their lives among the good things of the world—I mean the lives which they were living, not the life they hoped for as a reward—and on that account they have slept in the repose of hell and not in heavenly repose.[1] But let us pray rather to undergo toil here, so that we may deserve to gain the consolation of eternal rest in the kingdom of heaven. For prosperity and abundance constitute a powerful inducement to do wrong; they exalt a man to pride and induce him to forget his Creator. Think upon that rich man in the Gospel who reclined at table on coverings of fine purple, while the just Lazarus, a poor man, would gather the crumbs from his table.[2] Don't you think that the rich man is saying to God, "Depart from me; I desire not to know your ways"?[3] And, in truth, men of this sort do not desire to know the ways of the Lord. For if they desired to do so, they would come to know them; but because these ways are filled with toil, those that are incorrigible flee and turn aside from them. And so, like one who is intoxicated, the rich man does not recognize the Author of his salvation. Thereupon, turning to his fellow drinkers, he says, "Let us eat and drink.[4] What is the gain, if we should serve him? And what the advantage, if we should give heed to him?"[5] And so, he speaks in this way as one that is drunk with an abundance of worldly possessions, because the deserts of crime are not paid out immediately in the world. For he was reclining on his back, since all things were ready to hand for his pleasure; he was aware of his wickedness, and a penalty was reserved for it; only he supposed that God did not see the crimes of the wicked.

---

1 Cf. Job 21.13.
2 Cf. Luke 16.19–21.
3 Job 21.14 (Septuagint).
4 Isa. 22.13.
5 Job 21.15.

(5.18) Therefore holy Job replied to this belief of his: Do not think to be carefree and dissolute because the scourges of the Lord do not come to you even in this life. "The lamp of wicked men also is extinguished."[6] It gives light for a time, but it does not possess everlasting light. And although the world favors such men, because they do the will of him who possesses sovereignty in the world,[7] there generally comes a turning point in events, when sorrows come from heaven's wrath and indignation, so that the wicked are winnowed as chaff is by the wind.[8] The unjust are winnowed as chaff, the just as wheat. Therefore, heed the Lord as He says to Peter, "Behold, Satan has desired to winnow you as wheat; but I have prayed for you, that your faith may not fail."[9] Those who are winnowed as chaff fail, but that man does not fail who is like the seed that fell and sprang up, augmented and increased by very many fruits.[10] And so the prophet says, "Woe is me! For I am become as one who gathers the stubble in the harvest."[11] Thus wickedness is compared to the stubble, which is quickly burned, and to the dust. And so, Job said subsequently, "They will be like chaff driven by the wind,"[12] and at once he added a brief line and said, "or like dust that the wind has carried off."[13] Indeed, so that you may know that the wicked man swiftly crumbles and vanishes like dust, you find it said in the first psalm, "Not so the wicked, not so,"[14] that is, not like the just, "but like the dust, which the wind drives from the face of the earth."[15]

(5.19) Job also makes a distinction between the just man

---

6 Job 21.17.
7 Cf. John 14.30; 16.11.
8 Cf. Job 21.18.
9 Luke 22.31–32.
10 Cf. Luke 8.8.
11 Mich. 7.1 (Septuagint).
12 Job 21.18 (Septuagint).
13 *Ibid.*
14 Ps. 1.4.
15 *Ibid.*

and the wicked one. "One dies in the strength of his innocence, entirely in prosperity and favor, his inner parts are filled with fat, the marrow of them abounds. Another completes the course of this life in bitterness of soul and endures his end after having never feasted on anything good."[16] What can be repaid to such a man that is worthy of his merits? He is brought to the graves and keeps watch in his tomb.[17] And this is no slight punishment either, that he does not possess the repose of death but is carried to the tombs of the dead and not to the land of the living. For one who is living is not sought among the dead;[18] rather, he enjoys eternal life in the bosom of Abraham.[19] And so, the two men in dazzling apparel said to the women, "Why do you seek the living one among the dead?"[20] (5.20) Then Job enumerates the crimes of the wicked: they have transgressed the bounds and have ravaged the flock with the shepherd, they have driven away the ass of the orphan, they have taken the widow's cow for a pledge, they have reaped a field not their own, the weak have worked in their vineyards without wages and without food, they have made many to sleep naked by taking away their clothing, and have carried off the covering necessary to sustain their life.[21] These latter were wet with the dew of the mountains, and for want of shelter they took cover under a rock.[22] Orphans were torn from their mothers' breasts, and the fallen were pressed down, who should have been raised up.[23] The hungry were robbed of food[24] and the souls of little babies heaved heavy groans.[25]

---

16 Job 21.23–25 (Septuagint).
17 Cf. Job 21.32.
18 Cf. Luke 24.5.
19 Cf. Luke 16.22–23.
20 Luke 24.5.
21 Cf. Job 24.2–12.
22 Cf. Job 24.8.
23 Cf. Job 24.9.
24 Cf. Job 24.10.
25 Cf. Job 24.12.

(5.21) Could God not have known of such things, when nothing escapes His notice? "Hell is naked in his sight and there is no covering for the very wicked,"[26] because they cannot lie in hiding. "He stretches out Boreas in place of nothing, he suspends the earth on nothing, he binds up the water in his clouds, and the cloud does not burst under his feet.[27] The pillars of heaven leaped apart and were in dread at his rebuke. By power he restrained the sea, by knowledge he overthrew the monster of the sea. The bars of heaven are terrified at him; by a decree he doomed to death the apostate dragon. Who knows the strength of his thunder?"[28] Therefore, amid such great vices, "What hope is there for the wicked man? Will he be saved if he trusts in the Lord?[29] I will tell you what is in the hand of the Lord"[30] and cease "to heap vanities on vanities."[31]

(5.22) Job also describes the wretched lot of the wicked.[32] Even though they have many children, they are without a posterity, for they are lacking a succession of good and meritorious deeds; and that surely is the true posterity, which is not on earth but in heaven. Therefore such men have want as their inheritance and death as their succession. Although they have heaped up wealth,[33] they will beg; for when they have died, they will be in need in that they cannot find rest.[34] No one will take pity on their widows,[35] but these will remain abandoned and deprived of the consolation of any marital union. Even though money is collected like earth and gold has been prepared like clay, still their

26 Job 26.6.
27 Job 26.7–8 (Septuagint).
28 Job 26.11–14 (Septuagint).
29 Job 27.8 (Septuagint).
30 Job 27.11 (Septuagint).
31 Job 27.12 (Septuagint).
32 Cf. Job 27.14–15.
33 Cf. Job 27.14.
34 Cf. Job 27.15.
35 Cf. Job 27.15 (Septuagint).

substance will be as an empty cobweb, and all the inheritance of their line will be consumed as if by moths.[36] "The rich man, when he sleeps, shall have no increase; he has opened his eyes and now he is not."[37] He remains among sorrows. Therefore all things that exist in this world are nothing. Gold is in mines, silver is in mines; from the mine they are dug out[38] and into the mine they return. And what is the heart of a greedy man but a mine? It holds on to whatever it has received as if that had been buried, and conceals it in the veins and hiding-places of the earth, because it does not know how to make use of it. Gold is brought out from mines every day; who can bring forth from a greedy man?

(5.23) And so the empty craving for gold is profitless. Whatever one has gathered together slips away, and those men are indeed pitiable who have forsaken the way of the just and have forgotten it, since precious stones are in no way comparable to it. That way is difficult to search out, impassable to the proud, closed off to the boastful, level to the humble, and open to the wise. And so we ought to search for wisdom, that we may walk in the way of the just; for the adversary, who hastens through this world like a ravenous, roaring lion,[39] cannot pass over that way. But if a man wishes to search out wisdom, let him not seek it in the abyss,[40] like the philosophers who think that they can know its depths by their own initiative and their own ability. And let him not seek it in the sea[41]— for indeed where there is tempest and windstorm, there wisdom cannot be—but let him seek it there where there is tranquillity of heart and the peace that is beyond all understanding.[42]

---

36 Cf. Job 27.16–18.
37 Job 27.19.
38 Cf. Job 28.1.
39 Cf. 1 Peter 5.8.
40 Cf. Job 27.14.
41 Cf. *ibid*.
42 Cf. Phil. 4.7.

BOOK THREE

WE HAVE DISCUSSED the prayer of holy Job; now let us approach that prayer which we have found in the psalms. David himself spoke out in many passages in regard to worldly vanity; he often asserted that the supposed goods of this world were vain, especially in the thirty-eighth psalm, in which he says, "And indeed all things are vanity, every man living. Although man walks in the image of God, yet he is disquieted vainly. He stores up, and he knows not for whom he is gathering these things."[1] And in another passage he says, "How long shall sinners, O Lord, how long shall sinners glory?"[2]—because they have here a shadow of glory, but, when they have departed from life, they cannot gain the benefit of consolation. Still, the same David introduced into the collection Psalm 72. In it he declares, under the title Asaph,[3] that at first he almost fell, being afflicted with no little pain. For he saw that sinners were wealthy and rich in this world and enjoyed prosperity and abundance, whereas he, who had justified his heart,[4] was in afflictions and tribulations. He had committed a rather serious offense in the beginning; later he had been corrected and enlightened through the scourges of the Lord and had learned the course of true surrender by the gift of God's knowledge.

---

1 Ps. 38 (39).6-7.
2 Ps. 93 (94).3.
3 Cf. Ps. 72 (73).1.
4 Cf. Ps. 72 (73).13.

(1.2) But nowhere do I find that holy Asaph was troubled by any adversities, whereas holy David did indeed endure many that were severe and filled with dangers. For he speaks of his own toils, and on that account the psalm is titled, not as if it were "of holy Asaph," but as if "for holy Asaph," as is shown by the superscription. This is more clearly revealed from the Greek psalter, so that David appears himself to have given the psalm, which he had written, to this Asaph and to others as well, to be sung by them. But it is written in the very title that the psalms of David have ended.[5] Yet how have they ended? For after one has gone through the next ten psalms, the inscription of the titles includes "psalms of David" even to the very end.[6]

(2.3) "How good is God to Israel, to them that are right in heart!"[1] Growth in moral perfection is evident as a theme from the beginning of the psalm. Indeed, no one can truly proclaim that God is good but one who knows that goodness, not from his own successes and profits, but out of the depth of the heavenly mysteries and the height of God's plan. For it is to be weighed, not by the appearance of things present, but by the advantage of things to come. Consequently, to the just man God is always good. Whether tormented by bodily pain or overwhelmed by bitter punishments, he always says, "If we have received good things from the hand of the Lord, why

---

5 Cf. Ps. 71 (72).20.

6 The meaning of this obscure passage appears to be that after the next ten psalms (73-82), all of which make reference to Asaph in their titles, various psalms to the end of the psalter include the title "psalms of David." Actually, that title appears in Psalms 136, 138–40, and 142–43, although the name David appears also in the titles of Psalms 85, 90, 92–98, 100–103, 107–109, 130, 132, 141, and 144. It is interesting to note that Psalm 151, which concludes the Septuagint version, has in its title the phrase "psalm on David." (The Latin text of Ps. 151 may be found in the appendix to the Stuttgart Vulgate [cited above in *Death as a Good* ch. 11 n. 1] p. 1975.)

1 Ps. 72 (73).1.

do we not bear up under those which are evil?"[2] He rejoices
that he is being chastised here, so that he may gain consolation
for the future; he knows that one who has received good
things in this life has his reward.[3] The man who has not
struggled or been tried in the combat of various contests
will not be able to hope for future rewards. But the man who is
afflicted, be it justly or unjustly, rejoices in this world, either
because he is paying the price of his sins here, or because he
knows that it is a more abundant grace with the Lord if
he unjustly suffers misfortunes for Christ's name or for the
sake of some good work. It is written that "there is no glory,
if when you sin, you are punished and endure it, but if
when you do good and suffer, this is a grace with God. Unto
this, indeed, you have been called, because Christ also has
died for you, leaving you an example, that you may follow
in his steps, who did no sin, neither was deceit found in
his mouth; who, when he was reviled, did not revile in return, when he suffered, did not threaten."[4] And so the just
man, even if he is on the rack, is always just. Because he
justifies God and says that his suffering is less than his sins
warrant, he is always wise. For true and perfect wisdom
is not taken away by the torments of the rack, nor does it
lose its nature, because it casts out fear by its zealous and
loving purpose,[5] even as the wise man knows that he should
say that our sufferings in this body are unworthy of the reward of future glory, and that all the sufferings of this time
cannot equal the reward that is to come.[6] And thus, to him,
God, who knows the time of the harvest, is always good.
Therefore, like a good farmer,[7] he plows his field here with
the ploughshare of a rather severe abstinence, as it were. He

---

2 Job 2.10 (Septuagint).
3 Cf. Matt. 6.2.
4 1 Peter 2.20–23.
5 Cf. 1 John 4.18.
6 Cf. Rom. 8.18.
7 Cf. John 15.1.

clears his land here with the scythe of virtues that cuts off the vices, so to speak. He manures here by humbling himself even to the earth, for he knows that "God raises up the needy from the earth and lifts up the poor out of the dunghill."[8] Indeed, unless the Apostle Paul had been counted as dung, he could never have gained Christ for himself.[9] Such a man keeps watch over his crops here, so that he may store them away there without concern. And so, to him, God is always good because he always hopes for good things from God.

(2.4) Consider another point. "How good is God to Israel, to them that are right in heart!" Is God not good to all men, then? He is certainly good to all, because He is the Savior of all men, especially of the faithful. And so the Lord Jesus came that He might save what was lost;[10] He came, indeed, to take away the sin of the world,[11] to heal our wounds. But not all men desire the remedy, and many avoid it; else the sore may be stung by the drugs and lose its virulence. For that reason, He heals those that are willing and does not compel the unwilling. Therefore, those who desire the remedy regain their health. But those who resist the physician[12] and do not seek him out, cannot perceive his goodness, for they do not experience it. Now one who is healed is also restored to health, and thus the physician is good to those whom he has restored to health. Accordingly, God is good to those whose sins He has forgiven. But if someone has a sin that is incurable from a sore on his spirit, how can he value the physician as good, when he is avoiding Him? And therefore,

---

8 Ps. 112 (113).7.
9 Cf. Phil. 3.8.
10 Cf. Luke 19.10.
11 Cf. John 1.29.
12 The motif of Christ as physician occurs very frequently in Ambrose. For a listing of the relevant passages, see Gryson 287 n. 157, and add the passing reference to the good physician in *The Prayer of Job and David* 2.3.10, above. Studies have been done on this theme as it appears, most notably, in Augustine, but none as yet on its use by Ambrose.

as I said earlier, the Apostle aptly explained that God, "who wishes all men to be saved,"[13] is good to all men. And the special favor of God's goodness is reserved most of all for the faithful, who receive the assistance of His good will and of His grace. But also, when the psalmist said, "How good is God to Israel, to them that are right in heart!" he conveyed the sentiment of those who do not know how to entertain any other opinion concerning God, except that He is good toward all things and is in all.

(3.5) Indeed, in what follows, David sets out his own experience as he says, "But my feet were almost moved, my steps had wellnigh slipped, for I was envious in the case of sinners, when I saw the peace of sinners."[1] He is surely not speaking of bodily feet and bodily steps, but of the uprightness of the heart and of the step concerning which he says in another passage, "Let not the foot of pride come to me and let not the hand of sinners move me."[2] And so, we ought always to ask that the Lord may direct the footsteps of our spirits. Else they may fall, slip in a kind of morass of error, and be unable to maintain their firm hold. Moreover, the reason for David's fall is that he emulated the peace of sinners. But we ought to emulate what is good, not what is filled with shame, even as the Apostle Paul also put it when he said, "to emulate the good in a good thing always."[3]

(3.6) And do not be influenced by the fact that he counted peace as an evil. Indeed, in the Gospel, also, you find a peace which Christ rejects, as He Himself says, "My peace I leave with you, my peace I give to you; not as the world gives, do I give to you."[4] For there is a peace that does not have a stumbling block, and a peace that does. The one which

---

13 1 Tim. 2.4.

---

1 Ps. 72 (73).2–3.
2 Ps. 35 (36).12.
3 Gal. 4.18.
4 John 14.27.

does not have a stumbling block is from love; the one which does, from pretense. So also the prophet says, "Peace, peace; and where is peace?"[5] Let us therefore run away from the peace of sinners, for they conspire against the guiltless man, they come together to oppress him who is just,[6] they destroy the widow or overcome her modesty. (3.7) And so, "there is no rest to their death"[7]—not "avoidance," as is written in many of the Latin texts, but "rest." For when we labor upon some task, and are bent down upon it and inclined toward it, we ordinarily lean back and rest. But sinners who have committed grave offenses, and especially the impious, cannot lean back and rest; of them it is said, "Bend down their back always."[8] For those who did not cleave to Christ do not raise themselves up to heavenly things. Consequently, neither do those whose death is very evil rise up with Him, even as it is written, "The death of sinners is very evil."[9] But a man who dies together with Christ and is buried together with Him finds not only rest but also resurrection.[10] Of such a man it is very appropriately said, "You have healed all his infirmities in his illness,"[11] especially if he is a martyr, whose infirmity is undone by suffering and his death by resurrection.

(3.8) We have seen that rich man who was clothed in purple and fine linen.[12] In this world, he reclined at table and feasted elegantly every day, while the poor man Lazarus would gather what fell from his table. When he was in torments in hell, he could not lean back and rest; but with great difficulty he lifted up only his eyes to Abraham, not his whole body, and

---

5 Ezech. 13.10.
6 Cf. Wisd. 2.12.
7 Ps. 72 (73).4.
8 Ps. 68 (69).24.
9 Ps. 33 (34).22.
10 Cf. Rom. 6.4.
11 Ps. 40 (41).4.
12 Cf. Luke 16.19–24.

asked him to send Lazarus to dip the tip of his finger in water and to cool his tongue. Therefore "there was no rest to his death nor strength in his affliction."[13] For scourges have no value after death. (3.9) And so, while David was in this bodily life, he made himself ready for scourges, so that the Lord might receive him as one that had been chastised. Think again, I ask you, upon holy Job. He was covered all over with sores, afflicted in all his limbs, and filled with pain over his entire body. He dissolved clods of earth with the corrupt matter and the liquid from his wounds,[14] and since he could not rest in this body, he found death a repose. And so, thinking of his own case, he said, "Death is a repose for a man."[15] He, therefore, was not moved in his affliction, nor did he totter in the morass of his own speech, for "in all those things, he did not sin with his lips," even as Scripture testifies.[16] Rather, he found strength in his affliction, through which he was strengthened in Christ. And thus both Job and David, because they were scourged here, had strength in their afflictions, because "the father scourges the son whom he receives."[17] But those who are not scourged here are not received as sons there. And there "they are not in the toils of men and they shall not be scourged with men,"[18] so that they may be scourged forever with the devil.

(4.10) "Therefore their pride has got a hold over them, they are covered with their iniquity and their wickedness."[1] Iniquity affords a bad covering, and if anyone wishes to hold it over us, we ought to remove it; else he may begin to come into judgment with us. And if anyone tries to carry off our spiritual

---

13 Ps. 72 (73).4.
14 Cf. Job 2.7–8.
15 Job 3.23 (Septuagint).
16 Job 2.10.
17 Prov. 3.12 (Septuagint); Heb. 12.6.
18 Ps. 72 (73).5.

---

1 Ps. 72 (73).6.

tunic which we have received, remove the cloak of iniquity and take up the covering of faith and of patience, with which David covered himself in fasting, so that he would not lose the garment of virtue. Fasting is itself a covering. Indeed, unless a sober fasting had served to cover the holy Joseph, he would have been stripped by the wanton adulteress.[2] Had Adam chosen to cover himself with that fasting, he would not have been made naked. But because he tasted of the tree of the knowledge of good and evil contrary to heaven's prohibition and violated the fast imposed on him by taking the food of incontinence, he knew that he was naked.[3] Had he fasted, he would have kept the clothing of faith and would not have beheld himself uncovered. Let us not, therefore, clothe ourselves with iniquity and wickedness; else it may be said about one of us, "He clothed himself in cursing."[4] Adam clothed himself badly; while he searched for coverings of leaves, he received the sentence of a curse. (4.11) The Jews clothed themselves with a curse, for in regard to them it is written, "Their iniquity has come forth, as it were from fatness, they have passed on to the disposition of their heart."[5] For from "fat" is derived "fatty," that is, "rich." For just as a soul that is fed on good things and stuffed with virtues is filled "as with fat and richness," as it is written,[6] so iniquity, which proceeds, as it were, from fat, is not symbolized as thin and poor but as filled with vices. In fact, they did not fall into error by some chance misstep, but passed into sacrilege by plan and intent.

(5.12) "They have set their mouth against heaven, and their tongue has passed over the earth."[1] We learn the meaning

---

2 Cf. Gen. 39.12.
3 Cf. Gen. 3.6–11.
4 Ps. 108 (109).18.
5 Ps. 72 (73).7.
6 Ps. 62 (63).6.

---

1 Ps. 72 (73).9.

of "to set one's mouth against heaven" from the younger of the two brothers, who returned to his father and said, "Father, I have sinned against heaven and before you."[2] But those who think that freedom to sin is given to them by some inevitability of birth are setting their mouth against heaven. Such men usually spare neither heaven nor earth, that they may believe that man's life is governed by the course of the stars, as it were.[3] They leave nothing to providence, nothing to good character. And would that they also had returned like that one of the two young men—the good Lord would not have denied them a remedy! And yet, even if they do not wish to be healed, the Lord keeps open the option of a return, so that those in Israel who were driven out by the blindness of their own hearts may come back through the fullness of the Church. Thus they may spend the days of their lives, not in emptiness, but filled with good works and faith, when the Lord has filled them with His spiritual favor. Learn how they may return. "A partial blindness only has befallen Israel, until the full number of the Gentiles should enter and thus all Israel should be saved."[4] But it was fitting that the mystery be fulfilled, that God should shut up all things in unbelief,[5] that is, that He should refute and convict them. (For when two parties contend, if one is the stronger, it is said: "He has shut up the other.")[6] And thus, by His mercy, that people indeed went back among the heirs, so that the world might be made subject to God. But they

---

2 Luke 15.18.

3 The Christians rejected astrology as superstition, and also because of its close association with pagan thought. Therefore it is not surprising that attacks against it appear frequently in Christian authors. For a good survey of the subject see M. L. W. Laistner, "The Western Church and Astrology during the Early Middle Ages," *Harvard Theological Review* 34 (1941) 251–75; the anti-Christian arguments in general are treated by Courcelle, "Anti-Christian Arguments" 151–92.

4 Rom. 11.25–26.

5 Cf. Rom. 11.32.

6 Cf. 1 Kings 26.8.

were led astray by the delusion of their late wickedness, so that they would not believe that God had foreknowledge of things hidden. But that they may be redeemed at some time, the Lord has kept open for them the option of future salvation, and has said, "Therefore will my people return here."[7] What is "here"? It is "to me, to my equity and justice, to my worship." (5.13) "And it will fill the days of its life."[8] This you will interpret as follows, that the people which has believed is assuredly redeemed. According to this, even though those who have not believed are not redeemed, still the redemption of the people is granted as a special favor of God.

(5.14) Therefore those who were in sin said, "How has God known? And is there all knowledge in the Most High?"[9] Indeed, they suppose that knowledge is not in God, because sinners abound in worldly prosperity. And the Scripture still represents such men as saying, "Behold, these are sinners, and abounding in the world they have obtained riches."[10] You find this more clearly portrayed in the Gospel, where Simon the pharisee, seeing that the sinful woman had come into his house and had poured ointment over Christ's feet, said to himself, "This man, were he a prophet, would surely know who and what manner of woman this is who is touching him, for she is a sinner."[11] But God's patience is not prejudicial to truth, while His foreknowledge and providence are proved the more by this very fact, that one who is in sin abounds in worldly prosperity and success. Seeing this, one who is stronger laughs, but one who is incautious is moved and led astray.

(6.15) Indeed, the psalmist says that he himself said, "Then have I in vain justified my heart, and washed my hands

---

7 Ps. 72 (73).10.
8 *Ibid.*
9 Ps. 72 (73).11.
10 Ps. 72 (73).12.
11 Luke 7.39.

among the innocent."[1] This means: I see that sinners enjoy abundance, I see that all things are favorable and advantageous for them, whereas I am crushed and harassed by many trials. In vain, therefore, have I given myself over to innocence and devoted myself to the pursuit of a moderate way of life. And he aptly says, "I have washed my hands among the innocent," so as to appear not to be claiming the substance of innocence for himself, but to be engaged in the diligent pursuit of it.

(6.16) Meanwhile, he bears witness that talk of this sort has not proceeded from him without punishment. For he recounts that he was scourged all the day for having said that he had justified his heart to the Lord in vain.[2] But after the scourgings there ensued at once a correction of his perverse belief. For he says immediately, "My accuser is in the mornings,"[3] that is, in the open and clear. For the light of truth caught hold of him and did not allow him to keep the sentiments which he had expressed. And so the light of truth was poured forth over my spirit, and it disproved and refuted me because I had wrongly said, "I have in vain justified my heart." For I spoke those things as if I were situated in darkness, and my heart was stung to remorse at the remembrance of them. But from a remorseful heart, love was illuminated, so that it might become in my heart a blazing fire,[4] which made in me the beginning of the day in a spiritual sense. And consequently, when the day was illuminated and it dawned for me, and I found myself as it were amid many mornings, I understood that I was outside of the condition of the generation of God's children. I had believed at first that the Maker of the world, in His care for the generation of men, made all things for our advantage, those that are sorrowful

---

1 Ps. 72 (73).13.
2 Cf. Ps. 72 (73).14.
3 Ibid.
4 Cf. Jer. 20.9.

and those that give but little pleasure. Nevertheless, I was later confused by perverse opinions and lost the belief that was so good.

(6.17) And therefore I conferred with my heart and I said to myself, "if I will speak thus, that I have justified my heart in vain,"[5] and the voice of God replied to me and said, "Behold the generation of your children, to which I have made distribution."[6] This means: Behold, you find in the Scriptures, O you son of Adam, that I have made distribution to the generation of your children, that wealth may be granted to the wicked out of mere chance and not from some merit. Neither are the rewards of virtue the profits of a treasury, just as poverty, on the other hand, is not a punishment for sin. But such things come without distinction, for they roll along on a kind of flow of life that is like a river. (6.18) I considered that this was true and thought I knew it was true[7] and in complete harmony and accord with God's providence, but that I had been confused without cause in regard to such matters, in which I ought not to have occupied myself.

(7.19) Accordingly, because I thought that I had grasped the true belief and had acquired the knowledge of that matter, I said to myself, "This thing is a labor in my sight, until I go into the sanctuary of God and understand in the last."[1] This means: The only labor that remains for me is that I should go into the sanctuary of God, where the Cherubim is[2]—that is, the depth of knowledge—and should not be concerned with unsure and idle opinions, for "the talking of a fool is like a burden in the way."[3] Let us there-

---

5 Ps. 72 (73).15.
6 *Ibid.*
7 Cf. Ps. 72 (73).16.

1 Ps. 72 (73).16–17.
2 Cf. Exod. 25.17–22.
3 Sir. 21.16 (19).

fore enter into the sanctuary of holy knowledge and the inner
chambers of truth, that we may have no further labor, for
wisdom draws us away from the thought of labor. Indeed,
Jacob does not labor,[4] whereas the reason for labor is ignorance. For one who does not know that rewards have been laid
up for the just is not refreshed by his labors; rather, he is
bent and broken by labor that arises from his lack of knowledge. And so, let us enter the sanctuary of God, where the
Cherubim are, in whom there is remembrance of holy knowledge and of the true and eternal Light. (7.20) In the lampstand[5] there shines forth the symbol by which we may be
able to understand "in the last." In truth, the holy man
possesses knowledge at the last[6] and by his advance in age
he attains perfect wisdom, for he says, "O Lord, make me
know my end, and what is the number of my days, that I
may know what is wanting to me."[7] What other end is there
save that end when the kingdom is given over to God the
Father, when the secrets of wisdom are revealed?[8] This is the
end to our struggle that the psalmist was searching for when
he desired to know what was wanting to his perfection, for
the end is also the perfection of our learning and of our
endeavors.

(7.21) Such, then, is the first supposition of true knowledge,
that things in the world happen by chance. The second is, that
"on account of their subterfuges you have put to them"[9]
prodigious success, worldly profits and an abundance of riches.
Else, they might plead by way of excuse that they had been
less devout by reason of want or of some bitter pain or grief
and had been driven to the guilt of robbery and to the desire
to plunder under compulsion of poverty. For they were en-

---

4 Cf. Gen. 27.20.
5 Cf. Exod. 25.31–40.
6 Cf. Sir. 48.24 (27).
7 Ps. 38 (39).5.
8 Cf. Ps. 50 (51).8.
9 Ps. 72 (73).18.

riched with wealth and exalted with honors, not for tranquillity of life or the enjoyment of delight, but that complaining might be foreclosed and distress piled up.

(7.22) Accordingly, men of this sort are cast down while they are exalted.[10] Indeed, it is not a favor, but a catastrophe, when the use of a long-continuing gift is not withheld and the excuse for failure is taken away. For what complaint carried greater weight than that divine complaint which you find in the book of the prophet Michea, "O my people, what have I done to you or wherein have I grieved you or how have I wearied you? Answer me. Did I not bring you up out of the land of Egypt and deliver you out of the house of bondage?"[11] Behold how the wicked are cast down while they are lifted up, how their complaint is foreclosed and their punishment piled up. Summoned by heavenly favors, they ought not to have forsaken the Giver of prosperity and tranquillity of life but ought rather to have obeyed Him. But even as God's justice is great, so also is His vengeance stern. For a wicked man is frequently persistent in his wickedness, and in regard to him you find it written also in another passage, "I have seen the wicked highly exalted and lifted up over the cedars of Lebanon, and I passed by and behold! he was not; and I sought him, and his place was not found."[12] The swiftness of his annihilation is beyond belief. Of a sudden, you see a wicked man powerful in this life; while you are passing by, already he is not. How large is a shadow on the earth, and how short in duration! Take away your footstep and the shadow has passed away. And if there is some disturbance here, lift up the footstep of your spirit to the things which are to be, and you will discover that the wicked man whom you believed to be here, will not be there; for one who is

---

10 Cf. *ibid.*
11 Mich. 6.3–4 (Septuagint).
12 Ps. 36 (37).35–36.

nothing, is not. Indeed, "the Lord knows those who are his,"[13] but He does not recognize those who are not, because they have not recognized Him who is.[14]

(8.23) Therefore, in regard to the latter, David also says, "They have ceased to be and have perished by reason of their iniquity as the dream of one that wakes up."[1] This means: The wicked cease to be and they disappear as a dream does when one first wakes up from sleep, because they are in darkness and have walked in darkness;[2] not a trace of their good work remains, but they are like those who see a dream. Now one who dreams, dreams at night, whereas night is in darkness. The children of darkness are deprived of the Sun of Justice[3] and the splendor of virtue, for they sleep always and do not keep watch, and of them it is appropriately said, "They have slept their sleep and have found nothing."[4] For indeed, when their souls are separated from the body, and they are, as it were, released from the sleep of the body, they will find nothing, they will possess nothing, and they will lose what they thought they possessed. For although the unwise and foolish man may overflow with riches, he will leave his riches to strangers, and the glory of his house will not descend to hell together with him.[5]

(8.24) Subsequent events also go to show how the image of such a man is not found but perishes, since his image is not found in the city of the Lord, that Jerusalem which is above.[6] For the Lord has painted us to His image and likeness, even as He teaches us, saying, "Behold, O Jerusalem, I have

---

13 2 Tim. 2.19.
14 Cf. Exod. 3.14.

1 Ps. 72 (73).19–20.
2 Cf. Ps. 81 (82).5.
3 Cf. Mal. 3.20 (4.2).
4 Ps. 75 (76).6.
5 Cf. Ps. 48 (49).18.
6 Cf. Ps. 72 (73).20.

painted your walls."[7] If we have acted well, that heavenly image continues in us; if anyone acts badly, this image is destroyed in him, that is, the image of Him who came down from heaven, and there is in him the image of the earthly. On this account also the Apostle says, "Even as we have borne the image of the one that is earthly, let us bear also the image of the other that is heavenly."[8] Therefore, the images of the good continue to shine forth in that city of God. But if anyone has turned aside to graver sins and has not done penance, his image is destroyed or else cast out, even as Adam was cast out and excluded from paradise.[9] But whoever has conducted himself in a holy and honorable fashion enters into the city of God[10] and brings in his own image so that it may shine in that city of God. "O Lord, in your city you shall reduce their images to nothing,"[11] because those who have clothed themselves with the works of darkness cannot shine in the light. Let us adduce an example from the world. See how the images of good rulers continue in cities, whereas the images of tyrants are destroyed.[12]

(9.25) Considering these matters and reflecting upon them, the holy prophet was delighted, while before he had been troubled. For this reason he says, "For my heart has been delighted and my loins have been relaxed, and I am brought to nothing, and I knew not, and I am become as a beast before you, and I am always with you."[1] He is saying, "When I learned that God exercises His care and concern over human

---

7 Isa. 49.16.
8 1 Cor. 15.49.
9 Cf. Gen. 3.21–24.
10 Cf. Apoc. 3.12.
11 Ps. 72 (73).20.
12 The allusion may be to the statues of Gratian, preserved after his death in 383, or to those of Maximus or of Eugenius, destroyed in 388 and 394, respectively. In any case, the reference is too general in nature to be of much help in dating this work.

---

1 Ps. 72 (73).21–23.

affairs, my loins rested," and this means: After the great fatigue caused by my old ignorance, I rested through the knowledge of heavenly good and of grace. For there are loins of the soul, as it were, which are troubled in us through the exertion brought on by ignorance. But they are relaxed to find rest by the knowledge of heavenly teaching, and they are sustained by reliance on a kind of support furnished by heavenly precepts. "Then," he is saying, "I understood that I was fatigued in vain, because I did not know that which is true."

(9.26) "And I am become as a beast." He added, appropriately, "before you." Yes, by comparison with the dwellers in heaven, what is man but an irrational beast? For the stars also, although they are bright, vanish at the rising of the sun. Moses also says, "I am not qualified from yesterday, from when you have begun to speak with your servant. I have a weak voice and am slow of speech."[2] So likewise does man seem to be a dumb beast by comparison, I do not say to Christ, but to the angels. But even so, let no one despair, because the Lord preserves both men and beasts.[3] And consequently, because I have learned not from myself but from You, I will cleave to You always, so that I may cease to be a beast and You may say to me, "But do you stand here with me."[4] One who, by way of ignorance, pretended to the insensibility and lack of knowledge characteristic of a beast begins to be a man once he has been encompassed by the grace of God. Indeed, if he is capable of reason and of grace, he is proved a man by that very fact, and thus he rejoices that he has been separated from the dumb animals and has been admitted into the company of men, which God visits and protects. For what is man except that the Lord is mindful of him and that he is visited by the Lord?[5]

---

2 Exod. 4.10 (Septuagint).
3 Cf. Ps. 35 (36).7.
4 Deut. 5.31.
5 Cf. Ps. 8.5.

(10.27) For this reason David says, as if visited by Him, "You have held my right hand and in your will you have conducted me and have taken me up with glory."[1] This is the text we have received, and it is in accord with the Greek, for the Greek said *ekratēsas tēs cheiros*, that is "you have held the hand," *tēs dexiās mou* "my right hand." A man receives good guidance, when God takes hold of his right hand with His own hand. Such a one can say, "The Lord is at my right hand, that I be not moved."[2] Had Adam chosen to have the Lord at his right hand, he would not have been deceived by the serpent. But because he forgot God's command and fulfilled the will of the serpent, the devil took hold of his hand and made it to reach out to the tree of the knowledge of good and evil, to pluck things that were forbidden. In him, judgment was passed beforehand on all men, and the adversary began to stand by the right hand of every man. From this, there also came that model of the curse against Judas, "And may the devil stand at his right hand."[3] If that curse is severe, that blessing, whereby the bonds of the harsh curse are undone, is very momentous. For that reason the Lord Jesus, who had taken up man's cause and condition, set the devil at His right hand, just as we read in the book of Zacharia.[4] And so, where the inheritance of Adam stood, there Christ stood. Like a good athlete, He permitted Satan to stand at His right hand so that He could drive him back, and said, "Begone, Satan."[5] Consequently, the adversary was cast down from his place and departed; so that the devil may not stand at your right hand, Christ says, "Come, follow me."[6] Therefore, David foresaw the coming of the Lord, who came down from heaven to free us from the power of the adversary, and

---

1 Ps. 72 (73).23–24.
2 Ps. 15 (16).8.
3 Ps. 108 (109).6.
4 Cf. Zach. 3.1.
5 Matt. 4.10.
6 Matt. 19.21.

he said, "The Lord is at my right hand, that I be not moved."
But one who had the devil at his right hand was moved.
David was justified, then, in saying this also, "You have held
my right hand," that is, so that now I cannot sin, so that I
can take my stand in a trusty place, while before I was swaying
and my step was unsure. How aptly the Apostle said this!
For the Lord, seeing that he was troubled, stretched out His
right hand and did not allow him to falter but steadied him
to walk without fear.[7] And upon his deliverance, what else
did Peter say but these prophetic lines, "You have held my
right hand and in your will you have conducted me and have
taken me up with glory"? What is the right hand but the
power of the soul in operation? And if it is guided by the
will of the Lord, it desires nothing and is in want of nothing,
it demands none of the helps or aids of this world.

(11.28) Therefore the holy man says, "For what awaits me
in heaven? And besides you what do I desire upon earth?"[1]
This means: You are my portion, You are abundant to me
for all things, I have sought nothing but that I might possess
You as my share, I have not made myself subject to any
creature in the heavens, as the Gentiles do, and I have
desired none of the wealth and enticing pleasures of this
world. I have no want, for I have been taken up by You,
and there is nothing further for me to seek in the heavenly
bodies.[2] Possessing nothing, I possess all things,[3] because
I possess Christ, and Him the Father on high "has not spared,
but he has delivered him for us all; how has he not, then,
given us all things with him?"[4] even as the Apostle said.
For all things are in Christ, through whom are all things and

---

7 Cf. Matt. 14.30–31.

---

1 Ps. 72 (73).25.
2 Compare the earlier reference to astrology at 3.5.12, above.
3 Cf. 2 Cor. 6.10.
4 Rom. 8.32.

in whom all things hold together.[5] Therefore, possessing all things in Him, I seek no other reward, because He is the reward of all. And so, Christ said to him that was made perfect, "Take up your cross and follow me."[6] For one who follows Him is not led to perfection by the reward, but by perfection he is made perfect for the reward. For the imitators of Christ are not good by reason of hope, but for their love of virtue; for Christ is good by nature, not by reason of a desire for a reward. And, therefore, He suffered because it pleased Him to do good, and not because He sought an increase of glory from His passion. Thus one who desires to imitate Him does not do what is for his own advantage but what is for the advantage of others. It is not without reason, therefore, that he fails for himself, while for others he grows strong by the increase of virtue.

(11.29) And the psalmist says, appropriately, "My heart and my flesh have failed, God of my heart."[7] Indeed, abiding things cannot follow unless earthly things have failed. Therefore the flesh fails when fleshly things are put to death. And those who bear about in their flesh the dying of Jesus Christ[8] also fail, for the death of Christ works in them[9] so that every enticement to sin dies. From this it is inferred that the heart of man fails when evil thoughts, which proceed from the heart, are put to death. Thus forgetfulness may hide all earthly things, and, for those who are blessed with a clean heart and deserve to see God, there may come the God of their heart[10] that they may draw near to You and not separate themselves. For God, who is near, does not drive back those who draw near to Him;[11] He wishes to be for all men a cause of salvation

---

5 Cf. Col. 1.16–17.
6 Mark 8.34; Matt. 16.24; Luke 9.23; cf. Matt. 10.38.
7 Ps. 72 (73).26.
8 Cf. 2 Cor. 4.10.
9 Cf. 2 Cor. 4.12.
10 Cf. Matt. 5.8.
11 Cf. John 6.37; James 4.8.

and not of death. Indeed, He rejects no one except one who has decided to remove himself from His sight.

(11.30) "For behold, they that go far from you shall perish."[12] Each man by his own works either joins himself to Your goodness or removes himself from it. One who does such works that he is afraid to be detected in the examination of them is fleeing from God. Even so, one who thinks that he is not seen by the Lord God because he is covered with walls and encompassed with darkness[13] is seen nonetheless when it is said, "You have destroyed all those who go whoring from you."[14] A woman who goes whoring does not cleave to her husband and is neither one flesh nor one spirit with him[15] but separates herself and sets herself apart from him by her whoring. Even so, whatsoever soul does not cleave to God but goes whoring in submission to the vain worship of idols sets itself apart by a calamitous sacrilege and goes far from the Lord, whereas it ought to be near Him. Moreover, one who is separated from the Lord perishes. (11.31) For this reason the holy man, who fears the judgment of God, desires to cleave always to Christ and to put his hope in Him,[16] so that he may praise the Lord, to whom are honor, glory, and perpetuity from the ages, both now and always and forever and ever. Amen.[17]

---

12 Ps. 72 (73).27.
13 Cf. Sir. 23.18 (26).
14 Ps. 72 (73).27.
15 Cf. 1 Cor. 6.15–16.
16 Cf. Ps. 72 (73).28.
17 The same doxology appears at the conclusion of the fourth book.

BOOK FOUR

THE PRAYER OF DAVID

MANY INDEED HAVE COMPLAINED over human weakness and frailty, but the holy Job and holy David have done so in a fashion superior to the rest. The former is straightforward, forceful, sharp, and displays a loftier style, as one who has been provoked by severe afflictions. The other is ingratiating and calm and mild, of a gentler disposition, so that he truly reflects the disposition of the stag which he set out as a model for his imitation.[1] And do not be disturbed if I should appear to praise such a mighty prophet under the likeness of a wild animal, when there is read to you the maxim given to the Apostles, "Be wise as serpents, guileless as doves."[2]

(1.2) But granted that likenesses of that sort find support from holy models, and that the stag is by nature harmless and gentle, still, I think that the stag which the prophet is setting out for imitation in this passage is that stag of which Solomon, that apologist for paternal thought, said in Proverbs, "Let the loving stag and the graceful fawn confer with you."[3] For God's true Son represented in His very self the nature which God gave to animate creatures; He came into this world like a stag and, with a wonderful lack of guile, He associated with those who were preparing an ambush

---

1 Cf. Ps. 41 (42).2.
2 Matt. 10.16.
3 Cf. Prov. 4.1; much of the first part of Proverbs is cast in the form of an address from a wise man to his son. Prov. 5.19 (Septuagint).

for Him. Indeed, the guilelessness of stags is said to be such that even when they see that they are being harassed, they attach themselves to the very horsemen who have been assigned to the work of deception. These latter proceed, under pretense of flight and the appearance of friendship, to lead them right into the nets. So also the Lord, as if unknowing of the danger and not anticipating it, mingled with those Jews who were contriving a deceit for Him. And He received into His company the traitor Judas,[4] by whose lethal deception He came even to the snares of the cross and the nets of the passion. Thereupon, Christ turned to him and said, "Judas, do you betray the Son of Man with a kiss?"[5] Indeed, it was in this way that He came to the nets of the synagogue and willingly put them on; only He was not entangled or bound in them, for He looses all things.

(1.3) Indeed, He stood out over the nets.[6] And because His own had not received Him,[7] He called the Church and conferred His grace upon her, even as the most holy Church herself bears witness in the Canticles, saying, "I have adjured you, O daughters of Jerusalem, by the powers and virtues of the field, that you stir not up nor awake my love till he please."[8] She is therefore asking that her bridegroom be awakened by the daughters of Jerusalem in the fragrance of the field with which holy Jacob was fragrant,[9] that is, in a like faith and devotion, that He may hasten to the bride. She is asking that His love be awakened in her, indeed that He Himself be awakened, because the bridegroom is love. For "God is love,"[10] even as John said. But He did not permit Himself to be awakened by others, for He was hastening of His own accord,

---

4 Cf. Mark 3.19; Matt. 10.4; Luke 6.16.
5 Luke 22.48.
6 Cf. Cant. 2.9.
7 Cf. John 1.11.
8 Cant. 2.7 (Septuagint).
9 Cf. Gen. 27.27.
10 1 John 4.16.
11 Cf. Ps. 18 (19).6.

and, coming out of His bridal chamber, He rejoiced as a giant to run the way.[11] The bride saw Him and heard His voice as He approached; she suddenly turned and said, "Behold, he has come, leaping over the mountains, skipping over the hills."[12] He leaps over the greater and skips over the lesser, so as not to suffer hindrance to His devoted haste. "My cousin is like a gazelle or a young stag upon the mountains of Bethel."[13] Good is the stag whose mountain is the house of God;[14] He ran to it with such speed that He anticipated the wishes and longings of the bride. Indeed, where she had seen Him coming from afar, she suddenly recognized that He was in her presence, and in consequence she also says, "Behold, he is behind our wall, gazing through the windows, standing out through the netting. My cousin answered and said to me, 'Arise, come, my near one, my beautiful one, my dove, for behold! the winter is past, the rain is over, is gone; the flowers have appeared on the earth.' "[15] The winter is the synagogue; the rain, the people of the Jews, which could not look upon the sun; the flowers are the Apostles. The bridegroom continues, "The harvest of the pruning is come, the voice of the turtledove is heard in our land."[16] That harvest is the faith of the Church; the voice of the turtledove is modesty.

(1.4) Neither these alone[17] . . . but Christ also took on the likeness of a stag, because He came to the earth and trod upon that serpent the devil, without any harm to Himself.

---

12 Cant. 2.8. For further discussion of this Scripture verse, with specific reference to its use in this passage among others, see A. Olivar, in the article "Los Saltos del Verbo" (cited above, *Isaac* ch. 4 n. 74).
13 Cant. 2.9 (Septuagint).
14 Cf. Gen. 28.17–19. The name Bethel also appears in this same sense, "house of God," in *Isaac, or the Soul* 4.31 (translated in this volume) and *On Abraham* 1.2.6; 2.3.11; 2.5.21, and as "house of bread" in *Jacob and the Happy Life* 2.7.32 (in this volume).
15 Cant. 2.9–12.
16 Cant. 2.12.
17 The lacuna that Schenkl indicates after *solis* (our "alone") may, he grants, fall slightly later in the sentence. As for meaning, nothing is firm until "Christ took on . . ."

He exposed His heel to it[18] but did not experience its poisons. Consequently, it is said to Him, "You shall walk upon the asp and the basilisk."[19] Let us, then, also be stags, that we may be able to walk upon serpents. We shall be stags if we follow the word of Christ, which prepares the stags[20] and makes them not to fear the bites of serpents; and if by chance any have been wounded, it takes away their pain by destroying their sin. Concerning these stags the Lord says to Job, "Have you watched over the deer when they fawn? Have you numbered their months to full term, have you delivered their offspring or brought up their young devoid of fear?"[21] Learn how the young of such deer are devoid of fear. Let Isaia instruct you as he says, "And the little child shall thrust his hand into the den of asps, and they shall not hurt him."[22] And that you may know that he apparently means the children of the Church, he continues, "Will you send forth their young? Their progeny will be separated and they will be multiplied in their offspring. They will go forth and will not return back."[23] For "no one, having put his hand to the plow and looking back, is suitable for the kingdom of God."[24]

(1.5) Therefore, it was with good reason that the Lord became a stag, so that the word of the Lord might prepare such stags for Himself; of these He says, "In my name they shall cast out devils, they shall speak in new tongues, they shall take up serpents, and if they drink any deadly thing, it shall not hurt them."[25] Indeed they took up serpents, when His holy Apostles cast out the spiritual forces of wickedness[26] from their hiding places in the body by breathing on them and did not feel deadly poisons. When the viper came forth

---

18 Cf. John 13.18; Ps. 40 (41).10; Gen. 3.15.
19 Ps. 90 (91).13.
20 Cf. Ps. 28 (29).9.
21 Job 39.1–3.
22 Isa. 11.8–9.
23 Job 39.3–4.
24 Luke 9.62.
25 Mark 16.17–18.   26 Cf. Eph. 6.12.

from the bundle of sticks and bit Paul, the natives, seeing
the viper hanging from his hand, thought that he would
suddenly die.[27] But he stood unafraid; he was unaffected by
the wound, and the poison was not infused into him. Thereupon, they looked on him and judged that he had not been
begotten from the human condition, so to speak, but had
been brought forth, as it were, by the grace of God, and was
superior to men. Look upon the stag as He casts out the
vipers from their hiding places "with the spirit of God which
was in his nostrils,"[28] even as Job said. "Paul turned in the
spirit, and looking back he said with grief to the divining
spirit, 'I order you in the name of the Lord Jesus Christ to
go out from her forthwith.' And it went out that very
moment."[29] Look upon the stag when He came to baptism;[30]
made clean by the washing from the holy fountain, He cast
off all the poisons of persecution. Look upon the stag, the
Lord Jesus, when He came to John the Baptist. John said
to Him, "It is I who ought to be baptized by you, and do
you come to me?"[31] and He replied, "Let it be so now."[32]
And when He had said this, He went down with all eagerness
into the waters, for He thirsted after the salvation of the
people. But by now we have treated the stag sufficiently in
our introduction, even as the stag himself makes sport in the
beginning of the year according to popular custom.[33] Let us
proceed to what remains.

---

[27] Cf. Acts 28.3–6.   [28] Job 27.3.   [29] Acts 16.18.

[30] Cf. Ps. 41 (42).2.

[31] Matt. 3.14.

[32] Matt. 3.15.

[33] A playful allusion to a pagan custom whereby on New Year's Day
people roamed about disguised as stags or other animals, a custom
frequently inveighed against by Christian ecclesiastical authorities.
See H. G. J. Beck, The Pastoral Care of Souls in South-East France
During the Sixth Century (Analecta Gregoriana 51; Rome 1950)
281f. and, especially for bibliography, H. Leclercq, art. "Janvier
(Calendes de)," Dictionnaire d'archéologie chrétienne et de liturgie
7.2 (Paris 1927) 2147–53. There is a useful collection of relevant Latin
texts in Du Cange, Glossarium ad scriptores mediae et infimae Latinita-
tis, under the word cervula.

(2.6) David prays, as I said, by saying to the Lord, "Even as the stag pants after the fountains of water, so my soul pants after you, O God. My soul has thirsted after the living God. When shall I come, and appear before the face of God?"[1] The holy man is agitated and does not contain himself, for the grandeur of the soul is greater than the dimensions of anyone's body. Certain of the reward, he desires to fly away from the earth to heavenly things, even as he says in another passage, "Who will give me wings like a dove, and I will fly and be at rest?"[2] For snares are here, and the just man is hindered by them, even when he is not entangled in them; sorrow and anxieties are here, but joy is there, where grace is; yes, the chains of the body are here, and Paul eagerly desired to break them, that he might be divested of all entanglements and stand in freedom beside the Lord.[3] And so David's soul thirsted for this, that it might see God then, not through faith, but face to face,[4] and that it might not only be absent from the body[5] but might be freed from the body; for it thirsted to depart and to be with Christ, a lot by far the better,[6] because, for the just man, to die is gain.[7] And it is a great gain indeed to be without sin and not to be moved by the enticements of wrongdoing. Who is free of stain, when even a human life of but one day on earth is not without the contagion of wrongdoing?[8] Therefore, we suffer loss to our guiltlessness merely by living, whereas we gain an end to our sin by death. Therefore, a profit is gained by death, but by the act of living the interest due to sin is in

---

1 Ps. 41 (42).2–3.
2 Ps. 54 (55).7. This Scripture passage is developed by Ambrose at a number of points with specific reference to baptism. See R. T. Otten, "Caritas," 442–48, especially 446.
3 Cf. Phil. 1.23.
4 Cf. 1 Cor. 13.12.
5 Cf. 2 Cor. 5.8.
6 Cf. Phil. 1.23.
7 Cf. Phil. 1.21.
8 Cf. Job 14.4–5 (Septuagint).

creased, as if we were wretched debtors of an interest-bearing note. And the soul suffers a good thirst if it hastens to the fountain, not a fountain of water, but that of eternal life, of which David said in an earlier passage, "For with you is the fountain of life and in your light we shall see light."[9] And so, he had reason to hasten to come and appear before the face of God,[10] whose countenance is light,[11] because the Lord enlightens all men upon whom He looks.[12]

(2.7) "My tears have been my bread day and night, while it is said to me daily, 'Where is your God?' "[13] Tears are aptly called bread there, where a hunger for justice exists. "Blessed are they who hunger and thirst for justice, for they shall be satisfied."[14] And so there are tears which are bread and which strengthen the heart of man.[15] The maxim of Ecclesiastes is also appropriate to this discussion, "Cast your bread on the face of the water."[16] For the bread of heaven is there, where the water of grace is; it is right that those from whose belly rivers of living water flow[17] should receive the support of the Word and a nurture of a mystical kind. Likewise, also, this living bread is there,[18] where the water of tears and the weeping of repentance are. For thus it is written, "They set out in weeping, and I will bring them back in consolation."[19] Therefore, blessed are they whose bread is tears, for they have deserved to laugh, because "you who weep are blessed."[20] (2.8) "Mindful of these things, I poured out my soul upon

---

9 Ps. 35 (36).10.
10 Cf. Ps. 41 (42).3.
11 Cf. Ps. 4.7.
12 Cf. John 1.9.
13 Ps. 41 (42).4.
14 Matt. 5.6.
15 Cf. Ps. 103 (104).15.
16 Eccles. 11.1 (Septuagint).
17 Cf. John 7.38; 4.10.
18 Cf. John 6.51.
19 Jer. 31.9.
20 Luke 6.21.

me."[21] The holy man thinks of these externals and pours
forth his soul over himself. Thus his soul, once poured forth
over the body, may hide the weakness of his flesh and cover
his bodily appetite, and strength of soul and of spirit may
dwell everywhere.[22] For this reason also he says in a later
passage, "I shall pour out my prayer in his sight."[23] Where
prayer is poured out, there sins are covered.[24] But of what
things does he say that he is mindful? Surely of those which
he desired, to come and appear in the sight of God,[25] to
see that heavenly court of God where he would walk in spirit
and take pleasure at the anticipation of his entrance.

(2.9) "For I shall enter into the place of the wonderful
tabernacle, even to the house of God, with the voice of joy and
praise, the sound of one feasting."[26] He wept with good reason,
because he was dwelling on earth, while heavenly tabernacles
were his due and entry into a mighty court awaited him.[27]
In truth, he preferred that court alone to all the wealth of
his own kingdom, even as he bore witness, saying in another
passage, "One thing I have asked of the Lord, this I will
seek after, that I may dwell in the house of the Lord all
the days of my life and that I may see the delight of the
Lord."[28] The delight of the Lord is in the Church. The
Church is the image of things heavenly; and indeed, after the
shadow passed by, the image took its place.[29] The shadow
is the synagogue; in the shadow there is law, but in the
Gospel, truth. And thus, the image of truth shines forth in
the light of the Gospel. Therefore, the psalmist wept at the

---

21 Ps. 41 (42).5.
22 Cf. 2 Cor. 12.9.
23 Ps. 141 (142).3 (2).
24 Cf. Ps. 31 (32).1; Rom. 4.7.
25 Cf. Ps. 41 (42).3.
26 Ps. 41 (42).5.
27 Cf. Ps. 83 (84).2–3,11.
28 Ps. 26 (27).4.
29 Cf. Heb. 10.1; Col. 2.17.

postponement of good things that were filled to the full with grace and joy.

(3.10) Therefore David says also in a later passage, "Woe is me, that my sojourning is prolonged!"[1] And accordingly he made entreaty to the Lord because he was hastening on to better things. Yet even among the afflictions of the world, there was great consolation in things present and hope in those that would come. Yet who would not lift up his heart, when he could hope that a blessed share in the heavenly tabernacle was in store for him? But because things that are to come generally cause us weariness in our weakened condition, and those that are present generally cause distress, so also the soul of the holy psalmist was troubled by the surges rising up in his body.

(3.11) No wonder if the psalmist says that his soul was disturbed, when the Lord Jesus Himself said, "Now my soul is troubled."[2] For He that took on our infirmities also took on our feelings, wherein He was sad even unto death,[3] but not by reason of death. For the death that was freely chosen could not have held sorrow; in it was the future joy of all men and the refreshment of all. Concerning it the Scripture said, in another passage, "And I rose up and saw and sleep became pleasant to me."[4] Good is the sleep that has made the hungry not to hunger and the thirsty not to thirst and has prepared for them the pleasant savor of the mysteries. How then was Christ's soul troubled when He made the souls of others not to fear? He was sad, then, even unto death, until grace should be fulfilled. This is proved by His own testimony as He speaks of His death, "I have a baptism to be baptized with, and how distressed I am until it is accom-

---

1 Ps. 119 (120).5.
2 John 12.27.
3 Cf. Matt. 26.38.
4 Jer. 31.26.

plished!"[5] (3.12) And so, troubled by the hazardous turnings
of this world, David says, "Why are you sad, O soul, why do
you trouble me? Hope in God, for I will give praise to him,
the salvation of my countenance, and my God."[6] Therefore,
when we are distressed and apprehensive, let hope strengthen
us with the expectation of things that are to come. Look
to each phrase individually. "Hope, for I will give praise,"
he says; not "I give praise," but "I will give praise." This
means: I will give praise better at that time, when I shall
behold the glory of God with face unveiled and be transformed
into the same image.[7] (3.13) As he was consoling himself,
suddenly turning to himself, he says, "My soul is troubled
within myself"; that is, I, who ought to strengthen others, am
myself disturbed, and because I do not have strength of myself,
let us receive it from the Creator.

(4.14) "Therefore will I remember you, O Lord, from the
land of Jordan and Hermon."[1] He remembers from the land
of Jordan, in which grace increases the remembrance of pious
devotion. Naaman the Syrian went down into the Jordan and
was made clean of leprosy.[2] In the Jordan Christ was baptized,
when He established the form of saving baptism.[3] The name
Jordan means "descent,"[4] and the Lord Jesus made that
descent, while He made those who dwelt near the river Jordan
clean from the contagion of sin. This stream goes out from
Egypt and divides the promised land. Therefore one who is
troubled, if he takes good counsel, goes out from Egypt
and follows the way of light, for Hermon is interpreted

---

5 Luke 12.50.
6 Ps. 41 (42).6.
7 Cf. 2 Cor. 3.18.

1 Ps. 41 (42).7.
2 Cf. 4 Kings 5.1–14.
3 Cf. Matt. 3.13–17.
4 Ambrose uses the word in the same sense in *Abraham* 2.6.34 and
Commentary on Psalm 37, 10, and in a related sense in *Flight from
the World* 2.12 (translated in this volume).

to mean "way of the lamp." And so, go out first from Egypt, if you wish to see Christ's light. The Chanaanite woman went out from the territory of the pagans and found Christ; she said to Him, "Have pity on me, O son of David!"[5] Moses went out from Egypt and was made a prophet and sent back to the people, that he might free their souls from the land of affliction.[6] Moreover, the lamp is in the Body of Christ, and this is the lamp which shows you the way. For this reason also holy David says, "Your word is a lamp to my feet,"[7] a lamp, because it has enlightened the souls of all men[8] and shown the way in the darkness. The way of the lamp is the Gospel; it shines in the darkness, that is, in the world. For this reason also you find in another passage, "They shall be whitened with snow on Selmon,"[9] that is, in the shadow.

(4.15) The Jordan also represents Christ, who divides the land. Learn how He divides it: "And your own soul a sword shall pierce, to reveal the thoughts of many hearts."[10] For the sword is the divider of our souls, since it goes down into the innermost secret places of the heart and detects the thoughts of the mind. This sword is the living word of God. Indeed, in the Epistle to the Hebrews you read as follows, "For the word of God is living and strong, and, keener than every keenest sword, it penetrates even to the division of soul and spirit, of joints also and of marrow."[11] He is the fountain of Siloe, "which is called 'sent,' "[12] because Christ said that He had been sent from the Father. He is also that division which is produced from the fact that tribes of the Jews lived on both banks of the Jordan. For the Son of Man, who came

---

5 Matt. 15.22.
6 Cf. Exod. 2.11–4.17.
7 Cf. Ps. 118 (119).105.
8 Cf. John 1.9.
9 Ps. 67 (68).15.
10 Luke 2.35.
11 Heb. 4.12.
12 John 9.7.

down from heaven in later times, the true Jordan, the true
divider of the things of earth and those of heaven, gave
to the fathers a divided possession, one part to be possessed
on earth, and the other to be saved up for the rewards of the
life that is to come. Each of these tasks belongs to Christ
alone, whether to divide the things of heaven or to detect
things that are hidden. For the one who detects things that
are hidden divides those that are more profound, and this
indeed is a mark of divinity. Accordingly, you thus find it
written that God said, "I will rejoice and I will divide
Sichem."[13] This is that splendid portion, more excellent than
all, that Jacob allotted to his son Joseph. Thereupon he says,
"Now I give to you above your brothers, splendid Sichem
which I took from the hands of the Amorrites with my sword
and arrow."[14] The right of division was owing to the Lord
alone, and it is expressed in terms of the Word, that is, by
the spiritual sword of the true Solomon.[15] What is the
meaning of "to the Lord alone"? To the Father without
Christ? To Christ without the Father? Not at all. When I
speak of the Father, I do not make separation of the Son,
because the Son is in the bosom and the solitude of the
Father.[16] When I speak of the Son alone, I also associate the
Father, even as the Son also associated Him, saying, "Behold,
the hour is coming for you to leave me alone. But I am not
alone, because the Father is with me."[17] So also is the Father
called "the blessed and only Sovereign,"[18] in such a way that
the Son, who is always in the Father, is not separated from
Him.[19] Indeed, John says it very well, "In the beginning
was the Word,"[20] but He was not without the Father. And the

---

13 Ps. 59 (60).8.
14 Gen. 48.22 (Septuagint).
15 Cf. 3 Kings 3.24.
16 Cf. John 1.18.
17 John 16.32.
18 1 Tim. 6.15.
19 Cf. John 10.38.
20 John 1.1.

Father was God, but He was not without the Word, because "the Word was with God."[21]

(4.16) Such a Sichem is the Church; for Solomon chose her, whose hidden love he had discerned.[22] Such a Sichem is Mary, whose soul God's sword pierces and divides.[23] Such a Sichem is a "coming up," even as it appears in the meaning of the word.[24] As to what the "coming up" is, hear Solomon speaking in reference to the Church, "Who is she that comes up clothed in white, leaning upon her brother?"[25] She is radiant, a word expressed in Greek as *aktinōdēs*,[26] because she is resplendent in faith and in works. To her children it is said, "Let your works shine before my Father who is in heaven."[27] (4.17) Therefore, David is mindful of God from the land of Jordan and Hermon, "from the little hill."[28] What is that "little hill"? Let us consider if perhaps Christ's divinity is the great hill. Indeed, " 'I fill the heaven and the earth,' says the Lord."[29] If then Christ's divinity is the great hill, surely His incarnation is the small hill. Therefore Christ is both, being both a great hill and a lesser one—a great one indeed, because "great is the Lord and great is his power,"[30] and a lesser one, because it is written, "You have made him a little less than the angels."[31] Thereupon Isaia says, "We have seen him, and he had neither appearance nor beauty."[32] Nevertheless, from

---

21 *Ibid.*
22 Cf. 3 Kings 3.27.
23 Cf. Luke 2.35.
24 Contrast *The Patriarchs* 3.11, where Sichem means "shoulders," and *Joseph* 3.9, where the meaning is "shoulder" or "back." The meaning "coming up" appears otherwise unexampled in Ambrose.
25 Cant. 8.5 (Septuagint).
26 The word here translated as "radiant" is not the apparently unanimous reading of the manuscripts, *actuosa* (adopted by Schenkl), but Erasmus' *actinosa* (found in PL). Likewise *aktinōdēs* is Erasmus' correction of the confused Greek in the manuscripts, which led Schenkl to *enargēs*.
27 Cf. Matt. 5.16.
28 Ps. 41 (42).7.
29 Jer. 23.24.
30 Ps. 146 (147A).5.
31 Ps. 8.6.
32 Isa. 53.2 (Septuagint).

being great He became lesser, and from being lesser He became great. From being great He became lesser, because "though he was by nature God, he emptied himself and took on the nature of a slave."[33] From being lesser He became great, because Daniel says, "And the stone that struck the image became a great mountain and filled the whole earth."[34] If you seek to know who this stone is, acknowledge Him: "The stone which the builders rejected, the same is become the cornerstone."[35] He was the same nonetheless, and although He appeared small, He was great. Isaia shows his agreement with this fact, for he says, "A child is born to us, a son is given to us, whose beginning is on his shoulders, and he is called the Messenger of Great Counsel."[36] Christ is all things for your sake; a stone for your sake, that you may be built up, a mountain for your sake, that you may ascend. Come up upon the mountain, then, you that seek heavenly things.[37] For that reason He bowed heaven, that you might be nearer, for that reason He rose up onto the summit of the mountain, that He might lift you up.

(4.18) With reason, then, deep called upon deep, that that mountain might be made small, for concerning it the psalmist says, "Deep calls on deep at the noise of your cataracts."[38] The Old Testament was not strong enough for the redemption of this world; it called upon the New Testament and summoned it to help, as it were. The law cried out, announcing the Gospel. For the law was only half-filled and thus it was necessary that someone should come to fulfill it. "For Christ is

---

33 Phil. 2.6–7.
34 Dan. 2.35.
35 Cf. Ps. 117 (118).22; Isa. 28.16; Matt. 21.42; Luke 20.17; Acts 4.11; 1 Peter 2.6–7.
36 Isa. 9.5 (Septuagint). The Greek word *archē* in the Septuagint text may be translated either as "beginning," as it is here (Latin *initium*), or as "government."
37 Christ, the goal of man's ascent, is here seen as the means of ascent. The theme is frequent in Ambrose. See Otten, "Caritas" 442–48, especially 444; and compare *The Prayer of Job and David* 3.3.7, above.
38 Ps. 41 (42).8.

the consummation of the law unto justice for everyone who believes,"[39] and He came to fulfill the law, not to destroy it.[40] Listen to the psalmist telling how the law is a deep: "Your judgments are as a great deep."[41] At the same time, learn from this that each Testament contains the one wisdom, because Christ came to fulfill each as if it were His own. Further, I interpret the cataracts as depths of words and as the strength of heavenly discourse, and these have flowed forth to us like showers from the sky.[42] Therefore, the remedy for all weariness and the one refuge in temptations is Christ and God's Scripture.

(5.19) Indeed, David observed that the waves of the world were rising and coming over him, and we must endure many such waves on the sea of this life. But he is mindful of the mercies which the Lord promised in countless prophecies, and so he has recourse to prayer and makes entreaty of God. For he knows that God's mercy is commanded in the light,[1] that is, in the law, because "your statutes are a light,"[2] and that it is revealed, moreover, in temptations, as if in the darkness of the night. Accordingly, he is like a traveler who desires to return to his own country and to reach his destination; but still, since he is wearied by the rough road of this life, he calls upon his guide and implores relief.

(5.20) "With me is prayer to the God of my life. I will say to God: 'You are my support.' "[3] He does well now to seek the helps that are known to him, by calling upon both the Author of the promised gift and him who offers the familiar one. Thus, if man's merit fails to come to his help, God's

---

39 Rom. 10.4.
40 Cf. Matt. 5.17.
41 Ps. 35 (36).7.
42 Cf. Sir. 39.6 (9).

---

1 Cf. Ps. 41 (42).9.
2 Isa. 26.9 (Septuagint).
3 Ps. 41 (42).9–10.

example may not fail. Someone says, "When did God support him?" To demonstrate this, come with me to the beginning of Holy Scripture, and see how the Lord fashioned man out of the clay with His own hands,[4] for which reason also David himself says in a later passage, "Your hands have made me and formed me."[5] As if He were a potter, God worked on the fashioning of the flesh of man. And to Jeremia it is said, "Go down to the potter's house, and there you shall hear my words."[6] Now it often happens to a potter, in the fashioning of a vessel, that it falls from his hands and he gathers the clay anew to shape the vessel again. Indeed, Jeremia also says, "I went down and I saw how the vessel fell, which he was making with his hands."[7] And again he says, "He made a vessel of another sort, as it seemed good to him."[8] Therefore He is correctly called our support, because He supported us, He fashioned us, with His own hands. Those are the vessels of a human potter, some unto honor, others unto dishonor.[9] We are all vessels of clay; even if someone is a king, he is a vessel of clay, and even if he is an Apostle, he is a vessel. For this reason also Paul says, "We carry this treasure in vessels of clay,"[10] and the prophet says in reference to the king, "Conia is dishonored like a vessel which is useless,"[11] and he continues, "O earth, hear the word of the Lord, write this man down as disinherited."[12] As if by a paternal right, our God generally disinherits degenerate children. So also the earth writes down those who are the children of the earth. Consequently, when the Jews made accusation against the adulteress, the Lord Jesus wrote with His finger on the

---

4 Cf. Gen. 2.7.
5 Ps. 118 (119).73.
6 Jer. 18.2.
7 Jer. 18.3–4.
8 Jer. 18.4 (Septuagint).
9 Cf. Rom. 9.21.
10 2 Cor. 4.7.
11 Jer. 22.28 (Septuagint).
12 Jer. 22.29–30 (Septuagint).

earth.[13] But the just are not written down upon the earth, as we read, for to them it is said, "Rejoice, that your names are written in heaven."[14]

(5.21) Therefore the Lord supported us when He fashioned us; He supports us also when He bids us to be born. Consequently, the just man says, "You have supported me from my mother's womb."[15] Whose mother's? "Before I formed you in the womb, I knew you."[16] Those whom the Lord forms, He also supports; He supports them even in their coming forth: "And before you came forth from your mother's womb, I sanctified you."[17] He is our supporter, for He has supported us with His hands; He is called a supporter as the Creator of the human race; and He is our supporter, for He has supported us by His visitation, that He may protect us. In view of this, the psalmist himself says in another passage, "He that dwells in the aid of the Most High shall say to the Lord, 'You are my supporter and my refuge.' "[18] The first support is that of God's working in us, the second is that of His protection of us. Indeed, listen to Moses saying, "Spreading his wings, he received them and supported them upon his shoulders."[19] He supported them like the eagle, which was accustomed to examine its progeny, so as to keep and to bring up those whom it observed to possess the qualities of a true offspring and the gift of an undamaged constitution, and to reject those in whom it detected weakness of a degenerate origin even at that tender age.

(6.22) "Why have you forgotten me[1] and why have you re-

---

13 Cf. John 8.6, 8.
14 Luke 10.20.
15 Ps. 138 (139).13.
16 Jer. 1.5.
17 *Ibid.*
18 Ps. 90 (91).1–2.
19 Deut. 32.11 (Septuagint).

---

1 Ps. 41 (42).10.

jected me?"[2] God does not forget; indeed it is impossible
that He should forget, for all past and future events are
present to Him. But our sins have led Him to impose the
penalty of forgetfulness, that He might blot out those whom
He knew to be unworthy of His visitation. For "the Lord
knows them who are his."[3] Yet, when some commit wrongdoing, He says to them, "I did not know you."[4] Who then
can say to God, "Why have you forgotten me?" But nevertheless this sentiment is shared by the saints and by us who are
weak. The saint speaks as if aware of his own worth, and yet,
the more saintly he is, the humbler he is. But if the saint
speaks with great difficulty, what am I, a sinner, to say,
except to return to that complaint: Why have You forgotten
Your work,[5] why have You forgotten Your visitation, yes,
why have You forgotten my weakness? For what is man except
that You visit him?[6] Therefore do not forget one who is weak.
Remember, Lord, that You have made me weak, remember
that You have fashioned me as dust.[7] How will I be able
to stand, unless You direct Your care always so as to strengthen
this clay, so that my strength may proceed from Your countenance? "When you turn away your face, all things will be
troubled."[8] If You exercise Your care, woe is me! You have
nothing to behold in me but the contagion of sins. It is no
use either to be abandoned or to be looked upon, for even
while we are being looked upon, we are committing offenses.
Still, we can hold that God does not reject those whom He
looks upon, because He makes clean those whom He beholds.
A fire blazes before Him, that burns away sin.[9]

(6.23) It is good for us, therefore, that we are not rejected.

2 Ps. 42 (43).2.
3 2 Tim. 2.19.
4 Matt. 7.23.
5 Cf. Heb. 6.10.
6 Cf. Ps. 8.5 (4); Heb. 2.6.
7 Cf. Ps. 102 (103).14; Job 10.9.
8 Ps. 103 (104).29.
9 Cf. Joel 2.3.

Accordingly, David complains because he believed that he had been rejected, whereas before he had been supported. Indeed, he says in a later passage, "In you have I been strengthened from the womb."[10] But we also find it written previously, "I was cast upon you from the womb, from my mother's womb you are my God."[11] It is good also to be cast forth, but to be cast forth onto God. Indeed, in Psalm 21, this is said in reference to the person of Christ, who was truly cast forth onto the Father from the womb of a virgin; for earthly things did not receive Him at His dying. On this account, when He was on the cross and was breathing forth His spirit, He said to the Father, "Into your hands I commend my spirit."[12]

(6.24) Therefore, let none add the word "Lord,"[13] as the chanters do,[14] for I have found it neither in my Latin codex nor in the Greek one, nor, a reason clearer still, in the Gospel. Indeed, He had said previously, "Father, forgive them"[15] this sin, as if He were saying that He was commending His own spirit to the Father, into the hands of Him in whose bosom the Son is always.[16] And yet, even if they add that He said "Lord," let them consider that He says this like a man who finds himself dying.

---

10 Ps. 70 (71).6.
11 Ps. 21 (22).11.
12 Ps. 30 (31).6; Luke 23.46.
13 Ambrose's injunction may not have had full effect. The reading ". . . commendo, domine . . ." ["I commend, Lord"] appears in a 6th-century Old Latin psalter, probably of Italian origin, Paris, B. N. lat. 11947. See R. Weber, Le Psautier Romain et les autres anciens psautiers latins (Collectanea Biblica Latina 10; Rome 1953) 57 (cf. XVIII).
14 The employment of chanters (psaltae), who apparently constituted a separate order in the Church, was not incompatible with the congregational singing practiced at Milan. See Dudden 687 and, for the existence of an order of psaltae, Jerome, Letters 52.5 (translated by F. A. Wright in Select Letters of St. Jerome [Loeb Classical Library, Cambridge, Mass., and London 1963]).
15 Luke 23.34.
16 Cf. John 1.18.

(6.25) And so Christ was cast forth onto the Father from the womb, from His mother's womb. This means: it is established that that womb which cast Him forth is His mother's womb. Moreover, the Father says, "From the womb before the day star I begot you."[17] The Father did not indeed cast forth the Son, for the Son never came forth from Him, even as Christ says, "I was delivered up and came not forth."[18] The Father did not cast Him forth, for He is bound to Him by the unity of the same substance. Therefore, the passage can be read thus: "I was cast upon you from the womb, from my mother's womb,"[19] so that "You are my God, depart not from me,"[20] follows. It can also be read this way: "From my mother's womb you are my God," since, once I was in the womb, I never departed from You. I was with You; like Jona when he was in the belly of the fish, I prayed to You[21] on behalf of the people. And truly, Christ was with God from His mother's womb, according to what is written, "Before the child knew good or evil, it chose the good,"[22] and "Before the child called 'father' or 'mother,' he plundered the strength of Damascus and the spoils of Samaria,"[23] that by calling forth the Gentiles He might gain a kingdom for the Father out of a holy and devout worship.

(7.26) Let us look to what remains, "Why have you rejected me, and why go I sorrowful, while my enemy afflicts me and breaks my bones? They who trouble me have reproached me, while it is said to me day by day, 'Where is your God?' Why are you sorrowful, my soul?"[1] and so on. The first entreaty contains a complaint, because the possession

---

17 Ps. 109 (110).3.
18 Ps. 87 (88).9.
19 Ps. 21 (22).11.
20 Ps. 21 (22).12.
21 Cf. Jona 2.1–2.
22 Cf. Isa. 7.16.
23 Cf. Isa. 8.4.

1 Ps. 41 (42).10–12.

of goods was being deferred whereas the benefit of them was already needed. The second entreaty arose because the coming of Christ, awaited eagerly by the wise, and proclaimed by the law, and promised by the prophets, was being postponed. The hearts of the just were burning with a greater impatience for that very reason, because they knew that He would come for the redemption of all men . . .[2] yes, of the entirety of men, to open the way of virtue to them in the track of the Gospel, and to point out the paths of good works, even as He Himself said in Proverbs: "The Lord created me, the beginning of his ways."[3] Accordingly it was said to him, "Where is your God?" because Christ had not come till then but was hoped for. Therefore, the devil gave expression to his rage, to trample upon those he knew would believe in the Lord's coming, and he afflicted them with various misfortunes. And so David prays, in order that he might stir the Lord from His delay by a prophetic complaint, urge Him to hasten, and advise Him to bring His aid. We find a similarity to this prayer in a later passage also, where the psalmist likewise says, "O God, why have you rejected us unto the end?"[4] And in that passage he lamented tearfully, and quite openly, that God had forgotten His congregation and had thrown aside the scepter of His inheritance, and that enemies had risen up against the people of God;[5] of these he says, "And they that hate you have made their boasts in the midst of your solemnity."[6] Perhaps this short passage would seem to be referring to the Assyrians, who triumphed over the Jewish people, did there not follow, "They have set up their ensigns for signs, and I knew them not."[7] There are

---

2 The lacuna that Schenkl indicates here seems to do little damage to the sense and yet has not been convincingly filled.
3 Prov. 8.22 (Septuagint).
4 Ps. 73 (74).1.
5 Cf. Ps. 73 (74).2–3.
6 Ps. 73 (74).4.
7 Cf. Ps. 73 (74).4–5.

always ensigns in a war; they generally precede those who
are going to do battle and stand at the head of the military
column. Each individual unit or legion follows its own ensigns.
And if they have been scattered in the commotion of battle,
they return to that point where they have perceived their
ensigns to be, however far away they find themselves. Each
individual commander designates such ensigns and gives orders
that they be followed. But there are also other ensigns that a
conqueror of the enemy imposes, and he decrees that respect
be paid to them by captives, as it were. But one who is a
loyal soldier follows his own ensigns and does not recognize
those of a stranger.

(7.27) Let us consider with some care and attention what
these strange ensigns are. Christ has set His sign on the forehead of each one;[8] the Antichrist sets his sign there also, that
he may recognize his own. But as for him who is a Jew in
secret, to him the true believer says, "They have set up their
ensigns for signs, and I knew them not." The devil and his
servants set up their ensigns, but I did not know them, because
I was not a party to their deceits and I did not agree to their
dominion. Nabuchodonosor the Assyrian set signs upon the
Hebrew young men and changed their names.[9] He ordered
them to worship his statue,[10] to give up the feasts of their
fathers, to follow the religious usages of the Chaldeans, and
to neglect God's law. The king resolved upon this, but Daniel
determined in his heart to avoid the contagion of the king's
table.[11] Therefore, it was right and appropriate for him to
say that he did not know the ensigns of strangers. It had
been commanded that the Hebrew young men should worship
the king's statue; they replied to him, "We will not worship
your statue."[12] Therefore each one of them could have aptly

---

8 Cf. Apoc. 7.3; 9.4.
9 Dan. 1.6–7.
10 Cf. Dan. 3.4–6, 15.
11 Cf. Dan. 1.8–16.
12 Dan. 3.18.

said, "They have set up their ensigns for signs, and I knew them not"; that is, I have not tried them, I have not received them with any consent, I have not brought them into any association with myself. Consequently, we read also concerning the Son of God that He did not know sin.[13] And you find in another passage, "For he that keeps the commandment does not know the wicked word,"[14] when it is altogether clear that knowledge of wickedness is not culpable, but association with it is. David himself also says in a later passage, "But the malignant, that turned aside from me, I would not know."[15] Moreover, when the adversaries desired to set up these ensigns, he proclaims, "As if upon the way on the highest top, as if with axes in a wood of trees, they have cut down at once the gates thereof, with double-edged axe and hatchet they have brought it down."[16] What is the meaning of this? It surely shows that our faith ought not to be "upon the way," as it were; else the birds of the air may come and carry it off, even as that word of which you read in the Gospel that it ought not to be sown around ways and paths.[17]

(7.28) And so the adversaries, wishing to root out the faith of such a holy man—for they did not see their ensigns in his heart—attempted to set them up "upon the way," as it were, that is, on a passage. Moreover, the heart is "on the top," because "the eyes of a wise man are in his head."[18] And they set up their ensigns "as if in a wood of trees"— trees which are swiftly burned up by fire or cut down with axes.[19] For fire goes out from the wood and burns even the cedars of Lebanon.[20] Further, they thought that this should be done that they might defile the tabernacle of God's name

---

13 Cf. 2 Cor. 5.21.
14 Eccles. 8.5.
15 Ps. 100 (101).4.
16 Ps. 73 (74).5–6.
17 Cf. Luke 8.5.
18 Eccles. 2.14.
19 Cf. Ps. 73 (74).4–5; Jer. 46.22–23.
20 Cf. Zach. 11.1.

which is in us. For just as we are a temple of God,[21] so we are also a tabernacle of God, in which the feasts of the Lord are celebrated. Then do you, O man, keep a watch over the top of your head, so that "you may shatter the heads of the enemies, the hairy crown of them that walk about."[22] For they walk about in useless things, not in holy ones, and in a hairy crown, not in a crown of faith and devotion. And "if the spirit of him that has power ascends upon you," as you read in Ecclesiastes, "leave not your place."[23] In very truth, Christ set you higher, for He made you to the likeness of God.[24] Therefore hold to the higher place of faith and of holiness, which you have received from Christ. Thus, as one made higher, you may readily drive back the wicked spirit that ascends from lower things—I mean from those that are earthly and worldly—and may refuse to receive his ensigns in your heart. Let him not seize the entryways of your soul nor the entrances of your spirit and, "as if in a wood of trees," devastate with his fires those that are fragile and falling, or with his axes chop down the gates of your heart.[25]

Therefore let there be in us not a wood, but a vineyard. Let the door of our mouth and of our heart be shut with greater care, that the enemy may not enter in. He swiftly bursts open a door if he finds it accessible, whereas Christ knocks[26] and does not throw the door down, for "he has strengthened the bolts of your gates, O Jerusalem."[27] Christ knocks with His hand that you may open, whereas the adversary cuts the door down with axes; and therefore it is written, that hammer and axe should not enter into the house of God.[28] Pride and deceit ought to be outdoors, not inside;

---

21 Cf. 1 Cor. 3.16; 2 Cor. 6.16.
22 Cf. Ps. 67 (68).22.
23 Eccles. 10.4.
24 Cf. Gen. 1.26–27.
25 Cf. Ps. 73 (74).5–6.
26 Cf. Cant. 5.2; Luke 12.36.
27 Ps. 147 (147B).12–13 (1–2).
28 Cf. 3 Kings 6.7.

conflicts indeed ought to be outside;[29] but within, the peace
that surpasses all understanding.[30] Let not your soul be cut
with the iron, but even as Joseph's soul, so may your soul
pass by the iron.[31] Otherwise, your ruling part, which is
like a kind of tabernacle of the Word, may be destroyed at the
very beginning of faith and the entrance into spiritual learning. For the man who is established in habit and practice
continues unmoved, and he does not yield to the one who
is trying to ascend to the top by transforming himself into
an angel of light, as it were.[32] But if the latter does not see
his ensigns in us, he will not have the power to offer resistance.
Therefore, let not the enemy afflict us,[33] let him not break our
bones,[34] let us not fail to continue in Christ, that He may
say of us, "They continue with me now three days, and I
am unwilling to send them away fasting, lest they faint
on the way."[35] Blessed is the man to whom Christ has given
strength of heart, that he may not be able to fail, once set
on the track of this life. One who hopes in the Lord and gives
praise to Him with a profound love does not fail.[36] For even
that rider whose horse's heel was bitten by the serpent
was still not entrapped, although he fell backward, because
he looked for salvation from the Lord.[37]

(8.29) There is also a third entreaty, for although David
was set in the midst of men doing evil deeds, he eagerly
desires that his case be separated from contagion with them.[1]
Many suppose that this sentiment should be attributed to

---

29 Cf. 2 Cor. 7.5.
30 Cf. Phil. 4.7.
31 Cf. Ps. 104 (105).17–18.
32 Cf. 2 Cor. 11.14.
33 Cf. Ps. 41 (42).10.
34 Cf. Ps. 41 (42).11.
35 Matt. 15.32.
36 Cf. Prov. 28.25; Ps. 41 (42).6, 12.
37 Cf. Gen. 49.17–18.

---

1 Cf. Ps. 42 (43).1.

the Lord Jesus, because it belongs to Him alone not to fear judgment, as the one who overcomes when He is judged.[2] Indeed, He has a judgment from the unjust man, and into it Christ entered willingly, as you find it written, "O my people, what have I done to you? Or wherein have I grieved you?"[3] But since the Father has given all judgment to Him,[4] not indeed as if to one that was weak, but as if to a Son, what judgment can He undergo? If they think that the Son must undergo the Father's judgment, surely "the Father does not judge any man, but all judgment he has given to the Son, that all men may honor the Son even as they honor the Father."[5] The Father honors the Son, and do you put Him to judgment? We have expressed this thought here, so that no one would think that we substituted the figure of the psalmist in the Lord's place out of fear of inquiry. Holy David foresees in spirit that the Jews will rise up against the Lord in His passion; since he is not greatly afraid of the judgment upon his own faith, he beseeches that his own case be distinguished also from a nation of persecutors; else, the stock of the entire Jewish race could be implicated with those wicked heirs of his own race and posterity.

(8.30) Therefore he is troubled, and with good reason. He sees that his struggle is against flesh and blood, and that a severe shipwreck awaits him in his own self, that the storm is in his own body. And he could not endure it, unless he should have heaven's help and support, for a man has no sterner enemy than those of his household.[6] Moreover, what is so private as a man, and the weakness of his flesh, is to himself? And so, the psalmist hastens to pray with his whole heart that Christ may come, the strength of all men, to take

---

2 Cf. Ps. 50 (51).6.
3 Mich. 6.3 (Septuagint).
4 Cf. John 5.22.
5 John 5.22–23.
6 Cf. Mich. 7.6; Matt. 10.36.

up all weaknesses and make both one, to break down the enmities of spirit and flesh that contend against each other, by removing the wall that was dividing man's internal constitution so that it could not come together into harmony.[7] And so, because he had a battle in his own self and a battle from his neighbors, who had forgotten law and equity and were preparing the snares and ambushes of deceit, and because the remedy he hoped for was being postponed, David thought that he had been rejected.[8] It was as if the One who had promised that He would come as a remedy, refused to come. Like a man who had been called back from the hope of the dawning day into the depths of darkness, he prayed that the light would shine to drive away the gloom of this life, and that the eternal truth would be present to destroy the fallacious image of this world.[9]

(8.31) God lent His aid to these prayers, for He generally appears unexpectedly and reveals Himself to those who do not ask for Him, even as He says, "I became manifest to them who inquired not for me."[10] Assenting to his devout prayers, God anticipated the course of his desires by a swift operation. He suddenly brought the holy prophet into the Church and into His tabernacles in spirit,[11] and He set before his eyes the holy altar,[12] on which would be the redemption of the whole world and the forgiveness of all sins in the entire world.

(9.32) And so he sees in spirit those good and heavenly mysteries and that table which keeps away the snares of the destroyers. Even as he said in an earlier passage, "You have prepared a table before me against those that wear me out,"[1]

---

7 Cf. Eph. 2.14–15.
8 Cf. Ps. 42 (43).2.
9 Cf. Ps. 42 (43).3.
10 Isa. 65.1.
11 Cf. Ps. 42 (43).3.
12 Cf. Ps. 42 (43).4.

---

1 Ps. 22 (23).5.

he now says, "And I will go in to the altar of my God, to God, who gives joy to my youth."[2] He did well to say, as if he were Adam, "and I will go in." For we had been cast out of the paradise of the Lord, from which Adam, aware of his sin, turned away from the face of the Lord.[3] He continued appropriately, also, "and I will go in to the altar of God," as if he would return into the sight of God. For God had turned away from our offerings when He disapproved of the offerings of that murderer Cain.[4] Cain lay in hiding as a stranger from the sight of the Lord. His raging, brutal ferocity,[5] because the Lord had had regard for his brother's gifts,[6] left his own heirs under discredit. He had killed Abel, whose blood also cried to the Lord,[7] not only on his own behalf, but he had killed him on behalf of all of us. Then virtually no one's sacrifice won approval, because there was no one to do goodness, there was not even a single one,[8] since no faith was reserved for God nor any respect for the bond of brotherhood. The Lord Jesus came to raise up Adam; Abel also was raised up, for his offerings were pleasing to God. The Lord Jesus offered His own self, that is, the firstlings of His own body,[9] in a sprinkling of blood that speaks better than the blood of Abel spoke upon the earth.[10] God had regard to the offerings of Christ, for from Him He left to the good heirs the grace of reconciliation with Himself. Accordingly, holy David is right to say, taking the role of reconciled man, "And I will go in to the altar of my God, to God, who gives joy to my youth."[11]

---

2 Ps. 42 (43).4.
3 Cf. Gen. 3.8.
4 Cf. Gen. 4.5.
5 Cf. Vergil, *Aeneid* 10.898.
6 Cf. Gen. 4.4–6.
7 Cf. Gen. 4.8–10.
8 Cf. Ps. 13 (14).1; 52 (53).2.
9 Cf. Gen. 4.4.
10 Cf. Heb. 12.24.
11 Ps. 42 (43).4.

(9.33) If we can, let us also confirm this point—how the Lord first turned away from man's sacrifices and later was reconciled to him—by a citation from a second prophet. We find it written in the book of Isaia, where God speaks: "What is the multitude of your sacrifices to me? I am cloyed."[12] That means: I abound in my own, I do not seek yours, I do not desire whole burnt offerings of rams and the fat of lambs and the blood of bulls and of goats, and do not come so into my sight. And granted, Abel had offered out of the young of his flock a sacrifice in which he had pleased God,[13] but He did not require the symbolic sacrifice, for He was awaiting the true sacrifice; yes, the Lord's saving passion was being awaited. "For who required these things at your hands? You shall not be admitted to tread my court."[14] And later, " 'When you stretch forth your hands to me, I will turn away my face from you. But wash and be clean, take away the evil from your souls. Administer justice to the orphans and plead the cause of the widow and come, let us reason together,' says the Lord."[15] Therefore, it is clear that the Lord turned away from man's sacrifices earlier, and later was reconciled that He might be kind enough to have regard to our sacrifices.

(9.34) And so, then, the one who enters into the mercy of the Lord, goes in untroubled. Indeed, it is said to the good servant, "Enter into the joy of your lord,"[16] whereas it is said of the worthless servant, "Cast him into the outer darkness."[17] So also Adam was cast out from a heavenly homeland and from his dwelling in paradise and was banished to the island of sin. Therefore Scripture rightly says, "Be you renewed, O islands,"[18] because, just like islands, we are surrounded on

12 Isa. 1.11.
13 Cf. Gen. 4.4–5.
14 Isa. 1.12.
15 Isa. 1.15–18.
16 Matt. 25.21.
17 Matt. 25.30.
18 Isa. 41.1.

the sea of this world by waves of sin. Those islands were renewed by the forgiveness of sins through the coming of the Lord. That is, men at baptism found themselves, like islands, in the midst of the waters. Like islands, they were pounded by masses of water as the booming waves of their sins rebounded. They were like the islands on which the innocent earlier suffered many a shipwreck on the cliffs of deceit, for guile was in their heart and flattery on their lips. But then the Lord Jesus, in whom there is no guile,[19] came into the world. By His setting forth of heavenly teaching, He calmed the depths of human hearts and poured forth tranquillity upon the passions of every man. He took away the fence of discord,[20] and those who approached began to possess certain helps, like those afforded by safe havens. Thus, every man may anchor the vessel of his own repose in the love of neighbor or of brother and may remain by the shore in the recess of a devout heart, as it were.[21]

(9.35) And so, David has reason to cry, like a man renewed, "And I will go in to the altar of my God, to God, who gives joy to my youth."[22] Even as he had said earlier that he had grown old among his enemies, as we read in the sixth psalm,[23] here he says that youth has been restored to him after the lengthy old age of man's fall. For we are renewed through the regeneration experienced in baptism, we are renewed through the outpouring of the Holy Spirit, we shall be renewed also through the resurrection, even as he says in a later passage,

---

19 Cf. 1 Peter 2.22.
20 Cf. Eph. 2.14.
21 Imagery of storm and shipwreck is very frequent in patristic literature; see, for example, 1.7.21, above. On the harbor as symbolic of rest and security, see C. Bonner, "Desired Haven" (cited above, *Patriarchs* ch. 5 n. 4). A passage of similar tenor, combining many of the elements found here, occurs in verses 772–76 of the poem *On the Providence of God*, ascribed to Prosper of Aquitaine (Migne, PL 51.615–38; English translation by M. P. McHugh, *The Carmen de Providentia Dei* [The Catholic University of America Patristic Studies 98; Washington 1964]).
22 Ps. 42 (43).4.
23 Cf. Ps. 6.8.

"Your youth shall be renewed like the eagle's."[24] Learn the manner of our renewal: "You shall sprinkle me with hyssop and I shall be cleansed, you shall wash me and I shall be made whiter than snow."[25] And in Isaia, "If your sins be as scarlet, I shall make them white as snow."[26] One who changes from the darkness of sin into the light of virtue and into grace is properly renewed. Thus, one who earlier was stained with foul defilement may shine with a brightness that is whiter than snow.

(10.36) "I will give praise to you upon the cithara, my God."[1] Our soul has its own cithara, for Paul would not have said, "I will pray with the spirit, but I will pray with the understanding also; I will sing with the spirit, but I will sing with the understanding also,"[2] unless he had a cithara that resounded at the touch of the pick of the Holy Spirit. The cithara is our flesh when it dies to sin to live to God; it is a cithara when it receives the sevenfold Spirit in the sacrament of baptism. For while the tortoise is alive, it is sunk in the mire; but when it has died, its covering is adapted to the uses of song and the gift of holy instruction, to sound forth the seven changing notes in rhythmic measures.[3] Likewise, as regards our flesh, if it lives for bodily enticements, it is living in a kind of filth and in an abyss of pleasures. But if it dies to riotous living and incontinence, then it regains true life, then it begins to produce the fine melody of good works. Fine is the sound of chastity, fine is the sound produced by those

24 Ps. 102 (103).5.
25 Ps. 50 (51).9.
26 Isa. 1.18.

1 Ps. 42 (43).4 (5).
2 1 Cor. 14.15.
3 Cf. Vergil, *Aeneid* 6.646. A passage of similar nature appears in *Jacob and the Happy Life* 2.9.39 (translated in this volume). For further citations of passages in which Ambrose compares the seven notes of the scale to the seven gifts of the Holy Spirit, with references to Orpheus, see P. Courcelle, "Les Pères devant les enfers Virgiliens," especially 32 n. 8.

who fear God. Indeed, "their sound has gone forth into all the earth."[4] Fine is the sound of faith which "is proclaimed all over the world,"[5] as it is written. Let this sound go forth from us to God, just as it went forth also from the Thessalonians,[6] so that we may sing even when we are not singing and may proclaim the Lord in a symphony of good works, for to Him are honor, glory, and perpetuity from the ages, both now and always and forever and ever. Amen.[7]

---

4 Ps. 18 (19).5.
5 Rom. 1.8.
6 Cf. 1 Thess. 1.8.
7 The same doxology appears at the conclusion of the third book.

INDICES

GENERAL INDEX

Aaron, 156, 220, 335, 348

Abbott, W. M., 247 n.

Abel, 305, 319, 416–17

ability, 106, 143, 287, 317–19, 367

Abraham, 10, 23, 24, 96, 107–9, 189, 199, 203, 223, 256, 284, 300, 305, 338, 349, 365, 373–74

Absalom, 296

abstinence, 122, 147, 164, 173–74, 310, 351, 362, 370

abyss, 270, 347–49, 367, 419

accuser, 136, 343, 378; *see also* adversary, Antichrist, devil, Satan *and* serpent

Acylas, 48, 52

Adam, 3, 13, 35, 42, 56, 87, 97–8, 104, 105, 108, 125, 127, 128, 158, 194, 206, 260, 282, 357, 375, 379, 383, 385, 416–17

adulteress, 204-7, 308, 375, 404; *see also* harlot

adultery, 99, 119, 123, 207, 292, 320–21

adversary, 41, 45, 82, 135, 157, 205, 303, 331, 346, 359-60, 367, 385, 411–12; *see also* accuser, Antichrist, devil, Satan *and* serpent

Aeneas, 14 n.

Aeneas the paralytic, 199

Agar, 24

Alexandria, 102 n.

allegory: *see* exegesis, allegorical

almond tree, 220

aloe, 39, 41, 220

altar, 36, 61, 165, 181, 198, 415–16, 418

Aman, 213

ambition, 122

Ambrose

and authority of Church, 1–2

and city of God, 305 n.

concept of private property in, 143 n.

concept of redemption in, 125 n.

editions of works, vi, 5

influences on, 2–4

legal terminology in, 127 n.

life of, 1–2

preaching of, 2–4, 189 n., 253

relations with secular authorities, 1–2, 187, 209 n., 214 n.

translations of works, vi, 9, 69, 118, 188, 242, 280, 328

use of pagan philosophers, 2–4; *see also* Neoplaton-

ists, Philo, Plato, Plotinus, and Porphyry
works of:
Abraham, 10 n., 29 n., 52 n., 53 n., 102 n., 254 n., 289 n., 297 n., 391 n., 398 n.
Sermon against Auxentius, 2 n.
Cain and Abel, 60 n., 81 n., 254 n., 271 n.
Commentary on Psalm 37, 289 n., 398 n.
De Apologia prophetae David, 121 n.
Death as a Good, translated, 69–113, 35 n., 60 n., 107 n., 264 n., 320 n.
Exhortatio virginitatis, 307 n.
Explanatio psalmorum duodecim, 190 n.
Explanation of Psalm 118, 22 n., 25 n., 28 n., 43 n., 53 n., 54 n., 60 n., 81 n., 102 n., 156 n., 190 n., 244 n.
Explanation of the Gospel According to Luke, 24 n., 25 n., 35 n., 59 n., 241, 253 n.
Flight from the World, translated, 281–323; 83 n., 155 n., 159 n., 194 n., 339 n., 398 n.
Hexameron, 52 n., 84 n.
Isaac, or the Soul, translated, 9–65; 5, 81 n., 97 n., 155 n., 189 n., 298 n., 320 n., 391 n.
Jacob and the Happy Life, translated, 117–84; 11 n., 189 n., 298 n., 302 n., 391 n.
Joseph, translated, 187–237; 37 n., 156 n., 158 n., 248 n., 274 n., 316 n., 401 n.
Letters, 1 n., 11 n., 102 n. 209 n., 293 n., 297 n., 307 n., 339 n.
On the Mysteries, 37 n., 59 n.
On Naboth, 126 n., 307 n.
On Noe, 13 n.
Paradise, 53 n.
The Patriarchs, translated, 241–75; 193 n., 336 n., 401 n.
The Prayer of Job and David, translated, 329–420; 29 n., 170 n., 189 n., 289 n., 303 n., 323 n.
On the Sacraments, 15 n., 37 n., 59 n., 60 n., 81 n., 86 n., 256 n., 285 n.
On His Brother, Satyrus, 75 n.
On the Spirit, 254 n.
De Tobia, 127 n.
On the Death of Valentinian, 54 n.
Aminadab, 53–4
Amorrites, 248, 400
Anania, 142
Ananias, 226–27

angel, 24, 33, 36, 41, 45, 103–5, 155–56, 161, 173, 268, 270, 305, 350, 362, 365, 384, 401, 413

anger: *see* wrath

Anna, 272

Antichrist, 260–61, 410; *see also* accuser, adversary, devil, Satan, *and* serpent

Antiochus, 173–74

anti-Semitism, 242, 246, 336–37, 375

Apollo, 275

Apostles, 35, 61, 218, 233, 234, 243, 249, 256, 263, 264, 270, 274, 283, 284, 300–1, 314, 349, 389, 391–92, 404

apple tree, 58

Apuleius, 135 n.

Aquila, 48 n.

Aratus, 64 n.

Arians, 1, 117, 187, 209 n., 214 n.

Aristoxenus, 145 n.

ark, 44, 184, 294

Armstrong, A. H., 3 n.

Arnaldez, R., 3 n.

arrow, 142, 267, 319, 331, 400

Arusianus Messius, 279, 293 n.

Asaph, 368–69

Aser, 195, 263–64

asp, 313, 392

ass, 219, 233, 251, 254–55, 365

Assyrians, 409–10

astrology, 376, 386

athlete, 142, 303, 331, 353, 385; *see also* runner

Augustine, 1 n., 4, 9, 50 n., 53 n., 62 n., 63 n., 76 n., 106 n., 209 n., 280, 281 n., 292 n., 311 n., 371 n.

Auxentius, 1

avarice, 261, 295, 301; *see also* greed

axe, 411–12

Azaria, 142

Babylon, 44, 199

back, 193, 250–51, 363, 373, 401 n.

Bala, 245

Baldad, 352

balm, 198 n., 199

banquet, 84–7, 108, 122, 173, 212, 221, 223, 226, 254, 315

baptism, 31 n., 39 n., 60, 62, 69, 71, 124, 125, 131, 166, 226, 231, 262, 266, 307, 322, 393, 394 n., 397–98, 418–19

Bardenhewer, O., 79 n., 241 n.

barley, 56

Barnabas, 337

Basan, 261

basilisk, 392

basket, 321

Bathuel, 297

beast, 97, 102, 176, 198, 348, 384

Beck, H. G. J., 393 n.

bed, 27, 32, 34, 40, 78, 168, 169, 199, 245–46, 331–33

bee, 102

beggar, 202

Bellerophon, 123 n.

belly, 297, 312–13, 395, 408

Benjamin, 152, 218–31, 242, 273–74

Berger, A., 127 n.

Bethel, 29, 165, 391

Bethlehem, 120–21, 165

Beyenka, Sr. M. Melchior, O.P., 1 n., 297 n., 307 n., 339 n.

bird, 82–3, 212, 307, 350, 411

birdlime: see lime

birthright, 148, 319

bishop, 52

blessing, 36, 96–7, 147, 148, 149, 151–52, 168–69, 171–72, 195–96, 203, 224, 227, 239–75, 314, 316, 318–19, 356, 359, 385, 395, 413

blindness, 160, 168, 218, 225–26, 236–37, 246, 274–75, 281, 299–301, 376

blood, 11, 13, 37, 121, 127, 128, 131, 133, 136, 148, 161, 171, 177, 179, 183, 198, 200, 201, 217, 251, 255–56, 271, 293, 305, 311, 331, 343, 347, 416–17

boaster, 222, 347, 367, 409

Bonner, C., 257 n., 418 n.

Bonwetsch, G. Nathanael, 28 n.

Boreas, 366

bow, 248, 266, 319, 402

branch, 209, 254, 264–65, 344

brass, 264, 331

bread, 39, 46, 85, 86, 165, 195, 212, 216, 223, 256, 263–64, 318, 320, 391 n., 395

breast, 16, 19, 57, 60, 84, 266, 268, 306, 312–13, 339, 365

bull, 214, 247, 249, 270–73, 417

bullock, 265

burden, 18, 53–4, 80, 159, 195, 333, 357, 359, 379

burial, 41, 82, 86, 143, 165–66, 170, 197, 220, 263, 322–23, 347, 365, 367

Caesar, 262

Cain, 193, 310–11, 319, 347, 416

Caiphas, 246

Calligonus, 187, 209 n., 214 n.

Callinicum, 2

camel, 45

Campbell, J. M., 4 n., 81 n.

captivity, 97, 141–42, 143, 251, 273, 360, 410

cassia, 220

cataract, 402–3

catechumen, 69

cave, 297, 303

cedar, 27, 300, 381, 411

cement, 198-99, 219

centurion, 336

Cerberus, 94

Chadwick, H., 3 n.

chaff, 364

chains: see fetters

Chaldaeans, 11, 44, 410

Chanaan, 234, 258 n., 283, 399

chance, 121, 290, 375, 379–80

chanters, 407

chariot, 22, 53–5, 61, 63, 215, 216, 239

charity: see love

Charles, R. H., 104 n.

Charon, 94

Charrah, 297

chastity, 22, 30, 89, 126, 166,

189, 203–7, 225–26, 247–48, 249, 315, 321, 419
cheese, 341
Cherubim, 379–80
child: see children
children, 23, 62, 72, 95, 134, 140–42, 144, 149–50, 160, 161, 190–91, 199, 236, 243, 245, 259, 264, 284, 304–5, 306, 313, 317, 330, 339, 343, 347, 357, 359–60, 366, 378–79, 382, 392, 401, 402, 404, 408; see also infant
choir, 181
Chorrad, 307
Christ
    advent of, 15, 30 n., 129, 162, 165, 251, 345, 356, 371, 409, 414–15, 418
    as advocate, 133, 136, 290
    and allegorical exegesis, 3
    and Apostles, 61, 256, 263, 300–1, 349, 389, 392
    ascension of, 34, 112, 172, 210
    baptism of, 255, 393, 398
    birth of, 28, 164–65, 192, 221, 252–53, 267–69, 272, 339, 401–2
    as bread of salvation, 165, 263–64
    as bridegroom, 29–33, 36–42, 45–7, 52, 55–9, 84–7, 254, 266, 390–91
    and Church, 46, 169, 176, 216, 253–54, 265–66, 271–72, 390–91, 396
    as curse, 172, 314
    death of, 28, 131–35, 164, 171–72, 200, 230–32, 246–49, 263, 314–15, 322–23, 336–38, 370, 387, 397, 407
    and disciples, 46, 47, 102, 108–9, 124–25, 191–92, 230, 233–34, 284, 400
    as driver, 54–5
    and the Father: see God, and Christ
    as flower, 252–53
    and Jacob, 155–57, 160, 237
    as the Jordan, 399–400
    as judge, 38, 109, 136, 253, 291, 414
    as king, 36–7, 73–4, 191, 195, 229, 250–51, 291, 323
    as lamb, 128, 150, 200, 293
    lineage of, 249–50, 272, 359
    as love, 28, 37
    as Messenger of Great Counsel, 402
    as Messias, 27
    and money, 32
    and mystical body, 176, 271, 294
    passion of, 10, 133–34, 157, 162, 195–98, 200, 246–49, 251, 253, 255–56, 259, 262–63, 304–5, 322–23, 336–38, 346, 356, 370, 387, 390, 414, 417
    and the patriarchs, 195
    and Paul, 218–32, 273–75, 371, 393–94
    and Peter, 18, 53, 221, 338, 349, 364, 386
    as physician, 371
    and prayer, 49, 356

prefigured by David, 413–14

prefigured by Isaac, 10, 15

prefigured by Jacob, 160

prefigured by Jona, 296–97

prefigured by Joseph, 187–237, 266-73

prefigured by patriarchs, 239–75

as priest, 156, 250, 263, 285, 290–91, 293–94, 322

as prize, 54, 172 n.

raises dead, 37, 95, 131, 225–26, 246, 300, 339–40, 346, 373, 416

as redeemer, 107, 128, 133–36, 193, 196–97, 201, 217, 227–32, 248–50, 252–53, 256, 300, 312, 322, 336–39, 371, 373, 402, 409, 415–16

as refuge, 403

as reproach, 172

resurrection of, 28, 33–4, 63, 131, 144, 164, 166, 172, 191, 234-35, 249, 253, 259–61, 263, 270–71, 297, 322, 337–38, 345–46, 349, 418

as rider, 260

as seal, 59, 338

as Siloe, 399

as sin, 172

as Son of Man, 27, 41, 229, 295, 297, 312, 390, 399-400

and soul, 9, 15–23, 28–59, 394, 397, 412–13

as source of life, 64

as stag, 389–93

as stone, 402

as sun of justice, 19, 28, 132, 164, 337, 382

and synagogue, 160, 391

as victim, 271, 416

as vine, 27, 254–55

as Wisdom of God, 101

Christians, 2, 52, 151, 162, 279, 335, 371–72, 376 n., 401

Church, 2, 15, 22, 27, 28, 29, 31, 39, 46, 50, 52, 148, 151, 157, 160, 165–66, 169, 176, 181, 199, 216, 217 n., 231–32, 235, 244, 249, 253–54, 257, 265–66, 271–72, 274, 286, 298, 302, 305, 345, 376, 390–92, 396, 401, 415

Cicero, 13 n., 102 n., 135 n., 145 n., 295 n.

circus, 283

cithara, 90, 171, 183, 362, 419

cities of refuge, 283–90, 296, 322

clay, 78, 94, 97, 334, 339, 341, 366, 404, 406

Cleanthes, 64 n.

Cleophas, 61

clothing, 12, 21, 35, 45, 48, 58, 65, 132, 150–51, 158, 191, 200, 205–7, 210, 220, 222, 225, 228, 232–33, 255, 263, 294, 344–45, 355, 365, 374–75, 383, 401; *see also* robe, tunic and wedding garment

clouds, 108, 229, 302, 323, 345, 347, 357, 366

coals, 61, 355

cobweb, 367

Cocytus, 94

cold, 108, 306

column, Church as, 157, 166

commandment, 70-1, 88, 104, 111-12, 128-30, 148, 206, 231, 256, 286, 289, 292, 314, 316, 321, 375, 384, 411; see also law

compassion: see mercy

concupiscence, 45, 50, 53, 119-22, 128, 130, 131, 174

confession, 31; 37, 151, 212, 219, 236-37, 341-43, 357-58

confusion, 261, 281, 379

Conia, 404

conscience, 45, 64, 86, 92, 93, 99, 104, 105, 137, 145, 153, 321, 333, 341, 347, 355, 358

contest, 37, 38, 76, 282, 303, 331, 356-57, 370, 376, 380, 414-15

contract, 76, 201

Corinthian, 256, 258

counsel, 50, 91, 101, 137, 147, 149, 153, 167, 179, 196, 202, 214, 247-49, 266-67, 313, 322, 341, 343, 348, 360, 398, 402

courage, 144, 171, 177

Courcelle, P., 4, 9 n., 22 n., 42 n., 50 n., 59 n., 62 n., 64 n., 69 n., 71 n., 73 n., 79 n., 81 n., 85 n., 94 n., 95 n., 97 n., 102 n., 103 n., 109 n., 117 n., 119 n., 135 n., 170 n., 187 n., 210 n., 376 n., 419 n.

Couvée, P. J., 73 n.

cow, 213-14, 215, 361, 365

cowardice, 143

crops, 50, 306, 313, 344, 360, 371; see also harvest

cross, 28, 31, 54, 131, 132, 164, 166, 172, 195, 197-98, 220, 230, 232, 246, 255, 259, 265, 271, 284, 322-23, 330, 336-37, 356, 387, 390, 407

crown, 36-8, 103, 134, 207, 249, 270, 282, 296, 303, 353, 357; see also palm, victor's and wreath

cruelty, 153, 208, 231

CSEL: see Schenkl, K.

cup, 135, 147, 209, 211, 226-27, 322

curse, 170, 172, 258, 312-15, 347, 356-57, 375, 385

curtain of temple, 200

cypress, 27

Damascus, 408

Dan, 260-61

Daniel, 107, 142, 143, 166, 173, 410

darkness, 51, 72, 100, 108, 112-13, 177, 198, 257-58, 274, 302, 332, 361, 378, 382-83, 388, 399, 403, 415, 417, 419

David, 14, 46, 62, 73, 74, 98, 110, 120-21, 144, 151, 171, 190 n., 215, 250, 252-53, 272, 279, 282-83, 296, 300-1, 302-5, 308, 320, 330, 343, 348, 352, 356, 368-420

day, 31, 56, 62, 71, 73, 79, 107, 147 180-81, 208-9, 226, 295,

297, 331, 337–38, 344, 345, 378, 395, 408, 415

death, 10, 36, 37, 43, 60, 64–5, 67–113, 126, 128–36, 137, 140, 144, 154, 166, 168–84, 198, 204, 209, 210, 212, 217, 222, 230, 235, 236, 248, 250, 258, 261, 263–64, 265, 282, 286–87, 289–90, 291, 296, 300, 306–8, 309–10, 312, 314–15, 320–21, 322, 323, 329, 333, 336–37, 340, 344–46, 350, 359, 365–67, 370, 373–74, 387, 388, 394, 397, 407, 419

deceit, 45, 77, 148, 152, 160, 166, 174, 179, 208, 211, 213, 227, 309, 311–14, 329, 370, 385, 390, 410, 412, 415, 418

deer, 84, 392

Deferrari, R. J., viii, 1 n., 254 n.

denarii, 197

descent, 289, 398

desert, 30, 35, 46, 263, 304, 307

desertion, 194

devil, 41, 45, 88, 125, 136, 160, 200, 260–61, 273, 299–301, 303, 311, 354, 364, 374, 385–86, 391–92, 393, 409–13; see also accuser, adversary, Antichrist, Satan, and serpent

devotion, 24, 41, 44, 47, 61, 134, 149, 151, 161, 164, 176, 181, 183, 189, 216, 222, 230, 235, 251, 254, 259, 360, 390, 398, 412

dew, 41, 264, 270, 323, 365

Diederich, Sr. M. Dorothea, S.S.N.D., 4 n., 187 n.

Dina, 164, 247

disciples: see Christ, and disciples

discipline, 124, 204, 347

Doeg, 213

Dothain, 194, 316

dove, 30, 31, 48, 49, 183, 255, 303, 323, 389, 391, 394

doxology, 279 n., 323, 388, 420

dragon, 366

dream, 173, 191–92, 195, 208–15, 331, 333–34, 353, 382; see also sleep

drought, 148

drugs, 371

Dudden, F. Homes, 1 n., 9 n., 30 n., 68 n., 117 n., 143 n., 187 n., 209 n., 213 n., 241 n., 279 n., 327 n., 362 n., 407 n.

dung, 353, 371

dust, 102, 175, 183, 341, 364, 406

eagle, 17, 82, 305, 323, 341, 405, 419

ear, 15, 77, 78, 91, 99, 166, 252, 282, 297, 313

ears of grain, 214–15

earth, 14, 25, 29, 30, 35, 38, 48, 53, 61, 63, 73, 74, 78, 81, 82, 84, 88, 90, 102, 162, 180, 192, 230, 232, 235, 263, 267, 268, 270–72, 281, 283, 290, 297, 301–2, 307, 310–11, 312, 314, 315, 329, 331, 335–37, 339, 344–48, 353, 361, 364,

366, 367, 371, 374, 375–76, 381, 383, 386–87, 391, 394, 396, 400–2, 404–5, 412, 416, 420
Easter, 30 n., 69
Ecclesiastes, 359, 394
Edinger, H. G., 295 n.
Edwards, Mark, S. M., 118 n.
Egypt, 12, 167, 169, 172, 200–37, 243, 296, 306, 361, 381, 398–99
Eleazar, 117, 173–75
elements, the four, 48
Elias, 61, 107, 144, 258, 285, 307–08, 329–30
Eliphaz, 352
Eliseus, 144, 307
Emmet, C. W., 117 n.
Empedocles, 13 n.
emperor, 74, 163, 327, 348; see also ruler and tyrant
Enmity, well of, 23–4
enmity, 24, 29, 90, 154–58, 189, 191, 195–96, 200, 314
Enos, 11
ensigns, 409–13
envy, 81, 122, 190, 191, 196, 266–67, 322, 336, 372
Ephraim, 215, 216, 243–45, 271–72
Ephrata, 165
Epictetus, 93 n.
Epistles, Pauline, 2, 187
epithalamium, 36–7
equity, 377, 415
Erasmus, 328, 401 n.
Esau, 49–50, 123, 149–55, 161–62, 318–19
Esdras, 69, 102, 107, 142

eucharist, 223 n., 263 n.
Eugenius, Emperor, 383 n.
eunuch, 208–14
Eve, 34–5, 42, 127–28
evening, 108, 216, 273, 331
Evening Star, 335; see also star
exegesis, allegorical, 2–3, 9, 188
exile, 146, 155, 156
Exodus, the, 46, 61, 349
eye, 24, 40, 47, 59, 64, 77, 78, 88–9, 91, 98–9, 106, 111, 126, 147, 160, 168–69, 171, 182, 183, 193, 203–4, 224, 236–37, 251, 256, 275, 282–83, 297, 298, 301–2, 322, 332, 333, 360, 367, 373, 411, 415
Ezechia, 360
Ezechias, 141–42, 151

failure, 194 n., 316–17, 364, 381, 387, 413
faith, 21, 23, 24, 26, 31, 34, 37, 38, 39, 40, 44, 45, 47, 52, 54, 58, 59, 61, 74, 107, 108, 110, 111, 112, 134, 139, 140, 143, 148, 150–51, 156–57, 161, 162, 164, 165–66, 172, 175, 176, 178, 179, 181, 183, 189, 197, 199, 200, 206, 215, 216–17, 218, 219, 222, 223, 225–27, 235, 244, 251, 254, 256–57, 259, 265, 269, 272, 274–75, 287, 290–91, 293, 295, 296, 298, 299–300, 315, 319–20, 323, 338, 341, 349, 360, 362, 364, 375–76, 390–

91, 394, 401, 411–12, 414, 416, 420
famine: *see* hunger
farmer, 258–59, 275, 306, 370
fasting, 375, 413
fat, 195, 214, 365, 375, 417
fawn, 389, 392
fear, 25, 50, 53, 61, 62, 71, 79, 93–4, 107, 111, 112–13, 122, 125, 136, 140, 142, 144, 153, 162, 167, 171, 174, 175, 176, 177, 182, 202, 204, 217, 222, 225, 230, 234–35, 243, 257, 265, 288–89, 293, 306, 307, 320, 323, 329, 331–33, 347, 351, 353, 360–61, 366, 370, 386, 388, 392–93, 397–98, 414, 420
feet, 16, 21, 34–5, 42, 63–4, 98, 111, 112, 132, 197, 228, 230, 254, 264, 271, 300–1, 314, 349, 366, 372, 399
fetters, 72, 75, 76, 202, 208, 394
field, 14, 28, 39, 49–50, 56, 88, 147–48, 150, 203, 318–19, 365, 370, 390
fig tree, 31, 35, 58, 120, 148
Figueroa, G., 31 n., 151 n., 165 n.
finger, 43–4, 215, 374, 404
fire, 13, 35, 48, 60–2, 100, 178–79, 202, 220, 282, 311, 320, 329, 355, 378, 406, 411–12
firstborn: *see* birthright
fish, 297, 408
flattery 173, 418
flight, 14, 17–9, 29–30, 35–6, 44, 63–4, 82–4, 100, 193, 208,

277–323, 341, 346, 356, 363, 373, 388, 390, 394
flock, 20, 21, 22, 56, 156–57, 249, 298, 365, 417
flood, 183–84, 298, 311
flowers, 28, 30, 39, 56, 85, 147, 183, 252–53, 343, 391
food, 39–40, 79, 86, 122, 144, 148, 150, 164, 165, 173–74, 200–1, 210, 212, 216–17, 218, 220, 256, 263, 274, 307, 317–19, 341, 363, 365, 375
fool, 94, 152, 310, 322, 332–33, 342–43, 361, 379, 382
foot: *see* feet
footstep, 17, 21, 42, 189, 260, 282, 298, 310, 313, 322, 370, 372, 381, 388
forgetfulness, 88, 211–12, 216, 244, 330, 341, 363, 367, 385, 387, 405–6, 409
forgiveness, 10, 17, 30, 59–60, 70, 73, 82, 92, 109, 112, 131, 132, 134, 150–51, 157, 162, 164, 171, 190, 197, 221–22, 230, 236, 254, 258, 264, 289, 291, 296, 305–6, 314, 336, 340–43, 356, 371, 376, 407, 415, 418
fortitude, 53–4, 174, 340
fountain, 11, 24, 25, 26, 28, 33, 38–9, 62, 85, 86, 138, 198, 270, 287, 320, 393–95, 399
fox, 254 n.
fragrance, 16–7, 35–6, 39, 49, 56, 58–9, 85, 147–48, 151, 196, 198, 219, 232, 252–53, 282, 318, 390; *see also* smell, sense of

frankincense, 36; *see also* incense

fratricide, 146, 149, 154–55, 161, 194–95

free will, 119, 125–28, 152–53, 290

frugality, 144

fruit, 27, 31, 38, 39, 48, 49, 50, 52, 55, 56, 57 n., 70–1, 85, 120, 126, 147–48, 156, 159, 162, 166, 167, 191, 215, 221, 236, 259, 265, 270, 306, 319, 329, 332, 338, 364

fugitive, 283–90, 307, 331

Furies, 94

furnace, 62

fury: *see* wrath

Gad, 262–63

Galilee, 230

Gallagher, J., 247 n.

garment: *see* clothing *and* wedding garment

gate, 111, 121, 159, 221, 359, 411–12

gazelle, 32, 40

Gelenius of Prague, 342 n.

Gentiles, 62, 154, 161, 216, 226, 237, 253, 258, 272, 274, 318, 336, 376, 386, 408

Gera, 356

Gerara, 23, 24

giant, 17, 391

Gideon, 335

glory, 37, 38, 41, 47, 63, 64, 97, 98, 100, 103–6, 109, 112, 113, 133, 134, 144, 145, 163, 182, 183, 202, 209, 216, 221, 228, 265, 267, 272, 295, 296, 301–2, 309, 329–30, 333, 353, 361, 368, 370, 382, 385–86, 387, 398, 420

gluttony, 122–23

goat, 200, 306, 417

God

and Adam, 97–8, 375, 416–17

and Abraham, 107, 223, 300

and Christ, 28, 34–5, 37 n., 46, 59, 112, 172, 196–97, 200, 229, 234, 236–37, 251, 252, 253, 254–55, 261, 262, 263, 267–69, 272, 283, 286–87, 290, 293–95, 300, 350–51, 356, 386–87, 389, 393, 399–401, 407–9, 414, 416–17

clemency of, 286

as Creator, 182, 206, 227, 244, 286–88, 291, 341, 356, 363, 366, 378–79, 382–83, 398, 404–6, 409

and David, 14, 74, 98, 120–21, 155, 303–5, 320, 330, 343, 348, 352, 368–420

and Esdras, 107

glory of, 106, 388, 398, 420

goodness of, 19, 64, 92, 97, 110–11, 308–9, 369–72, 388

as husbandman, 254–55

and Jacob, 25, 107, 157, 161–73, 235, 296–302, 317–20

and Job, 329–67, 374, 392

and Joseph, 123, 193, 196–97

as judge, 178, 272, 340–41,
346–47, 354–55, 358, 388,
414
justice of, 269, 290–91, 377,
381
knowledge of 11, 17, 286,
321, 332, 347, 350–51,
366, 377, 382, 406
as love, 59, 269, 286–87, 390
and man, 87–8, 340–41, 345,
353, 361, 366, 368, 371–
72, 378–79, 380–84, 387–
88, 403–6, 409, 411–12,
415–20
as painter, 83–4
patience of, 92, 377
as potter, 404
and prayer, 35–6, 327–420
as president of contest, 357
prophecies of, 146, 403
as protector, 54–5, 264, 266,
268, 330, 342, 403–7
as refuge, 286–87, 315, 405
and soul, 21–2, 42, 48, 54,
82, 86–7, 97–8, 100, 101,
102, 315–16, 388, 394–96
vengeance of, 75, 381
as watchman, 84
Goliath, 74
gold, 15, 19, 62, 83, 87, 88,
128, 159, 179, 196–97, 216,
217, 232, 234, 259, 301, 339,
349–50, 366–67
Gomorra, 361
Gorce, D., 9 n., 10 n., 22 n.,
118 n.
Gospel, 2, 16, 33, 46, 47, 56,
73, 125, 144, 156, 190, 197,
217, 219, 225, 231, 246, 253,

290–91, 301, 314, 321, 332,
346, 357, 363, 372, 377, 396,
399, 402, 407, 409, 411
grace, 10, 11, 15, 16, 17, 20,
24, 28, 30, 35, 37, 39, 40, 46,
50, 74, 82, 85, 96, 110, 125,
128–33, 136, 137, 138, 139,
144, 145, 146, 147, 148, 149,
152, 154, 155, 156, 157, 158,
160, 164, 166, 167, 170, 171,
178, 181, 189, 190, 191, 196,
197, 201, 203, 210, 215, 218,
219, 221, 225, 226, 227, 228,
233, 235, 237, 245, 249, 250,
251, 253, 254, 256, 258, 259,
261, 265, 266, 267, 270–71,
274–75, 295, 306–7, 309–10,
315, 316, 323, 330, 335, 342,
360, 362, 370, 372, 384, 390,
393–95, 397–98, 416, 419
grain, 46, 49, 167, 217–19, 222,
231, 259, 264
grape, 20, 49, 148, 171, 209,
251, 255
Gratian, Emperor, 383 n.
grave: see tomb
Great Bear, 335; see also star
greed, 72, 87, 89, 91, 111, 201–
2, 249, 333–34, 366–67; see
also avarice
Greek, 291
Gregory the Great, St., 27 n.
Gryson, R., 69 n., 151 n., 156
n., 263 n., 290 n., 371 n.
guilt, 42, 78, 81, 95, 98, 125,
126, 127, 128, 130, 133, 146,
179, 196, 203–6, 213, 221,
225, 282, 287–89, 323, 334,
342, 344, 380, 411

Hadot, P., 3 n., 9 n., 69 n.
Haides, 102
hail 108
hair, 173, 175, 197, 412
Ham, 258
hammer, 412
hand, 15, 18, 22, 28, 43–4, 59, 77, 78, 100–1, 108, 123, 126, 143, 168–69, 171, 172, 195, 197–98, 199, 205, 206, 209, 210, 227, 229, 230, 234, 236–37, 244, 248, 250–51, 266, 299–300, 304, 308–9, 310, 318, 321, 337, 338, 341–42, 345–46, 347, 349, 357, 363, 366, 369, 372, 377–78, 385–86, 392, 393, 400, 404–05, 407, 412, 417
harbor, 81, 93, 96, 135, 167, 175, 181, 257, 298, 323, 418
harlot, 26, 88–9, 99, 126, 210, 248, 282, 308, 388; see also adulteress
harp, 145
Harris, V., 2 n.
hart, 28, 32, 40, 99, 320
harvest, 30, 219, 306, 364, 370, 391; see also crops
haven: see harbor
head, 41, 45, 56, 59, 176, 181, 182, 212, 215, 244, 266, 270–71, 273, 294, 310, 314, 411–12.
health, 140, 144, 170, 354, 371
hearing, 15, 77, 89, 91, 99, 166, 167, 183, 275, 282, 297
heart, 16, 29, 32, 36, 40, 43, 44, 49, 59, 60, 61, 62, 77, 78, 86, 88, 92, 96, 97, 99, 101, 106, 124, 125, 126, 132, 133, 144, 145, 151, 159, 162, 163, 167, 175, 177, 181, 189, 198, 203, 204, 220, 224, 227, 230, 234, 235, 247, 249, 258, 261, 269, 281–82, 288, 292, 297, 308, 313, 322, 330, 332–33, 337, 339, 340, 341, 347, 353, 361, 363, 367, 368–69, 371–72, 375–76, 377–79, 383, 387, 395, 397, 399, 409–13, 418
heat, 100, 343
heaven, 17, 18, 19, 21, 28, 29, 33, 41, 48, 52, 54, 61, 76, 77, 79, 82, 104, 107, 135, 143, 145, 147, 152, 165, 170, 178, 180, 227, 229, 230, 231, 256, 261, 263–64, 266, 267, 268, 270–71, 289, 290, 293–96, 299, 301, 305, 310, 311–12, 315, 329–30, 333, 335, 337–38, 344–45, 348, 352, 357, 362–64, 366, 375–76, 383–84, 385–86, 394–97, 400–2, 405, 414; see also paradise
Hebrew, 12, 44, 65, 207, 209, 210, 220, 223, 292, 296, 306, 317, 336, 399, 410; see also Israel and Jew
heel, 260, 262, 314–15, 392, 413
heifer: see cow
hell, 35, 102, 111, 183, 210, 346, 348, 362–63, 366, 373, 382
Hellenistic Age, 3
helmet, 176
Henoch, 61
heretic, 257, 327, 362

Hermon, 37, 38, 398–99, 401

Herod, 253

hill, 28, 40, 171, 196, 266, 269–70, 272, 346, 391, 401

Hippolytus, 9, 28 n., 241

hireling, 79, 331–32; *see also* servant

holiness, 144, 153, 156, 177, 181–84, 195, 230, 250, 262, 296, 309, 405, 412

Holy Spirit, 33, 35, 61, 107, 125, 169, 212, 231, 232, 234, 254, 255, 275, 304, 345–46, 360, 418–19

Homer, 3, 123 n.

honey, 31, 39, 85–7, 102, 183, 219

hope, 11, 26, 38, 139, 142, 167, 208, 221, 223, 259, 283, 304, 323, 329, 331–32, 334, 336, 370–71, 387, 388, 397–98, 409, 413, 415.

horns, 249, 270–73

horse, 22, 53–5, 61, 64, 260–61, 283, 329, 413

horseman, 260–61, 390, 413

humility, 23, 77, 124, 127, 161, 219, 223, 289, 367, 371, 406

hunger, 91, 165, 167, 169, 202, 210, 214–19, 263, 329, 332, 334, 365, 397

hunting, 150, 318–19, 395

husbandman: *see* farmer

Hydra, 94

hymns, antiphonal singing of, 1

hyssop, 419

idols, 161, 165–66, 299, 302, 388, 410–11

ignorance, 50, 111, 128, 133, 299, 310, 336, 343, 380, 384

Ihm, M., 279 n.

imagination, 14, 93, 333

immortality, 81, 100, 105, 124, 165, 169, 170, 182

impiety, 92, 133, 151, 308, 341, 373

impudence, 99; *see also* insolence

impunity, 207

impurity, 27, 99, 205, 248; *see also* incontinence

incarnation: *see* Christ, birth of

incense, 35–6, 156, 198, 220, 347; *see also* frankincense

incontinence, 375, 419; *see also* impurity

India, 184

infant, 106, 306, 344, 365, 394; *see also* children

ingratitude, 128, 204, 243

inheritance, 98, 105, 107, 110, 127, 134, 146, 182, 190, 221, 243, 247, 248, 253, 258, 259, 332, 357, 359, 366–67, 376, 385, 404, 409, 416

iniquity, 27, 33, 61, 76, 86, 108, 111, 112, 126, 158–59, 215, 259, 300–02, 306, 309, 341–42, 346, 354, 361, 374–75, 382

injustice, 24, 53, 71, 79, 133, 208, 213, 353–54, 361, 370

Injustice, well of, 23–4

innocence, 35, 70, 100, 104, 133, 311, 343, 365, 378

insensibility, 306, 384

insolence, 86, 205, 245–46; *see also* impudence

integrity, 39, 45, 80, 289, 315; *see also* uprightness

intemperance, 78, 155, 161

iron, 140, 264, 413

Isaac, 9–65, 96, 108, 118, 148–54, 189, 235, 241 n., 244, 297, 300, 317–19

Isaia, 61, 173, 193, 210, 392, 402

island, 417–18

Ismaelites, 196–97

Israel, 22, 54, 147, 165, 170, 193, 195, 228, 235, 237, 242, 244, 245, 246, 249, 260, 262, 264, 266, 267, 268, 295, 369, 371–72, 376; *see also* Hebrew *and* Jew

Issachar, 258–59, 275

Ixion, 94

Jacob, 24, 26, 36, 49, 65, 73, 96, 107, 108, 117–18, 123, 124, 146–73, 189, 191–93, 200, 217–18, 222, 228–37, 241–42, 243–75, 279, 296–302, 317–20, 380, 390, 400

James, 178, 336

jealousy, 149

Jeremia, 60, 142, 173, 199, 220, 313 n., 404

Jerome, 407 n.

Jerusalem, 46, 83, 134, 191, 412

Jerusalem, daughters of, 35–7, 45, 148, 390

Jerusalem, heavenly, 33, 46, 63, 305 n., 382–83

Jesse, 252

Jew, 3, 11, 27, 46, 58, 102 n., 120, 151, 153–54, 195, 198, 200, 214, 216, 221, 227–29, 231–32, 234–37, 244, 245–47, 252–53, 257, 272, 290–91, 335–36, 375–77, 390–91, 399–400, 404, 409, 410, 414; *see also* Hebrew *and* Israel

Jezabel, 307

Job, 96, 329–67, 374, 389

John the Baptist, 43, 152, 262, 279, 307, 345, 393

John the Evangelist, 33, 58, 112, 178, 235, 336, 350

Jona, 3, 296–97, 408

Jordan, 28, 255, 258, 283, 288–89, 398–401

Josaphat, 339–40

Joseph, 20, 26, 118, 123, 152, 158, 167–68, 171, 172–73, 187–237, 243–45, 266–71, 316, 375, 400, 413

Josias, 151

Josue, 254, 260, 335, 348

joy, 11, 15, 90, 92, 104–5, 141, 144, 168, 169, 180, 191, 254, 255, 256, 265, 282, 302, 309, 315–17, 329, 338–40, 344, 370, 391, 394, 396–97, 400, 405, 416–18

Juda, 165, 171, 195–97, 219, 228, 236, 250–53

Judas, 197, 260–61, 385, 390

Judea, 198, 216, 235, 305

judgment, 20, 80, 81, 92, 93, 102–4, 136, 137, 149, 153, 158, 223, 227, 261, 262, 272, 291, 315, 321, 336, 339–40, 343–44, 346–47, 354–56, 358–60, 362, 374, 385, 388, 403, 414

Jupiter, 84

justice, 14, 20, 25, 39, 46, 53–4, 61, 78, 89, 101, 111, 125–27, 138, 140, 149, 158, 159, 174, 207, 223, 227, 262, 269, 282, 291, 293, 295, 299, 306, 309, 322, 342, 354, 357, 360, 377, 381, 395, 403, 417

Justina, Empress, 1

kindness, 153, 161, 204, 209, 211, 223, 342, 417

kingdom, 18, 21, 37, 38, 45, 63, 108, 109, 151–52, 169, 200, 211, 232, 253, 285, 296, 306, 345, 363, 380, 392, 396, 408

kiss, 15–6, 40, 57, 197, 282, 390

knowledge, 11, 16–7, 25, 51, 62, 70, 77, 85, 88, 91, 110, 128, 129, 131, 200–1, 206, 216, 235, 263, 273, 286–87, 294, 297–98, 307, 312, 317, 332, 336, 347, 350–51, 354, 362, 366, 368, 375, 377, 379–80, 384, 385, 411

Laban, 156–60, 297–302

Lactantius, 145 n.

lacunae in the Latin text, 94 n., 98 n., 103 n., 167 n., 211

n., 294 n., 332 n., 339 n., 342 n., 391 n., 409 n.

Laistner, M. L. W., 376 n.

lamb, 57, 150, 152, 198, 293, 417

lamp, 33, 100, 181, 200, 227, 345, 364, 399

lampstand, 380

lantern, 142

laughter, 10, 174, 317, 340, 355–58, 377, 395

law, 13, 17, 27, 32, 33, 46, 55, 72, 76, 104, 119, 121, 122–23, 124, 127–33, 147, 153–54, 156, 160, 161, 172, 173, 174, 175, 176, 178, 181, 195, 198, 199, 215, 217, 219, 227, 246, 254, 262, 273, 283, 285, 286, 288–89, 291–92, 296, 307, 311, 335, 396, 402–3, 409–10, 415; *see also* commandment

Lazarus, 95, 108, 225, 363, 373–74

leaves, 375

Lebanon, 26, 37, 42, 300, 381, 411

Leclercq, H., 393 n.

leisure, 33, 145, 180

Lent, 2

leopard, 37, 176, 254 n.

leprosy, 398

Lesousky, Sr. M. Alphonsine, O.S.U., 281

Levi, son of Jacob, 62, 124, 170, 247–50, 271

Levi, priest, 250

Levites, 283–86, 336

Lia, 160

life, 12, 25, 30, 35, 38, 45, 62,

64, 70–81, 85, 86, 87, 89, 90, 91–6, 97, 98, 99, 100, 109, 110–13, 125, 128, 129, 136, 137, 138, 140, 143, 144, 147, 156, 163, 167, 168, 170, 174, 178, 179, 180, 181, 198, 217, 218, 219, 221, 222, 230–31, 233, 234–35, 236, 250, 255, 263–64, 282, 285–87, 290, 293, 295, 296, 300, 302, 306, 308–10, 312, 313, 314–15, 320, 323, 330, 331, 337, 340–41, 343–45, 347, 352, 353, 359, 360, 361–62, 363–65, 368, 370, 374, 376–77, 378, 379, 381, 394, 395–96, 400, 403, 413, 415, 419

light, 20, 25, 28, 31, 38, 41, 46, 47, 51, 52, 57, 61, 63, 64, 79, 90, 100, 104–6, 108, 110, 113, 142, 151, 160, 180, 181, 183, 192, 202, 218, 223, 225, 227, 248, 252, 257–58, 270, 274, 294, 302, 309, 312, 332, 337–38, 345, 362, 364, 378, 380, 383, 395–96, 398–99, 403, 413, 415, 419

lightning, 108, 311–12, 362

lily, 28, 46, 56

limb, 171, 174, 178, 182, 341, 374

lime, 83

lion, 37, 171, 173, 195, 250–53, 254 n., 261, 262, 342, 347, 367

lips, 16, 88, 363, 374, 418

Lloyd, A. C., 3 n.

loaves of proposition, 46

logismos, 123 n.

Lot, 279, 282, 299, 321–22

love, 16, 25, 26, 27, 28, 31, 37, 40, 41, 42, 43, 52, 54, 55, 56, 58–62, 82, 83, 85, 88, 108, 133, 135, 136, 137, 138, 148, 149–50, 155, 168, 175, 176, 181, 183–84, 190–92, 195, 197, 202, 204–05, 221, 224, 227, 234, 236, 267, 269, 274, 286, 287–89, 293, 294, 308, 309, 370, 373, 378, 387, 390, 401, 413, 418

lust, 22, 75, 83, 99, 126, 147, 202–07, 248, 261, 282, 292, 295, 298, 320

McGuire, M. R. P., viii, 1 n., 75 n., 126 n., 143 n., 307 n.

Machabees, 173–84

McHugh, M. P., 418 n.

Macrobius, 13 n., 264 n.

Maes, B., 53 n., 71 n., 292 n.

Mamre, 223

man
  free, 127–28, 153–54
  happy, 146
  just, 19, 141, 143, 144, 163, 192–95, 204–5, 291–92, 303, 305, 311, 335, 340–43, 352, 354, 356, 360–61, 364–65, 367, 369–70, 373, 380, 394, 405, 409
  rich, 201–2, 261, 306, 310, 333, 363, 366–67, 373
  unjust, 334, 341–43, 352, 413–14
  wicked, 291, 300–1, 334, 340, 341–42, 350, 353, 359, 363–67, 379–83

Manasse, 168–69, 216, 243–45, 271–72

manure, 371

marriage, 24, 36–7, 41, 85, 146, 160, 254, 298 n., 313 n., 362, 366

martyr: *see* martyrdom

martyrdom, 60, 181, 183, 373

Mary of Cleophas, 34

Mary Magdalene, 34

Mary, mother of Christ, 43, 44, 252–53, 267–69, 272, 275, 359, 401, 407–8

Maximus, 1, 383 n.

mercy, 17, 29, 53, 70, 89, 90, 157, 165, 172, 178, 179, 181, 190, 208, 221, 231, 258, 274, 286, 289, 294, 306, 341, 376, 399, 403, 417

Merlan, P., 3 n.

Mesopotamia, 296–97

Messius: *see* Arusianus Messius

metaphor, 4, 81 n., 257 n.

Metzger, B. M., 104 n.

Michea, 381

Migne, J. P., vii, 5, 327 n.

Milan, 1, 2, 187, 263 n., 407 n.

milk, 40, 57, 86, 171, 180–81, 215, 251, 256, 268, 341

mind, 12, 13, 19, 21, 26, 29, 51, 64, 76, 78, 84–5, 87, 119, 121–22, 123, 130, 131, 137, 138, 140, 145, 156, 170, 224, 226, 281–82, 287, 299, 355, 399

Mineans, 352

mirror, 106, 188, 189

mist, 264, 345

moderation, 14, 54, 64, 122, 129, 144, 148, 152, 174, 249, 288, 311, 378

modesty, 124, 164, 189, 203–7, 208, 224, 373, 391

Momigliano, A., 79 n., 102 n., 103 n., 109 n.

Monachino, V., 263 n.

money, 32, 144, 149, 153, 190–91, 196–97, 201, 219–20, 222, 227–28, 234, 249, 262, 301, 331–32, 360, 365, 366–67

Monica, 9

moon, 51, 52, 58, 108, 135, 152, 183, 191–92, 249, 266, 270

morality, systems of, 102 n.

Moretus, H., 241 n.

Moricca, U., 69 n., 187 n., 241 n., 279 n., 327 n.

Morino, C., 52 n., 125 n., 305 n.

Mornay, Philippe de, 69 n.

morning, 226, 273, 331, 378

moroseness, 83

Moses, 21, 24, 26, 46, 60, 107, 144, 172, 190 n., 221, 235, 241 n., 242, 250, 254, 259, 270–72, 279, 292, 294, 296, 300, 314, 335, 348–49, 384, 399, 405

moths, 367

Mount Choreb, 307

Mount Sion, 305

mountain, 28, 37, 40, 49, 171, 196, 266, 269–70, 305, 335–36, 346, 365, 391, 402

mules, 213

murder, 146, 164–65, 246, 274, 283–90, 310–11, 347, 416
music, 89–91, 145, 170–71, 362, 419–20; *see also* song
myrrh, 36, 39, 41, 43, 85–6, 220
mysteries, 15, 20, 26, 27, 33, 35, 40, 46, 146, 154, 164, 165, 192, 196, 198, 201, 210, 216, 218–19, 222, 223, 227, 230, 231, 236, 243, 244, 255, 265, 266–69, 283, 298–99, 335, 353, 362–63, 369, 376, 397, 415
myth, 79 n., 94

Naaman, 398
Naboth, 126 n.
Nabuchodonosor, 410
Nahasson, 54
nail, 83, 246, 322
nakedness, 206–7, 210, 365, 366, 375
Nathan, 250
Nathanael, 58
neck, 23, 54, 154, 215, 231, 246, 251, 265
nectar, 84, 87
Neoplatonists 3, 14 n., 69
Nephthali, 171–72, 257–58, 264–65
net, 29–30, 83, 84, 99, 204, 295, 302, 390–91
New Testament, 2, 103 n., 187, 217 n., 243, 259, 268, 279, 335, 402–3
New Year's Day, 393 n.
Niederhuber, J. E., 69 n.

night, 31, 32, 34, 40, 78, 79, 101, 147, 226, 235, 257–58, 274, 295, 297, 304, 331–33, 337–38, 345, 382, 395, 403
nightingale, 102
Nun, 254, 260, 335, 348
nut, 52

oak, 220, 223
Oath, well of, 23, 25, 235
obedience, 125, 126, 128, 134, 148, 174, 181, 302, 346, 381
Ochozias, 340 n.
oil, 18, 31, 33, 215, 217, 264
ointment, 16–7, 36, 85, 86, 148, 157, 197, 316, 377
old age, 72, 94–7, 103, 166–70, 173–76, 180, 218, 223, 225, 228, 237, 267, 343, 359–60, 418
Old Testament, 2, 5, 12, 48 n., 103 n., 104 n., 151, 190 n., 243, 259, 268, 279, 335, 402–3
Olivar, A., 28 n., 391 n.
olive tree, 49, 148
O'Neill, W. H., 3 n.
organ, 90
Origen, 3, 9, 48 n., 52 n., 69, 264 n.
orphan, 126, 365, 417
Orpheus, 170 n., 419 n.
Otten, R. T., 31 n., 37 n., 55 n., 60 n., 69 n., 175 n., 303 n., 322 n., 394 n., 402 n.

pain, 122, 123, 124, 140, 142, 144, 162, 220, 247, 282, 313, 330–31, 339–40, 354, 368–69,

374, 380, 392; *see also* suffering
Palanque, J. R., 1 n., 9 n., 35 n., 69 n., 117 n., 187 n., 241 n., 279 n., 327 n.
palm, victor's, 54–5, 103, 140; *see also* crown *and* wreath
palm tree, 55
parable, 32
paradise, 18–9, 39, 56, 70–1, 79, 85, 108, 124, 170, 181, 201, 232, 282, 321, 348, 383, 416–17; *see also* heaven
pardon: *see* forgiveness
Paredi, A., 1 n., 2 n., 4 n., 9 n., 69 n., 117 n., 241 n., 279 n., 327 n.
Pasch, 30, 152
passions, 15, 19, 22, 30, 42, 49, 50–1, 53, 83, 88, 91, 98–9, 111, 112, 119–26, 130–32, 134, 137, 153, 163, 170, 174, 204, 232, 246, 282, 285, 297, 343, 354, 397, 418; *see also* pleasure, bodily
patience, 11, 23, 92, 139, 141, 142, 144, 155, 176, 259, 291, 298, 375, 377
patriarch, 36, 39, 61, 96, 107, 150, 152–53, 162, 165, 168, 189, 192–93, 195–200, 217–37, 239–75
Paul, 3, 13, 18, 20, 28–9, 61, 75, 76, 107, 110, 112, 127, 218–32, 235, 242, 243, 273–75, 279, 293, 321, 329, 348, 356, 371, 393–94, 419
Paulus, 274
peace, 23, 32, 48-9, 54, 72, 84,

112, 141, 148, 157, 162–63, 222, 230, 233, 247, 271, 301, 309, 315, 367, 372–73, 413; *see also* tranquillity
pearl, 217
Pelagius, 280
perfection, 19, 25, 42, 49, 51, 56, 59, 106, 117, 138–43, 158, 295, 369, 380, 387
perseverance, 32, 100, 104, 152, 175, 223, 257, 298
Peter, 18, 53, 63, 111, 162, 199, 217, 221, 235, 318, 330, 336, 338, 349, 364
Pharao, 22, 172, 202–37, 296
Pharisees, 46, 197, 316
Philemon, 110, 225
Philo, 3, 52 n., 53 n., 71 n., 187, 279, 328
philosopher, 55, 102, 107, 110, 187, 367
physician, 358, 371
piety, 23, 96, 101, 109, 152, 176, 197
Pilate, 229
pillar, 335–37
pillar of fire, 61
pillow, 345
pilot, 96, 142, 257
pipe, 90
plane tree, 156–57
Plato, 3, 9, 42 n., 71 n., 84–5, 87, 102 n., 107, 320, 322 n.
works of:
Apology, 107 n.
Gorgias, 95 n.
Phaedo, 71 n., 100 n., 107 n., 145 n.

Phaedrus, 53 n., 55 n.
Republic, 102 n., 295 n.
Symposium, 62 n., 63 n., 85 n., 87 n., 320 n.
pleasure, bodily, 12, 14, 17, 44–5, 50–1, 71–2, 75–7, 82, 88, 98–9, 122–23, 137, 140, 153, 163, 232, 281–82, 297, 343, 363, 386, 419; *see also* passions
Pleiades, 335
Plotinus, 3, 9, 50 n., 62 n., 69
ploughshare, 370
plow, 259, 361, 392
poison, 35, 129, 161, 260–61, 313–14, 341, 392–93
polemic, anti-Christian, 103 n., 109 n.
pomegranate, 38, 52, 148
Porphyry, 3, 9, 13 n., 65 n., 69, 71 n., 89 n.
port: *see* harbor
Portalupi, F., 69 n., 280 n.
Porus, 84
potter, 404
poverty, 96–7, 126, 143–45, 146, 157, 169–70, 202, 217, 243, 263, 331–32, 365, 371, 379, 380
power, 19, 21, 22, 34, 37, 43, 63, 87–8, 93, 100, 103, 109–10, 120, 122, 143, 144, 148, 153, 166, 168, 169, 172, 176, 177, 179, 196, 203, 204, 208, 209–12, 227, 230–31, 234, 252–53, 259, 262, 264, 266, 267, 272, 273, 281, 286–88, 290–91, 294, 297, 299, 303–4, 315, 334–35, 340, 341, 346, 350, 358, 366, 381, 385, 386, 390, 401, 412, 413
prayer, 35–6, 40, 46, 88, 106, 172, 173, 180, 182, 194, 196, 198, 220, 304, 308, 325–420
preaching, 2–3, 22, 73, 189, 219–20, 225, 228, 232, 234, 243, 274, 281, 314, 321
pride, 27, 122, 127, 128, 133, 222, 224, 310, 342, 363, 367, 372, 374, 412
priest, 143, 166, 173, 200, 213, 220, 227, 229, 246–49, 250, 262, 263, 274, 283–86, 289–90, 293–94, 320–21, 322, 336
Priscillian, 362 n.
prison, 73, 104, 172–73, 207–13, 274
Prodigal Son, 376
property, 65, 72, 87, 126, 143 n., 156–60, 167, 201–2, 203, 333
prophecy, 23, 29, 144, 145, 146, 150, 153–54, 162, 165, 166, 168, 171–72, 178, 192, 200, 207, 212, 227, 235–36, 243–75, 297, 346, 386, 403, 409
proposition, loaves of, 46
proselyte, 153, 292
Prosper of Aquitaine, 81 n., 418 n.
providence, 230, 289, 376–77, 379, 383-85, 403–07
prudence, 17, 53–4, 119, 121, 158, 167, 174, 298, 302, 343
psalms, signing of, 1
psalter, Greek, 198, 369, 407
psalter, Latin, 407

psaltery, 171, 183, 360, 362
Publius, 274
punishment, 60, 80, 92–5, 103, 137, 173–84, 213, 254, 286, 291–92, 312–15, 321, 333, 334, 353–54, 358, 361, 363, 365, 369–70, 374, 378, 379, 381, 406
purity, 21, 59, 106, 188, 189, 309
pyre, funeral, 101
Pythagoreans, 145 n.

Quasten, J., 241 n.

Rachel, 24, 160–61, 165–66, 274, 298 n., 302
rack, 174, 370
rage: see wrath
rain, 30, 85, 108, 391
ram, 306, 417
raven, 304
reason, 117, 119–24, 131, 137, 138, 175, 177, 224, 225, 344, 352, 384, 417
Rebecca, 9, 10–1, 14–5, 23, 45, 118, 148–50, 155, 296–98, 301, 318
redemption: see Christ, as redeemer
repentance, 32, 44, 92, 125 n., 128, 129, 133, 135–36, 246, 259, 291, 307, 323, 342, 383, 395
resurrection, 34, 37, 63, 81–2, 94–5, 105, 131, 139, 144, 164, 166, 171, 172, 191, 235, 249, 259, 261, 263, 270, 305, 315,

339–40, 344–46, 349, 373, 418
reward, 56, 102, 103, 105, 107, 110, 133, 134, 136, 137–40, 144, 147, 172, 173, 175, 176, 215, 231, 233, 258-59, 291, 317, 330, 342, 354, 357–59, 362–63, 370, 379–80, 387, 394, 400
riches: see wealth
ring, 215
river, 22, 44, 379, 395
robber, 18, 65, 108, 159
robbery: see theft
robe, 42, 171, 215, 251, 255; see also clothing
rock, 31, 94, 148, 344, 358, 365; see also stone
rod, 220, 252
Rome, 290
Room-enough, well of, 23–4, 26
rowing, 175 n.
Ruben, 195, 219, 245–46, 249, 250
ruler, 36, 202, 358, 383; see also emperor and tyrant
runner, 340; see also athlete

sabbath, 46, 306, 315
sack, 222, 226–28
sackcloth, 222, 251, 254
sacrifice, 10, 59, 74–5, 156, 215, 235, 271, 306, 319, 416–17
sacrilege, 158, 166, 194, 213, 216, 246, 311, 375, 388
saffron, 39

Sallust, 293 n.

salvation, 3, 31, 54, 59, 135, 147, 155, 164, 165, 174, 193, 200, 218, 220, 221, 227, 229, 232, 246, 249, 257, 259, 260–61, 267, 273, 283, 286, 288, 290, 292–93, 305, 307, 311, 317, 337, 361, 363, 372, 377, 387, 393, 398, 413

Samaria, 26, 408

Samson, 260, 357

sanctuary, 379–80

sandals, 254, 271, 300–1, 314

Sanir, 37, 38

Sara, 317

Satan, 45, 159, 286, 300, 311–12, 362, 364, 385; see also accuser, adversary, Antichrist, devil and serpent

Saul, 14, 272, 296, 303

Savage, J. J., 52 n., 53 n., 60 n., 84 n., 254 n., 271 n.

Schenkl, K., 5, 55 n., 94 n., 98 n., 103 n., 167 n., 187 n., 211 n., 294 n., 327, 328 n., 332 n., 339 n., 342 n., 391 n., 401 n., 409 n.

Schulte, F. X., 280 n.

scribes, 246–49, 262

Scripture, 2, 5–6, 49, 61, 70, 74, 86, 95, 97–8, 102, 103, 105, 124, 147, 187, 189, 204–6, 226, 266, 327, 329, 379, 397, 403–4, 417

scythe, 371

sea, 55, 81, 96, 167, 172, 184, 256–58, 259, 265, 323, 335, 338, 344, 347, 349, 366–67, 403, 418

Second Sophistic, 4, 81 n.

seed, 43, 87, 169, 171, 245, 250, 252, 313–14, 360, 364

Segor, 305

Selmon, 399

Semei, 356

Septuagint, 5–6, 369 n., 402 n.

sepulcher: see tomb

Seraphim, 61

serpent, 35, 54, 161, 260–61, 311–15, 385, 389, 391–92, 413; see also accuser, adversary, Antichrist, devil and Satan

servant, 44, 73, 108, 120, 142, 146, 153, 155–56, 165, 176, 193, 196, 201–07, 211–12, 213, 221, 223, 268, 270, 274, 292, 296, 300, 331, 356, 384, 410, 417; see also hireling and slavery

sexual intercourse, 11–2

shadow, 28, 40, 56, 58, 64, 111, 132, 151, 198, 258, 302, 304, 331, 343, 368, 381, 396, 399

shame, 97, 103–4, 121, 179, 180, 204, 208, 261, 323, 342, 343, 354, 359, 372

sheaf, 191

sheep, 150, 156, 192–93, 228, 267, 273–74, 298, 316, 362

sheepskin, 144

shepherd, 21, 22, 56, 249, 274, 365

ship, 63, 96, 142, 152–53, 256–58, 323, 338–39, 341, 418

shipwreck, 93, 96, 135, 142, 175, 183, 257, 298, 338, 343–44, 414, 418 shoe, 228, 264

shoulder, 193, 248, 258–59, 274–75, 401 n., 405

Shuhites, 352

Sibinga, J. Smit, 241 n.

Sibyl, 14 n.

Sichar, 26

Sichem, 193, 247–48, 400–1

Sidon, 256, 258

sight, 54, 74, 77–8, 89, 91, 98–9, 106, 168–69, 194, 209, 224, 226, 236, 244, 246, 275, 282, 297, 301, 335, 341, 343–44, 345, 366, 388, 416–17

Siloe, 399

silver, 15, 19, 61, 83, 87, 88, 91, 128, 159, 179, 197, 217, 220, 226–27, 234, 259, 301, 303, 339, 349, 367

Simeon, prophet, 72, 73, 193

Simeon, son of Jacob, 124, 170, 247–49

Simon the pharisee, 197, 316, 377

Simonetti, M., 241 n.

singing: see song

Sion, 134

Sirach, 331

Sirens, 183

slavery, 21, 74, 87, 98, 125, 126–28, 130, 143, 152–54, 166, 174, 201–07, 273, 331, 381, 402; see also servant

sleep, 40, 41, 86–7, 95, 145, 146, 162, 166, 210, 212, 253, 260–61, 303, 333, 344, 362–63, 365, 367, 382, 397; see also dream

sloth, 218

smell, sense of, 99, 282, 297; see also fragrance

snare, 30, 59, 77, 78, 83, 88–90, 99, 177, 204, 302, 394, 415

snow, 100, 399, 419

Socrates, 107

Sodom, 299, 311, 321–22, 361

soldier, 88, 96, 125, 142, 163, 273, 410

solitude, 78, 145, 285–86, 400

Solomon, 22, 25, 27, 33, 36, 85, 86, 138, 151, 250, 308, 339, 389, 400–1

song, 90–1, 102, 145, 170–72, 181, 183, 369, 407, 419–20; see also music

Sonny, A., 91 n.

Sophar, 352

Sophistic, Second, 4, 81 n.

sore, 179, 330–31, 353, 371, 374

Soulignac, A., 117 n.

sparrow, 302, 304–5

speech, 48, 88, 99, 129, 142, 170, 177–78, 205, 220, 224, 228, 275, 295, 318, 341, 343, 348, 355, 357, 374, 384, 392, 416

spheres, harmony of, 52

spices, 85

spider, 215

springtime, 39

staff, bishop's 52

stag, 138, 389–94

Stahl, W. H., 13 n.

star, 52, 105, 107, 108, 135, 183, 191–92, 335, 338, 376,

384, 386, 408; *see also* Evening Star *and* Great Bear
statue, 327, 410
steed: *see* horse
Stephen, 225
stone, 31, 199, 219, 305, 331, 402; *see also* rock
storax, 156
storm, 30, 137, 142, 162, 167, 257, 343–44, 357, 367, 414, 418
stubble, 364
stumbling-block, 372–73
suffering, 60, 134, 137, 173–84, 190, 212, 216, 296, 313, 329–30, 352–67, 370, 373, 397, 399; *see also* pain
Sulamite, 54
Sullivan, J. J., 75 n.
summer, 108
sun, 26, 27, 28, 52, 58, 64, 91, 92, 105, 106, 107, 108, 135, 164, 191–92, 266, 270, 302, 332, 335–38, 345, 384, 391
Susanna, 166, 207, 320–21
swan, 183
swine, 173–74
sword, 44, 124, 153, 248, 286, 399, 400–1
synagogue, 2, 31, 36, 151–52, 160, 199, 210, 221, 234, 345, 390–91, 396

Taormina, L, 50 n.
Tartarus, 94
taste, sense of, 27, 77, 99, 297
teaching, 25, 35, 48, 95, 122, 125, 130, 131, 154, 175, 176, 200, 220, 227, 232, 313, 316, 356, 384, 418, 419
teeth, 171, 251, 256, 260
Temanites, 352
temperance, 14, 53–4, 89, 101, 122–23, 124
temptation, 25, 30, 33, 38, 41, 42, 45, 52–3, 72, 88, 99, 163, 173–74, 177, 190, 207, 210, 260–61, 281–83, 295, 297–98, 308, 330–31, 343–44, 353, 363, 394, 403
Tertullian, 241
text of Ambrose, followed above, 5; readings of, 52 n., 55 n., 79 n., 94 n., 98 n., 101 n., 103 n., 167 n., 211 n., 264 n., 271 n., 294 n., 332 n., 339 n., 342 n., 391 n., 401 n., 409 n.
Tharsis, 55 n., 296, 323, 339
theater, 283
theft, 111, 143, 196, 292, 380
Theodosius, 1–2
Thessalonians, 420
Thessalonica, 2
thief: *see* robber
thigh, 164, 299
thirst, 91, 217, 320, 334, 393–95, 397
Thompson, T., 15 n., 17 n., 37 n., 59 n., 81 n., 86 n., 256 n., 285 n.
Thomson, Charles, 6 n.
thorns, 20, 28, 30, 35, 148
thunder, 366
thunderstorm, 108
Tityos, 94
tomb, 28, 34, 82, 97, 101, 159,

165–66, 169, 170, 253, 336, 340, 365

tongue, 99, 177–78, 233, 322, 340, 374, 375, 392

torrent, 52, 64, 137, 147, 307

tortoise, 419

touch, sense of, 77, 99, 419

tranquillity, 31, 32, 81, 105, 145, 147, 155, 162–63, 166, 202, 257, 309, 315, 367, 381, 418; *see also* peace

treachery: *see* deceit

treasure: *see* wealth

Trinity, 156, 302

trumpet, 273, 335

truth, 77, 78, 89, 93, 99, 109, 110, 143, 157, 166, 173, 176, 177, 208, 225, 250, 257, 260, 291, 309, 316–17, 322, 332, 357, 362, 377–78, 380, 384, 396, 415

tunic, 191, 195, 198, 200, 206, 374–75; *see also* clothing

turpentine tree, 165–66

turtledove, 391

tyrant, 173–84, 260, 352, 383; *see also* emperor *and* ruler

Ulysses, 183 n.

unbelief, 143, 161, 164, 166, 175, 177, 212, 227, 229, 234, 236, 246, 251, 295, 299, 320, 341, 362, 376–77

understanding, 62, 64, 124, 129, 162, 216, 287, 299, 304, 309, 320, 334, 335, 348, 367, 380, 413, 419

unicorn, 270–73

uprightness, 89, 106, 314, 372; *see also* integrity

usury, 111, 159

Valentinian II, Emperor, 1, 187, 209 n., 213 n.

vanity, 13–4, 15, 25, 37, 72, 91-2, 281, 283, 307, 317, 361, 366, 368

Vatican Council, Second, 247 n.

vengeance, 75, 124, 165, 190, 233–34, 247–48, 291, 305, 311, 355, 381

Venus, 84

Vergil, 4, 187, 327–28

works of:

Aeneid, 14 n., 21 n., 35 n., 83 n., 94 n., 95 n., 124 n., 162 n., 168 n., 170 n., 175 n., 183 n., 225 n., 257 n., 288 n., 416 n., 419 n.

Eclogues, 21 n., 87 n., 153 n., 215 n.

Georgics, 83 n., 159 n., 162 n., 271 n., 317 n., 361 n.

village, 56

vine, 27, 35, 52, 157, 171–72, 209, 251, 254–55, 264–65

vineyard, 20, 147–48, 365, 412

viper, 307, 392–93

virgin birth: *see* Christ, birth of

virginity, 39, 89, 164, 248

virtues, four cardinal, 53–4

von Campenhausen, Hans, 1 n.

vulture, 94

walnut bough, 156
war, 13, 22, 96, 123–24, 163, 182–83, 273, 409–13
watchman, 33, 45, 84, 258
water, 11, 24, 25, 26, 28, 33, 36, 48, 86, 120–21, 137, 138, 142, 147, 156, 198, 217, 245–46, 249, 255–56, 257, 265, 302, 305, 320, 338, 344, 349, 351, 366, 374, 393–95, 418
wave, 142, 152, 162, 167, 175, 296, 298, 338, 349, 403, 418
wealth, 19, 63, 72, 84, 143–44, 157, 159, 169–70, 172, 179, 222, 243, 260–61, 263, 286, 291, 295, 296, 298–99, 308, 323, 333, 353, 359–61, 363, 366–67, 368–69, 377–82, 386, 396, 404
Weber, R., 104 n., 369 n., 407 n.
wedding garment, 45, 87; see also clothing
weeping, 71–2, 79, 110, 143, 182, 183, 197, 224, 225–26, 228–29, 282, 316, 321, 332, 341–42, 346–47, 395–97, 409
well, 23–7, 86, 138, 156, 194
wheat, 56, 227, 364
wheel, 178
widow, 36, 89, 111 n., 225, 365, 366, 373, 417
Wiesner, W. T., 69 n.
Wilbrand, W., 2 n., 9 n., 155 n., 241 n.
wilderness: see desert
William of St. Thierry, his

Commentary on the Canticle of Canticles, 5, 12, 15–22 passim, 25, 32, 36–39 passim, 41, 43, 46, 47, 48, 51, 53, 55, 58, 63, 84, 147, 264, 272
Willis, G. G., 279 n.
wind, 39, 85, 142, 214–15, 257, 339, 351, 364
windstorm, 108, 367
wine, 16, 19, 27, 40, 86–7, 171, 195, 211, 212–13, 217, 251, 255, 256, 264, 319–20, 322
wing, 60–2, 82, 257, 295, 302–04, 323, 394, 405
winter, 30, 39, 108, 306, 391
wisdom, 77, 78, 92, 122–24, 125, 131, 150, 152–54, 156, 158, 172, 173, 215–16, 232–33, 263, 269, 272, 287–88, 295, 297–99, 310, 317, 319–20, 334, 347–51, 352–53, 359, 361, 367, 370, 380, 403
wolf, 198, 254 n., 273–75
womb, 23, 43, 59, 103, 180, 181, 252, 259, 266, 268–69, 306, 313, 361, 405, 407–08
worm, 331
wound, 41, 86, 93, 97, 99, 108, 126, 128, 142, 163, 178, 179, 183, 220, 247, 260–61, 333, 353, 357, 358, 360, 371, 374, 392–93
wrath, 53, 79, 83, 124, 146, 153, 154–55, 161, 170, 176, 194–95, 208, 233–34, 246–47, 307, 311, 323, 334–35, 340, 343–44, 346, 353, 364, 409

wreath, 96; *see also* palm, victor's, *and* crown
Wright, F. A., 407 n.
writing, 27, 76, 132, 235, 262, 343, 369, 404–5

yoke, 53–4, 125, 154, 246, 251, 273
youth, 17, 82, 94, 103, 123, 166–67, 169, 174, 175, 218, 225, 298, 332, 343, 410, 416, 418–19

Zabulon, 256–58
Zacchaeus, 193
Zacharia, 385
zeal, 29, 60, 97, 106, 135, 165, 181, 183, 232, 288, 311, 370
Zeus, 64 n.
Zucker, L. M., 127 n.

INDEX OF HOLY SCRIPTURE

(Books of the Old Testament)

Genesis
—: 2, 187
1.26–27: 412
1.26: 288
1.31: 287
2.2–3: 180
2.7: 13, 404
2.9: 79, 85
2.16–17: 70
3.3: 124
3.5: 35
3.6–11: 375
3.6: 357
3.7: 35, 206
3.8–13: 35
3.8: 104, 194, 416
3.10–11: 158
3.10: 206
3.14: 312 (ter)
3.15: 314, 392
3.17–19: 314, 315
3.19: 81
3.21–24: 383
3.21: 42, 206
4.1–16: 319
4.4–6: 416
4.4–5: 417
4.4: 319, 416
4.5: 416
4.8–10: 416

4.10: 177, 305
4.11–12: 347
4.14: 311
4.15: 310
4.16: 193, 194
5.6–11: 11
5.18–24: 11
5.24: 61
6.3: 12
9.18–27: 258
9.25–26: 243
10.15: 258
12.1: 284
16.4: 10
18.1–15: 107
18.1: 223
18.11–15:10
18.11: 317
19.1–11: 299
19.12–22: 321
19.12–29: 305
19.26: 282, 305
21.1–2: 10
21.6: 10
21.10: 10
21.14: 24
22.1–19: 10
22.1: 109
24: 10, 203
24.16: 11

451

24.22: 15
24.53: 15
24.60: 15
24.62: 15
24.63: 11, 14, 15, 319
24.65: 45
25.8: 96
25.21: 23
25.22: 23
25.23: 23, 36, 150
25.27: 50, 150, 318
25.28: 150
25.29–34: 148
25.31–32: 123
26.18: 23
26.19–20: 23
26.21: 23
26.22: 23, 25
26.24: 25
26.25: 23
26.32–33: 23
26.46: 12
27.1–40: 244
27.1–17: 148
27.1–14: 317
27.3: 319
27.4: 318
27.5: 318
27.9: 150, 319
27.10: 317
27.11: 50
27.12: 148
27.13–14: 148
27.14: 150
27.15–29: 317
27.15: 150
27.17: 150
27.18–29: 148
27.20: 318, 380

27.22: 151, 318
27.27–40: 96
27.27: 36, 39, 49, 147, 151 (bis), 318, 390
27.30: 151
27.35: 152
27.36: 319
27.38–40: 152
27.40: 153, 154
27.41–28.7: 146
27.41–28.5: 320
27.41: 146, 149, 154
27.42–45: 155
27.43: 296, 297 (bis)
27.44: 297
27.45: 298
28.1–4: 319
28.2: 297 (bis)
28.10–12: 155
28.12: 146, 299
28.17–19: 391
29.2: 24, 156
29.2: 156
29.9–10: 24
29.9–15: 156
29.16–21: 146
29.17: 160
29.18, 30: 160
29.22–27: 160
29.26–30: 160
29.28–30: 298
29.30: 160
29.32: 219
29.35: 219
30.23: 160
30.25–43: 298
30.31–35: 156
30.37–43: 156
30.43: 157

31.1: 157, 302
31.3: 157
31.25–30: 160
31.32: 158, 160
31.33–35: 160, 299, 301
31.33: 158
31.34–35: 161
31.34: 302
31.35: 161
32.1–2: 107
32.2: 161
32.3: 161
32.4–21: 161
32.14–21: 146
32.14: 162
32.22–33: 299
32.23–25: 163
32.26: 164
32.28–29: 147
32.32: 164 *(bis)*
32.33: 164
33.1–2: 161
33.3: 161
34.1–31: 124
34.1–5: 164
34.13–31: 247
34.13–17: 164
34.25–29: 165
34.30: 124, 165
35.1: 165
35.2–4: 165
35.4: 166
35.18: 274
35.19: 165
35.20: 157, 165
37.3–4: 191
37.3: 267
37.4: 190
37.5–8: 191

37.8: 191
37.9: 192
37.10: 192
37.11–14: 192
37.14: 193
37.15: 194
37.17–18: 316
37.18: 194 *(bis)*
37.19–20: 194
37.20: 195
37.21–22: 195
37.22: 198
37.23: 198
37.24: 198
37.25–28: 196
37.25: 198 *(bis)*, 199
37.26–27: 195
37.27: 196, 198
37.28: 197
37.31–33: 198
37.31: 200
37.34: 200 *(bis)*
37.36: 200
39.1–20: 123
39.1: 200
39.5: 203
39.6–7: 203
39.6: 203
39.7: 204 *(bis)*
39.8–9: 123
39.8: 204 *(bis)*
39.10: 205
39.11–12: 205
39.12–18: 207
39.12: 158, 205 *(bis)*, 375
39.19–20: 207
39.21–23: 208
40: 173
40.1–4: 208

40.1: 208
40.8–15: 209
40.14: 211, 212
40.16–19: 212
40.16: 212
40.23: 211
41.1: 211
41.9–13: 213
41.9: 212
41.14–15: 213
41.25–32: 214
41.42: 215 (bis), 216
41.43: 216
41.51: 216, 244
41.52: 216, 244
41.55–56: 202
41.55: 216
41.56: 167, 216, 234
41.57: 216
42.1–2: 167, 218
42.3: 218
42.4: 218
42.7: 220
42.20: 152
42.25–28: 219
43.1–14: 219
42.11: 219
43.12: 220
43.13: 167
43.15: 20, 220
43.19–24: 221
43.21: 222
43.23: 222 (bis)
43.25: 223
43.26: 223
43.27: 223
43.28: 223
43.29: 220, 224 (bis), 225
43.30–31: 224

43.30: 224
43.31: 223
43.32–34: 223
43.33: 226
43.34: 226 (bis), 227
44.2: 226
44.3: 219
44.11–12: 226
44.12–13: 228
44.12: 226
44.33–34: 228
45.2: 228
45.3: 229
45.4–5: 230
45.4: 229
45.5: 230, 231
45.9: 230
45.10: 231
45.14: 231
45.16–20: 231
45.22: 232 (bis)
45.23: 233 (bis)
45.24: 233
45.25–26: 234
45.26–28: 168
45.26: 234
45.28: 235
46.1: 235
46.2–4: 235
46.4: 169, 236
46.26–27: 65
46.27: 236
47.9: 73
47.28: 168
47.29–31: 168
48.1–49.28: 168
48.1: 243
48.2: 36
48.8–20: 243

48.10: 168
48.13–20: 244
48.17–18: 169
48.18–19: 245
48.19: 169 *(bis)*
48.20: 245
48.22: 248, 400
49: 36, 242
49.1–2: 237, 245
49.1: 169
49.3–4: 245
49.4: 249
49.5–7: 124
49.5: 247
49.6: 170, 247
49.7: 170, 249
49.8–12: 251
49.8–10: 195
49.8–9: 171
49.10: 253
49.11–12: 171
49.13: 256
49.14–15: 258
49.16–17: 260
49.17–18: 413
49.19: 262
49.20: 195, 263
49.21–22: 171
49.21: 264
49.22–26: 266
49.22: 196
49.26: 171, 196
49.27: 274
49.28: 96
49.29–31: 170

Exodus
1.19: 317
2.11–4.17: 399
2.11–15: 296
2.15–22: 24
2.15: 172
3.4: 60
3.5: 21, 254, 271, 300, 301, 314
3.6: 300
3.14: 382
4.10: 384
12.4–5: 200
12.11: 152
12.35–36: 306
13.21: 61
14: 296
14.10–22: 349
14.21: 172
20.12: 243
20.13: 119
25.5–9: 294
25.16–17: 294
25.17–22: 379
25.20–21: 294
25.31–40: 380
25.37: 181
33.3: 246 *(bis)*
33.20: 106

Leviticus
11.4–47: 123
20.18: 11
23.25: 46
25.6: 315
25.10: 197

Numbers
1.7: 54
2.3: 54
12.8: 29
17.16–26: 156

17.23 (8): 52, 220
19.11: 111
21.9: 54
23.10: 82
24.5–6: 22
35.6: 284 *(bis)*
35.11: 283
35.13–14: 283
35.25: 284, 322
35.32: 322

Deuteronomy
5.31: 384
6.5: 288, 309
6.13: 161
8.17: 88
10.12: 306
11.6: 263
13.4: 306, 307
14.3–21: 273
15.6: 153, 154
15.9: 88
27.17: 126
30.15: 70, 309
32.11: 405
32.13: 31
32.15: 214
32.18: 244
32.39: 273
33: 242
33.6: 250
33.8: 250
33.12: 274
33.13–17: 271
33.17: 272
33.19: 259
33.20–21: 262
33.22: 261

33.23: 265
33.24–28: 264

Josue
5.15 (16): 254
20.6: 289

Judges
13.2: 260
15.20: 260
16.4–22: 357

1 Kings (1 Samuel)
2.10: 272
17.40–54: 74
18.7: 272
19.18: 14, 296
21.6: 46
21.7: 213
22.1: 303
22.18: 213
26.8: 376

2 Kings (2 Samuel)
15.14: 296
16.5–14: 356
23.15: 121
23.16–17: 121 *(bis)*
24.17: 75

3 Kings (1 Kings)
3.24: 400
3.27: 401
6.7: 412
10.22: 339
17.5: 307
17.6: 307
19.2: 307
19.4: 307, 308

19.5–7: 307
19.8: 307 *(bis)*
19.14: 285
21: 126

4 Kings (2 Kings)
2.11–12: 329
2.11: 61
2.12: 54
5.1–14: 398
20.17–18: 142
20.19: 141

1 Paralipomenon
22.9: 37

2 Paralipomenon
20.35–37: 340
20.37: 339

1 Esdras
7.6: 142

4 (2) Esdras
—: 69, 102, 107
5.42: 103
5.53: 103
7.32–33: 102
7.32: 103
7.78–87: 106
7.91–99: 104
7.96: 105
7.99: 105
7.100: 105
7.101: 106
14.9: 107

Esther
3.1: 213

3.8: 213
3.9: 213
7.10: 213

Job
—: 328
1.13–19: 330
2.1–6: 331
2.7–8: 353, 374
2.7: 330
2.9–10: 330
2.10: 370, 374
2.11: 352
3.3: 71
3.23: 374
4–37: 352
4.8–9: 334
4.8: 361
4.19: 334
4.21: 334
5.9: 347
5.13: 334
5.16: 334
6.4: 331
6.9: 331
6.11–14: 331
7.1–6: 331
7.1–2: 79
7.1: 78
7.4: 79
7.6: 79
7.13–14: 331
8.9: 302
9.2–11: 335
9.6: 336, 338
9.8: 338
9.17–20: 340
9.22–24: 340
9.25–26: 341

458 INDEX

9.25: 310
9.28: 341
9.33: 341
10.2–7: 341
10.8–12: 341
10.9: 78, 406
10.11: 78
10.13–16: 342
10.14–15: 78
10.17: 78
11.7: 347
13.19–20: 358
13.26: 343
14.1–5: 344
14.4–5: 394
14.5: 106
14.7–11: 344
14.12: 344
14.13–17: 346
15.20: 353
16.18: 347
17.1–2: 347
17.11: 347
19.4: 355
19.5–6: 355
19.7: 355, 356 *(bis)*
19.8: 355
19.25–26: 339
20.5: 353
20.7–9: 353
20.15: 353
20.23: 353
20.28–29: 353
21.2–3: 358
21.7–9: 359
21.7: 359 *(bis)*
21.8: 360 *(bis)*
21.9: 360
21.10: 361

21.11–13: 362
21.13: 363
21.14: 363
21.15: 363
21.17: 364
21.18: 364 *(ter)*
21.23–25: 365
21.32: 365
24.2–12: 365
24.8: 365
24.9: 365
24.10: 365
24.12: 365
26.6: 366
26.7–8: 366
26.11–14: 366
27.3: 393
27.8: 366
27.11: 366
27.12: 366
27.14–15: 366
27.14: 366, 367 *(bis)*
27.15: 366 *(bis)*
27.16–18: 367
27.19: 367
28.1: 367
28.8: 347
28.12–14: 347
28.18: 350
28.21: 350
28.22: 350
28.23: 350
28.24–25: 351
28.27: 351
28.28: 351
29.13: 96 *(ter)*, 97
29.14: 158
33.2: 177
33.16: 124

38.1: 357
39.1–3: 392
39.3–4: 392
42.7: 357
41.17: 346

Psalms (the enumeration of
the Septuagint and Vulgate
is used)
—: 2, 5, 187, 369
1.1: 147
1.2: 147
1.3: 147
1.4: 364 (bis)
3.6: 95, 253
4.5: 32, 78, 120, 333
4.6: 110
4.7: 395
6.8: 418
7.4–6: 159
7.5: 190
7.15: 361
8.5 (4): 406
8.5: 13, 342, 384
8.6: 401
8.7: 268
9.14: 111
11.7: 61 (bis), 220
13.1: 416
15.2: 63, 155
15.8: 385
15.10: 348
16.8: 304
16.14: 87
17.12: 32
17.26–27: 100
17.29: 100
17.31: 201
18.3: 32

18.5: 235, 420
18.6–7: 17
18.6: 57, 390
20.13: 193
21.11: 407, 408
21.12: 408
21.13: 214
21.23: 251, 270
22.1: 216
22.2: 265
22.3: 89
22.5: 215, 226, 415
22.6: 110
23.4: 91
24.7: 343
24.13: 98
24.15: 193
25.2: 62
26.4: 63, 138, 396
26.13: 98, 110, 308
27.9: 229
28.6: 273
28.9: 392
29.2: 47
29.10: 136
29.12: 222
30.6: 84, 407
31.1: 305, 396
31.5: 133
32.17: 283
33.12: 125
33.14: 99
33.15: 301 (bis)
33.16: 84, 224
33.22: 95, 373
35.7: 384, 403
35.10: 320, 395
35.12: 372
36.5–6: 20, 223

36.35–36: 300, 381
38.5: 380
38.6–7: 368
38.12: 215
38.13: 73
38.14: 73
39.5: 283
39.7: 294
39.13: 301
40.4: 373
40.10: 260, 392
41: 328
41.2–3: 11, 320, 394
41.2: 28, 389, 393
41.3: 320, 330, 395, 396
41.4: 395
41.5: 320, 396 *(bis)*
41.6: 398, 413
41.7: 398, 401
41.8: 402
41.9–10: 403
41.9: 403
41.10–12: 408
41.10–11: 330
41.10: 405, 413
41.11: 413
41.12: 413
42: 328
42.1: 413
42.2: 406, 415
42.3: 415 *(bis)*
42.4 (5): 419
42.4: 415, 416 *(bis)*, 418
43.6: 273
44.2: 268
44.3: 271
44.9: 220
47.7–8: 339
47.7: 340

47.9: 340
48.18: 333, 382
49.11: 148
50.6: 414
50.7: 342
50.8: 348, 352, 380
50.9: 215, 419
50.19: 339
52.2: 416
54.1: 304
54.2: 304
54.7: 303, 304, 394
54.8: 304
57.4–6: 313
58.7: 216
59.4: 339
59.8: 400
61.2: 89
62.6: 375
62.9: 14
62.12: 133
63.8: 142
64.5: 110, 145
65.10: 179
65.12: 179
67.14: 303
67.15: 399
67.22: 412
67.28: 257
68.24: 373
68.32–33: 249
70.6: 407
71.20: 369
72: 328, 368, 369
72.1: 368, 369
72.2–3: 372
72.4: 373, 374
72.5: 374
72.6: 374

72.7: 375
72.9: 375
72.10: 377 *(bis)*
72.11: 377
72.12: 377
72.13: 368, 378
72.14: 361, 378 *(bis)*
72.15: 379 *(bis)*
72.16–17: 379
72.16: 379
72.18: 380, 381
72.19–20: 382
72.20: 333, 382, 383
72.21–23: 383
72.22 (23): 348
72.23–24: 385
72.25: 386
72.26: 387
72.27: 388 *(bis)*
72.28: 388
73–82: 369
73.1: 409
73.2–3: 409
73.4–5: 409, 411
73.4: 409
73.5–6: 411, 412
74.4: 336
75.6: 212, 261, 382
75.7: 261
76.3: 315
81.5: 382
83.2–3: 396
83.6: 282
83.11: 396
85: 369
87.3: 194
87.7: 198
87.9: 408
88.28: 172

90: 369
90.1–2: 405
90.4–6: 257
90.13: 392
92–98: 369
92.1: 50, 266, 294
93.3: 368
97.6: 273
100–103: 369
100.4: 411
101.7–8: 304
101.26–27: 345
101.27: 255
102.1: 17
102.5: 17, 82, 419
102.14: 406
103.2: 50
103.15: 86 *(bis)*, 395
103.19: 135
103.28: 309
103.29: 406
104.17–18: 413
106.23: 338
107–109: 369
108.6: 385
108.18: 375
109.2: 251
109.3: 268, 408
109.4: 250, 293
110.10: 125, 361
112.7: 371
114.7–9: 111
114.7: 98
114.8: 98
114.9: 98
115.4 (13): 227
115.6: 74, 95
115.7–8: 74
115.8: 75

117.22: 402
117.24: 338
118:22
118.36: 281
118.37: 283
118.73: 404
118.81: 317
118.105: 399
118.109: 101
118.131: 16
118.140: 201
119.5: 397
123.5: 52, 137
123.7: 51, 302
125.6: 191
126.3: 259
126.5: 359
128.3: 251
128.8: 316
130: 369
132: 369
136: 369
136.1: 44
138–140: 369
138.1–2: 303
138.1: 303
138.9: 303
138.12: 338
138.13: 405
140.2: 36, 156, 198, 220, 347
140.5: 215
141: 369
141.3 (2): 396
141.4: 89, 302
141.5: 302
142–143: 369
142.2: 106
143.3–4: 13
143.5: 304

143.7: 304
144: 369
146.4: 338
146.5: 401
147.12–13: 412
148.3: 192
148.14: 249
151: 369

Proverbs
—: 25, 27, 389
1.7: 125
1.28: 350
3.12: 374
4.1: 389
4.25: 89, 99
5.8: 322
5.15–18: 138
5.15–16: 25, 156
5.15: 24, 33
5.18: 25
5.19: 138, 389
5.20: 89
6.25: 99
6.26: 99
7.5: 308
7.21: 99
8.22: 356, 409
9.2: 319
9.4: 320
9.5: 216, 320
10.26: 302
11.25: 12, 49
11.29: 153
14.21: 306
15.1: 357
16.24: 86
17.6: 143
18.17: 343

20.9: 106
21.1: 101, 308
22.7: 153, 154
22.20: 27
23.33: 322
24.11: 126
25.9: 90
26.4: 322
27.11: 355
27.13: 355
28.25: 413
31.22: 233

Ecclesiastes
—: 25
1.2: 283
1.9–10: 91
1.18: 91
2.6: 26
2.14: 411
2.17: 91
4.1–2: 92
4.1: 72
4.2–3: 72
4.12: 321
5.12–13: 359
6.3–5: 72
6.3: 361
7.2 (3): 282
7.25–26: 92
8.5: 411
9.6: 26
10.4: 412
11.1: 395
11.2: 181

Canticle of Canticles
—: 9, 25, 27, 55, 84
1.2–3: 16

1.2: 15, 40
1.3–4: 17
1.4: 18, 19
1.6: 19, 20
1.7: 20
1.8: 20, 21
1.9: 22
1.12–13: 56
1.16–17: 27
2.1: 28
2.3: 27, 40
2.4: 27
2.5: 28
2.7: 148, 390
2.8: 28, 40, 391
2.9–12: 391
2.9: 29 *(ter)*, 32, 40, 390, 391
2.10: 29, 30
2.11: 30 *(bis)*, 39
2.12: 30 *(ter)*, 391
2.13–14: 31
2.13: 31
2.14: 31
2.16–17: 56
2.16: 46
2.17: 56
3.1: 32, 34, 40
3.2: 32, 40
3.3: 33
3.4: 33, 35
3.5: 35
3.6: 35, 36
3.7: 36
3.10–11: 36
3.11: 37
4.8: 37, 42
4.12–13: 38, 85
4.12: 12
4.15: 26

4.16: 39 *(bis)*, 85
5.1–2: 86
5.1: 39 *(bis)*, 86
5.2: 40 *(bis)*, 41 *(bis)*, 412
5.3: 42, 132
5.4–5: 43
5.4: 43
5.5: 41
5.5–6: 41
5.6: 44
5.7: 45
5.8: 15
5.10: 272
5.16: 51
6.2: 56
6.4: 46, 47
6.5: 47
6.8 (9): 48
6.9: 48, 51, 58
6.10 (9): 266
6.10: 58
6.11: 52 *(bis)*
6.12: 53, 54
7.6–7: 55
7.8: 55
7.10: 55, 56
7.12: 56
7.14: 57
8.1: 57
8.2: 35, 57 *(bis)*, 148
8.3: 56
8.5: 58 *(ter)*, 401
8.6: 31, 44, 59, 60 *(ter)*, 183
8.7: 137, 184
8.10: 84 *(bis)*
8.13: 84
8.14: 84

Wisdom
1.13: 79, 81
2.12: 195, 373
4.8–9: 167, 218
5.6: 223
7.9: 349

Sirach (Ecclesiasticus)
1.16: 125
6.13: 90
8.10 (13): 355
9.13 (20): 30, 78, 302
11.28: 95
21.16 (19): 333, 379
23.18 (25–26): 332
23.19 (28): 332
23.18 (26): 51, 178, 388
24.3 (5): 269
27.11–12: 152
27.13 (14): 332
35.17 (21): 347
39.6 (9): 403
40.20: 86
48.24 (27): 380

Isaia
1.11: 299, 417
1.12: 417
1.15–18: 417
1.18: 419
1.19: 309
3.9–10: 249
5.1: 272
6.1: 256
6.6–7: 61
6.8: 193
7.9: 348
7.16: 259, 408
8.4: 259, 408

9.1–2: 258
9.5 (6): 259, 402
10.22: 154
11.1: 252
11.8–9: 392
19.11: 267
22.13: 363
24.18: 29
26.9: 403
26.17–18: 361
27.3: 32, 83
28.16: 402
29.7: 333
29.8: 210, 334
31.9: 134
35.3: 199, 310
38.19–20: 360
40.11: 56
41.1: 417
42.1: 268
43.25: 109
43.26: 342
45.8: 323
48.20: 44
49.16: 83 *(bis)*, 84, 383
49.18: 255
50.1: 201
50.11: 202
52.6: 229
52.7: 21, 301
53.2: 401
53.3–5: 259
54.1: 305
55.1: 217
58.6: 76
60.8: 323
60.9: 323
62.11: 255
65.1: 229, 415
65.2: 229, 251
65.17: 344

Jeremia
1.5: 269, 405 *(bis)*
1.11–12: 220
2.13: 11, 198
4.19: 313
9.20 (21): 282
11 (12).19: 150
16.1–4: 313
18.2: 404
18.3–4: 404
18.4: 404
20.9: 60, 378
22.28: 404
22.29–30: 404
23.24: 401
31.9: 395
31.26: 397
37–38: 142
46.22–23: 411
51.8–9: 199

Lamentations
4.19: 323
4.20: 64

Ezechiel
1.15–20: 178
13.10: 373
13.18: 345
18.4: 51, 71
18.20: 51
21.5 (20.49): 32
33.18: 111
33.19: 112
34.23: 56
37.9: 339

Daniel
  1.6–7: 410
  1.6: 142
  1.8–16: 410
  2.35: 402
  3.4–6: 410
  3.15: 410
  3.18: 410
  3.19–96: 142
  3.50: 62
  6.2–29: 173
  12.3: 107
  13: 207
  13.22: 321
  13.34–35: 321
  13.42–43: 321
  13.44–62: 321
  13.45–61: 126
  13.54: 166
  14.9–22: 143
  14.33–39: 173

Osee (Hosea)
  10.11: 215
  10.12: 25
  10.13: 215
  11.1: 219
  13.14: 350

Joel
  2.3: 406

Amos
  5.14–15: 308

Jona
  1.3: 296
  2.1–2: 408

Michea
  2.9–11: 305
  4.4: 148
  5.1 (2): 29, 165
  6.3–4: 381
  6.3: 414
  6.6: 306
  6.7: 306
  6.8: 306
  7.1: 364
  7.6: 414

Habacuc
  3.8: 54
  3.15: 55
  3.18: 19

Zacharia
  3.1: 385
  9.9: 219, 255
  11.1: 411

Malachia
  3.3: 62
  3.20 (4.2): 20, 28, 132, 164,
    265, 337, 382

2 Machabees
  6.18–31: 173
  7: 175
  7.18: 179
  7.21–23: 180
  7.24: 179
  7.25–26: 180
  7.27–29: 180
  7.27: 181
  7.30–36: 180
  7.30: 180

7.41: 173, 181
9: 184

4 Machabees
—: 117, 123 n.
1.1–2: 119
1.6: 120
1.14: 122
1.15–17: 122
1.20: 122
1.21–24: 122
1.25: 119
1.26: 122
1.33–34: 122
1.35: 123
2.1–3: 123
2.5–6: 119
2.19: 124
2.20: 124
2.21–22: 122
3.2–5: 120
3.5–16: 121
3.12: 121
3.17–18: 121
5.4: 173
5.5–13: 173
5.14–38: 174
6.1–10: 174
6.11–15: 174

6.16–23: 175
6.24–30: 175
8.3: 175
8.5–8: 175
8.9–15: 175
8.28–9.9: 176
9.10–25: 176
9.26–31: 177
10.1–12: 178
10.12–11.1: 178
11.1–13: 179
11.13–12.1: 179
12: 180
13.11–18: 182
14.4: 182
14.5: 182
14.6–8: 183
14.7–8: 181
14.20: 181
15.8: 181
15.11–12: 181
15.20: 182
15.21: 183 *(bis)*
15.26–27: 182
15.31–32: 184
16.13: 183
17.5: 183
17.14–15: 184
18.5: 184

(APOCRYPHAL OLD TESTAMENT BOOKS)

4 (2) Esdras. *See* Esdras.

4 Machabees. *See* Machabees.

(BOOKS OF THE NEW TESTAMENT)

St. Matthew
—: 187
1.3: 250
2.15: 219
3.1: 307
3.7: 307, 323
3.9: 199
3.11: 62
3.13–17: 398
3.14: 393
3.15: 393
4.4: 318
4.10: 289, 385
4.16: 111
5.6: 395
5.8: 387
5.10: 138
5.12: 357
5.15: 227
5.16: 48, 401
5.17: 296, 403
5.28: 99, 126, 282, 298
5.44: 190
5.48: 295
6.2: 370
6.10: 311
6.21: 159, 308
6.34: 73
7.8: 33
7.16–20: 20
7.23: 406
8.11: 108, 109
8.20: 27
8.22: 98
9.4: 88
9.16: 344, 345
9.20–22: 263

9.22: 112
10.4: 390
10.9–10: 234, 301
10.10: 314 (bis)
10.16: 311, 323, 389
10.23: 295
10.24: 270
10.28: 65, 82, 101
10.29–30: 54
10.32: 261
10.33: 261
10.36: 414
10.37: 161
10.38: 387
10.39: 38
11.12: 152, 306, 345
11.27: 350
11.28: 18, 30, 194, 333
11.29: 11, 124
12.1: 46
12.25: 200
12.38–42: 3
12.40: 297, 337
12.48: 285
12.49–50: 270
13.8: 259
13.12: 88
13.13: 32
13.45–46: 217
14.25–26: 349
14.25: 338
14.28–33: 349
14.28: 338
14.29–31: 338
14.29: 349
14.30–31: 386
14.31: 338, 349

14.34–36: 263
15.22: 399
15.24: 193, 228, 267
15.32: 413
15.36: 263
16.18: 111
16.19: 18
16.24: 387
16.26: 83
17.1–13: 107
17.1–8: 47
17.3: 144, 259
17.4: 63
17.5: 46
18.21: 162
18.22: 162
19.21: 385
21.1–7: 255
21.7: 233
21.23–24: 262
21.25: 262
21.42: 402
22.1–14: 87
22.12–13: 45
22.15–22: 262
22.17–21: 262
22.30: 41
22.32: 300
22.37: 309
23.32: 200, 248
23.37: 62
24.12: 108
24.16: 305
24.19: 306
24.20: 306 (bis)
24.27: 312
24.28: 305
25.1–13: 217
25.8–9: 33

25.9: 217
25.21: 417
25.30: 417
25.33: 22
25.43: 208
26.12: 197
26.14–15: 196
26.15: 261
26.28: 90
26.31: 249
26.38: 397
26.59–61: 200
26.60–68: 336
26.63: 229
26.64: 172, 229
26.65: 200
27.5–6: 196
27.42–43: 195
27.51–53: 336
27.51: 200
27.54: 336
28.1: 34
28.5–6: 34
28.9: 34, 112
28.10: 34, 112, 230
28.18: 230
28.19: 125, 231
28.20: 47, 231, 349

St. Mark
2.23: 46
3.17: 178
3.19: 390
4.8: 259
4.21: 227
5.35–43: 36
6.8–9: 301
6.8: 234
8.34: 38, 387

8.38: 261
10.18: 64, 309
14.5: 197
16.17–18: 392

St. Luke
—: 187
1.27: 253
1.35: 275
1.44: 43
2.21–40: 193
2.26: 72
2.28–29: 72
2.29–31: 193
2.29: 73
2.35: 399, 401
3.2: 307
3.7: 323
3.29: 250
3.31: 250
4.1: 255
4.4: 318
4.18–19: 294
6.1: 46
6.2: 46
6.3–5: 46
6.16: 390
6.19: 299
6.21: 395
6.28: 356
7.11–17: 36
7.35: 44
7.36–38: 316
7.39: 377
7.45: 16
7.47: 16, 60, 197
8.1: 232
8.5: 411
8.8: 364

8.21: 285
8.46: 34
8.48: 112
9.3: 234, 301
9.23: 284, 387
9.26: 261
9.58: 41, 56
9.62: 392
10.3: 198
10.4: 314 (bis)
10.18: 311, 362
10.20: 405
10.30: 108
10.34: 18
11.27: 268
11.33: 227
12.19: 89
12.20–21: 310, 359
12.20: 101
12.33: 359
12.36: 412
12.49: 61
12.50: 398
13.7–9: 120
13.7: 31
14.18–24: 87
14.18: 108
15.11–16: 332
15.18: 376
16.19–24: 373
16.19–21: 363
16.22–23: 365
16.23: 108
17.7: 300
17.21: 21
17.24: 312
18.19: 64
18.29: 284
19.1–10: 193

19.4: 193
19.10: 371
19.17: 296
20.17: 402
21.23: 306, 339
22.3: 261
22.31–32: 364
22.35: 234
22.48: 390
22.54–62: 53
22.61: 53
23.30: 346
23.34: 230, 336, 356, 407
23.43: 108
23.44–45: 336
23.46: 100, 407
24.3: 34
24.5–6: 112
24.5:34, 365 *(bis)*
24.10: 34
24.32: 61
24.36: 230
24.38–39: 230

St. John
—: 187
1.1: 33, 112, 350, 400, 401
1.4: 79, 108
1.5: 332
1.9: 106, 108, 294, 337, 338,
   395, 399
1.11: 390
1.16: 294
1.18: 112, 237, 269, 350, 400,
   407
1.19: 200
1.26: 57
1.27: 254

1.29: 172, 279, 293, 300, 322,
   371
1.32: 255
1.33: 62
1.47–50: 58
1.51: 155
3.14: 54
3.19–20: 332
3.29: 254
3.30: 267
4.5–6: 26
4.6: 24, 194
4.7: 27
4.10: 395
4.12: 24
4.21–26: 27
5.22–23: 414
5.22: 136, 414
5.28–29: 340
6.27: 59
6.35: 263
6.37: 387
6.38–40: 47
6.48–50: 264
6.51: 165, 264, 395
7.38: 395
8.6: 405
8.8: 405
8.34: 153, 201
8.51: 113
8.56: 256, 338
9.6–7: 236
9.7: 399
9.29: 267
10.11: 56
10.14: 194
10.15: 350
10.18: 100
10.38: 288, 400

11.11: 95
11.25: 95, 345
11.33: 225
11.35: 225
12.5: 197
12.14–15: 219
12.24–25: 218
12.27: 90, 397
12.31: 301
13.18: 260, 392
13.23: 58
13.36: 18
14.2: 102, 108
14.3: 108
14.6: 87, 89, 109, 110
14.18: 47
14.23: 42
14.27: 162, 233, 301, 372
14.30: 45, 82, 160, 299, 364
14.31: 82, 283, 307
15.1: 27, 255, 370
15.3: 286
15.22: 129
16.11: 364
16.15: 300
16.21: 339
16.32: 286, 400
17.3: 286
17.21: 49
17.22–23: 49
17.24: 109
18.4: 109
18.5: 229
18.6: 228
18.8: 229
18.31: 198
18.32: 198
18.37: 37, 229
19.23–24: 198

19.31: 46
19.34: 255
19.39: 41
20.17: 34, 112
20.19: 230
20.27: 299

The Acts of the Apostles
2.2–3: 61
2.32–33: 234
3.1–11: 199
3.6: 199, 217, 349
4.11: 402
4.32: 49
5.17–18: 234
7.58: 225
9.1–2: 274
9.3–9: 274
9.3–7: 61
9.3: 20, 28, 225
9.5: 225
9.6: 225
9.8–9: 218
9.8: 275
9.12: 227
9:15: 110, 226, 274
9.17: 227
9.18: 226 *(bis)*, 227
9.34: 199
9.40: 199
10.10–16: 318
10.38: 294
13.7–12: 274
15.20: 166
16.18: 393
17.28: 64, 97, 110, 309
20.28: 217
28.3–6: 393
28.7–10: 274

Romans
  1.8: 256, 420
  1.15–17: 291
  1.17: 291
  1.18–25: 166
  1.20: 287, 291
  1.32: 92
  2.1: 92
  2.2: 291
  2.3: 92
  2.4: 92, 291
  2.5: 93
  2.12: 291
  2.13: 292
  2.14–15: 132
  3.19: 133, 292
  3.20: 133, 292
  3.25: 293
  4.7: 396
  4.17: 300
  5.14: 3
  5.20: 133, 152, 258
  6.1–11: 236
  6.2: 36, 71
  6.3: 131
  6.4–5: 323
  6.4: 43, 71, 134, 166, 322, 373
  6.6: 323
  6.8: 131
  6.11: 36, 131
  6.13: 126
  6.16: 126
  6.17–18: 125
  6.19: 126
  6.20: 227
  6.21: 127
  6.23: 126
  7.7–8: 128

  7.13: 130
  7.14–23: 130
  7.14–15: 12
  7.14: 130 (bis), 335
  7.16–17: 13
  7.23: 13, 76, 90
  7.24–25: 130
  7.24: 13, 77
  8.3: 193
  8.7: 89, 131
  8.10: 132
  8.15: 134
  8.17: 134
  8.18–23: 135
  8.18: 105, 134, 329, 370
  8.29: 42, 64, 288
  8.30: 136
  8.32: 37, 135, 136 (bis), 193, 386
  9.21: 404
  9.27: 154
  10.4: 403
  10.7: 349
  10.11: 251
  10.15: 21, 301
  10.18: 235
  11.1: 218
  11.5: 285
  11.20: 348
  11.25–26: 237, 376
  11.26: 249
  11.32: 376
  11.33: 263, 347
  12.19: 155, 234
  13.10: 28, 55
  13.12: 31, 226, 257

1 Corinthians
  2.2: 232

2.4: 232
2.14: 360
2.15: 13, 362
3.2: 39, 57, 256
3.6: 275
3.16: 412
4.7–8: 222
4.7: 128
4.12: 356
5.5: 286
6.15–16: 388
6.18: 295
6.19–20: 217
7.22: 127
7.23: 217
7.29–31: 316
7.40: 335
9.11: 360
9.16–18: 321
9.24: 18, 55
11.3: 59, 176, 270
11.5–10: 45
11.28: 264
13.5–7: 60
13.5: 60
13.12: 43, 106, 394
14.15: 419
15.9–10: 275
15.12–19: 235
15.20: 172
15.22–24: 105
15.27: 268
15.31: 329
15.42: 81, 179
15.45–49: 3
15.45: 125
15.47: 125
15.49: 383
15.55: 323, 350

2 Corinthians
2.15–16: 31, 198
2.15: 232
3.3: 292
3.6: 154, 290
3.13–18: 227
3.18: 228, 398
4.7: 339, 404
4.10–12: 76
4.10: 82, 315, 387
4.12: 76, 387
4.16: 76, 139
4.18: 77
5.8: 38, 394
5.21: 172, 201, 411
6.10: 386
6.11: 258
6.16: 412
7.5: 49, 413
7.10: 139
8.9: 263
10.5: 273
11.14: 160, 362, 413
11.32–33: 321
12.2–4: 232, 321, 348
12.3–4: 18
12.4: 19
12.9: 354

Galatians
2.9: 337
2.16: 133, 221
2.19: 71
2.20: 282, 315
3.13: 172, 314
3.27: 60
4.4: 285
4.18: 372
4.19: 59

4.22–31: 154
4.26: 63
4.27: 305
5.7: 260
5.16: 132
5.19–20: 90
5.25: 132
6.8: 360
6.14: 27, 43, 75, 323

Ephesians
  1.22: 270
  2.14–15: 415
  2.14: 24, 29, 48, 139, 418
  2.16: 139
  2.19: 44
  3.19: 294
  4.13: 225
  4.15–16: 294
  4.15: 270
  4.22: 323, 359
  4.23: 17
  4.26: 28
  5.16: 310
  5.23: 270
  5.30: 176
  6.12: 38, 87, 163, 251, 392

Philippians
  1.21: 73, 74, 79, 394
  1.23–24: 74
  1.23: 71, 75, 79, 95, 144, 394
    (bis)
  1.26: 26
  2.6–7: 196, 402
  2.9: 172
  2.10: 191
  3.3: 133
  3.8: 282, 371

3.14: 54, 282
3.20: 76, 77, 145, 170, 231
4.7: 163, 309, 367, 413

Colossians
  1.13: 37
  1.15: 39
  1.16–20: 290
  1.16–17: 387
  1.17: 271
  1.18–19: 271
  1.18: 172, 272, 345
  1.20: 271
  2.9: 43, 47, 64, 135, 210, 294,
    299
  2.12: 43, 82, 322
  2.14: 201, 322
  2.17: 396
  2.21–22: 77
  3.1–2: 131, 315
  3.3–4: 64, 112
  3.3: 310
  3.9–10: 206
  3.9: 132, 359
  3.16: 57

1 Thessalonians
  1.8: 420
  4.13: 139

2 Thessalonians
  3.1: 17

1 Timothy
  1.13: 61
  1.19: 257
  2.4: 201, 372
  3.15: 157, 166
  5.6: 111

5.11: 225, 362
5.17: 220
6.15: 400
6.16: 47, 63

2 Timothy
  1.8: 31
  2.5: 357
  2.9: 17
  2.19: 53, 194, 382, 406
  4.8: 103, 282

Titus
  3.5: 60

Philemon
  6: 110
  9: 225
  11: 233
  15: 110

Hebrews
  1.1–9: 294
  1.11: 65
  2.6: 406
  3.5–6: 221
  4.12: 399
  4.14: 293
  6.10: 406
  7.2: 37
  7.9–10: 284
  7.14: 250
  7.21: 293
  7.23–24: 293
  7.25: 293
  7.26: 293 (bis)
  8.1: 47
  9.27: 80
  10.1; 132, 396

10.5: 294
11.37: 144, 173
12.2: 47
12.6: 374
12.22–24: 305
12.22: 33, 63
12.24: 416

James
  1.17: 309
  4.8: 387

1 Peter
  1.12: 33
  1.18–19: 128, 217
  2.6–7: 402
  2.9: 285
  2.20–23: 370
  2.22: 45, 418
  4.8: 288
  5.8: 367

2 Peter
  3.13: 135, 337

1 John
  2.1–2: 290
  2.1: 133
  4.16: 390
  4.18: 25, 370

Apocalypse
  1.5: 172, 345
  3.12: 383
  3.20: 42, 57
  3.21: 55
  5.5: 252
  7.3: 410
  8.3: 36

8.4: 36
9.4: 410
14.6: 350

21.1: 135, 337
21.5: 345
22.5: 345

THE FATHERS OF THE CHURCH SERIES

(A series of approximately 100 volumes when completed)

VOL. 1: THE APOSTOLIC FATHERS (1947)
- LETTER OF ST. CLEMENT OF ROME TO THE CORINTHIANS (trans. by Glimm)
- THE SO-CALLED SECOND LETTER (trans. by Glimm)
- LETTERS OF ST. IGNATIUS OF ANTIOCH (trans. by Walsh)
- LETTER OF ST. POLYCARP TO THE PHILIPPIANS (trans. by Glimm)
- MARTYRDOM OF ST. POLYCARP (trans. by Glimm)
- DIDACHE (trans. by Glimm)
- LETTER OF BARNABAS (trans. by Glimm)
- SHEPHERD OF HERMAS (1st printing only; trans. by Marique)
- LETTER TO DIOGNETUS (trans. by Walsh)
- FRAGMENTS OF PAPIAS (1st printing only; trans. by Marique)

VOL. 2: ST. AUGUSTINE (1947)
- CHRISTIAN INSTRUCTION (trans. by Gavigan)
- ADMONITION AND GRACE (trans. by Murray)
- THE CHRISTIAN COMBAT (trans. by Russell)
- FAITH, HOPE, AND CHARITY (trans. by Peebles)

VOL. 3: SALVIAN, THE PRESBYTER (1947)
- GOVERNANCE OF GOD (trans. by O'Sullivan)
- LETTERS (trans. by O'Sullivan)
- FOUR BOOKS OF TIMOTHY TO THE CHURCH (trans. by O'Sullivan)

VOL. 4: ST. AUGUSTINE (1947)
- IMMORTALITY OF THE SOUL (trans. by Schopp)
- MAGNITUDE OF THE SOUL (trans. by McMahon)
- ON MUSIC (trans. by Taliaferro)

479

ADVANTAGE OF BELIEVING (trans. by Sr. Luanne
Meagher)
ON FAITH IN THINGS UNSEEN (trans. by Deferrari
and Sr. Mary Francis McDonald)

VOL. 5: ST. AUGUSTINE (1948)
THE HAPPY LIFE (trans. by Schopp)
ANSWER TO SKEPTICS (trans. by Kavanagh)
DIVINE PROVIDENCE AND THE PROBLEM OF EVIL
(trans. by Russell)
SOLILOQUIES (trans. by Gilligan)

VOL. 6: ST. JUSTIN MARTYR (1948)
FIRST AND SECOND APOLOGY (trans. by Falls)
DIALOGUE WITH TRYPHO (trans. by Falls)
EXHORTATION AND DISCOURSE TO THE GREEKS
(trans. by Falls)
THE MONARCHY (trans. by Falls)

VOL. 7: NICETA OF REMESIANA (1949)
WRITINGS (trans. by Walsh and Monohan)
SULPICIUS SEVERUS
WRITINGS (trans. by Peebles)
VINCENT OF LERINS
COMMONITORIES (trans. by Morris)
PROSPER OF AQUITANE
GRACE AND FREE WILL (trans. by O'Donnell)

VOL. 8: ST. AUGUSTINE (1950)
CITY OF GOD, Bks. I-VII (trans. by Walsh, Zema;
introduction by Gilson)

VOL. 9: ST. BASIL (1950)
ASCETICAL WORKS (trans. by Sr. M. Monica
Wagner)

VOL. 10: TERTULLIAN (1950)
APOLOGETICAL WORKS (vol. 1), (trans. by Arbes-
mann, Sr. Emily Joseph Daly, Quain)
MINUCIUS FELIX
OCTAVIUS (trans. by Arbesmann)

VOL. 11: ST. AUGUSTINE (1951)
COMMENTARY ON THE LORD'S SERMON ON THE
MOUNT WITH SEVENTEEN RELATED SERMONS
(trans. by Kavanagh)

480

VOL. 12: ST. AUGUSTINE (1951)

    LETTERS 1-82 (vol. 1), (trans. by Sr. Wilfrid Parsons)

VOL. 13: ST. BASIL (1951)

    LETTERS 1-185 (vol. 1), (trans. by Deferrari and Sr. Agnes Clare Way)

VOL. 14: ST. AUGUSTINE (1952)

    CITY OF GOD, Bks. VIII-XVI (trans. by Walsh and Mother Grace Monahan)

VOL. 15: EARLY CHRISTIAN BIOGRAPHIES (1952)

    LIFE OF ST. CYPRIAN BY PONTIUS (trans. by Deferrari and Sr. Mary Magdeleine Mueller)

    LIFE OF ST. AMBROSE, BISHOP OF MILAN, BY PAULINUS (trans. by Lacy)

    LIFE OF ST. AUGUSTINE BY POSSIDIUS (trans. by Deferrari and Sr. Mary Magdeleine Mueller)

    LIFE OF ST. ANTHONY BY ST. ATHANASIUS (trans. by Sr. Mary Emily Keenan)

    LIFE OF ST. PAUL, THE FIRST HERMIT; LIFE OF ST. HILARION; LIFE OF MALCHUS, THE CAPTIVE MONK (trans. by Sr. Marie Liguori Ewald)

    LIFE OF EPIPHANIUS BY ENNODIUS (trans. by Sr. Genevieve Marie Cook)

    A SERMON ON THE LIFE OF ST. HONORATUS BY ST. HILARY (trans. by Deferrari)

VOL. 16: ST. AUGUSTINE (1952)—Treatises on Various Subjects:

    THE CHRISTIAN LIFE, LYING, THE WORK OF MONKS, THE USEFULNESS OF FASTING (trans. by Sr. M. Sarah Muldowney)

    AGAINST LYING (trans. by Jaffee)

    CONTINENCE (trans. by Sr. Mary Francis McDonald)

    PATIENCE (trans. by Sr. Luanne Meagher)

    THE EXCELLENCE OF WIDOWHOOD (trans. by Sr. M. Clement Eagan)

    THE EIGHT QUESTIONS OF DULCITIUS (trans. by Mary DeFerrari)

VOL. 17: ST. PETER CHRYSOLOGUS (1953)

    SELECTED SERMONS (trans. by Ganss)

    ST. VALERIAN

    HOMILIES (trans. by Ganss)

VOL. 18: ST. AUGUSTINE (1953)
    LETTERS 83-130 (vol. 2), (trans. by Sr. Wilfrid Parsons)

VOL. 19: EUSEBIUS PAMPHILI (1953)
    ECCLESIASTICAL HISTORY, Bks. 1-5 (trans. by Deferrari)

VOL. 20: ST. AUGUSTINE (1953)
    LETTERS 131-164 (vol. 3), (trans. by Sr. Wilfrid Parsons)

VOL. 21: ST. AUGUSTINE (1953)
    CONFESSIONS (trans. by Bourke)

VOL. 22: ST. GREGORY OF NAZIANZEN and ST. AMBROSE (1953)
    FUNERAL ORATIONS (trans. by McCauley, Sullivan, McGuire, Deferrari)

VOL. 23: CLEMENT OF ALEXANDRIA (1954)
    CHRIST, THE EDUCATOR (trans. by Wood)

VOL. 24: ST. AUGUSTINE (1954)
    CITY OF GOD, Bks. XVII-XXII (trans. by Walsh and Honan)

VOL. 25: ST. HILARY OF POITIERS (1954)
    THE TRINITY (trans. by McKenna)

VOL. 26: ST. AMBROSE (1954)
    LETTERS 1-91 (trans. by Sr. M. Melchior Beyenka)

VOL. 27: ST. AUGUSTINE (1955)—Treatises on Marriage and Other Subjects:
    THE GOOD OF MARRIAGE (trans. by Wilcox)
    ADULTEROUS MARRIAGES (trans. by Huegelmeyer)
    HOLY VIRGINITY (trans. by McQuade)
    FAITH AND WORKS, THE CREED, IN ANSWER TO THE JEWS (trans. by Sr. Marie Liguori Ewald)
    FAITH AND THE CREED (trans. by Russell)
    THE CARE TO BE TAKEN FOR THE DEAD (trans. by Lacy)
    THE DIVINATION OF DEMONS (trans. by Brown)

VOL. 28: ST. BASIL (1955)
    LETTERS 186-368 (vol. 2), (trans. by Sr. Agnes Clare Way)

VOL. 29: EUSEBIUS PAMPHILI (1955)
ECCLESIASTICAL HISTORY, Bks. 6-10 (trans. by Deferrari)

VOL. 30: ST. AUGUSTINE (1955)
LETTERS 165-203 (vol. 4), (trans. by Sr. Wilfrid Parsons)

VOL. 31: ST. CAESARIUS OF ARLES (1956)
SERMONS 1-80 (vol. 1), (trans. by Sr. Mary Magdeleine Mueller)

VOL. 32: ST. AUGUSTINE (1956)
LETTERS 204-270 (vol. 5), (trans. by Sr. Wilfrid Parsons)

VOL. 33: ST. JOHN CHRYSOSTOM (1957)
HOMILIES 1-47 (vol. 1), (trans. by Sr. Thomas Aquinas Goggin)

VOL. 34: ST. LEO THE GREAT (1957)
LETTERS (trans. by Hunt)

VOL. 35: ST. AUGUSTINE (1957)
AGAINST JULIAN (trans. by Schumacher)

VOL. 36: ST. CYPRIAN (1958)
TREATISES (trans. by Deferrari, Sr. Angela Elizabeth Keenan, Mahoney, Sr. George Edward Conway)

VOL. 37: ST. JOHN OF DAMASCUS (1958)
FOUNT OF KNOWLEDGE, ON HERESIES, THE ORTHODOX FAITH (trans. by Chase)

VOL. 38: ST. AUGUSTINE (1959)
SERMONS ON THE LITURGICAL SEASONS (trans. by Sr. M. Sarah Muldowney)

VOL. 39: ST. GREGORY THE GREAT (1959)
DIALOGUES (trans. by Zimmerman)

VOL. 40: TERTULLIAN (1959)
DISCIPLINARY, MORAL, AND ASCETICAL WORKS (trans. by Arbesmann, Quain, Sr. Emily Joseph Daly)

VOL. 41: ST. JOHN CHRYSOSTOM (1960)
HOMILIES 48-88 (vol. 2), (trans. by Sr. Thomas Aquinas Goggin)

VOL. 42: ST. AMBROSE (1961)
HEXAMERON, PARADISE, AND CAIN AND ABEL (trans. by Savage)

VOL. 43: PRUDENTIUS (1962)
POEMS (vol. 1), (trans. by Sr. M. Clement Eagan)

VOL. 44: ST. AMBROSE (1963)
THEOLOGICAL AND DOGMATIC WORKS (trans. by Deferrari)

VOL. 45: ST. AUGUSTINE (1963)
THE TRINITY (trans. by McKenna)

VOL. 46: ST. BASIL (1963)
EXEGETIC HOMILIES (trans. by Sr. Agnes Clare Way)

VOL. 47: ST. CAESARIUS OF ARLES (1964)
SERMONS 81-186 (vol. 2), (trans. by Sr. Mary Magdeleine Mueller)

VOL. 48: ST. JEROME (1964)
HOMILIES 1-59 (vol. 1), (trans. by Sr. Marie Liguori Ewald)

VOL. 49: LACTANTIUS (1964)
THE DIVINE INSTITUTES, Bks. I-VII (trans. by Sr. Mary Francis McDonald)

VOL. 50: OROSIUS (1964)
SEVEN BOOKS AGAINST THE PAGANS (trans. by Deferrari)

VOL. 51: ST. CYPRIAN (1965)
LETTERS (trans. by Sr. Rose Bernard Donna)

VOL. 52: PRUDENTIUS (1965)
POEMS (vol. 2), (trans. by Sr. M. Clement Eagan)

VOL. 53: ST. JEROME (1965)
DOGMATIC AND POLEMICAL WORKS (trans. by John N. Hritzu)

VOL. 54: LACTANTIUS (1965)
THE MINOR WORKS (trans. by Sr. Mary Francis McDonald)

VOL. 55: EUGIPPIUS (1965)
LIFE OF ST. SEVERIN (trans. by Bieler)

VOL. 56: ST. AUGUSTINE (1966)
THE CATHOLIC AND MANICHAEAN WAYS OF LIFE
(trans. by Donald A. and Idella J. Gallagher)

VOL. 57: ST. JEROME (1966)
HOMILIES 60-96 (vol. 2), (trans. by Sr. Marie
Liguori Ewald)

VOL. 58: ST. GREGORY OF NYSSA (1966)
ASCETICAL WORKS (trans. by Virginia Woods
Callahan)

VOL. 59: ST. AUGUSTINE (1968)
THE TEACHER, THE FREE CHOICE OF THE WILL,
GRACE AND FREE WILL (trans. by Russell)

VOL. 60: ST. AUGUSTINE (1968)
THE RETRACTATIONS (trans. by Sr. Mary Inez
Bogan)

VOL. 61: ST. CYRIL OF JERUSALEM, VOL. 1 (1969)
INTRODUCTORY LECTURE (trans. by Stephenson)
LENTEN LECTURES 1-12 (trans. by McCauley)

VOL. 62: IBERIAN FATHERS, VOL. 1 (1969)
MARTIN OF BRAGA, PASCHASIUS OF DUMIUM,
LEANDER OF SEVILLE (trans. by Barlow)

VOL. 63: IBERIAN FATHERS, VOL. 2 (1969)
BRAULIO OF SARAGOSSA, FRUCTUOSUS OF BRAGA
(trans. by Barlow)

VOL. 64: ST. CYRIL OF JERUSALEM, VOL. 2 (1970)
LENTEN LECTURES 13-18 (trans. by McCauley)
MYSTAGOGICAL LECTURES (trans. by Stephenson)
SERMON ON THE PARALYTIC (trans. by Stephenson)
LETTER TO CONSTANTIUS (trans. by Stephenson)

VOL: 65: ST. AMBROSE: SEVEN EXEGETICAL WORKS
(1972)

ISAAC, OR THE SOUL

DEATH AS A GOOD

JACOB AND THE HAPPY LIFE

JOSEPH

THE PATRIARCHS

FLIGHT FROM THE WORLD

THE PRAYER OF JOB AND DAVID

Date Due

BJJH
